Management of Foreign Exchange Risk

Second edition

Edited by
Boris Antl
and
Richard Ensor

Published by Euromoney Publications

Published by
Euromoney Publications Limited,
Nestor House, Playhouse Yard,
London EC4

ISBN 0 903121 30 1

Text set in 10/12 Linotron 202 Bembo, printed and bound
in Great Britain at The Pitman Press, Bath

Contents

List of exhibits

Introduction

Listen in to the discussion at almost any gathering of company treasurers today, whether it be a small private meeting or a larger conference or convention, and it is a reasonable bet that you will hear the members debating and arguing about one prevailing subject: foreign exchange risk, and its management. Add bankers to the group, and the subject will remain the same, but this time the odds are that the two sides will be trying to learn as much as possible from each other and in particular their respective views on exchange rate movements in the future. The reason for this current pre-occupation with this particular problem is not difficult to track down. It is not, as many commentators have imagined and asserted, that both company treasurers and bankers are obsessed with finding new ways of making quick and easy profits, and that they find the currency markets of today ideal for that purpose. It is not that they are all inherently speculators, and find themselves in a world where, because of the instability of currency markets and the massive amount of short-term liquidity available for that purpose, speculation is possible on a vast scale. The reason is quite the reverse, and in fact, much more mundane.

Ask, then, the treasurer of almost any international or multinational company why he finds foreign exchange risk so important today, and he will point, first, to the growing importance of multinationals and their activities in the world economy; then to the great instability in currency markets in recent years, and especially since 1973; and finally to the increasing problems for companies which have to operate on a worldwide basis in an era of flexible or floating exchange rates. The instability of currency markets in recent times is legion, and it would be impossible for me to retell it all here. It is, however, just worth recording that as I write, a little over a decade after the famous crisis move of August 1971, when President Nixon severed the link between the U.S. dollar and gold, the dollar is still the object of doubt as to its value against other currencies. In between, against the Deutschemark and sterling for example, we have seen swings of 15% or more, first one way and then the other, in periods of only a few months at a time. All of this, to say the least, has made the business of conducting international trading more than a little difficult.

The significance of the problem to an international company can be highlighted by first considering one or two figures relating to my own company, Imperial Chemical Industries PLC. We convert foreign currency assets, and long-term liabilities, and foreign currency current assets, into sterling at year-end rates. The movement on the fixed assets and long-term liabilities is taken to reserves, but any difference between year-end and start of year values for current assets of our overseas subsidiaries resulting from currency movements is taken to profit and loss account. In 1976 this resulted in a credit of £58 million; in 1977 in a "loss" of £29 million; a swing of £87 million between one year and the next, simply due to currency movements — and not reflected in cash flows at all. Similarly, if you look at our long-term loan capital — currently just over £1,300 million in total — you will find that currency fluctuations caused an increase in the figure of loans of £110 million in 1976. But in the four subsequent years, 1977 to 1980, they brought about a reduction totalling some £220 million — movements affecting our gearing, but nothing to do with actual borrowing operations, or repayments. And

1

these very significant repercussions of currency fluctuations on our accounts were over and above the impact of currency movements on our export realizations, our import payments, and the profits made by our overseas subsidiaries in their own markets, and in their own currencies. Little wonder that this is a problem which is of constant concern to us. It is, unfortunately, compounded by the fact that companies find that currency fluctuations affect them in at least three different ways, i.e. there are three different types of risk they have to consider. First, there is the accounting risk, to which I have already referred. Some companies continue to measure their currency exposures by reference to up-to-date accounts, though they do not necessarily include every currency asset and liability in their sums. Secondly, there is the economic risk, which most of us would equate with transactions in the near future, or with cash movements. For many of us this is the real risk the company must face and contend with, and it is the one which ICI's systems are designed to measure and evaluate. And thirdly, there is the market valuation risk, or the impact of currency movements on the value of the company in the equity market. One can summarize that risk by saying that, generally speaking, equity investors prefer to see steady growth in a company's earnings. But a company hedging quite successfully against its economic risks could, nevertheless, show substantial fluctuations in its earnings as reported under accounting conventions. The question which then has to be answered is: "Which risk prevails — the economic one, or the market valuation one? Should one aim, in one's currency operations, at stabilizing earnings, even if it means not necessarily maximizing them?"

If that is the broad nature of the problem, is it perhaps one which will not be with us for much longer? Is it likely to disappear, or at any rate to become easier to cope with, as stability returns to the world's money and currency markets? I must say I for one doubt it; it seems to me that the current liquidity in the system, plus the general malaise of uncertainty, must spell instability for some time to come. Up to the end of 1973 there was a reasonable balance in the whole system, but since then we have seen a massive distortion in the distribution of resources, a build-up of non-productive liquidity, a huge accumulation of debt on the part of the lesser-developed countries, and the most serious recession since World War II. The world's leaders are finding it virtually impossible to see a way through this labyrinth, seeming to have no weapon with which to control the resultant expansion of credit than ever higher interest rates. We, I think, having noted that sterling has left the arena as an international currency, that the dollar is highly volatile, and that the Deutschemark is most reluctant to step forward to play a part, must reckon on the future being pretty much like the recent past. In these circumstances we must do something; we must calculate our currency exposures, one way or another, consider them, and then decide whether to hedge or not.

Thus, for several reasons, I believe the re-issue of this book to be particularly timely. By collecting together a number of papers, written by experts with different backgrounds, considering specific aspects of the problem, we hope it will help company treasurers, and in turn the bankers and others who try to serve them, to arrive at their own answers to the major questions which anyone involved in foreign exchange exposure management must surely ask of himself and his colleagues. They are:

(1) How should we measure our foreign currency exposures? What is the relevance of the accounting (or translation) approach, in contrast to the economic (or transaction) method? (Chapter 1).

(2) Is it possible to develop a reasonably efficient system for forecasting rates, or must we admit that the vagaries in the system, at any rate in the short run, are always likely to defeat us? (Chapters 2 and 3).

(3) Having measured our exposures, what technique or techniques do we use in coping with them? (Chapter 4).

(4) What management considerations arise in dealing with the problem in these ways? For example, should the activity be centralized, or decentralized? How do we control it within the total scheme of organization? (Chapter 5).

2

As I have said already, I am sure that this is a problem which is going to remain with us for a number of years. The debate will go on, new approaches will be suggested, and new techniques for matching, covering, and so on, will be devised, but if this book at the very least poses the right questions, and suggests just a few of the possible answers, it will have made a major contribution.

A. W. Clements
London, April 1982

CHAPTER ONE
Measuring foreign exchange risk

1. Definition and measurement
Boris Antl

Foreign exchange exposure arises when a corporation has transactions denominated in currencies other than its own or when it has net assets or liabilities outside the home country. As foreign exchange rates change, the value of the transactions or the value of the net assets or liabilities abroad changes when translated into the parent currency. Accordingly, foreign exchange gains and losses arise.

The magnitude of the recorded gains and losses will depend to a large extent on how exposure is defined; accounting standards used in major industrial countries vary and, accordingly, definitions of exposure do as well. Furthermore, companies themselves, even if using the same accounting standards, define exposures in various ways using different concepts. Thus, some may be concerned about transaction exposure while others will be primarily interested in translation exposure; some define exposure before-tax, others after-tax; some use today's exposure while others, pro-forma exposure.

The purpose of this section is to outline some of the basic concepts in exposure management as they will be used in this book. We proceed by first outlining the main accounting conventions used in major countries and defining some of the most important concepts used by corporations. The following parts of this section discuss and analyse exposures generated by various items of the balance sheet. Once exposures have been analysed from a static viewpoint, the income statement is brought into the equation and a more dynamic approach is introduced by the concept of pro-forma exposure. Finally, the various definitions and concepts are related to hedging strategies which are discussed in greater detail in other parts of the book.

To avoid unnecessary repetition, the exchange rate assumptions are identical in all of the examples used in this section. For convenience, they are summarized in Exhibit 1.

I. Accounting standards and exposure management concepts

There are five main accounting conventions used to translate financial statements denominated in foreign currencies: (1) closing, or current, rate method; (2) current/non-current method; (3) monetary/non-monetary method; (4) temporal method; and (5) functional currency method. Each of these methods looks to an item's specific attribute to categorize it as either exposed, employing the current exchange rate, or non-exposed, employing the historical rates of exchange.

> 1. The *closing rate method* translates all the assets and liabilities in the financial statements at the current rate. The rationale underlying this method is that the subsidiary's activities are being conducted in a foreign environment and its cash flows are denominated in a

Exhibit 1.1.1: Exchange rate assumptions and abbreviations used

At the beginning (time t^0) and at the end of the exposure period (time t^1), the exchange rates are as follows:

$$t^0 .... TC1 = LC1 \quad\quad = PC1$$
$$t^1 .... TC1 = LC0·8889 = PC0·8$$
$$LC1 = PC0·9$$

In other words, on the last day of the exposure period, LC depreciates by 10% against PC, and TC depreciates by 20% against PC.

For consistency we use the following abbreviations:

PC	—	currency of the parent company
LC	—	local currency of the subsidiary
TC	—	third currency (other than LC or PC)
FX	—	foreign exchange
ER	—	exchange rate
BT	—	before-tax
AT	—	after-tax
A/R	—	account receivable
A/P	—	account payable
T/P	—	tax payable
R/E	—	retained earnings

foreign currency. It is not a conglomeration of individual parts at risk, but the sum of the parts. The entire operation, the firm's net investment, is considered exposed.[1]

2. The *current/non-current* method classifies items based on the maturity, or holding period, within the subsidiary's books. All current items are translated at the current exchange rate, while non-current items are translated at historical rates. Accordingly, all current assets and liabilities are considered to be exposed to exchange risk while non-current items are not. Potentially unrealistic exchange gains and losses are thus avoided as long-term debt and fixed assets are not re-translated at each balance sheet date.

3. Under the *monetary/non-monetary* translation convention, the distinction between exposed and non-exposed is made on the basis of the financial nature of the item. All monetary items, where monetary is defined as fixed in the number of foreign currency units, are translated at the current exchange rate. All non-monetary items, essentially inventory and fixed assets, are translated at the historical rates of exchange. The rationale of this method is that as monetary items are fixed in terms of foreign currency units, any change in the exchange rate will result in a change in the base currency value. Non-monetary items are forms of wealth whose money value can change; price inflation or deflation is assumed to compensate for any changes in currency values.

4. The *temporal method* is very similar to the monetary/non-monetary. It is based on the concept that the subsidiary is an extension of the activities of the parent. The translation process reflects transactions of the group as though it were a single enterprise, using the base currency as a unit of measure. Under this method, all accounts which are measured on a historical basis are translated at the exchange rate in effect when these accounts were initially recorded. In a similar fashion, those accounts measured on a current (or market) basis are valued at the exchange rate in effect at the date of the balance sheet.

5. The *functional currency* approach accepts multiple currency measurement bases in consolidated financial statements. Accordingly, under this standard each entity measures and reports its results in its functional currency, and FX gains and losses determined in relation to the various functional currencies are included in current income. Following the remeasurement of an entity's results in the functional currency, all functional currency assets and liabilities are translated into the parent currency at the *current exchange rate*. The

---

[1] In a literal sense, equity is not translated at the current rate, although obviously it is in a net investment sense or the balance sheet would not balance.

resulting translation adjustments are not included in net income but charged to a separate component of stockholders' equity. The accounting results achieved are thus compatible with the expected economic results (a strengthening of a functional currency results in gains and vice-versa) while operating margin distortions (due to applying historical exchange rates to non-monetary accounts) are eliminated.

As there is no commonly accepted definition of foreign exchange exposure, a firm's attitude towards risk, and the steps it takes to manage its exposure, will depend upon how it defines exposure. Management must decide what is exposed and must select appropriate exchange rates for translating each item on the balance sheet and income statement. From an exposure management viewpoint, these exposures are frequently defined as (1) transaction, (2) translation, or (3) consolidated after-tax.

1. *Transaction exposure* relates to actual transactions in foreign currencies, while translation exposure deals with the valuation of overseas operations. Transaction exposure frequently occurs at both the parent and the subsidiary level. For the parent it occurs whenever a transaction is denominated in a currency other than the parent currency; at the subsidiary level it arises when a transaction is denominated in a currency other than the local (functional) currency. These gains or losses, whether at the parent or subsidiary level, are taxable or tax-deductible by the local tax authorities. The point is that transaction exposure has a tax impact and affects directly the cash flows of the trading entity.

2. *Translation exposure* is a major issue only from the consolidated viewpoint. Translation gains and losses are recognized for accounting purposes by the consolidated entity upon translating the foreign subsidiary's financial statements (as reported in local currency terms) to the parent currency. Translation gains or losses do not normally represent immediate cash gains or losses. Translation exposure can also frequently be assumed to have no tax effect upon consolidation; the parent currency translation gain or loss has no tax effect for the subsidiary, and the parent often does not provide for tax effects of foreign earnings considered to be reinvested. Each company's tax position must be evaluated to avoid making unwarranted assumptions, but for illustration purposes it is assumed below that translation gain or loss has no tax effect.

3. *Consolidated after-tax exposure*, as the term indicates, combines the translation component and the tax effect of the transaction component of the exposure from a consolidated after-tax viewpoint. Accordingly, this definition of exposure, though not an accounting concept, accounts properly for the gain, loss and the tax effects of movements of the individual currencies *vis-à-vis* the parent currency. The concept of after-tax exposure is used by corporations with a centralized exposure management function.

In addition to the above concepts some firms may measure exposure using a *country* approach; others may use a *currency* approach. Those firms which approach the measurement of transaction and translation exposure by the country concept are managing foreign exchange risk from a decentralized perspective. Those firms which use the currency concept are managing foreign exchange risk on a global basis. Country and currency exposure measures yield two very different values but the total exchange gain/loss is equivalent. The obvious difference of the two exposure measures is that the exchange gain/loss computed from country exposure is based on cross-rates, while the exchange gain/loss computed from currency exposure is based on straight exchange rates.

Finally, the corporate treasurer should be aware that whereas accounting results are historically oriented, exposure is computed on a *pro-forma* basis. There must be an anticipatory element to properly quantify the risks inherent in operations conducted in a foreign currency. In this sense, transaction exposure for the firm should not only identify the existing book exposure, but also the exposure arising from future transactions. This subject is treated in more detail in Parts VI and VII of this section.

II. Current monetary assets and liabilities

Current monetary exposure arises when a corporation holds current monetary assets and/or liabilities denominated in a foreign currency on its own books and/or when it operates abroad and generates current monetary assets and/or liabilities on the subsidiary's books.

The following paragraphs discuss current monetary exposure from the parent's, the subsidiary's and the consolidated viewpoints.

Parent's exposures in foreign currencies

In this example, presented in Exhibit 1.1.2, let us assume that the only exposure on the parent's books is an account receivable of TC 1,000. This account receivable is worth PC 1,000 on 31/12/X0. As the TC devalues by 20% vs. the PC on 31/3/X1, the receivable is then worth PC 800 and a before-tax transaction loss of PC 200 is recorded by the parent company (line 4). This loss is assumed to be taxable at the rate of 40% and results in a net after-tax loss of PC 120 (line 6) and an after-tax negative cash impact of PC 120 (line 7).

Exhibit 1.1.2: Parent's exposure: transaction

	31/12/X0	31/3/X1
(1) Exposure (TC)	1,000	1,000
(2) ER (PC/TC)	1·0	0·8
(3) PC equivalent	1,000	800
(4) FX gain/(loss) BT		(200)
(5) Tax (40%)		80
(6) FX gain/(loss) AT		(120)
(7) Cash impact AT		(120)

Subsidiary's exposures

Whereas exposures on the parent's books impact only the parent, exposure on the subsidiary's books may affect either the subsidiary, the consolidated results or both. To understand fully the impact of a subsidiary's exposures it is useful to differentiate between at least two categories of exposure; those denominated in (i) local currency, and (ii) foreign currencies.

1. Local currency exposure

In this example, we assume that the only exposure on the subsidiary's books on December 31, 19X0, is an account receivable of LC 1,000. From the consolidated viewpoint, this receivable is originally worth PC 1,000, as illustrated in Exhibit 1.1.3. On March 31, the PC value of the receivable decreases to PC 900 and a translation loss of PC 100 is recognized in consolidation (line 4). This loss is a valuation loss and has no immediate cash impact. The subsidiary is not affected, as the receivable is denominated in the local currency.

Exhibit 1.1.3: Subsidiary's exposure: translation

	31/12/X0	31/3/X1
(1) Exposure (LC)	1,000	1,000
(2) ER (PC/LC)	1·0	0·9
(3) PC equivalent	1,000	900
(4) FX gain/(loss)		(100)

2. Translation of third currency exposure

Translation of third currency exposure and the related gains and losses can be analysed by two different approaches.

Under one approach — referred to as indirect — the third currency amount is first translated into the local currency and then retranslated from the local currency into the parent currency. Under an alternative approach — referred to as direct — the third currency exposure on the subsidiary's books is translated directly into the parent currency, using the cross-rate between the TC and the PC. The two approaches are shown and reconciled below with the following data:

A receivable of TC 100 is booked by the subsidiary at time t^0. At time t^1, when the books of the subsidiary are consolidated with the parent's books, the translation loss can be computed as follows:

Indirect approach

t^0 .... TC1 = LC 1 = PC 1   TC 100 = LC 100   = PC 100

t^1 .... TC1 = LC 0·8889 = PC 0·8   TC 100 = LC 88·89 = PC 80

Foreign exchange loss (LC 11·11)   (PC 20)

Direct approach

t^0 .... TC = PC 1   TC 100 = PC 100

t^1 .... TC 1 = PC 0·8   TC 100 = PC 80

Foreign exchange loss   (PC 20)

Reconciliation of the two approaches at time t^1

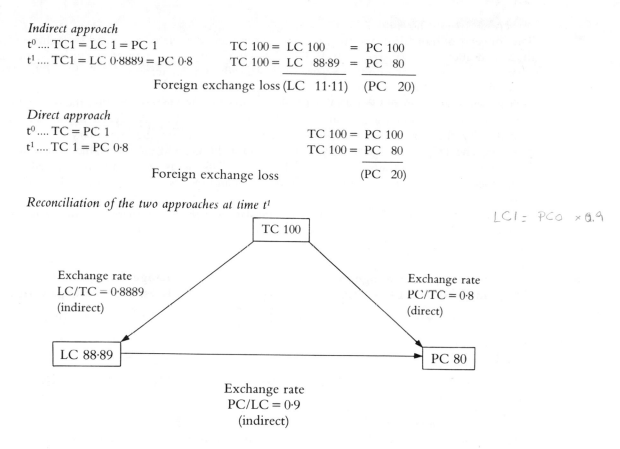

$LCI = PCO \times 0.9$

The subsidiary's exposure of TC 100 in the above example yields a translation loss of PC 20 for the parent, regardless of which of the two approaches is used. Whereas the direct approach identifies only the translation loss in terms of PC, the indirect approach identifies also the transaction loss of the subsidiary in terms of LC. The transaction loss for the subsidiary is LC 11·11 and the translation loss for the parent, PC 20.

The distinction between the above identified transaction and translation gains/losses is important for understanding the functional currency approach to translation of foreign currency financial statements. Using the data from the above example, although the net impact under the functional currency approach is identical, the breakdown between transaction and translation impact is not. This is because the functional currency approach accepts multiple currency measurement bases in consolidated statements. Under the functional currency approach, the consolidated statements reflect (1) the PC equivalent of the transaction loss as measured on the subsidiary's books in LC terms, and (2) the translation adjustment in PC terms to balance the translated consolidated statements. This is illustrated in the table below.

	(1) Transaction component	(2) Translation component	(3) = (1) + (2) Net impact
t^0	FC 100 = LC 100	LC 100 = PC 100	
t^1	FC 100 = LC 88·89	LC 100 = PC 90	
FX impact in LC	(LC 11·11)		
ER (PC/LC) at t^1	PC 0·9		
FX impact in PC	(PC 10)	(PC 10)	(PC 20)

These figures indicate that the *net impact* of a foreign currency transaction under the functional currency approach is identical to that derived above by using either the direct or the indirect translation approaches.

3. Third currency after-tax exposure

The concepts of translation and transaction exposures and the related gains and losses have been illustrated above in a tax-free world. The following analysis is on an after-tax basis. In this example, assume that the only exposure of the subsidiary is an account receivable of TC 100. This account receivable is thus worth LC 100 or PC 100.

From the parent's viewpoint, as the TC depreciates by 20% against the PC, the receivable is now worth PC 80 and a translation loss of PC 20 (assumed not to be taxable by the parent) is recorded by the parent (see right-hand column below). From the subsidiary's viewpoint, however, the TC has depreciated by 11·11% against the LC and the receivable is now worth LC 88·99 resulting in a transaction loss of LC 11·11. This loss is assumed to be tax-deductible under local law (at the rate of 60% in this example) and results in a tax credit of LC 6·67 (see below).

This tax credit is consolidated — after its translation at the appropriate exchange rate — by the parent and, added to the translation loss of PC 20, yields an after-tax loss of PC 14 to the parent.

LC gain (loss)	Change in ER vs. LC	Exposure	Change in ER vs. PC	PC gain (loss)
(LC 11·11) ⟵	−11·11% ⟵	TC 100 ⟶	−20% ⟶	(PC 20)
LC 6·67 ⟶		tax effect (×PC 0·9) ⟶		PC 6
		After-tax gain (loss)		(PC 14)

The after-tax loss of PC 14 shown in this example can be interpreted as follows: if the receivable of TC 100 was collected by the subsidiary at time t^1 and was immediately remitted to the parent, it would be worth to the parent PC 86 (vs. PC 100 at time t^0). This valuation is the sum of the value of the receivable, i.e. PC 80, and the PC equivalent of the tax credit received by the subsidiary, i.e. PC 6.[2]

III. Inventory exposure

As mentioned earlier, accounting methods differ in the treatment of inventory. Essentially, the difference is between those which translate inventory at current rates and those which use historical rates. Although the overall economic impact of inventory exposure will be much the same under both methods, a key difference between them is in the deferral of accounting gains or losses when inventories are carried at historical rates, and the immediate recognition if inventories are carried at current rates. This difference is illustrated below.

Inventory carried at current rate

We assume that a subsidiary purchases inventory worth LC 100 when the exchange rate is LC 1·00 = PC 1·00. This inventory is financed by a payable of LC 100. If both the inventory and the payable are carried at current rates, no exchange exposure exists. The underlying assumption is that if the local currency depreciates, both the payable and the inventory will be smaller in terms of the parent currency and that the smaller revenues (in parent currency equivalents) generated by the sale of the inventory will be used to pay the smaller payable (parent currency equivalent).

---

[2] This example can be viewed from a different angle, and the foreign exchange loss of PC 14 can be derived from the concept of after-tax currency exposure. See *The Management of Foreign Exchange Risk*, 1st edition, edited by R. Ensor and B. Antl, Euromoney Publications, London, 1978, pp. 13–16.

Inventory carried at historical rate

If these inventories are carried at the historical rate, the subsidiary's exposure will be the LC 100 payable (a short position) as the inventory is assumed not to be exposed. A gain of PC 10 will be recorded upon translation and consolidation at time t^1.

When the inventory is sold (say in the following accounting period) for its cost of LC 100 at the new exchange rate (PC 0·90), the consolidated company would record an operating loss of PC 10. This may be shown as follows:

	LC	ER	PC
Sales	100	0·9	90
Cost of goods sold	100	1·0	100
Pre-tax profit (loss)	LC0		(PC10)

Thus the historical translation of inventory required by some accounting methods may result in swings in reported income, e.g. a foreign exchange gain during the current period and a corresponding decrease in earnings during the following period.[3]

IV. Fixed assets

Translation methods also differ in the treatment of fixed assets. Again, the difference is between those which translate the asset at current rates and others which use historical rates. As in the case of inventories, the net impact of fixed asset exposure is the same under both methods, the key difference between them being in the immediate recognition of accounting gains or losses when the asset is carried at current rates and their deferral if it is carried at historical rates.

Fixed assets carried at current rate

If the fixed asset is carried at current rates of exchange, then the underlying assumption is that if the local currency depreciates, the asset will be less valuable in terms of the parent currency. Accordingly, smaller revenues in parent currency equivalents will be generated by the goods it produces for sale. More specifically, under the current rate method, by purchasing a fixed asset, exposed monetary assets are converted into exposed fixed assets and translation gains or losses are accrued each time the books of the subsidiary are translated and consolidated. For instance, given our exchange rate assumptions, if a fixed asset is valued at LC 1,000 or PC 1,000 on December 31, 19X0, it gives rise to a translation loss of PC 100 on December 31, 19X1.

Fixed assets carried at historical rate

Under the historical rate method, investment in fixed assets results in freezing the parent currency value of a local currency-denominated asset. It is assumed that the asset maintains its intrinsic value in terms of the parent currency, and foreign exchange gains or losses are foregone as current monetary assets are transferred into a historically valued fixed asset. Accordingly, returning to the previous example, by investing LC 1,000 in a fixed asset on December 31, 19X0, the company has eliminated its monetary exposure of LC 1,000, thereby foregoing a potential translation loss of PC 100.

To summarize: the foreign exchange impact of fixed asset exposure is identical under the two methods, regardless of the resale value of the asset. The only difference is in the timing of recognition of that impact, with the current rate method reporting it as exchange rates change, and historical method deferring it until its sale. Care should be exercised in applying either the historical or current rates to fixed assets. The book value of the asset may grossly over- or understate its market or replacement value, and upon sale of the asset unexpected gains or losses may have to be reported.

---

[3] For a detailed discussion of inventory exposure see *Currency Risk and the Corporation*, edited by Boris Antl, Euromoney Publications, London, 1980, pp. 32–5.

V. Long-term debt

Long-term debt consists of present obligations that are not payable within the current period. Bonds payable, mortgage notes payable, long-term notes payable and pension obligations are examples of long-term liabilities.

Two basic accounting alternatives are available when treating long-term debt. By translating the debt at historical rates, no loss or gain is recognized or, through translation at current rate, a gain or loss is recognized at the time of the devaluation or revaluation. The historical rate method mis-states the value of long-term liabilities. Here, as long-term debt does not change its value during a currency movement but retains its historical value, it is assumed not to be exposed. In reality, however, at some point in the future it must be repaid in de- or revalued currency and the company will recognize a gain or loss. Thus, if long-term debt is translated at historical rates, the balance sheet is distorted and the evaluation of gains or losses incurred is difficult. In the case of a depreciating currency, translating long-term liabilities at historical rates creates a hidden reserve which can make a balance sheet misleading.

Under the current rate method, it is assumed that long-term monetary liabilities could theoretically be exchanged for liabilities in the parent's currency through the foreign exchange market. They are considered vulnerable to exchange movements and are valued at the current rate. This valuation — if gains or losses are currently recognized — results in substantial swings in reported income if exchange rate changes are significant over the life of the debt. From a translation point of view, a long-term debt of FC (foreign currency) 100 million issued on 31/12/19X0 would impact the financial statements of a borrower as follows:

	FC	ER (PC/FC)	PC	FX gain (loss)
31/12/19X0	100,000,000	1·0	100,000,000	—
31/12/19X1	100,000,000	0·9	90,000,000	10,000,000
31/12/19X2	100,000,000	1·1	110,000,000	(20,000,000)
31/12/19X3	100,000,000	1·0	100,000,000	10,000,000
31/12/19X4	100,000,000	1·0	100,000,000	0
			Net FX impact	PC 0

Although the net impact of the long-term debt of FC 100 million over the four-year period is nil, the company will report a gain of PC 10 million in 19X1, a loss of PC 20 million in 19X2, a gain of PC 10 million in 19X3, and zero gain/loss in 19X4, increasing or decreasing the owners' equity in line with currency fluctuations in each period.

The discussion indicates that, depending on the translation method used, long-term debt can completely reverse the foreign exchange exposure of a company. For example, if the foreign currency devalues against the parent currency, a leveraged firm reports a translation gain. Such a gain, however, reflects economic reality only where the devaluation clearly improves the firm's international trading position. Further, if the all-current translation method were used, a translation loss would be recorded, assuming the company is in a net asset position. Can one seriously say that a difference in translation method results in an economic loss in one case and an economic gain in the other?

VI. Income statement

Income statement exposure quantifies the negative or positive impact of currency fluctuations on the operating income and/or the translation adjustment of a reporting entity. As the value of a foreign currency changes relative to the currency of the reporting entity, the revenues and expenses from operations within a country, when expressed in the reporting currency, show an increase or decrease. This increase or decrease is generally not reported as a foreign exchange gain or loss. Instead, it is usually quantified as an operating variance, affecting the operating income, as discussed in detail in Chapter 5, section 7. Concomitantly, however, the revenues and expenses generate assets and liabilities on the books of the reporting entity. The net assets generated impact the translation adjustment of the reporting entity if, at the end of the exposure period, they are translated at an exchange rate different from the transaction rate at which they had been originally recorded. This translation adjustment is conceptually identical to the one discussed in part II of this section.

If revenues and expenses are denominated in a currency other than the parent currency, the PC equivalent of revenues and expenses will be altered if the exchange rate between the local currency (LC) and parent currency changes during the exposure period. The income statement and balance sheet exposure, and the relationship between the two using different assumptions as to the timing in exchange rate changes, is considered in Exhibit 1.1.4. Scenario 1 assumes that the local currency devalues by 10% at the end of the exposure period; Scenario 2, a devaluation of 10% at the beginning of the period. Scenario 3 assumes a gradual depreciation of the LC over the period, with a 10% depreciation by the end of the period.

Stable foreign currency — control statement: If the exchange rate between the local currency and the parent currency does not change over the exposure period, the results in terms of the parent currency will represent exactly the PC equivalent of the LC earnings. In our case, where the exchange rate remains at par throughout the period, the LC and PC results are identical. This situation is presented as the control statement in Exhibit 1.1.4, where sales of LC 10,000 have no impact on either the operating variance or the translation adjustment (columns 5 and 6).

Local currency devalues at the end of the period: If the local currency devalues on the last day of the accounting period, the parent will report a translation loss of PC 1,000. This is because the net assets generated by the net income at the exchange rate of PC 1·0 are translated at the end of the period at the exchange rate of PC 0·9. The translation loss of PC 1,000 is shown under Scenario 1 in the Exhibit (column 6).

Local currency devalues at the beginning of the period: If the LC devalues at the beginning of the period, revenues will be recorded at the exchange rate of PC 0·9. Since the exchange rate remains at PC 0·9 throughout the whole quarter, the income generated during the period will remain on the books on March 31, 19X1, at the same exchange rate of PC 0·9. No translation gain/loss will be reported and the decline in income would show as a negative variance of PC 1,000 as illustrated under Scenario 2 (column 5).

Local currency depreciates gradually over the period: If the local currency depreciates gradually over the exposure period, revenues and expenses generally will be translated at the lower average exchange rate of the period. Furthermore, if the local currency continues to decline after the revenues and costs have been booked at the average rate, the assets generated, i.e. LC 9,500 will decline in value when expressed in PC terms and result in a translation loss. In Scenario 3, the total decline of PC 1,000 in income (column 7) is due to a negative variance of PC 500 (column 5) and a translation loss of PC 500 (column 6).

Reconciliation of impact recognition: The above analysis indicates that the timing of the exchange rate changes influences the manner in which the impact of foreign exchange fluctuations is reported. Column 7 indicates that the net impact of the exchange rate changes is identical under the three scenarios where the local currency depreciates by 10% against the parent currency by the end of the accounting period. The key difference between the three situations is, therefore, only a matter of accounting cosmetics.

Exhibit 1.1.4: Income statement exposure

Item	(1) LC revenues	PC equivalent stated at: (2) Opening rate	(3) Transaction rate	(4) Closing rate	PC impact analysis: (5) Operating variance	(6) Translation adjustment	(7) Total impact
Control statement	10,000	10,000	10,000	10,000	0	0	0
Scenario 1	10,000	10,000	10,000	9,000	0	(1,000)	(1,000)
Scenario 2	10,000	10,000	9,000	9,000	(1,000)	0	(1,000)
Scenario 3	10,000	10,000	9,500	9,000	(500)	(500)	(1,000)

VII. Pro-forma exposure

As corporations engage in commercial activities, they accrue expenses and revenues, settle liabilities and collect receivables, pay dividends, borrow and make capital investments. Their exposure changes over time as individual transactions are recorded.

It is, therefore, not merely today's exposure that may give rise to foreign exchange gains and losses in the future. As a result, an increasing number of companies are forecasting their exposures with the view of protecting earnings expected to be reported in the future.

A simple example shows how pro-forma exposure is computed. Starting with the balance sheet in the following table, the company has projected the following income statement and identified transactions which will affect future exposure. We assume the following pro-forma income statement of the subsidiary:

Sales	LC 250
Cost of goods sold	100
Expenses	50
Pre-tax earnings	100
Tax (60%)	60
After-tax earnings	40
Dividend	20
Change in retained earnings	LC 20

The following forecast of anticipated transactions can then be prepared:

Item	Cash	Inventory	LC A/R	Fixed assets	PC A/P	LC A/P	T/P	R/E
t^0	100	0	100	200	300	0	0	100
Expenses						50		(50)
Buy inventory		100				100		
Sell inventory		(100)	250					150
Collect A/R	200		(200)					
Pay A/P	(100)					(100)		
Accrue tax							60	(60)
Pay dividend	(20)							(20)
t^1	180	0	150	200	300	50	60	120

Using the current rate method, the *projected* after-tax foreign exchange loss is PC 12 (PC 120 × −0·10). It is brought about by the same factors as the loss of PC 10 (PC 100 × −0·10) with the static balance sheet, except that the additional LC 20 in retained earnings caused an increase in the exposure from LC 100 to LC 120. In other words, the additional positive exposure of LC 20 gave rise to the additional loss of PC 2.

VIII. Exposure definitions and hedging strategies

It is not within the scope of the preceding discussion to come to a conclusion for an ideal definition of foreign exchange exposure for a corporation's operating purposes. Accounting standards and corporate practices are so diverse that it would be inappropriate to indicate an optimal approach. Each company must, therefore, select the definition which reflects best the economic reality of its own operations. Once the exposure is defined, however, that definition will affect the amount, and possibly the direction, of the hedge. It is possible for a company to be short from a monetary/non-monetary viewpoint due to long-term debt. It may be balanced if inventory is included in the exposure definition, and long under the functional currency approach. Motivated by the first definition, the company would be buying forward. In the second case, it would do nothing, and in the third case it would sell forward. Those hedging techniques, their cost and accounting implications, are discussed further in this chapter and in Chapter 4.

2. Exposure identification
Friedrich W. Meierjohann

Most companies which operate in a multicurrency environment, have ideas — which often take the form of very sophisticated models — about how they should react to identified exposures. Many of these ideas, however, are never executed because the companies still believe that active currency exposure management is a speculative business, and that conservative management principles require that a company accepts currency exposure as and when it is incurred.

The damage caused by these so-called conservative management principles, which tend to prevent active exposure management, may be substantial. However, it may be less than the damage which could be caused by active management of the exposure as it is understood. Most companies know how to respond to an identified exposure, whereas the process of the identification of the exposure is not very sophisticated.

Usually, the analysis of the possible earnings effects of a company's currency exposure does not present the full picture but is limited to selected aspects. Under certain circumstances, this approach may lead to conclusions which are exactly the opposite of the conclusions of a complete analysis. For example, the currency exposure associated with a specific new product line (e.g. a product supplied under a long-term purchase contract by a foreign vendor who bills in a foreign currency) ought to be compared with the currency exposure associated with all programmes of the company. If the exposure analysis is limited to the currency exposure of the new product line, the company is likely to decide to cover an exposure which may already be offset by a reverse exposure of an existing product group.

The most common restriction in the identification of a currency exposure is to limit the analysis to the balance sheet at a given moment and to neglect commitments for future transactions, such as sales, purchases, manufacturing, investments, etc. Companies which apply this restriction recognize the need to protect the results of past operations, which are reflected in the balance sheet, whereas they cannot see the need to protect the earnings from future operations by currency management activities, since they believe in their ability to respond to future exchange market situations with changes in their marketing and product supply strategy. They even fear that commitments in respect of currency management, such as forward contracts, might affect their ability to react to new developments in the markets for their products.

This approach, which is encouraged by the usual accounting and reporting rules, may be valid under very special circumstances, but it neglects a currency exposure which definitely exists. If a company wants to determine its real currency exposure, it must try to establish how its earnings could be affected by future exchange rate fluctuations. The balance sheet translation exposure cannot be more than one element in such a study.

The analysis of the earnings exposure due to exchange rate movements seems to be simple and straightforward, but it is not. The usual approach is to start with the currency content of each element (sales, costs of goods sold, expenses, etc.) of the anticipated consolidated earnings statement for a future period, which may be a quarter, a year, five years or an even longer period.

Exhibit 1.2.1 shows the situation of a U.S. company which has a French subsidiary. U.S. vendors supply half the products sold by the subsidiary, the other half is manufactured by the subsidiary. About 10% of the products which the U.S. parent sells in the American market, are bought from various vendors in France which bill in French francs. The Exhibit analyses the earnings effects of a 10% appreciation of the French franc against the dollar. It shows that the higher dollar value of the purchases by the U.S. parent from the French vendors, of the costs of the manufacturing by the French subsidiary and of the other expenses incurred by the French subsidiary will reduce corporate earnings by $15 million in the case of a 10% appreciation of the French franc versus the U.S. dollar. This adverse effect, however, will be more than offset by the increase in the dollar value of the sales of the French subsidiary ($20 million).

The calculations illustrate to the management of the company that a 10% appreciation (or depreciation) of the French franc, which is the invoicing currency for 25% of the worldwide sales, will result in a fluctuation of worldwide consolidated earnings of less than 7%. The company may be willing to live with an exposure of this size. It could be reduced further by

16

Exhibit 1.2.1: The model which leaves out too much

| | Before appreciation of the French franc | | | After appreciation of the French franc | | | |
	U.S. company	French subsidiary	Consolidated	U.S. company	French subsidiary	Consolidated	Variance
			($ million)				
Sales							
$ content	600	—	600	600	—	600	—
Ffr content	—	200	200	—	220	220	20
Cost of sales							
$ content	432	80	512	432	80	512	—
Ffr content	50	80	130	55	88	143	13
Expenses							
$ content	60	—	60	60	—	60	—
Ffr content	—	20	20	—	22	22	2
Earnings							
before tax	58	20	78	53	30	83	5

certain operating decisions. The U.S. company could increase its purchases from French vendors, the French subsidiary could bill certain customers for certain products in dollars instead of French francs, and/or replace purchases from U.S. vendors with purchases from vendors in France. Or the company might engage in hedging operations, such as dealings in forward contracts.

This example is an oversimplification. The economic reality is more complicated. Most companies are exposed in more than one foreign currency. This may cause calculation problems, but does not change the basic logic. More important is a simplification in the logic which may cause wrong conclusions. The model neglects the effects of exchange rate movements on managerial decisions. Let us consider the most typical complications.

1. The French subsidiary sells products (steel, chemicals, etc.), which have a world price expressed in dollars. If the French franc appreciates against the dollar, the prices in French francs, at which the subsidiary can sell its products, will be affected; the subsidiary must lower its prices, or it will lose sales. The consequence may be that the dollar value of the sales of the French subsidiary will not be influenced by a fluctuation in the exchange rate, even though the invoicing currency is not the dollar. The situation is different if shipments are made under long-term contracts without a price adjustment clause.

2. The calculation was based on the assumption that the exchange rate movements do not have volume effects. This is not very realistic. If exchange-rate movements reduce or increase costs, the company can reduce or is forced to increase its selling prices, and such decisions will affect its sales volume which, in turn, will affect manufacturing unit costs due to changes in capacity utilization.

3. The example assumed major purchases by the U.S. parent company from French vendors. If they are made under short-term contracts and these vendors can be replaced with U.S. suppliers on short notice, the French franc currency exposure with regard to these supplies can be neglected.

4. The model disregards the inter-relationship between inflation and exchange rates. It does not recognize that increases of costs incurred in a foreign currency, which are caused by currency appreciation, may be offset by savings due to a lower inflation rate of the foreign currency, whereas the advantages of a deteriorating exchange rate of a foreign currency may be more than compensated by the medium and long-term effects of a higher inflation level.

5. The most serious reservation about this model, however, is that it neglects the time factor. Exchange rate changes may affect the earnings of one company immediately, whereas for another company the effects are delayed. One company may have long-term contracts with its customers but be able to change its suppliers at short notice. A competitor may sell under contracts of a short-term nature but be committed

by longer-term contracts with his suppliers. It is obvious that the exposure of the two companies is quite different.

6. The timing of the exchange rate adjustment is an additional complication. This is important, since the direction and possibly even the extent of future exchange rate adjustments may be predictable, but the timing is not. A given currency may be critically overvalued, but government policies and central bank intervention may delay the necessary rate adjustment for years.

It is essential for any company which has operations in more than one currency to know the currency content of its expected business transactions and to determine how parity changes would affect planned earnings. Then it can have a plan for decisions and actions to be taken if expected parity changes actually occur. This will increase the speed at which the company can react, possibly a critical advantage over a puzzled competitor.

All this, however, does not accomplish much more than to make the management aware how much, or how little, exposed its company and its earnings are. It does nothing to protect the earnings. A company may develop very sophisticated plans about how it will react if exchange rates begin to move in a certain way, but there is no assurance that such reactions will be possible and meaningful under the future circumstances; there may be new products, new export markets, new competitors, new production methods, new government regulations, and all this may force the company to look for different solutions, when the rate adjustment actually occurs.

The only coverage of the earnings against the effects of future currency fluctuations is an operating structure in the various currencies which protects the earnings no matter whether expected exchange rate adjustments actually occur or not, and no matter whether the currencies involved appreciate or depreciate.

The translation of this principle into business practice means that a company should develop a structure of currency contents in its business operations which ensures that the adverse effects of any exchange rate movements on selling prices, sales volumes, and product costs is fully offset by the effect of the currency appreciation or depreciation on the value (expressed in the base or accounting currency) of the transactions in the various foreign currencies, and *vice-versa*. Since exchange rate forecasts have only a limited reliability, it is extremely risky to base a business plan for a future period on assumptions about future exchange rate developments, which may or may not materialize.

It is more useful to base the business plan on the present set of exchange rates, to determine separately how exposed the earnings are if certain expected or unexpected exchange rate movements occur, and to take what steps may be possible to reduce this exposure.

Let us look at our earlier example, and make a few additional assumptions:

— The U.S. company anticipates, in the case of a 10% appreciation of the French franc, that it will be able to negotiate a 5% price reduction with its French suppliers. The cost increase of the supplies from France, expressed in dollars, will be passed on in a 5% selling price increase in the market, which will result in a 10% decline in the sales volume of the imported products.

— The French subsidiary, in turn, would pass on the absolute amount of the reduction of the cost of the imported products, expressed in French francs, in its selling prices, but expects that this will not increase its sales volume by more than 5%.

The results of this calculation are presented in Exhibit 1.2.2. The analysis indicates that a 10% appreciation of the French franc would affect worldwide earnings only by an amount of $2 million or less than 3% of the planned profit. These amounts, and especially the effects on the French subsidiary, are quite different from those suggested in Exhibit 1.2.1. If additional calculations for the whole range of the possible appreciation (as well as depreciation) of all currencies in which the company is involved confirm that the maximum exposure does not exceed this amount, the company may be well advised to stay away from protective arrangements, like forward contracts or long-term obligations towards foreign suppliers.

The currency management concepts, under which most companies operate, are orientated towards expectations about future exchange rates, but neglect the earnings effects of managerial decisions in response to future actual exchange rate developments. Such concepts at best may be

Exhibit 1.2.2: Taking price movements into account

| | Before appreciation of the French franc | | | After appreciation of the French franc | | | |
	U.S. company	French subsidiary	Consolidated	U.S. company	French subsidiary	Consolidated	Variance
			($ million)				
Sales							
$ content	600	—	600	597	—	597	(3)
Ffr content	—	200	200	—	216	216	16
Cost of sales							
$ content	432	80	512	432	84	516	4
Ffr content	50	80	130	47	88	135	5
Expenses							
$ content	60	—	60	60	—	60	—
Ffr content	—	20	20	—	22	22	2
Earnings before tax	58	20	78	58	22	80	2

able to produce speculative profits but cannot protect a company against earnings fluctuations due to exchange rate movements.

The currency exposure management concepts used by most companies reflect the thinking in terms of positions, typical of the banking industry, which may not be applicable to the more complex situation of the industrial sector.

3. Country and currency exposure

Gail F. Lieberman

The external forces which affect the multinational firm are sufficient in themselves to disrupt international financial planning, and any internal planning should take account of them. One of the first steps is the definition and measurement of the foreign exchange risk, i.e. a loss due to fluctuation of exchange rates. The amount on which a company reports the loss is the exposed position, or exposure.

Multinational firms use two different measurements of exposure: a country approach, or a currency approach. Most firms are concerned with two categories of foreign exchange risks: those due to transaction effects and those due to translation effects. Those firms which approach the measurement of transaction and translation exposure by the country concept are managing foreign exchange risk from a subsidiary's viewpoint. Those which use the currency concept are managing foreign exchange risk on a global basis. The difference between the two methods implies, at the very least, the possibility of non-uniformity in communication and reporting. The implications for planning are far more serious.

The country approach to the measuring of exposure as suggested in this section is similar in concept to the functional currency approach as embodied in FAS-52 (see sections 4 and 5 of this chapter). The currency approach, on the other hand, uses a single unit of measurement, as implied by the now discarded FAS-8.

Country exposure

Exhibit 1.3.1 illustrates a typical balance sheet for the United Kingdom. All accounts are in thousands of U.S. dollars. Using the general definition of exposure under the monetary/non-monetary translation method, country exposure is calculated from the accounts which are on the local country's books, adjusted for tax effects. The exposure in the United Kingdom is found by, first, netting the $70 million liability from the $30 million asset position and, second, adjusting for the tax effects of the $10 million account denominated in dollars and the $10 million account denominated in lire. The exposure in the United Kingdom is a liability of $30 million computed as shown in Exhibit 1.3.2, equation 1.

Assuming no other accounts on Italy's books — the exposure in Italy is an asset of $10 million, computed as shown in Exhibit 1.3.2, equation 2. The exposure in the United States is 0.

If a devaluation of the pound and lire is assumed at 6% and 3% respectively, the exchange

Exhibit 1.3.1: Balance sheet summary report

	Total	Current rates ($ thousand)	Historical rates
Assets			
Cash	1,000	1,000	—
Receivables	15,000	15,000	—
Inter-company receivables	—	—	10,000
Inventories	10,000	—	10,000
Net fixed assets	50,000	—	50,000
Other assets	14,000	14,000	—
Total assets	90,000	30,000	60,000
Liabilities			
Loans	50,000	50,000	—
Payables	—	—	—
Payables to U.S. in $	10,000	10,000	—
Inter-company payables	—	—	—
Payables to Italy in lire	10,000	10,000	—
Capital/reserves	15,000	—	15,000
Retained earnings	5,000	—	5,000
Total liabilities	90,000	70,000	20,000

Exhibit 1.3.2: Country v. currency exposure calculation

	($ thousand)
Country exposure — U.K.	
$30{,}000 - 70{,}000 - (1 - 0.5) \times (0 - 20{,}000) = -30{,}000$ (1)	
Country exposure — Italy	
$10{,}000$ = $10{,}000$ (2)	

Currency exposure — pound	
$30{,}000 - 70{,}000 - (1 - 0.5) \times (0 - 20{,}000) =$ $30{,}000$ (3)	
Currency exposure — lire	
$10{,}000 + (1 - 0.5) \times (0 - 10{,}000)$ = $5{,}000$ (4)	

gain in the United Kingdom is $1,950,000 as shown in Exhibit 1.3.3, equation 5. The exchange gain due to exposure in the United Kingdom is calculated by:

(1) multiplying the $40 million sterling exposure by the 6% devaluation of sterling *vis-à-vis* the dollar;

(2) tax affecting the $10 million liability at the U.K. tax rate of 50% and multiplying it by the 6% devaluation of sterling *vis-à-vis* the dollar;

(3) tax affecting the $10 million lire liability at the U.K. tax rate of 50% and multiplying it by the cross rate of 3% between sterling and lire.

The exchange loss in Italy of $300,000 is found by multiplying the $10 million lire asset by the 3% devaluation of lire *vis-à-vis* the dollar as shown in Exhibit 1.3.3, equation 6. The total exchange gain to the company is $1,650,000.

Exhibit 1.3.3: Country v. currency exposure gain (loss) calculation

Lire devalues 3%; pound devalues 6%

	($ thousand)
Country exposure — U.K.	
$-40{,}000\,(-0.06) + 5{,}000\,(-0.03) + 5000\,(-0.06) = 1{,}950$ (5)	
Country exposure — Italy	
$10{,}000\,(-0.03)$ = -300 (6)	
Country exposure — total	= $1{,}650$

Currency exposure — pound	
$-30{,}000\,(-0.06)$ = $1{,}800$ (7)	
Currency exposure — lire	
$5{,}000\,(-0.03)$ = -150 (8)	
Currency exposure — total	= $1{,}650$

Currency exposure

Currency exposure is calculated from all accounts which are on the books of subsidiaries located in the country of currency, and all accounts which are denominated in local currency, no matter where located. The first part of the definition is equivalent to the country definition of exposure (current assets minus current liabilities less the tax effects of foreign currency on local books). The second part of the definition aggregates all the net asset positions denominated in local currency on other subsidiaries' books adjusted for taxes. Using the information provided in Exhibit 1.3.1, the pound exposure is the same as the exposure in the United Kingdom because there is no sterling on any books outside the United Kingdom.

The lire exposure, however, is very different. There are $10 million in lire receivable on Italy's books and $10 million in lire payable on the United Kingdom's books. The lire exposure is computed by adding the net asset position on Italy's books of $10 million to the net liability position of $5 million which has been adjusted for the U.K. tax rate. The lire exposure is $5 million computed as shown in Exhibit 1.3.2, equation 4.

The two measures of exposure can be reconciled by comparing the total exchange gain from the currency exposure definition with the exchange gain calculated earlier. Assuming the same exchange fluctuations, the exchange gain due to a fluctuation in sterling is $1·8 million, as shown in Exhibit 1.3.3, equation 7. The exchange gain is calculated by multiplying the $30 million sterling liability exposure by the 6% devaluation of sterling *vis-à-vis* the dollar. The exchange loss due to a fluctuation of lire is $150,000, as shown in Exhibit 1.3.3, equation 8, and is found by multiplying the $5 million lire asset exposure by the 3% devaluation of lire *vis-à-vis* the dollar. The total exchange gain to the company is $1,650,000, the same gain that resulted using the country definition of exposure.

Country and currency exposure measures yield two very different values but the total exchange gain/loss is equivalent. The obvious differences of the two exposure measures are:

(1) the exchange gain/loss computed from country exposure is based on cross rates, while the exchange gain/loss computed from currency exposure is based on straight rates;
(2) the country definition of exposure groups non-homogeneous accounts together into a single measure, whereas the currency definition of exposure groups all accounts which are affected by a fluctuation of the currency under consideration.

Both country and currency exposure have the same total exchange gain/loss because the currency exposure definition is an arithmetical regrouping of the elements of the country exposure. For example, a lire foreign currency liability on the United Kingdom's books is usually multiplied by the cross rate of pounds and lire to obtain the exchange gain/loss in the United Kingdom according to the country exposure definition. This transaction can be separated into two components. One part of the transaction is the contribution to sterling exposure due to the account being affected by a fluctuation of sterling *vis-à-vis* the dollar. The other part of the transaction is the contribution to lire exposure due to the account being affected by a fluctuation of lire *vis-à-vis* the dollar. All the accounts that are affected by a fluctuation of sterling comprise the sterling exposure. The same is true for the lire exposure.

Advantages and disadvantages

Country and currency exposure implies more than a regrouping of terms. The country exposure measures the exchange risk and exchange gain/loss in each country, while currency exposure measures the global exposure and exchange gain/loss in each currency. The former exposure concept implies a decentralized exposure management programme and the latter exposure concept implies a centralized exposure management programme. The firm which is making decisions based solely on the country exposure definition is viewing each country as an independent entity not interacting with any subsidiaries in other countries.

Those firms which do not engage in cross-border trading say that this is a valid picture, but this argument can be fallacious. Assume, for example, that a U.K. subsidiary borrows lire directly from a bank in Italy, and the firm uses a country definition of exposure. The lire foreign currency liability in the United Kingdom is an offset to exposure by the U.K. tax rate multiplied by the Euro-lire loan. However, there is a corresponding offset to a lire asset exposure of which the Italian subsidiary is unaware. The account is not on the Italian subsidiary's books; they have no way of knowing about the lire liability in the United Kingdom. So if the lire is forecast as weak, the Italian lire subsidiary might enter into a forward contract or over-finance itself. Then the total hedging and financing cost to the parent company is increased.

Those firms which engage in cross-border trading are affected to a greater extent. If payables extended to Italy are invoiced in lire, there is an offset to an asset exposure in the United Kingdom multiplied by the lire liability. On Italy's books there is an asset exposure in lire. It is quite possible that the Italian subsidiary might again overprotect itself if only because it cannot be sure what the British subsidiary is planning.

On the other hand, the firm which is making decisions based solely on the currency exposure definition is viewing its operations on a global basis. Financing and hedging costs are being minimized because the interaction among currencies is being taken into account. However, there are disadvantages to this method of management. First, there is a loss of incentive to the local manager. By accepting exposure management directives from the parent, the local

22

manager may quite conceivably be asked to take a loss position for the good of the entire company. The parent firm must often rely on local managers for information about the events affecting currency outlooks. If the local managers are no longer responsible for decisions, the communication link may be strained. Second, the company which uses the currency definition of exposure does not have knowledge of the exchange gain/loss in each country. The global currency gain/loss is known but has to be disaggregated, so that losses and gains can be traced to the initiating transactions and appropriate chargebacks made. Third, though the use of straight rates rather than cross rates greatly simplifies the gain/loss calculation, the gains/losses due to cross rate movements are buried in the straight rate adjustments. Thus, gains/losses due to cross rate changes are more difficult to detect.

Recommendation

Summarizing the advantages and disadvantages of country and currency exposure concepts, it is apparent that the currency exposure concept is essential for planning. If the currencies are viewed on a global basis, financing and hedging costs are minimized. The currency exposure value is more meaningful than the country exposure measure because it can be multiplied by the straight rate to yield the exchange gain or loss. Using straight rates is also a welcome simplification. The advantages of the country exposure concept are the disadvantages of the currency concept of exposure. The country exposure concept allocates the exchange gain/loss where the account is booked, while the currency concept of exposure determines the exchange gain/loss due to the movement of a given currency. The country exposure measure allows for incentive at the local level. Which measure, then, should the company use?

For planning and reporting purposes the advantages of the currency definition of exposure greatly outweigh the country definition of exposure. The parent corporation will be know-ledgeable about the global position in each currency and, therefore, will not be incurring needless financing and hedging costs because of sub-optimal strategies. However, FAS 52 implies that the country exposure measure should be used. Currency exposure can be employed at the corporate level.

For example, if a financing and hedging strategy which minimized costs due to interest charges and expected foreign exchange losses was found to cause an abnormally large loss position on one country's books (and this was unacceptable for one reason or another) the optimal strategy would be adjusted so that an acceptable loss position would result. All that is necessary to implement this recommendation is to calculate and evaluate both country and currency exposure for each planning decision. For more complicated international financial planning strategies, computer programmes have been developed to simulate and optimize hedging strategies. These programmes can be extended to include this recommendation.

4. Accounting standards

Björn Holm

The consolidation of foreign subsidiaries into the books of the parent company creates problems which arise partly from methodological reasons and partly from the subsidiaries' structure of assets and financing. The methods of handling these problems vary sharply from each other, and produce unequal effects on the profit and loss account. In addition, there may be problems in the understanding of the conversion effect.

We shall study three methods, all widely used to treat the exchange rate problem. The following scheme sums up how they work.

	Converted at closing rate[1]	Converted at historic rate[2]
1. Closing rate method	All items including depreciation	—
2. Current/non-current method	Current assets and current liabilities	All other assets and liabilities Depreciation
3. Monetary/non-monetary method	Cash, debtors, all liabilities	Inventory Fixed assets Depreciation

[1] The rate existing at year end.
[2] The rate in force before the change.

Let us now show how they work in practice. I have used two fictitious subsidiary currencies B and C, and one fictitious currency A for the consolidating company. B-currency appreciates (25%) and C-currency depreciates (25%) in relation to A-currency. Otherwise the examples are identical.

In Exhibit 1.4.1 we see in the first column of figures (t^0) what the accounts of subsidiary B looked like before being consolidated into the books of A. The three following columns show the accounts after being converted to currency A at the new or historic exchange rate as applied by the different methods.

Exhibit 1.4.1: B-currency appreciates by 25%

($B^0 = 2/3A$, $B^1 = 5/6A$)

		Closing rate method	Current/ non-current method	Monetary/ non-monetary method
Profit and loss account	P/L t^0	P/L t^1	P/L t^1	P/L t^1
Sales	15,000 B	12,500 A	12,500 A	12,500 A
Costs + financial charges	12,000 B	10,000 A	10,000 A	10,000 A
Depreciation	600 B	500 A	400 A	400 A
Taxes	1,200 B	1,000 A	1,000 A	1,000 A
Net profit	1,200 B	1,000 A	1,100 A	1,100 A
Balance sheet	t^0	t^1	t^1	t^1
Cash	300 B	250 A	250 A	250 A
Accounts receivable	3,000 B	2,500 A	2,500 A	2,500 A
Inventory	3,000 B	2,500 A	2,500 A	2,000 A
Fixed assets	6,000 B	5,000 A	4,000 A	4,000 A
	12,300 B	10,250 A	9,250 A	8,750 A
Accounts payable	1,500 B	1,250 A	1,250 A	1,250 A
Local loan	3,600 B	3,000 A	2,400 A	3,000 A
Share capital (4,000 A)	6,000 B	4,000 A	4,000 A	4,000 A
Net profit	1,200 B	1,000 A	1,100 A	1,100 A
Gain (+), loss (−) on exchange		1,000 A	500 A	−600 A
	12,300 B	10,250 A	9,250 A	8,750 A

24

At the bottom of the Exhibit we can see the great variation of the effects of the methods, going from a gain of 1,000 A by the closing rate method to a loss of 600 A according to the monetary/non-monetary method. The closing rate method is perhaps the easiest to understand and also the most logical. Since the subsidiary currency B has appreciated, there should be a gain for the shareholder, because his holdings are by definition the net of the assets and the liabilities.

When using the current/non-current method, the size of the working capital plays a vital part in establishing the magnitude of the exchange rate effect. Thus, the higher the working capital the higher the gain, and vice-versa. The monetary/non-monetary method shows a loss of 600 A. This is a strange result, compared with the other two. It is a bit difficult to understand that we incur a loss, if the local currency of the country we have invested in appreciates. The method is conservative since it immediately realizes all latent losses on external financing.

There is evidently an argument for a more smooth timing of showing these losses. One way would be to realize only the losses of those parts of the external financing that fall due during the next one-year period. The method favours high share capital financing, since the higher it is the lower the exchange loss will be.

Inventory is a non-monetary item and is thus valued at the historical rate. This procedure has an important bearing upon the profit margin as it is calculated in A-currency before and after the appreciation.

In another example, subsidiary B sells regularly at a profit margin of $33\frac{1}{3}$%. The year-end inventory of 3,000 B is thus sold to customers during the first part of the next year for 4,500 B. These transactions result in a profit margin of 46·7% when shown in A-currency (sales 3,750 A minus year-end inventory 2,000 A = 1,750 A or 46·7%). I do not think it is a good procedure to have distortions of the profit margins on account of exchange rate changes.

If we look at Exhibit 1.4.2, we see exactly the reverse situation, the closing date method giving a loss of 1,000 A and the monetary/non-monetary method a gain of 600 A. A decline in the investment value on account of depreciation follows from the closing rate method.

A positive working capital gives a loss if the current/non-current method is used.

Exhibit 1.4.2: C-currency depreciates by 25%
($C^0 = 2/3A$, $C^1 = 1/2A$)

		Closing rate method	Current/ non-current method	Monetary/ non-monetary method
Profit and loss account	P/L t^0	P/L t^1	P/L t^1	P/L t^1
Sales	15,000 C	7,500 A	7,500 A	7,500 A
Costs + financial charges	12,000 C	6,000 A	6,000 A	6,000 A
Depreciation	600 C	300 A	400 A	400 A
Taxes	1,200 C	600 A	600 A	600 A
Net profit	1,200 C	600 A	500 A	500 A
Balance sheet	t^0	t^1	t^1	t^1
Cash	300 C	150 A	150 A	150 A
Accounts receivable	3,000 C	1,500 A	1,500 A	1,500 A
Inventory	3,000 C	1,500 A	1,500 A	2,000 A
Fixed assets	6,000 C	3,000 A	4,000 A	4,000 A
	12,300 C	6,150 A	7,150 A	7,650 A
Accounts payable	1,500 C	750 A	750 A	750 A
Local loan	3,600 C	1,800 A	2,400 A	1,800 A
Share capital (4,000 A)	6,000 C	4,000 A	4,000 A	4,000 A
Net profit	1,200 C	600 A	500 A	500 A
Gain (+), loss (−) on exchange		−1,000 A	−500 A	600 A
	12,300 C	6,150 A	7,150 A	7,650 A

The monetary/non-monetary method produces a gain of 600 A. The conservative bias of that method in the appreciation example of Exhibit 1.4.1 turns into an optimistic bias in Exhibit 1.4.2, and at once realizes all the gains on external financing, thus resulting in a substantial exchange profit compared to the other two methods, which show a loss.

We meet the same problem regarding the profit margins of products sold because of the inventory valuation at historical rate. Taking the same example as before, we get a decrease in the margin for the sale of the year-end inventory (sales 2,250 A minus year-end inventory 2,000 A = 250 A or 11·1%).

More long-term effects occur when we look at the impact of depreciation of fixed assets. In the case of currency appreciation it could be argued that the current/non-current and monetary/non-monetary methods inflate the profit on depreciation of fixed assets. In the future these assets must be replaced and neither method retains enough profit for that purpose. In the case of currency depreciation, the situation is the reverse since the two methods deflate the profit.

To avoid the problems associated with each method, we should have an operation consisting of cash and accounts receivable and financed by accounts payable and share capital. In such a case the methods coincide. However, each method has its own underlying philosophy, from the simplicity of the closing rate method to the more theoretical approach of the monetary/non-monetary method, and there are arguments for and against each one.

5. FAS 52 — accounting implications
Douglas E. Bender

Since the adoption of FASB Statement No. 8 (FAS 8) in 1975, U.S. multinational companies have been attempting to adapt to the temporal approach (essentially the monetary/non-monetary approach) to foreign currency translation as required by that Statement. This approach required that foreign currency translation gains and losses:

— all be measured against the common basis of the dollar,[1] and
— be calculated for monetary assets and liabilities but not for non-monetary accounts.

In addition, FAS 8 required that foreign currency translation gains and losses be included in income.

These requirements produced the following distortions in reported results of operations, which have led a number of critics to question the relevance, reliability and predictive value of the accounting answers produced under FAS 8.

Economically compatible results
Critics of FAS 8 argued that translation should, at a minimum, produce positive accounting results (i.e. gains) when foreign investments are enhanced by a strengthening of the foreign currency against the dollar. Thus, a German subsidiary should appear to have more value as the Deutschemark rises in value against the dollar because the investment or future sales at a constant Deutschemark price could be converted into more dollars.

Often, however, the opposite accounting result was produced under FAS 8 because Deutschemark debt was translated at the higher current exchange rate while non-monetary assets such as inventory or fixed assets were translated at low historical rates, and the resultant translation loss was included in income. Additionally, the enhanced value of future sales is not considered by the historical cost accounting model. As a result, a net translation loss was frequently reflected in the accounts despite an appreciating investment.

Operating margins
Another perceived distortion caused by the monetary/non-monetary approach arose from the matching of sales measured at current prices and translation rates against cost of sales measured at historical costs and translation rates. Thus, under FAS 8, exchange rate movements resulted in reporting increasing or decreasing operating margins solely because of the lag in inventory turns.

Volatility of earnings
A third concern with the FAS 8 approach arose from the requirement that all translation gains and losses be included currently in income. Although exchange rate movements are frequently short-term in nature, at any reporting date the measured gain or loss may be significant. Because such gains and losses are unrealized and frequently short-term in nature, some believe that reflecting them currently in income tends to obscure long-term trends which are more relevant in predicting profitability of the enterprise and return of capital.

FAS 8 was superseded by the issuance of FASB Statement No. 52[2] (FAS 52) in December 1981, after three years of intensive research, analysis and public comment. To correct the perceived distortions created by FAS 8, the FASB adopted the following objectives for translation in FAS 52:

"a. Provide information that is generally compatible with the expected economic effects of a rate change on an enterprise's cash flows and equity.

---

[1] Dollar in this chapter refers to the U.S. dollar and is assumed to be the reporting currency in all cases.
[2] Statement of Financial Accounting Standards No. 52, *Foreign Currency Translation*, Financial Accounting Standards Board, Stamford, Connecticut, December 1981.

b. Reflect in consolidated statements the financial results and relationships of the individual consolidated entities as measured in their functional currencies in conformity with U.S. generally accepted accounting principles."

The functional currency approach

The approach adopted to achieve the objectives of FAS 52 is called the functional currency approach. It presumes the following:

— An enterprise may operate and generate cash flows in a number of separate economic environments.
— Each of the enterprise's operations can be identified as operating in one primary economic environment, generally either the local environment or the parent company's environment. The currency of that primary economic environment is the functional currency for those operations.
— The enterprise may commit to a long-term position in a specific economic environment and does not currently intend to liquidate that position.

The functional currency approach is a radical change from the FAS 8 approach. Because it accepts multiple measurement bases in consolidated financial statements, two steps may be required to prepare dollar financial statements. First, the results of operations in each environment are to be measured in the functional currency of that environment. ("Measured in the functional currency" has the specific meaning that gains and losses included in income are determined only in relation to accounts denominated in that currency.) This first step is automatically accomplished if the accounts of the specific foreign operation are maintained in the functional currency (i.e. if the local currency is the functional currency). However, if they are not (e.g. if the accounts are maintained in Deutschemarks, but the dollar is determined to be the functional currency), it will be necessary to remeasure the results of operations in the functional currency (e.g. dollars).

Translation to dollars is the second step of the two-step process necessary to prepare dollar financial statements under FAS 52. Mechanically, the functional currency approach calls for translation of all functional currency assets and liabilities into dollars at the current exchange rate. Use of the current rate for all accounts is responsive to both the economically compatible results and operating margin distortions because those distortions arose from the translation of non-monetary accounts at historical rates. The resultant translation adjustment has to be recorded directly in shareholders' equity in an attempt to alleviate the volatility of earnings distortion. The need for translation is obviated if the dollar is determined to be the functional currency.

Because measurements are made in multiple functional currencies under FAS 52, determination of the functional currency of a specific foreign operation can have a significant effect on reported income.

If the functional currency of a specific foreign operation is determined to be the local currency, assets and liabilities are translated at current exchange rates while equity accounts are translated at historical rates. Because the translation process is performed only for the purpose of preparing financial statements of the reporting enterprise, and the process does not anticipate that the foreign currency accounts will be liquidated and exchanged into dollars, translation adjustments are not included in income but are deferred as adjustments to the equity (net worth) section in the financial statements of the reporting enterprise.

Essentially, the translation process expresses functional currency net assets at their dollar equivalent — using the current exchange rate — and creates an adjusting entry to balance the dollar net worth. The translation adjustment does not affect net income until a specific foreign net investment is wholly or substantially liquidated. At that time, the component of the translation adjustment account related to that specific net investment is relieved from the translation adjustment account and included in the determination of gain or loss on sale of the investment.

If the functional currency of a specific foreign operation is determined to be the dollar, all transactions must be remeasured to dollars by assuming that an exchange of currencies will occur at the exchange rate prevailing on the date of the remeasurement. This will produce a foreign exchange gain or loss if the exchange rate fluctuates between the date of the original transaction and the date of the assumed (or actual) exchange. Foreign exchange gains or losses are similar to other trading activities and are included in income.

Remeasurement under FAS 52 is very similar to translation under FAS 8. When the functional currency of a foreign entity is deemed to be the dollar, an effect on earnings comparable to the effect under FAS 8 should be expected from the remeasurement process. Because FAS 8 was based on the premise that financial statements of a U.S. enterprise should be measured in a single unit of currency (i.e. the dollar), translation was a one-step process that encompassed both remeasurement to dollars and expression as dollars. Under the functional currency approach, which accepts multiple units of measure, remeasurement is required only when:

— the functional currency is that of a highly-inflationary economy (cumulative inflation of approximately 100% or more over a three-year period), in which case the accounting must presume the dollar as the functional currency;

— the accounts of an entity are maintained in a currency other than its functional currency; or

— an entity is a party to a transaction which produces a monetary asset or liability denominated in a currency other than its functional currency.

Hedging strategy and exposure

Hedges are designed either directly, by entering into a forward exchange contract to buy or sell one currency for another, or indirectly, by managing the exposed[3] net asset or liability position (e.g. by borrowing or billing in dollars rather than the local currency).

With the adoption of the monetary/non-monetary approach in FAS 8, many companies reported foreign exchange gains and losses in income for the first time. Although the adoption of FAS 8 neither increased nor decreased the true economic exposure to foreign exchange risks (i.e. the risk that foreign exchange rate movements will affect future cash flows), FAS 8 did create an accounting exposure to foreign exchange risks (i.e. the risk that foreign exchange rate movements will affect reported income through the translation process). As a result, hedging strategies became increasingly important as management sought to minimize the effect of exchange rate fluctuations on reported income.

Similarly, the adoption of FAS 52 will not change a company's true economic exposure to foreign exchange risks. However, because accounting exposure is significantly different under FAS 52 from what it was under FAS 8, hedging policies may require fundamental reconsideration. For a foreign entity with the local currency as the functional currency:

— Accounting exposure as previously defined will be significantly reduced if not eliminated. Under these conditions, some companies may elect to avoid the cost of hedges altogether. However, if accounting exposure were considered to include the translation adjustment deferred in the equity section, such exposure may have increased substantially since non-monetary assets (inventory and property accounts) are now translated at current rates and are accordingly exposed. Some companies may choose to hedge this exposure to protect reported equity.

— Gains and losses on remeasurement of dollar denominated intercompany payables and receivables (except those of a long-term investment nature) are not eliminated in consolidation and, accordingly, directly impact income. Under FAS 8, with its single unit of measure premise, intercompany transactions were self-hedged (except for possible tax effects).

— Exposure to foreign currency commitments and other foreign currency transactions is the same, and is accounted for in the same manner, as under FAS 8.

For foreign entities with the dollar as the functional currency, accounting exposure remains essentially equivalent to that under FAS 8, except that deferred taxes are now considered monetary and accordingly affect the exposed net asset position.

---

[3] Only monetary assets and liabilities are exposed for accounting purposes under FAS 8.

6. U.K. accounting standards

Richard Mathews

Over recent years, the U.S. Financial Accounting Standards Board (FASB), the Canadian Institute of Chartered Accountants (CICA) and the Accounting Standards Committee (ASC) in the U.K. have attempted to develop an internationally accepted approach to the subject of foreign currency translation. The introduction of FAS 52 in the United States in December 1981, and the anticipated adoption of an amended ED 27 in the U.K. in 1983, are the results of the above efforts. This section outlines the principles underlying ED 27 and highlights the major areas of contention.

ED 27 was issued in October 1980, and was originally intended to be implemented in 1982. However, the delayed introduction of FAS 52 in the United States, and the major objections to certain sections of ED 27 have forced the postponement of its adoption. It now seems likely that a new draft will be issued in April or May, which will be adopted in January 1983.

The net investment concept forms the basis of ED 27. Under this concept "the assets and liabilities of foreign subsidiaries are translated at the closing rate of exchange and incorporated into the holding company's consolidated balance sheet. Exchange differences which give rise to cash flows, i.e. those resulting from business transactions, are reported as part of the profit or loss for the year. Other exchange differences which do not give rise to cash flows, because they result from re-translations of the holding company's long-term investments in the foreign subsidiary, are reported as reserve moments."

The major proposals of ED 27 are:

1. Operating gains or losses of foreign subsidiaries are to be translated at an average rate for the year in the consolidated profit and loss account.
2. Foreign subsidiaries' balance sheets are to be translated at the closing rate for consolidation purposes, with the exception of those subsidiaries deemed to be an extension of the parent company. In this case, the temporal method will apply.
3. Translation differences arising from the conversion of subsidiaries' balance sheets into the consolidated accounts will be taken to reserves.
4. Exchange gains/losses on foreign currency debt will be taken to the consolidated profit and loss account unless local currency debt is used to finance an equity investment. In this case, exchange differences will be taken to reserves.

The exposure draft was issued by the ASC in October 1980, and at the public hearings on ED 27 held in London during February 1981, the following major comments were made:

1. The application of the closing rate method to historical cost data does not produce useful results and distorts the true financial state of a company's overseas operating units. It has been argued that the above method is not consistent with SSAP (Statement of Standard Accounting Practice) 16 and that to reflect realistically the operating performance of overseas subsidiaries, the closing rate method should be applied only to current cost data. ED 27 makes only a fleeting reference to this subject.
2. The cover concept contained in the draft is too restrictive. The concept was first developed in ED 16 which was published in 1975. It stated that where a foreign loan was used to finance the purchase of fixed assets, exchange differences on the loan could be offset against exchange differences on the asset. ED 27 has defined the cover concept in a narrower sense as follows:

   "Where an equity investment in a foreign subsidiary has effectively been financed by the proceeds of a foreign loan raised by the holding company, the holding company may be covered in economic terms against any movement in exchange rates. Any increase or decrease in the amount outstanding on the loan as a result of exchange movements will probably be covered by a corresponding change in the value of the net investment. It would be inappropriate to record an accounting profit or loss in these circumstances when exchange rates change."

   ED 27, therefore, stipulates the following conditions for offsets to be made between differences on foreign loans and the re-translation of the net investment:

(a) the loan is dominated in the same currency as the investment;

(b) exchange differences on the loan can be offset only to the extent of the differences arising on the re-translation of the investment;

(c) the closing rate method of translation must apply between the holding company and overseas subsidiary for consolidation purposes;

(d) the accounting treatment used should be applied consistently.

It has been suggested that ED 27 be amended to include a wider definition of the cover concept. For example, the new U.S. exposure draft refers to "foreign currency transactions that are intended to be, and are effective as, economic hedges of a net investment in a foreign entity". Recent comments on ED 27 by an *ad hoc* committee of the Council of the Association of Certified Accounts specifically recommended that the restriction to "holding" company referred to in paragraph 57 should be broadened to include any operating unit, and the offset permitted in the following subsection extended to include hedging transactions in parallel currencies. A broader interpretation of the cover concept would be consistent with the fact that most multinational companies attempt to manage foreign currency risk on a global basis. In this respect, ED 27 is also lacking in that it does not address the question of the treatment of forward exchange contracts.

3. The use of the average rate method to translate subsidiaries' profit and loss accounts is misleading. Several companies made strong representations against the use of an average rate to translate subsidiaries' profit and loss accounts. BAT Industries Limited specifically stated: "We believe that the main objective of consolidated accounts is to indicate to shareholders of the parent company the effect of the group's trading performance on their interest. In the final analysis the parent company's shareholders are interested in the profits available to cover dividends and those that remain to finance growth. On this basis it follows that the concern of the shareholders is for the parent to receive a stream of dividends to go toward covering that company's distributions. It appears to us that the use of an average rate for translating currency profits is incompatible with this main objective of the consolidated accounts and we therefore advocate the use of the closing rate for translating currency profits".

4. The inclusion of the unrealized gains on long-term debt in the profit and loss account conflicts with the provisions of the 1980 Companies Act. The example contained in paragraph 65 of ED 27 results in an unrealized gain on the translation of a U.S. dollar loan to the parent company, which is reported in the profit and loss account as a profit for ordinary operations. Under the provisions of the 1980 Companies Act relating to dividend distribution, it would not be consistent in the above example to base a dividend report on a combination of realized and unrealized income.

The majority of U.K. companies already use the closing rate method for translation purposes. However, the treatment of the gains/losses associated with the translation process will be standardized under the new draft. So, because of the direct impact upon earnings which will result from translation differences on foreign borrowings, U.K. companies will tend to use sterling to a greater extent to fund overseas expansion. Alternatively, the cover concept will also encourage local currency borrowing where possible to obtain an offset of translation differences on the debt and the equity investment it related to. Revisions to the draft should include an explanation of how to calculate the average exchange rate to translate subsidiaries' profit and loss accounts.

7. Cash flow exposure: a case study[1]

Joseph G. Blake

In recent years, the headlines of the financial papers have reported the adverse impact of foreign exchange fluctuations on the income of many companies. In 1979 Rolls-Royce reported substantial losses because of a fixed-dollar contract with an American customer. Laker Airways, which had expanded quickly, was declared bankrupt in early 1982. At the time of the bankruptcy the company owed $255 million. While not the primary cause of the bankruptcy, the currency risk of these borrowings contributed to the bankruptcy.

On first consideration, one might conclude that a prudent treasurer never borrows foreign currency. Speculation about currency is to be avoided and these examples clearly are proof of the axiom. However, for companies with large international activity the issue is not that simple. The answer in each case will be influenced both by the facts and the style of management of a company.

First, let us summarize the major facts in the Laker story. In 1978–79 Laker Airways arranged to borrow $124 million from the U.S. Export-Import Bank to help finance the purchase of 11 DC-10s. The loans were made at exchange rates of between $2·10 and $1·80. The rate of interest was less than 10% and had a term of nine years. In January 1981, Midland Bank International led a syndicated loan to the company of $131 million to purchase three A-300 airbuses. This loan was over 10 years at a rate of around 10%.

During the 1981–82 financial year, Laker Airways was obliged to pay the equivalent of £47 million in principal and interest. In the summer of 1981 Laker paid £23·5 million and requested a delay until late 1982 of the balance which otherwise would have been due between January and March 1982. Laker budgeted a rate of U.S.$2·25. In late 1981, the spot rate ranged between U.S.$1·80 and $1·95. About one-third of Laker's revenues were in foreign currency, whereas the balance was in sterling. In addition, Laker had substantial expenses for fuel, navigation and landing fees denominated in dollars. Under U.K. tax law, exchange gains and losses related to funding are not recognized. Consequently, there would have been no tax relief if Laker Airways eventually realized an exchange loss.

Net cash flow

Four elements of currency exposure are important: liquidity, transaction exposure, translation exposure, and economic exposure. Of these four elements, translation exposure was not very important to Laker Airways. It was a private company, and yearly fluctuations due to translation exposure were not critical. Net cash flow was critical to the company. This fact was highlighted by the rapid growth of the company, its highly competitive fare programmes, and the tough economic environment in which the industry operated. As one might expect, its gearing ratio was also higher than many other comparable airlines. Considering these factors, Laker Airways needed to manage its transaction exposure and liquidity aggressively to maximize cashflow and reduce current borrowing costs. This approach would have been consistent with both the facts and the style of its management.

We now need to ask a simple question — should Laker Airways have borrowed such large amounts of dollars and so obviously mismatched revenues and expenses? During the 1970s, the long-term sterling debt market vanished. Sterling interest rates have traditionally been higher than U.S. dollar rates and the rates of interest on the finance for these planes was attractive.

Nonetheless, Laker Airways' situation was similar to Rolls-Royce's. Rolls-Royce reported large losses because of a fixed-rate dollar contract with Lockheed. Unfortunately, Rolls-Royce did not arrange long-term dollar finance to match its revenues under contract. Consequently, Rolls-Royce lost money on every engine sold under the contract and also had to fund the losses at the highest rates of interest in modern British history.

---

[1] This section was first printed in the March 1982 issue of *The Treasurer* and appears, amended, by kind permission of *The Treasurer*.

Economic exposure

Laker and Rolls-Royce are not unique examples. A major American oil company operating in the North Sea elected to fund its U.K. operations in sterling, ignoring that oil is priced in dollars. This decision merely compounded its exposure in sterling because most of its local expenses — salaries, rates, utilities — were also in sterling. If a company has large, long-term revenue sources in a foreign currency, it has an economic exposure that cannot be ignored.

However, these examples do not mean that one should only fund a company with a foreign currency because of a long-term revenue source in that currency. Currency borrowings are another source of funding. Currently, money market conditions dictate that the treasury examine raising funds in other than sterling if only for short periods. However, there should be a clear financial advantage, such as relatively low rates of interest on Deutschemarks during a period of upward pressure on the pound.

When combined with forward contracts, the use of short-term borrowings can be quite advantageous. For example, several large U.K. companies, such as Rolls-Royce, are using the U.S. commercial paper markets and forward contracts to reduce effective borrowing costs. Normally, the cost of commercial paper is the cheapest way to borrow dollars. The rates are usually less than prime rate or Libor. At various times, U.S. interest rates have risen above sterling rates. Consequently, when sterling sold at a premium against the dollar in the forward markets, a top-rated U.K. company could borrow in the commercial paper market and buy dollars forward to satisfy the maturity dates of the paper. As a result, the effective borrowings cost would have been less than sterling for the same period.

Currency exposure is not just another risk associated with international business. It is also an opportunity to earn substantial rewards. For long-term borrowings, the treasurer should borrow currencies which he can anticipate in subsequent periods as revenues. If a company expects substantial revenues in Deutschemarks during a five- or 10-year period, it can always borrow the amount expected today and match payments of the borrowing to the expected revenue in subsequent years. If a treasurer considers that German interest rates are normally lower than in the U.K., and the likely dramatic effect on sterling of changes in the world oil markets, then this alternative is probably the most prudent option. If the past is any guide, there will be savings of interest and effective cover of the currency exposure.

The bankruptcy of Laker Airways was primarily due to commercial judgements rather than its currency borrowings. Its plans for growth were too ambitious, if not unsound. However, let us assume the company had developed a more conservative expansion plan in the U.S. market. Undoubtedly, there would have been larger dollar revenues earned from an increasing number of American passengers. If Laker's corporate plan had forecast the growth of the U.S. market realistically, Laker's treasury should have borrowed dollars which matched the anticipated dollar revenue.

Swapping liabilities and obligations

Assuming the corporate plan was sound and the terms of the dollar borrowings were attractive enough to justify the mismatch of revenues and liabilities, could Laker have taken action to ensure that the currency risk was not too burdensome? Rolls-Royce and Laker had similar problems which might have provided an opportunity which was mutually beneficial. Rolls-Royce has dollar revenue and Laker dollar debt. Possibly, these two companies could have arranged their own long-term forward contracts and solved their currency exposure problems in a mutually beneficial way.

Such contracts would obviously require some sophisticated analysis. However, swaps between large international organizations are not unknown. Recently, IBM exchanged long-term Swiss franc debt on its books with the World Bank. The World Bank gave IBM dollar liabilities and assumed IBM's Swiss franc obligations. Consequently, IBM reported substantial transaction gains.

The role of the budgeted exchange rate and the forward markets should also be considered. Laker budgeted for an exchange rate of $2·25 during its current financial year. Laker was obliged to pay $85·6 million during the current year. In January 1981, market conditions clearly indicated an opportunity to exceed budgeted expectations. For example, the pound was trading between $2·35 and $2·40. On January 15, 1981, the spot rate was $2·401. However, the forward rate for six months was $2·4385, and for 12 months $2·4430. Therefore, large savings could have been realized in 1981 if pounds had been sold forward for dollars. Budgeted exchange rates are to be used not only for planning but also for decision–making.

If there is a single lesson to be learned from this analysis it is that currency exposure management and funding management require continuous review. Obviously, large companies can afford sophisticated treasury staff to perform this function. But even large companies often need to rediscover the wheel. Likewise, smaller companies need to be aware that sophisticated financial techniques are not the monopoly of multinational giants. These techniques can often be used just as effectively by smaller companies, who do not need to have an international treasurer. They merely need to know what the issues are, and discuss them with their bankers.

Regardless of the size of the company, currency exposure requires management to address certain issues and to make specific choices. No one solution will satisfy every company, nor will it always be appropriate for a specific organization.

8. Accounting standards and exposure management

Michael Adler and Bernard Dumas

How should we define economic exposure to foreign exchange risk? Should we hedge any exposure, however defined? Should the proposed shift from the Financial Accounting Standard 8 temporal method of translation to the closing rate method change our hedging practices?

Companies' answers to these questions vary widely. Some define exposure in accordance with the FAS 8 definition, as net local currency monetary assets, plus, in some cases, some measure of their transactions and commitment exposures. A second group aims to identify and hedge economic exposures, defined as net local currency monetary assets plus inventories. Apparently inventories are added because they are typically rolled over through the cash account several times a year. A third group ignores translation exposures altogether (on the generally faulty grounds that exchange rate changes are frequently self-reversing) and chooses to hedge only large foreign currency transactions. A fourth group considers that what the parent has at risk abroad is its net investment, defined as its net worth, in each subsidiary. Hedging decision rules in this last case are seldom specified precisely; there is a tendency to define exposure not from the parent's but rather from the subsidiary's viewpoint.

Use of simulation methods

Once we have defined exposure, how do we manage it? Here again practice is diverse. Some firms attempt centralized global management. They often discover that special provisions have to be made to preserve local managerial incentives. Managers do not like to have their performance evaluated on dimensions which are beyond their control. Others, acknowledging these pressures, decentralize and put each tub on its own bottom. Local managers are set free to hedge their own exposures, presumably so as to protect their incomes measured in the parent's currency. In at least one case, this decentralized approach is paralleled by a headquarters activity which nets the individual decisions and attempts to adjust the total to conform to overall corporate exposure targets.

These firms cannot all be right, at least not all the time. To bring order to the chaotic state of current thinking, a possible first step is to define the concept of economic exposure to exchange risk and to relate it to various accounting-based definitions. A second is to analyse the financial objectives that hedging may serve and the circumstances in which acquiring protection can prove valuable to the firm and its stockholders.[1] A third is to analyse the implications of the economic approach to exposure management for the debate surrounding the proposed introduction of the current rate translation method in the U.S., the U.K. and the EEC.

Economic exposure should ideally be defined and measured as the amount of foreign currency which represents the sensitivity of the future, reference currency market value of any asset, liability, security or firm to variations in the future exchange rate, on a specific future date. A hedge is the foreign currency transaction (e.g. forward contract) which renders that reference currency market value independent of the exchange rate.

From the viewpoint of its stockholders, a firm's economic exposure can be identified with a measure of the sensitivity of its future stock price to future randomness of the exchange rate. This sensitivity can be measured statistically, by regression analysis, using past data. For managerial purposes, however, this approach is not very useful, and not merely because past data may not predict the future. The difficulty is that, to manage exposure, treasurers must orchestrate a variety of financial and operating plans whose probable effects on the firm's stock price, individually and jointly, are extremely hard to determine.

---

[1] (a) M. Adler and B. Dumas, "Simulating a Firm's Exposure to Exchange Rate Changes," mimeo, Colombia University (1980a).

(b) M. Adler and B. Dumas: "Foreign Exchange Risk Management," in B. Antl, ed., *Currency Risk and the Corporation* (London, Euromoney Publications, 1980), 145–57.

(c) M. Adler and B. Dumas, "The Exposure of Long Term Foreign Currency Bonds," *Journal of Financial and Quantitative Analysis*, November 1980, 973–94.

Simulations using managerial cash flow projections and accounting data can produce useful approximations (Exhibit 1.8.1). The value of the firm can be proxied in terms of either the level of the future cash balance or of the future book value of stockholders' equity at the target date. Neither choice is theoretically ideal.

Exposure in this approach is simply measured as the coefficient in a regression of the proxy value of the firm on the exchange rate. Consider how this technique works in the straightforward case of a local currency 1,000 foreign currency, receivable due in one year. Here we know exactly what the exposure is. It is LC 1,000 and that also is the size of the calculated regression coefficient. A hedge in the form of a forward sale of LC 1,000 renders constant the future dollar value of the receivable, regardless of how the exchange rate moves (Exhibit 1.8.2). Being constant, this dollar value is certainly also independent of the exchange rate, as required by the definition above. The technique, however, also works similarly for any risky asset, liability or security whose dollar value after hedging is not certain. The remaining uncertainty is unrelated to the exchange rate.

Some treasurers may object to simulation methods for planning on the grounds that they are cumbersome and costly. In the past, this has been true. However, managers now have

Exhibit 1.8.1: Simulating and measuring exchange risk exposure

(1) Simulation

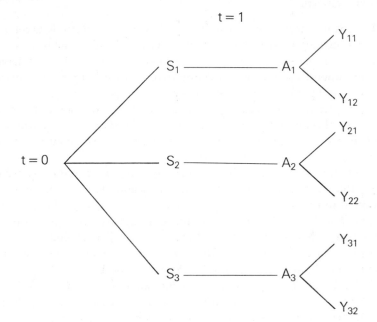

Notation: time 0 = decision planning date;
time 1 = target date or planning horizon;
S_s = possible levels or ranges of the exchange rate at t = 1;
A_j = set of (optimal) actions at t = 1 given that S_s occurred;
Y_{sj} = proxy value of the firm given the combination, S_s and A_j.

(2) Measurement: Define exposure as the size of the forward contract which renders Y_{sj} statistically independent of S_s.

Method: Statistical regression: regress $Y_{sj} = a + bS_s +$ random error.

Result: The regression coefficient, b, measures the exposure *ex-ante*.

Caveats:
(a) The measure is exact if Y_{sj} and S_s are linearly related.
(b) *Ex-ante* exposure can be measured up to the precision of a statistical estimate, but not in an exact accounting sense.
(c) The exposure coefficient, b, includes the impact of excluded risks which are perfectly correlated with S. It would change were other variables to be incorporated.

relatively cheap access to global information systems such as those installed by the major banks and for their customers, who frequently employ them for projections. The further step, to more formal simulation, seems short. Whether it will be taken depends on the value of the additional information that the procedure can provide. We claim that it improves on current practice in the following ways.

The simulation approach is global. It involves comparisons among the various future values of the entire firm, proxied in cash or equity terms, each of which is associated with a possible level of the future exchange rate. That is, the approach enables the treasurer to estimate his global exposure, in advance of any financial or real decisions, as the statistical association between the possible values of the firm as a whole and the exchange rate. The approach is global also in the sense that the exchange gain or loss associated with economic exposure thus determined can further be decomposed into components which include translation and transaction gains and losses — a traditional concern — plus the gain or loss produced by the impact of the exchange rate change on volume. This last is widely ignored. Our simulation methods, however, automatically encompasses all such effects (Exhibit 1.8.3).

The aim of hedging

Measuring exposure via simulation and regression permits the treasurer to hedge away completely his exchange risk as it is seen at the time of his decision. A hedge in the amount of this exposure will render the future proxy value of the firm independent of the exchange rate (though not riskless because the hedged value will itself still be uncertain). Hedging economic exposure, however, will not produce zero accounting exchange gains and losses except by coincidence. Reported exchange gains and losses are invariably measured as the difference between the beginning and ending values of some set of financial statement accounts. This difference can be measured only after the fact. Consequently, it cannot be hedged in advance and can be reduced to zero, if ever, only by profitable speculation. The temptation, or pressure, to gamble on the exchanges is one a treasurer should perhaps resist.

What is the aim of hedging? This is a matter of theoretical and empirical analysis, the results of which seem largely to accord with treasurers' intuitive judgements. Some executives state their goal as making decisions which improve their stock price. Were the financial markets perfect, however, they would not be able to do so by hedging. In the absence of imperfections such as transactions costs and default risks, the value of a forward contract would be zero at the instant at which it was initiated. The market would therefore place a value of zero, i.e. not respond at all to a treasurer's announcement of his intention to hedge, regardless of the risk or the firm's exposure. In practice financial markets contain imperfections, but their severity and impact is so hard to measure as to make it extremely difficult to design a value-improving hedge. There have been no direct tests of the effect of hedging on stock prices. Indirect tests suggest that the effect is probably minor.[2]

Most treasurers believe that value maximization is either not practicable, or should not be their only goal. Besides, many work in companies where it is considered vital to increase and stabilize reported income. The result in the United States has been a tendency on the part of some treasurers to choose a strategy of hedging the worst possibility, so as to reduce the likelihood of having to report translation losses in income, as is required by FAS 8. There is some question as to the validity of the objective, and of the strategy. The treasurers themselves complain that the amount of hedging they feel impelled to do is excessive and uneconomic. Empirically, there is no evidence that any additional earnings variability introduced by FAS 8 has caused security returns to suffer.[3] It seems that forward contracting to avoid reporting losses will not improve stock prices unless, perhaps, managers have access to superior forecasts or inside information which enables them consistently to produce exchange trading profits. Most treasurers admit that they cannot forecast exchange rates. Why, then, do they submit to the demand that their forward exchange transactions produce countervailing profits?

---

[2] Roland E. Dukes, "The Empirical Investigation of the Effects of FASB Statement No. 8 on Security Return Behaviour," Financial Accounting Standards Board, December 1978.

[3] Roland Dukes, *op. cit.* Apparently investigators judge either that they can compensate for corporate exposure by hedging for themselves or that reported exchange gains and losses have little effect on firms' bankruptcy risks.

Exhibit 1.8.2: Exposure and hedging when there are three states of nature and a fixed amount — LC 1,000 — due in the future

(1) **To show:** Exposure is the regression coefficient of the future dollar value of the LC position in a regression of that position on the exchange rate. In this case, no simulation is required.

(2) **Definitions:** Y_s = Dollar value of LC 1,000 in state s at time t

S_s = Future spot exchange rate in state s

(3) **Regression:** $Y_s = a + bS_s$, where here, $a = 0$ and

$b = cov(Y_2, S_s)/Var(S_s)$

p_s = Probability of state s

$\bar{Y} = \Sigma_s p_s Y_s$

$\bar{S} = \Sigma_s p_s S_s$

$cov(Y_2, S_s) = \Sigma_s p_s (Y_s - \bar{Y})(S_s - \bar{S})$

$Var\ S_s = \Sigma_s p_s (S_s - \bar{S})^2$

(4) **Data:**

States	P_s	S_s	Y_s	$S_s - \bar{S}$	$Y_s - \bar{Y}$	$(S_s - \bar{S})^2$	$(Y_s - \bar{Y})(S_s - \bar{S})$
1	1/3	0·25	$250	0·025	$50	0·000625	0·625
2	1/3	0·225	$225	0	0	0	0
3	1/3	0·20	$200	−0·025	−$50	0·000625	0·625

(5) **Calculated regression coefficient:**

$$b = \frac{cov(Y_s, S_s)}{Var\ (S_s)} = \frac{(2/3)\ (0·625)}{(2/3)\ (0·000625)} = LC\ 1,000 = exposure$$

(6) **To hedge:** Sell LC 1000 @ F, cover @ S_s: proceeds = $1,000 (F − S_s)

(7) **Results**

	State 1	State 2	State 3
Dollar value of LC 1,000	$250	$225	$200
Dollar proceeds of contract	(1,000) (F − 0·25)	(1,000) (F − 0·225)	(1,000) (F − 0·20)
Dollar value of position	(1,000) F	(1,000) F	(1,000) F

Exhibit 1.8.3: Defining and hedging economic exposure, measured in terms of the future cash balance

(1) **Assumptions:** (a) Initial exchange rate, $S_0 = \$0·25/LC$, at time 0.

(b) Cash balance prior to exchange rate change = LC 500.

(c) At time 0, expect an exchange rate change at time t.

(d) Time t exchange rate may be either $0·25/LC or $0·20/LC.

(e) Depending on the time t exchange rate, the cash balance will differ as planned sales, purchases, production and taxes change.

(2) **Simulation**

Data	Time 0	State 1	State 2	Difference
Exchange rate	$0·25/LC	$0·25/LC	$0·20/LC	$−0·05/LC
LC cash balance	LC 500	LC 1,000	LC 1,500	LC 500
Dollar value of cash balance	$125	$250	$300	$50

(3) **Economic exposure** = $50/(0·20 − 0·25)$/LC = − LC 1,000

(4) **To hedge:** Buy LC 1,000 @ F, cover @ S_s: proceeds = $1,000 ($S_s$ − F)

(5) **Results**

	State 1	State 2
Time t cash balance in U.S.$	250	300
Dollar proceeds of contract	(1,000) (0·25 − F)	(1,000) (0·20 − F)
Time t cash balance in U.S.$	$500 − (1,000)F	$500 − (1,000)F

(6) **Decomposition of time t cash balance:**

(a) Choose state 1 as the reference state: 0 subscripts initial CB.

(b) Variation to be explained: $(CB_2)S_2 - (CB_1)(S_1)$, where

$$(CB_2)S_2 - (CB_1)S_1 = CB_1(S_2 - S_1) + (CB_2 - CB_1)(S_2 - S_1) + (CB_2 - CB_1)S_1$$
$$CB_1 = CB_0 + (CB_1 - CB_0)$$
$$CB_2 = CB_0 + (CB_2 - CB_0)$$
$$\therefore\ (CB_2)S_2 - (CB_1)S_1 = CB_0(S_2 - S_1) + (CB_2 - CB_0)(S_2 - S_1) + (CB_2 - CB_1)S_1$$

Exhibit 1.8.2 (cont)

(c) Using example data:

    (i) CB Variation to be explained: $(1,500)(0 \cdot 2) \times (1,000)(0 \cdot 25) = \$50$
    (ii) Translation loss $= CB_0 S_2 - S_1) = (500)(0 \cdot 20 - 0 \cdot 25) = - \$25$
    (iii) Transaction loss $= (CB_2 - CB_0)(S_2 - S_1) = (1,000)(0 \cdot 20 - 0 \cdot 25) = - \$50$
    (iv) Operations gain $= (CB_2 - CB_1)S_1 = (500)(0 \cdot 25) = \$125$
    (v) Reconciliation: $\$125 - \$50 - \$25 = \$50$

(7) **Observations**

(a) Total, i.e. economic, exposure is measured on the basis of comparisons of the U.S.$ cash balance in different states of nature at a future date.

(b) The translation loss in this two-state example is identical to the accounting definition. This is because the reference state is one with no devaluation, i.e., $S_1 = S_0$, which is always a possible assumption.

(c) The transaction loss is the product of two parts. The first is the transaction exposure, $(CB_2 - CB_0)$; this difference between the CB in the non-reference state and the initial CB is equal also to $(CB_2 - CB_1) + (CB_1 - CB_0)$ and is affected by all the economic factors and corporate decisions which affect cash flows in both states. The second is the exchange rate between the non-reference and reference states, $S_2 - S_1$, at a single point in future time.

(d) The operations gain is equal to the exchange rate in the reference state times the difference between the CBs in the non-reference and reference states. This difference is due to the change in local operations occasioned by the exchange rate variation. There is no operations exposure. This quantity has not before been displayed in the literature.

Improved reporting

What should be the aim of hedging? What do treasurers have in mind when they insist on their concern for parent currency cash flows? They identify transaction exposure as their main problem, especially as it relates to large commitments, but why? The answer seems to be that they are avoiding default. The treasurers of large firms as a rule deny that default is even a remote possibility for their firms. But their efforts would not be so directed if they did not fear defaults, at least subliminally.

The risk of bankruptcy can be reduced by hedging so as to minimize the variability of cash flows (for each given level of the firm's expected returns). Managers should view this as part of a strategy to diversify their global portfolio of risks. Minimizing cash–flow variability may not require a perfect exchange risk hedge if exchange rates are imperfectly correlated with other sources of uncertainty. Avoiding default seems to be the most justifiable of all the possible reasons for hedging. It is, so far, the only strategy which can lead to the calculation of an optimal hedge. The simulation planning method is ideally suited to the task.[4]

Such techniques will require of managing boards the courage largely to ignore accounting exchange gains and losses, and the understanding that an economically correct programme of exposure management can produce uncertain (i.e. random) reported results. Current practice is unlikely to change for as long as treasurers aim (or are obliged) to manage their financial statements instead of their risks and opportunities.

Accountants assume, often correctly, that the goal of improving reported results governs managerial behaviour. Reacting to treasurers' dissatisfaction with FAS 8 and the temporal translation method in general, the accounting standards boards in the United States and Great Britain, acting cooperatively, last autumn recommended changing to the current rate/net investment method. Almost immediately articles appeared in *Euromoney* and elsewhere, predicting major changes in corporate hedging practices.[5] This may happen, but it should not.

---

[4] The early lead in the application of simulation to default risk analysis was taken by Gordon Donaldson, "A New Framework for Corporate Debt Policy," *Harvard Business Review*, March-April, 1962.

[5] John B. Gianotti, and D. P. Walker, "How the new FAS 8 will change exposure management," *Euromoney*, November, 1980.

No radical change would occur if firms were already managing their exposures correctly by minimizing the variability of cash flows with the objective of reducing default risk. Such a strategy can be conducted independently of any translation conventions, except the rule that cash flows be translated at the rate in effect on the date they occur.[6]

Assessing techniques

The debate on which translation technique is best has become confusing. For purposes of managerial decisions neither method serves well. From a purely technical accounting point of view the temporal method seems superior.

The temporal and current rate methods often produce opposite results. Say that net monetary assets are negative, net worth is positive and the home currency devalues. The former generates an exchange loss and the latter a gain. This difference arises from the different quantities each method deems exposed: net monetary assets in one case and net worth in the other. Proponents of current rate method argue that it preserves more faithfully than the temporal method the structure of the local currency accounts, and therefore reflects better the operations of the foreign subsidiary. Further, they argue that the current rate method represents better what the parent has at risk — its investment in the subsidiary measured by the subsidiary's net worth. The temporal method, in their opinion, mistakenly views the assets of a foreign subsidiary as if they had individually been purchased for home currency by the parent. Accordingly, it is irrelevant to measure the local currency translation exposure as the subsidiary's net local currency monetary assets.

Proponents of the temporal method counter that, in a different sense, it is more general. It extracts the exchange rate used to translate individual assets and liabilities from the rule (acquisition cost or current price) governing the original posting of the local currency balance sheet accounts. The temporal translation method can therefore accommodate any set of valuation conventions. Specifically, it would imply the current rate method if all local currency assets and liabilities were carried at current prices. Seen in this light, choosing between translation rules depends on the logically prior choice of a system of accounting measurement, that is, of the underlying method of valuing assets and liabilities. Applying the closing rate to historic cost account is, accordingly, inconsistent.

So stated, the differences between the contending parties appear irreconcilable. To proponents of the temporal method, the current rate approach unreasonably treats fixed assets as if they were perfectly exposed. To proponents of the current rate method, the temporal approach, equally unreasonably, fails to recognize that the parent's exposure is limited to its share of the subsidiary's equity. In this view the subsidiary's net monetary assets in its own functional currency (i.e. the currency in which it does business and keeps its accounts) are not the source of the parent's exposure. The exchange rate could change and possibly leave the subsidiary's operations and default risk unaffected. To the subsidiary as an entity, changes in the reference currency value of its local net monetary assets need not matter.

In this debate it is possible to distinguish two threads which can perhaps usefully be separated. One concerns the exposure of individual assets and liabilities. The second relates to the definition of the extent of the parent's possibly indirect exposure to exchange risk through its subsidiary.

Let us consider the parent as if there were no intervening subsidiary. Assume that it owns monetary and fixed assets located and operated abroad. What is its exposure to exchange risk?

All existing translation methods answer this question by defining some assets and liabilities as perfectly exposed to exchange rate variations and others as perfectly unexposed. Under each convention, exposed accounts are then translated at the current rate and the others at the historical rate. The question is whether the logic can be reversed. Are accounts which are translated at the current rate necessarily perfectly exposed, and those translated at historical rates unexposed?

---

[6] M. Adler and B. Dumas, "Simulating a Firm's Exposure to Exchange Risk," *op. cit.*, especially sections 2 and 3. Simulations of the cash balance will be the same regardless of whether the temporal or closing rate convention is used.

Link between exposure and translation rate

Preliminary theoretical analysis shows that only non-interest bearing, nominally fixed, foreign currency accounts, such as cash and accounts receivable or payable (each for the date it is due) are fully exposed. The reference currency values of these items vary directly with the exchange rate. All other assets and liabilities, physical or financial (including interest-bearing, long-term foreign debt) are also generally and individually exposed, in the sense that future exchange rate variations can cause each of their future reference currency market values to change. However, they will not be perfectly exposed if their reference currency market values do not vary one-for-one with changes in the exchange rate. The implication of these propositions for present purposes is simple. Economically speaking there need be no connection between the degree of an asset's exposure and the choice of the exchange rates used to translate its book value when consolidating financial statements. The whole question of linking the notion of exposure to the rate used for translation would disappear were all foreign currency accounts to be posted at their current local currency market prices. These would be translated at the current exchange rate, whether they were exposed or not.

If a correct definition of exposure is independent of the choice of translation convention, so also should be the issue of what the parent has at risk. Suppose that, instead of conducting its foreign operations directly, the parent incorporates a subsidiary as a separate legal entity. The subsidiary does business exclusively in local currency. It holds no foreign currency assets or liabilities and makes no sales or purchases outside its territory from the parent or third parties. Again, the parent's exposure is best defined as the sensitivity to variations in the exchange rate of the market price in its own currency for which it could sell its shares in the subsidiary to outside investors.

Importance of liquid items

In the absence of an incorporated subsidiary, the definition remains the same, but for the substitution of the words "foreign operations as a unit" for "shares in the subsidiary". What is crucial is not so much that the subsidiary's exposure does not matter, but that the parent's economic exposure is not, and cannot be, defined from the subsidiary's point of view.

When exposure is defined thus in economic rather than in accounting terms, the argument over which balance sheet item serves as a better indicator loses much of its force. Both the net monetary position and net worth have a role to play. The subsidiary's local currency net monetary position may influence economic exposure to the extent that its value in reference currency affects the market's (potential) valuation of the subsidiary. Liquid items may matter if the subsidiary goes bankrupt or into liquidation. The incorporation of the subsidiary as a distinct legal entity may separate its default risk from the parent's. To the extent that the parent remains liable, exchange rate changes may affect the reference currency value of the parent's liability, if there is a bankruptcy in which the subsidiary's local currency net monetary assets are used to offset the claim of local creditors.

The subsidiary's local currency net monetary position cannot, therefore, automatically be ignored in connection with exposure defined in terms of the subsidiary's market value in reference currency. On the other hand, the translated book value of the parent's share in the subsidiary's net worth, whether measured by the closing rate or temporal approach, is clearly, at best, an imperfect approximation to that market value. As such, it can serve as a proxy target in measuring economic exposure.

However, for practical purposes it may be possible approximately to define exposure in a simulation approach as the sensitivity of either the (future) book value of equity or of the future cash balance to variations in the (future) exchange rate. Selecting between these two may depend upon which is a better signal of changes in default risk. This choice, however, has absolutely nothing to do with prior claims in favour of one translation convention or another. Either the current rate or the temporal method may be employed. Both permit a decomposition of the change in income or cash flow among components, at least one of which reflects a conventional exchange gain (a local currency monetary position times an exchange rate change) while others reflect operating performance. Using the cash balance proxy has the great advantage of being independent of any accounting convention but only at the cost of ignoring the capital gains and losses on monetary items with maturities beyond the planning horizon.

The arguments used by the supporters of the alternative translation methods may seduce the unwary into believing that the current rate and temporal methods portray alternative views of reality between which one must choose. Closer analysis reveals, however, that economic exposure is captured by neither method.

The two methods merely offer alternative measures, up to an accounting definition, of the component of the change in income which was due to the changes of the exchange rate in the past, between the present and the previous reporting dates. Both, however, ignore key aspects of the total effect. Neither, therefore, reflects accurately what the firm gained or lost because of the exchange rate. The true economic gain or loss may not, as a practical matter, be measurable. Without knowing what it would have been in the absence of the exchange rate change, however, one cannot tell which method produces the closer approximation.

Economic exposure can be defined for firms as the sensitivity of their future share prices to the future exchange rate. It can be measured only approximately and only after some balance sheet magnitude has been, somewhat arbitrarily, selected as the objective to be protected. None serves perfectly. Once such a selection has been made the variations in the objective associated with exchange rate changes must be projected. These variations can be further decomposed into gains or losses of the usual kinds, associated with translation, transactions and operations. This decomposition may be useful for the purpose of decentralizing exposure management.

The fact that exposure exists and can, perfectly or approximately, be measured, does not imply that it must be hedged. If the treasurer's objective is to serve his shareholders, hedging may matter mainly to the extent that it can be used as an instrument to reduce taxes and the risks of costly bankruptcy.

If his objective is speculative gain or the avoidance of losses, he should transact forward only when he is highly confident that he has superior forecasts of, or inside information on, the future course of exchange rates. If, finally, his objective is stabilizing net income, the required hedging will involve both gains and losses on the forward contract needed to offset the predicted variations.

CHAPTER TWO
Forecasting exchange rates

1. The value of forecasts

Gunter Dufey and Rolf Mirus*

Accurate forecasts of exchange rates can be of tremendous help to managers who must assess costs and set prices in the face of international competition, not to mention the speculative profits that investors with access to successful forecasts could reap. It is not surprising, therefore, that extensive efforts have been made to predict changes in exchange rates. But to what extent can such efforts be expected to be successful? What is the worth of forecasts, and how can they be evaluated?

The starting point of this analysis is the concept of market efficiency and the potential use of the forward exchange rate as a forecast. Since the forward rate may be regarded as the market's aggregate prediction of the future spot exchange rate, it is necessary to ask how forecasting services manage to coexist when such an inexpensive forecast is available. Specific forecasting techniques will then be analysed in order to help users of such forecasts understand the nature of and the assumptions behind the various models. Throughout, the forward exchange rate is used as a benchmark — both in the discussion of theoretical issues and in the performance appraisal of commercial forecasts.

Market efficiency and forecasting

Much of the literature on market efficiency has originated in connection with the analysis of stock prices. Unfortunately, when drawing analogies between the stock market and the foreign exchange market, one is apt to generalize too quickly, ignoring some subtle differences.[1] In conjunction with stock price determination, three versions of the concept of efficiency are encountered: weak, semi-strong, and strong. The concept of weak efficiency asserts that past price changes do not contain unexploited information about future price changes; the concept of semi-strong efficiency requires that all publicly available information be reflected in the current prices; the concept of strong efficiency assumes that all available information, both public or private, is embedded in current prices.

Applied to exchange markets, the concept of strong efficiency may be too restrictive. It is possible to argue that transactors in the U.S. stock market have access to much more information of a standardized nature (required by the SEC) and much more information from insiders than is the case for traders in foreign exchange markets. Moreover, foreign exchange

---

* Helpful comments by I. H. Giddy, R. Grosse, and A. Tschoegl are acknowledged.
[1] The following points have been made by S. W. Kohlhagen, *The Behavior of Foreign Exchange Markets — A Critical Survey of the Empirical Literature*, New York University Monograph Series in Finance and Economics, 1978-3; and R. M. Levich, "Analyzing the accuracy of foreign exchange advisory services: theory and evidence," in R. M. Levich and Clas Wihlborg, *Exchange Risk and Exposure*, Lexington, Mass.: Lexington Books, 1979.

traders may and do rely on inside information without having to disclose it. As a result, the requirement assumed in the strong efficiency concept of perfect information at zero cost is less likely to be fulfilled in foreign exchange markets than in stock markets.

Notwithstanding these technical points, it can be shown both on theoretical and to a lesser extent on empirical grounds that transactions costs, political intervention, and risk premiums can cause a deviation of the forward rate from the market's expected future spot rate without indicating inefficiency or market failure. However, given the current state of theoretical and empirical knowledge, it is difficult to ascertain the size and direction of any bias contained in the forward rate. One can, therefore, as a point of departure, use the forward rate provided by an efficient market as a low cost forecast.[2] This is, in fact, the basis of the class of forecasts referred to as "market based".

At this point it becomes possible to provide a theoretical justification for the existence of commercially available exchange rate forecast services. If the forward rate deviates from the expected spot rate, it might be worthwhile to devote resources to obtaining more precise estimates of future spot rates. Since a number of forecasting services have been in existence for some time, and since they have been using resources for the task, the pragmatic view would be to accept that they must be worth their price, in some sense; perhaps they produce a better estimate of the future spot rate than that represented by the forward rate, or perhaps the purchaser obtains other benefits. This view is attractive at this point in the discussion because it obviates the need for a performance evaluation of the commercial services relative to the forward rate. With respect to the users of commercial forecasts, the implication is that they are earning speculative returns as a consequence. However, it must be remembered that market efficiency is not a static concept, i.e. the market is not efficient *per se*; but prices of financial assets established by the buy-and-sell decisions of profit-seeking agents who act as if the market was *not* efficient. In addition, successful transactors will be quickly imitated so that prices adjust to the point where forecasting efforts, at best, yield a return commensurate with the resources employed and the risks taken. The fact that forecasting services are used is, therefore, not incompatible with efficient markets, but does not imply that it is worthwhile for anyone to develop or purchase forecasts of exchange rates.

As in any other competitive market, the expenditure of resources for currency forecasts must be founded on concrete expectations that (1) specific and identifiable market imperfections exist; (2) such imperfections are not already reflected in prevailing rates; and (3) conditions permit the profitable exploitation of the forecasts, i.e. the actions will not be quickly imitated, or government regulations do not permit acting on the forecast to the extent desired.

The following survey of forecasting models shows that it is difficult even to meet the first two preconditions.

Forecasting techniques: what the user should know

Traders' intuition

Forecasting of economic data requires a model, i.e. a set of relationships among variables, one of which is the variable to be forecast. Such models may be unspecified; they are simply ingrained in the mind of the long-term observer of the processes that generate the data. In foreign exchange forecasting, this is particularly true of successful professional traders, who develop a "gut feel" for the implications of new pieces of economic and political information *vis-à-vis* the future spot rate. These models are so complex that the traders themselves are usually unable to describe them adequately, and their attempts to describe how they arrive at their opinions about future spot rates tend to yield answers that are inconsistent or naive. Nevertheless, their failure to make explicit the complex relationships they have observed in the foreign exchange markets does not mean that their actions do not reflect a high degree of sophistication. Their success at surviving in a competitive business is the best indicator of the their respective models.

---

[2] While the forward rate may be available at zero marginal cost to a market participant, it is not "free", in the sense that the aggregate traders and others have devoted resources to its determination. This point is made by John H. Makin, "Techniques and success in forecasting exchange rates: Should it be done? Does it matter? The long and the short of it," in R. G. Hawkins, R. M. Levich and C. G. Wihlborg (eds), *Internationalization of Financial Markets and National Economic Policy* (JAI Press, 1982).

44

Formal models

Formal, structured models are the specific concern of this note. The widespread availability of computer facilities has promoted the development and use of forecasting models based on relationships that are stated in explicit mathematical terms. Because of the usefulness of exchange rate forecasts, there have been numerous attempts to construct foreign exchange forecasting models.[3]

Forecasting models can be divided into two categories — extrinsic and intrinsic. In extrinsic models, the underlying assumption is that there are fundamental causal factors which influence the variable of interest — i.e. the future spot rate. In intrinsic models, a forecast of the future spot rate is based on information derived from its past values.

Extrinsic models can be further distinguished by the underlying theoretical framework. Specification of the theoretical framework is needed to identify the most appropriate factors, or variables, and to specify the precise nature of their interaction. Broadly, three subgroups of extrinsic models can be distinguished: (1) models based on balance of payments analysis; (2) models of the national economy focusing on changes in aggregate demand; and (3) so-called monetary models. Exhibit 2.1.1 contains a schematic presentation of the forecasting models analysed here.

Exhibit 2.1.1: Schematic presentation of foreign exchange forecasting models

A. Informal models

B. Formal models

Extrinsic models
Based on relationships of
foreign exchange rate with
other variables

Intrinsic models
Based on past values
of foreign exchange rate

1. Partial equilibrium models (balance of payments models)

2. Equilibrium models (simulation models)

Aggregate demand
models

Monetary
models

Various time series models
Moving averages,
Box-Jenkins techniques
Momentum models

C. Market-based model

Based on the assumption of
efficient processing of information

Models based on fundamental balance of payments analysis endeavour to forecast the individual items in a country's external accounts, such as the current account balance. This approach is thought to capture the demand for and supply of foreign exchange, thereby providing indications of its price, the exchange rate.

Balance of payments models are plagued by a number of inherent difficulties. One problem stems from the fact that any change in the exchange rate tends to affect all the components of the balance of payments. Thus, while a deficit in the trade balance will put downward pressure on the exchange rate, this change in the rate will, in turn, impact on the trade balance. And, while some of these feedback effects are reasonably stable and can be built into the model, others are not. Further, there are interactions among the components of the balance of payments which are quite elusive. For example, a change in the trade balance may be

---

[3] In early 1978, there were several specialized firms offering foreign exchange forecasts. These organizations and their offerings have been extensively descibed in the article, "Mobbing up the treasurer," *Euromoney*, August 1978, pp. 13–41. See also "Forecasters are tougher, more mature — or missing," *Euromoney*, August 1979, pp. 32–52.

supplemented or supplanted by various capital flows. By the same token, exchange rate changes may induce offsetting or compounding changes in various kinds of capital flows.

Last, but not least, the presumption behind this kind of forecasting is that it is easier to predict the components of the balance of payments than the exchange rate itself — a questionable assumption. To illustrate, it may be possible to forecast with a reasonable degree of accuracy that a country will experience a deficit in its current account. However, a relatively small percentage of deviation in that forecast may lead to a substantial difference between the actual and forecast spot rates in percentage terms.

As long as there is systematic government intervention in the foreign exchange markets, as is the case when the rate is fixed, the feedback effects of changing exchange rates on the various components of the balance of payments can be neglected. But when exchange rates are changing in a system of free or managed floating, it is necessary to move toward so-called full equilibrium models,[4] where the predicted variable, the future exchange rate, is the result of the interactions of all those variables that are considered to be determinants of the future rate.

The usual approach, well developed in economic model building, is to construct a set of equations that describes the economy (or several economies) and can be solved simultaneously to yield the desired variable, here the exchange rate. In its simplest form, the exchange rate, S, is expressed as a function of endogenous (Y) and exogenous (X) variables:

$$S = f[Y(1), \ldots, Y(n); X(1), \ldots, X(m)].$$

The distinction is important because one set of variables (Y) is determined by the model, but the forecaster must provide an estimate of the exogenous variables (X).

Depending on the choice of variables and the specification of their interrelationships, one can distinguish between aggregate demand models and monetary models. The former are more complex; since they rely on changes in output, it is necessary to specify many different relationships. One such foreign exchange model, for example, specifies relationships involving such variables as trade balances, relative inflation rates, real growth rates, relative capacity utilization, short-term interest rates, government deficits, foreign exchange reserves of central banks, relative wage and price performance, and others.[5]

It is important to recognize that the various relationships are specified on the basis of past experience. And one of the crucial determinants for the success or failure of such a forecasting model is the stability of such relationships over time. In defence of model builders, it must be said that they pay a great deal of attention to problems stemming from this source. Thus the more sophisticated models of this kind have built into them an elaborate analysis of errors produced by each equation in the model in order to adjust as soon as possible for changes in the hypothesized economic structures. Still, with so many relationships interacting, it is easy for errors to occur because of "misspecification", i.e. the model fails to represent reality properly because either the wrong variables have been chosen, relevant ones have been omitted, or the interrelationships are not correctly stated. Furthermore, it is extremely difficult to rank the performances of different models because of extensive correlation of forecast errors for the variables predicted by the various models.[6]

Monetary models, based on a more comprehensive view of exchange rate changes, try to avoid some of these problems by concentrating on considerably fewer variables. The fundamental notion underlying all of the monetary models is that an excess supply of money in the economy — measured in relation to other economies — will also increase the supply of that country's currency in the foreign exchange market and therefore depress the exchange rate.

The output of all equilibrium models — regardless of their theoretical base — depends on an estimation, i.e. forecast, of the exogenous variable(s) that must be provided by the user of the model. Thus, to make such models useful for forecasting, it is necessary either to forecast the exogenous variables or to find a lagged relationship between the exogenous variable(s) and

---

[4] Partial equilibrium models neglect feedback effects.

[5] Michael K. Evans and John F. Norris, "International business and forecasting," *Columbia Journal of World Business*, Winter 1976, pp. 28–35.

[6] This point is made by W. Allen Spivey and William J. Wrobleski, *Econometric Model Performance in Forecasting and Policy Assessment* (Washington, D.C.: American Enterprise Institute, 1979), p. 3.

the exchange rate. Typically, aggregate demand models treat government spending, taxes, exports, and investment as exogenous variables, while monetary models require either a forecast of the money supply or specification of a constant, lagged relationship between changes in the money supply and other variables.

The role of the government with respect to exchange rate forecasting models is particularly important because governmental actions can produce the crucial lags needed to make models that simulate the "equilibrium exchange rate"[7] into true forecasting models. Under a system of "fixed" but adjustable exchange rates (typical of the Bretton Woods system) or even a system of managed floating where the authorities "lean against the wind" by intervening in the foreign exchange market, it is government action that provides for delays in the reaction of the exchange rate to changes in the economic fundamentals, and this permits successful forecasting.[8]

In fact, when government intervention is predictable, not only will econometric models be quite successful, but much cruder models will also yield successful forecasts. In such an environment, simple examination of balance of payments trends and other "fundamentals", such as relative rates of inflation and trade patterns, provides a measure of the pressure on the value of a currency. Then, changes in the level of foreign exchange reserves of the central bank, as well as an analysis of the country's access to credit facilities provided by the IMF or the international markets, indicate the time when a situation will become critical. The final and crucial step is to predict which of the limited policy options decision makers of the particular country will resort to in a crisis: reinforced attempts at internal deflation, imposition of additional exchange controls, or devaluation.

The success or failure of foreign exchange forecasting under such circumstances depends very much on that final step. An investment in analysis of the power structure and of the economic ideology of key decision makers in various countries could pay off in the form of successful forecasts.[9]

With the move toward a system of flexible exchange rates in the international financial environment, which implies less or less predictable government intervention in markets, the so-called intrinsic class of formal forecasting models has attracted renewed attention. Unlike extrinsic models, which are based on causal relationships among two or more exogenous variables, intrinsic models rely on statistical relationships between the variable to be forecast and past values of the same series. The idea is to identify and to extricate from historical data the underlying processes that generate new data.

Applied to exchange rate forecasting, this concept implies that the future exchange rate can be predicted from the behaviour of the exchange rate in the past. Specifically, forecasting models of this type assume the existence of some pattern or relationship that can be identified and subsequently used for forecasting. This has led to the application of a number of time series techniques, each of which is designed to identify the "pattern", or statistical dependence, of foreign exchange rates over time. Essentially, such techniques range from naive fitting of trendlines to sophisticated time series models, where, through a sequence of filtering models and diagnostic analysis, the forecaster attempts to detect any dependencies that can be used for forecasting.

As an illustration of a time series forecast, an outline will be given of foreign exchange forecasts based on autoregressive, integrated moving-average (ARIMA) processes, generally referred to as Box-Jenkins models.[10] ARIMA models incorporate many other time series techniques and are therefore representative of all forecast models based on such methods.

The first step involves the preliminary specification of a model that tentatively identifies the underlying process. Often, it is necessary subsequently to perform first-order differentiation

[7] The exchange rate that would prevail for given exogenous variables, provided the model is correctly specified.

[8] A point clearly recognized in M. Murenbeeld, "Economic factors for forecasting foreign exchange rate changes," *Columbia Journal of World Business*, Summer 1975, p. 81.

[9] For a report by one of the most successful practitioners of the art of currency forecasting in this era, see Robert B. Shulman, "Are foreign exchange risks measurable?" *Columbia Journal of World Business*, June 1970, pp. 57–8.

[10] For an illustration, see Ian H. Giddy and Gunter Dufey, "The random behavior of flexible exchange rates," *Journal of International Business Studies*, Spring 1975, pp. 17–39. For another early application of Box-Jenkins techniques to foreign exchange forecasting, see Rolf Mirus, "Speculation in the forward exchange market: the Canadian dollar since 1970," *Recherches Economiques de Louvain*, Fall 1975, pp. 303–11.

and/or other transformations to obtain a zero trend in the mean and variance of the time series, which is a prerequisite for the application of this technique. Once the model has been selected, its parameters are estimated, using, for example, non-linear least squares methods. The autocorrelations of the residuals and the significance of the variables are then carefully checked. If the residuals show significant autocorrelation, it indicates that systematic economic information remains in the series, and the model must be adjusted. The final model, having filtered out of the time series all systematic relationships, thus leaving only random disturbances, or "white noise", can subsequently be used for forecasting. The model is projected forward and the expected values of future exchange rates are computed.

The application of such forecasting techniques is greatly facilitated nowadays by the many forecasting packages that are available in large-scale computer systems. The focus here is on the assumptions that are crucial for the user of such exchange rate forecasts who is contemplating venturing his own funds or those of his company's shareholders on the output of such models.

The attractiveness of Box-Jenkins forecasting techniques is that the sophisticated fitting of the model is capable of capturing much of the information contained in the series of historical data. This is an improvement over extrinsic models, in which important information may be left out as a result of choosing the wrong variables, or misspecifying the interrelationships of variables. Unfortunately, like all time series models, Box-Jenkins techniques rely on information contained in the data of the past. And the structure extracted from such data may or may not hold for the future.

In the past few years commercial services have begun to offer exchange rate forecasts based on the concept of "momentum".[11] These forecasts, while promulgated by so-called "chartists", in effect are based on the same rationale as time series analysis. Their essential feature is to obtain the rate of change, i.e. momentum, from a series of exchange rates and, by projecting the rate of change forward in time, to predict future spot rates.[12]

Together with the basic logic, this method shares the problems of time series analysis: the presumption that relationships or "structures" derived from past data will prevail into the future; the sensitivity of the results to the point of departure of the analysis; and the lack of cause and effect reasoning. These deficiencies notwithstanding, the secretiveness of the sellers regarding the process by which they arrive at their forecasts gives them an image of black box magicians which some people find attractive.

Performance criteria and related problems

The question inevitably arises: are forecasts worth their cost? To some cynics, the corporate managers who buy foreign exchange forecasts are simply buying "handholding services"; the forecast of a prestigious institution can, after all, serve as a convenient scapegoat when foreign exchange losses occur. To other observers, it is not clear even what the costs of the forecasts are, because they may be part of a bundle of services provided to clients by financial institutions.

If exchange markets are not strong-form efficient, advisory services may be able to uncover information leading to the identification of structural changes in the economy, resulting in better forecasts than the forward rate. For example, it might be possible to predict changes in the stance toward, and mode of official intervention in, the exchange market on the basis of information acquired from private sources. Since the theory explaining systematic deviations of the forward rate from the expected future spot rate is of relatively recent vintage, and because empirical tests may be going on for some time, it is likely that forecasting services will continue to exist side by side with the forward rate.

But what constitutes a good forecast? How well has the forward rate performed? What is known about the performance of forecasting services? The following is an attempt to provide answers to these questions.

---

[11] For discussion of momentum based forecasts see Chapter 2, section 5.
[12] For a description of the momentum approach see Martin J. Pring, *International Investing Made Easy*, New York: McGraw-Hill, 1981, pp. 81–90.

Criteria for performance[13]

What constitutes a good forecast may be considered a trivial question. To illustrate that it is not quite so simple, a numerical example, which compares the forward rate and two other forecasts of the future spot rate to the actual later spot rate, is shown in Exhibit 2.1.2.

Exhibit 2.1.2: Hypothetical constellation of spot, forward, forecast and future spot rates

Spot rate $S(t)$	Forward rate $F(t)$	Forecast 1 $E1(S(t + 1))$	Forecast 2 $E2(S(t + 1))$	Future spot rate $S(t + 1)$
2.00	1.95	1.94	1.99	1.96

One possible criterion for forecasting accuracy is the mean absolute forecast error (MAFE). By this standard, the ranking of the three forecasts would be F, E1, E2, where the error coincides with the mean, since there is only one observation. When the mean squared forecast error (MSFE), which is also a possible criterion, is used, the ranking remains unchanged: the first forecast service is to be preferred to the second. However, a closer look reveals that while the mean absolute and squared forecast errors for Forecast 2 are greater, the forecast is on the "right" side of the forward rate. When the forward rate is 1·95 and Forecast 2 is 1·99, the signal is to buy foreign currency forward for 1·95 and later to sell it at 1·99, for a 0·40 profit per unit (if unlevered). The actual profit will turn out to be 0·01. By contrast, both MAFE and MSFE of Forecast 1 are smaller, but the signal for action is in the wrong direction: to sell forward at 1·95 and later to buy at 1·94. When the spot rate turns out to be 1·96, a loss of 0·01 will actually be incurred.

From the point of view of the hypothetical speculator in the example above, it is crucial whether the direction of the forecast is on the right side of the forward rate. By this criterion, Forecast 2 is ranked ahead of Forecast 1.

This point can be made differently by following the considerations of a financial manager with a long or short position in the foreign currency. He would have to assess the constellation of the forward rate relative to the commercial forecast, in order to make the speculative decision of whether or not to hedge.

In such a situation, even though both forecasts are in the right direction (here, both are forecasting a depreciation of the foreign currency), they can have different impacts. On the basis of Forecast 1, a financial manager with a 100 long position in the foreign currency would sell 100 forward. The result would be an actual loss of:

$$F(t) - S(t) = 1·95 - 2·00 \text{ per unit, plus an opportunity loss of } F(t) - S(t + 1) = 1·95 - 1·96 \text{ per unit,}$$

in the sense that if he had not hedged, the loss would have been smaller. However, on the basis of the forecast, hedging was indicated.

The second forecast implies a smaller depreciation than the forward rate; hence no hedging is indicated. The actual loss is:

$$S(t + 1) - S(t) = 1·96 - 2·00,$$

and an opportunity loss (or gain) does not result.

The conclusion that follows from these examples is that a useful criterion for the evaluation of a forecast service should be its ability to predict the direction of exchange rate movement, relative to either the current spot rate or the current forward rate. But that would be only the first test a given forecast would have to pass. Subsequently, the relevant questions become: how large are the profits earned relative to alternatives, and how risky are such investments? The

---

[13] These ideas are expressed in Sangkee Min, "Performance evaluation of foreign exchange forecasting techniques," *The Seoul National University Economic Review* 13, 1 (1980), pp. 83–96.

nature of these questions indicates how difficult it will be, in practice, to provide conclusive answers.

Empirical evidence

In contrast, it is relatively easy to say something about the directional accuracy of the forward rate as a predictor of future spot exchange rates. Recent research,[14] covering the period 1967–79 and the currencies of nine major trading nations, finds that the forward rate is successful in anticipating the direction of change approximately 50% of the time; in other words, it is not a very good predictor. Managers relying on the forward rate as an estimate of the future spot rate, therefore, are exposed to substantial risks.

Some preliminary evidence finds commercial services inferior to the forward rate when judged in terms of mean squared forecast errors.[15] When the proportion of correct predictions of the direction of change is assessed, however, there is evidence that some commercial services have outperformed the forward rate. As shown in the previous sub-section, the direction of change is a more appropriate performance standard than mean absolute or squared forecast errors; and so the question remains whether the profits obtained from successful commercial forecasts are sufficiently large to justify the risk involved.

Given the preliminary nature of the performance evaluation of commercial forecasts, and given the unsettled theoretical issue of the nature of the bias separating the forward rate from the expected spot rate, the conclusions for the practitioner are somewhat less than clear cut:

1. It is possible that the forward rate is about as good a forecast as one can find. However, its accuracy is poor because unexpected events swamp its predictions.
2. It is possible that the forward rate does not reflect the expected future spot rate. If the expected deviation represents the price of risk it is again not worthwhile to purchase forecasts.
3. Only if and when the *ex ante* deviation exceeds the risk premium by a sufficient margin is it worthwhile to forecast.

Either way, substantial risks are likely to remain, not the least being the difficult task of forecasting the successful forecasting service.

Summary and conclusions

Throughout this overview, the fact that forward exchange rates are readily available for many currencies was used as a justification for studying the information possibly contained in them. If there is no *ex ante* risk premium, the forward rate is the approximate forecast in an efficient market.

If forward rates represent the market's expected future spot rates, then they do indeed provide low cost forecasts. If not, it is important to determine whether there is a predictable bias, for if so it could be taken into account, thus preserving the low cost nature of the forecast. If the bias is highly variable and itself difficult to predict, additional justification for purchases of forecasts may exist.

What holds true for markets that are approximating efficiency holds even more true for inefficient markets or currencies for which forward markets do not exist. After ferreting out the low cost forecast, perhaps from black market exchange rates or interest differentials from grey credit markets, it may become apparent that expenditures for forecasts are worthwhile; if government has historically reacted in a certain fashion, there could be payoffs for discovering

---

[14] Richard M. Levich, "Are forward exchange rates inbiased predictors of future spot rates?" *Columbia Journal of World Business*, Winter 1979, pp. 49–61.

[15] Richard M. Levich, "Analyzing the accuracy of foreign exchange advisory services: theory and evidence," in Richard M. Levich and Clas G. Wihlborg, *Exchange Risk and Exposure*, Lexington, Mass.: Lexington Books, 1979. An earlier study reached similar conclusions but both the statistical techniques used and the theoretical justifications left much to be desired. See Stephen H. Goodman, "Foreign exchange rate forecasting techniques: implications for business and policy," *Journal of Finance*, May 1979, pp. 415–38.

and acting on such knowledge. The large foreign exchange losses that can be gleaned from the data reported by a number of central banks[16] appear to support this conclusion.

The fact that most forecasting services seem to focus on the currencies of a few industrialized countries where there are many active transactors and where effective government restrictions in both foreign exchange and credit markets are minimal, makes it less likely that promises of speculative gains can be realized. This is perhaps the reason the output of such services is sold to third parties rather than being acted upon by their creators.

[16] From 1973 to 1979 the combined foreign exchange losses of the monetary authorities in the United Kingdom, the United States, Germany, Japan and Switzerland have exceeded $10 billion. See Dean Taylor, "Betting against the central banks," *Euromoney*, Nov. 1980, pp. 121–3.

2. Fundamental analysis

David Kern*

It is now generally accepted that the old convention of measuring the value of each currency against the dollar has become inadequate in a world of floating, or frequently changing, exchange rates. The only acceptable alternative is to calculate the changes in the value of various currencies in a way that takes into account their relative importance in world trade or in each other's bilateral trade. Various trade-weighted or effective indices are now published regularly; there are some technical differences between these models, but they all provide a more reliable measure of the "true" changes in the relative position of each currency than a simple calculation, which only takes into account changes against one single currency such as the U.S. dollar.

Most of the existing trade-weighted statistics used at present cover less than 20 years, and to analyse such a relatively short period it is quite legitimate to use weights based on trade flows in one particular year. However, if we try to carry out a similar sort of calculation over a very long period, the choice of the appropriate weights raises many conceptual and statistical difficulties, because the composition of international trade may have changed considerably over time. The neatest solution would be to use different weights for each year, but this is computationally too cumbersome.

The simple alternative used in this section is to apply the most recent available weights, in this case 1979, to the entire period covered, from 1953 to 1981. This is clearly a rough approximation which is theoretically untidy, but such a simplified method appears to provide a perfectly adequate measure of the post-war exchange rate history.

Historical record

A casual look at the movements of the various currencies over the past three decades reveals many well-known features. However, there have also been a number of important developments which have not been adequately noted, and which must be properly understood if the difficult international monetary problems of the late 1970s and early 1980s are to be tackled sensibly. Exhibit 2.2.1 summarizes the broad historical experience since 1953 of 18 countries which account for the bulk of the non-Communist international trade. Exhibit 2.2.2 gives a more detailed description of the year-to-year movements in eight major OECD currencies: those of the U.S., Canada, Japan, Germany, France, Italy, Switzerland and the U.K. The basic trends during the 28 years between 1953 and 1981 can best be appreciated by looking separately at four periods: (a) 1954 to 1961; (b) 1962 to 1969; (c) 1970 to 1978; (d) 1979 to 1981. Unless otherwise specified, all the figures in Exhibit 2.2.1 are expressed as annual averages.

The year 1953 was chosen as the starting point for the historical comparison because, by that time, the international upheavals associated with the Korean War were coming to an end, and the effects of the 1949 major parity adjustments were already completed. During the eight-year period ending in 1961, exchange rates were initially remarkably stable, and until the end of 1956 the international parity structure remained virtually fixed. Thereafter, however, there were a number of important adjustments, most notably the devaluations of the French franc between 1957 and 1959, and the revaluations of the Deutschemark and the Dutch guilder in 1961. These changes provided a stable starting point for the second eight-year period, covering the years 1962 to 1969. However, from about 1964 onwards, serious pressures started to build up, and in spite of strong official resistance, the U.K. was forced to devalue sterling in November 1967. This move signalled the beginning of a lengthy period of upheaval and instability in international monetary affairs. The French franc was devalued again in August 1969 while the Deutschemark was forced upwards in October of that year.

The third period, covering the nine years between 1970 and 1978, witnessed many dramatic changes in the international currency markets. Starting with the floating of the Canadian dollar

---

* The author is grateful to Geoff Brown, a member of Economic Analysis Section, National Westminster Bank, for his useful research assistance.

Exhibit 2.2.1: Historical experience of 18 currencies' trade-weighted exchange rates
Index: 1953 average = 100

	Average					Total % change	Average % change per annum (inclusive)				
	1953	1961	1969	1978	1981	1953–81	1954–81	1954–61	1962–69	1970–78	1979–81
United States	100	103.0311	106.9877	88.5357	95.1989	−4.80	−0.18	0.37	0.47	−2.08	2.45
Canada	100	97.4874	92.3873	82.7924	79.9685	−20.03	−0.80	−0.32	−0.67	−1.21	−1.15
Japan	100	101.2220	103.6826	163.4438	161.7324	61.73	1.73	0.15	0.30	5.19	−0.35
Switzerland	100	103.4898	106.0339	195.1892	199.6506	99.65	2.50	0.43	0.30	7.02	0.76
Germany	100	110.9053	117.3363	185.3231	187.0427	87.04	2.26	1.30	0.71	5.21	0.31
France	100	71.6735	69.0210	60.8991	57.4658	−42.53	−1.96	−4.08	−0.47	−1.38	−1.92
Italy	100	108.2038	109.9413	58.3753	48.6297	−51.37	−2.54	0.99	0.20	−6.79	−5.91
Netherlands	100	107.8776	110.5096	132.5802	129.2504	29.25	0.92	0.95	0.30	1.27	−0.84
Belgium	100	105.9711	108.0635	126.1367	120.5526	20.55	0.67	0.73	0.24	1.73	−1.50
Denmark	100	102.2949	97.3772	104.4987	88.6775	−11.32	−0.43	0.28	−0.61	0.79	−5.33
Austria	100	99.7142	100.6348	118.8610	123.3387	23.34	0.75	−0.04	0.11	1.87	1.24
Sweden	100	104.5570	110.5136	99.1549	97.8971	−2.10	−0.08	0.56	0.70	−1.20	−0.43
Norway	100	101.9453	108.3637	126.3983	124.2137	24.21	0.78	0.24	0.77	1.72	−0.58
Finland	100	72.8319	57.5055	46.8393	49.2320	−50.77	−2.50	−3.89	−2.91	−2.25	1.68
Spain	100	70.2336	62.2093	46.7842	43.4427	−56.56	−2.93	−4.32	−1.51	−3.12	−2.44
Australia	100	100.8172	102.4295	83.9113	88.3655	−11.63	−0.44	0.10	0.20	−2.19	1.74
South Africa	100	101.7585	104.1834	66.9537	71.9005	−28.10	−1.17	0.22	0.29	−4.79	2.41
U.K.	100	104.0250	90.2084	53.5092	63.3239	−36.68	−1.62	0.49	−1.77	−5.64	5.77

Source. National Westminster exchange-rate index, 18 countries, 1979 trade weights and geometric calculations.

Exhibit 2.2.2: Currency experience since World War II

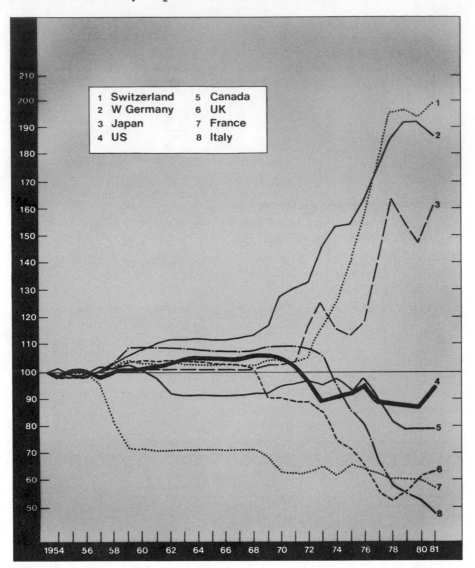

1	Switzerland	5	Canada
2	W Germany	6	UK
3	Japan	7	France
4	US	8	Italy

Source. National Westminster Bank trade-weighted index: 18-country model, 1953 = 100, geometric calculation, 1979 trade weights, annual averages.

in June 1970, a succession of crises led to the final collapse of the old Bretton Woods system during 1971, and the gradual and somewhat reluctant emergence of managed or "dirty" floating during 1973. The first oil crisis, which erupted late in 1973, added considerably to international monetary instability, and many countries experienced a most unpleasant combination of high inflation, recession, payments imbalances and currency instability.

The most dramatic features of this period were the sterling crisis of 1975–6 and the more serious dollar crisis of 1977–8. It is significant that both these crises were brought to an end by the adoption of rigorous monetary and fiscal policies. In the U.K., a firm economic package preceded the 1976 IMF loan, while in the case of the United States, the pursuit of tough money supply policies followed the appointment in 1979 of Paul Volcker to the chairmanship of the Federal Reserve Board.

The main features of the fourth period, from 1979 to 1981, were the emphasis on forceful anti-inflation policies and the continuation and intensification of exchange rate volatility. The establishment of the European Monetary System (EMS) in 1979 was an attempt to create a more stable currency bloc within Western Europe, but so far it can only be regarded as, at best, a limited success. A second oil crisis towards the end of 1978 and in 1979 (following the Iranian

54

revolution and compounded by the Iran/Iraq war) only served to heighten the problems of subdued growth, inflation, and payments imbalances. The last two or three years have seen growing uncertainties in the international monetary situation, with increasing international tensions. Following the events in Afghanistan and Poland, we have witnessed unprecedented volatility in interest and exchange rates and the importance of political factors during periods of acute uncertainty. The adoption of tougher monetary policies in many countries, particularly in Britain and the United States, has produced historically high levels of interest rates which have resulted in some highly important changes in the traditional relationships between currencies. During the last three years, the earlier, virtually uninterrupted, rises of currencies such as the Deutschemark, Swiss franc and yen have been, at least temporarily, reversed while the dollar and sterling have recovered some of the ground lost earlier in the 1970s.

To put recent events in a longer-term historical context, it is worth remembering that although the problems were less severe before 1970, exchange rate stability in the past was often more apparent than real. Indeed, abortive attempts to protect an unrealistic parity structure (for example, the attempt to protect sterling during the period 1964–7) masked large imbalances and massive intervention, which added to the underlying instability in the system.

The figures in Exhibit 2.2.1 show that, contrary to commonly-held views, the French franc exhibited a tendency for larger and earlier devaluations than any of the other major currencies, including sterling and the lira. Until 1975 the index value (1953 = 100) of the French franc was lower than that of any of the other major currencies, and its relative position has only improved marginally in the last six years. In retrospect, it is clear that France has always adopted a policy of giving the first priority to domestic growth targets, and, unlike Britain, has rarely attempted to defend an overvalued currency.

The fundamental factors

It is perhaps not surprising that standard economic theory does not offer a fully satisfactory explanation for the complex relationships determining movements of the various exchange rates. Nevertheless, theory does provide a useful conceptual framework which can be used as a convenient starting point for assessing the various factors involved. One of the oldest and most attractive approaches to this subject focuses on the relationship between the different rates of inflation experienced by the various countries and the relative performances of their currencies. Conventional economics, as well as commonsense, seemed to suggest that if the rate of inflation in country A is consistently higher than that in country B, this will, in due course, be reflected in a corresponding depreciation of currency A against currency B. While there were always legitimate differences of opinion about the most appropriate inflationary index, or about the time lags involved, the general validity of this principle was, nevertheless, usually accepted by academics as well as by practical businessmen. Consequently, foreign exchange dealers often reacted adversely to news that the inflationary outlook was likely to worsen in a particular country.

However, other factors are also thought to be relevant, most notably the balance of payments, interest rates, cyclical pressures and the forward markets; and one obvious difficulty is to assess the relative importance of these factors in determining currency movements. The historical relationships between exchange rate movements, inflation and other economic factors are summarized in Exhibit 2.2.3.

Inflation differentials

The figures in Exhibit 2.2.3 provide strong support for the view that there is a close statistical relationship between inflation and currency movements. A more detailed assessment of this relationships can be found later, in section 3 of this chapter. However, the link between changes in prices and in exchange rates is particularly noticeable if inflation is measured in terms of wholesale prices; by contrast, the relationship is considerably weaker when the more widely publicized consumer prices are used.

The figures suggest that the experience of the various countries has differed quite considerably. In the case of Germany and Switzerland, a low rate of inflation has been associated with a rapidly appreciating currency, irrespective of the specific price index used; at the weaker end of

Exhibit 2.2.3: Economic background to exchange rate movements

	Annual average for period 1954–81 inclusive							
	U.S.	**Canada**	**Japan**	**Germany**	**France**	**Italy**	**Switzerland**	**U.K.†**
Average % annual change in trade-weighted exchange-rate index	−0.18	−0.80	1.73	2.26	−1.96	−2.54	2.50	−1.62
Average % annual change in wholesale prices	4.66	4.62	3.16	2.67	5.06	6.74	2.39	6.87
Average % annual change in consumer prices	4.47	4.61	5.86	3.34	6.37	7.36	3.46	7.22
Average % annual change in export prices	4.80	5.09	1.68	2.72	5.60	6.02	2.41	6.75
Balance of payments current account ($ billion)*	1.80	−1.68	1.07	0.96	−1.31	−0.07	0.74	0.59
Average % annual change in industrial production	3.68	4.63	9.95	4.70	4.58	5.89	3.32**	1.32
Average end-year official discount rate — % per annum	5.41	6.59	6.33	4.32	6.30	6.45	2.77	8.09

† Some 1981 figures for UK are estimated.
 * The balance of payments figures are for the period 1956–81 inclusive, except for France which covers only 1960–81 inclusive.
** Switzerland, industrial production, 1960–81 inclusive.

Sources. National Westminster exchange rate index; International Financial Statistics; IMF.

the currency spectrum, Italy, France and the U.K. have combined high rates of inflation and large declines in exchange rates, whether one uses consumer or wholesale prices. However, in Japan it is clear that consumer price inflation provides a poor explanation of its relative position, while wholesale prices provide a more consistent explanation for the various exchange rate relationships. A different measure of inflation, which is sometimes thought to explain exchange rate movements, is the index of export prices; the results are as good as those obtained with wholesale prices.

The balance of payments

The figures in Exhibit 2.2.3 also provide support for the hypothesis that there is a limited link between exchange rate movements and the balance of payments on goods and services. However, the relationship is by no means conclusive. Traditional surplus countries such as Germany, Japan and Switzerland have experienced large rises in their currencies; but some countries with depreciating currencies — such as Italy, the U.K. and, to a lesser extent, the U.S. — have been in rough balance or have recorded surpluses over the long term. It is too often forgotten that, for many countries, current deficits and surpluses will tend to balance over the long term and situations of large-scale chronic imbalances are an exception rather than a rule.

International payments imbalances became unusually large following the first oil crisis of 1973–4. Since that time the substantial balance of payments surpluses of the major oil-exporting nations (OPEC) have been counter-balanced by large and persistent deficits amongst the oil-importing countries. However, it is important to distinguish between the relatively affluent and strong industrialized nations, which can usually obtain fairly easily the necessary funds to finance their deficits, and the poorer, less-developed countries (LDCs) which are particularly vulnerable to the pressures arising from high energy prices.

In the aftermath of the oil glut, which became apparent in the spring of 1982, there were exceptional uncertainties regarding OPEC's long-term balance of payments prospects. Looking ahead, there is now a reasonable chance that oil-induced payments imbalances will gradually diminish, given the more subdued oil market conditions likely to prevail during the next few years. However, there can be little doubt that payments imbalances and their financing will remain a serious international problem for the foreseeable future. The fact that many less-developed countries will have to service and repay a large amount of existing foreign currency indebtedness will inevitably add to the financial burdens facing them.

One of the main causes for the violent upheavals seen on the foreign exchange markets over the past few years has been the very unequal balance of payments performances of the major economies, with sharp and abrupt swings between deficits and surpluses. Exhibit 2.2.4 illustrates the nature of these swings in the case of the United States, West Germany, Japan, the U.K. and France, and the implications for their respective currencies. The U.S. position switched from massive deficits in 1977 and 1978 to a position of rising surplus in 1979–80. In contrast, West Germany and Japan moved over the same period from a position of sizeable surpluses to one of massive deficits. The U.K. has also experienced large balance of payments swings in recent years, but the improvement in its position has largely been due to the steady increase in North Sea oil revenues.

Exhibit 2.2.4: Balance of payments and exchange rate movements

	1977–78		1979–80		1981	
	Cumulative current account balance ($ bn)	% change in trade-weighted* exchange rate	Cumulative current account balance ($ bn)	% change in trade-weighted* exchange rate	Estimated current account balance ($ bn)	% change in trade-weighted* exchange rate
U.S.	−28.2	−7.0	+5.1	+5.2	+7.0	+11.2
Germany	+12.9	+12.9	−22.0	−0.8	−7.8	+3.2
Japan	+28.4	+44.7	−19.5	−1.7	+4.8	−1.2
U.K.	+1.7	+5.1	+5.5	+25.6	+16.0	−8.5
France	+0.2	+2.6	−6.7	−2.0	−7.5	−7.0

*Nat West trade-weighted index, covering 31 countries, using 1979 trade weights (geometric calculation).
Source. OECD, IMF, and own calculations.

Interest rates

In recent years, particularly in 1980 and 1981, interest rates have emerged as a very important, if not dominant, influence on currency movements. The growing importance of interest rate differentials as the key short-term factor in the foreign exchange markets can be directly related to the greater emphasis which has been placed on the pursuit of tight monetary policies in recent years, in an effort to combat inflation, especially in the U.K. and United States. Throughout 1981, for instance, the international currency markets were dominated by events in the United States, particularly the high level of U.S. interest rates and the consequent strength of the dollar resulting from President Reagan's economic policies.

The close link between interest and exchange rates reflects fundamental economic forces as well as technical market relationships. One of the most crucial issues facing people responsible for financial decisions are the implications of prevailing interest rates for prospective movements in currency values. In theory, people holding assets in a weak currency, the value of which is expected to decline, should demand a higher rate of interest to compensate them for the likely capital loss. Conversely, those holding strong currencies with an appreciation prospect should be prepared to accept a lower yield, because the capital value of their assets is likely to appreciate. Bankers who are familiar with the technicalities of the foreign exchanges will know that, in a free money market, differences in interest rates are automatically reflected in the forward exchange market, where currencies are traded for delivery on future dates. For example: if three-month sterling interest rates are 2% higher than three-month dollar rates, three-month forward sterling will automatically show a 2% per annum discount against the dollar.

The technical details of the forward exchange market are of concern only to specialists in this field. However, the question whether interest rates provide us with correct signals about future currency trends is a fundamental issue for most businessmen, bankers and governments. In a theoretical world, where people have perfect foresight, an interest rate gap would exactly match a future exchange rate movement. Unfortunately, in practical situations, we are always faced with many uncertainties and a change in interest rates may be open to conflicting interpretations.

Exhibit 2.2.5: Interest differentials and currency movements

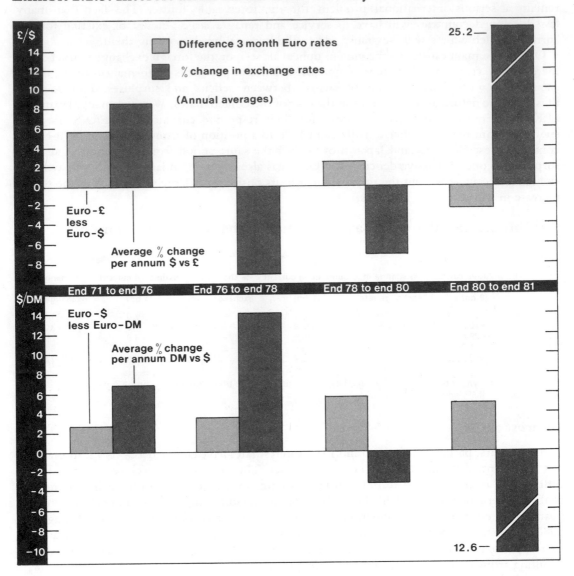

Source. National Westminster Bank, Economic Analysis, International and Statistics sections.

Exhibit 2.2.5 summarizes the relationship between key interest and exchange rates over the past decade. In the case of sterling, until the end of 1976 the higher level of U.K. rates provided a correct indication that the pound was likely to decline against the dollar, but the interest gap grossly underestimated the extent of sterling's actual fall. However, between end-1976 and end-1980 the pound rose sharply against the dollar, although the interest rate gap in favour of sterling rates remained substantial.

A similar pattern can be observed in the dollar/Deutschemark relationship, though the turn-round in the fortunes of the dollar occurred around the end of 1978. Until that time the higher level of U.S. interest rates grossly underestimated the weakness of the dollar. In the following two years the dollar rose sharply, although the gap in favour of American interest rates became even larger. Exhibit 2.2.5 demonstrates quite clearly that the relationships between interest and exchange rates have altered quite substantially, for both sterling and the dollar, over the past few years. The reasons for this transformation are still open to debate, particularly in the light of developments seen during 1981. Nevertheless, in both cases the change has been directly linked to the fact that the financial markets have shown greater confidence in the determination of Britain and the United States to persevere in the fight against inflation. The sharp rises in interest rates over the past three to four years have been interpreted not only as a reflection of underlying inflationary pressures, but also as a first step in a determined effort to bring down the rate of price increases.

Although the significance of interest rates and their volatility in recent years is undeniable, their longer-term impact on currency movements remains more questionable for a number of reasons. First, although interest rates have frequently been used as an important weapon in the exchange rate strategy of most countries, their main task was usually to offset and moderate the influence of more fundamental and basic factors, rather than to exert an independent influence of their own. Secondly, interest rates were occasionally used in order to achieve domestic policy aims, while disregarding the international consequences of such policies. This has often been the case in the United States, reflecting its relatively low dependence on foreign trade, and its past ability to pursue a balance of payments policy of "benign neglect". Thirdly, it is not easy to distinguish between a change in interest rates which simply reflects previous inflationary pressures, and a policy-induced change which is intended to counteract and reverse these very pressures.

Policy issues

Finally, let us consider the relationship between the real growth of the various countries (as expressed, for example, by the rate of increase in industrial production), and the relative performance of their currencies. Unfortunately, economic theory does not provide us with unambiguous hypotheses or expectations on this subject. For example, while it is plausible to argue that a country can achieve a relatively high level of economic growth by devaluing regularly, it is equally reasonable to take the view that a country whose growth rate is relatively fast can expect to see steady increases in the value of its currency. Thus, whereas Japan and Germany combined a higher rate of economic growth with a rapid rate of currency appreciation, in the case of France and Italy the rapid rate of economic growth coincided with large falls in the value of their currencies. At the other extreme, however, the United Kingdom, in spite of the rapid decline in the value of its currency until end-1976, experienced a very low relative rate of economic growth.

It appears that relative rates of inflation, if properly defined, show a good systematic relationship with the performance of different currencies. However, economic factors alone cannot explain adequately the post-war exchange rate experience. This requires a broader understanding of both the gradual changes in the power structure within the Western World over the past three decades, and the conflicting policies pursued by the major countries.

Many important features in post-war international monetary history were a direct result of the exchange rate pattern established immediately after the war at Bretton Woods. The key factors were that the parities of two of the defeated countries, Germany and Japan, were fixed at levels which were clearly undervalued, while the massive amount of economic aid, particularly from the United States, enabled them to reconstruct their economies with remarkable speed. The relative competitiveness of their currencies made it possible for the two countries to establish a sound basis for export-led growth, and also created the necessary conditions for both countries to achieve a strong balance of payments position and steady increases in their foreign exchange reserves. Against this background, it is not surprising that over the period between 1953 and 1981, Germany and Japan achieved larger exchange rate appreciations than the other major countries, with rises of 87% and 62% respectively. The rise in the Swiss franc was even larger, 100%, but Switzerland is a relatively small country influenced by special factors.

The rises experienced by these currencies were particularly striking until end-1978 and, in spite of the past few years' reversals, their overall performances appear remarkable. It seems probable that the initial low level of the Deutschemark and the yen exchange rates played a major role in creating in both countries the necessary conditions for a rapid and sustained economic recovery. Such an initial effect is perfectly consistent with the subsequent developments, whereby a high rate of growth in output and productivity largely based on rapidly rising exports provided the necessary background for a steady appreciation in the value of Germany's and Japan's currencies. The favourable influence of a competitive exchange rate could not operate on its own, without the right mix of domestic policies; but it is difficult to envisage either country's rapid economic progress without the original benefits of an undervalued currency.

59

In sharp contrast to Germany and Japan, the effective value of the currencies of some of the countries who won the war was set at rates which were overvalued, particularly in the case of the United Kingdom. This absence of exchange rate competitiveness, together with a misconceived determination to uphold an unrealistic parity for sterling, can be blamed for the dismal economic performance. The United Kingdom was often prepared to sacrifice domestic economic targets, such as growth and employment, in a misguided effort to preserve the stability of the monetary system; and only the pressure of market forces eventually caused the abandonment of these policies. The Bretton Woods value of the U.S. dollar was also probably too high; but, given the dominant position of the United States in the Western economic and monetary system, the initial lack of exchange rate competitiveness did not create serious problems, particularly as long as the United States was able to pursue its domestic policies without being significantly affected by international monetary considerations. However, towards the late 1960s, the United States was forced to alter its policy when it became clear that the cost in terms of growth and employment was serious. The Americans became increasingly reluctant to accept the domestic consequences and foreign exchange upheavals associated with the maintenance of a grossly overvalued dollar.

In contrast, France was always determined to give paramount importance to its domestic policy targets. From 1957 until the mid-1970s, France followed an effective strategy of devaluing its currency regularly, and by large amounts, whenever its balance of payments was under pressure. At the same time, the nation's high growth rate was one of the post-war success stories. Since the mid-1970s, France has appeared more concerned with currency stability, and has given strong political support to the EMS, and to previous attempts to link European currencies in various snakes. President Mitterand, elected in 1981, and his socialist government are clearly giving more emphasis to economic growth and to reducing unemployment within the EMS framework, but these aims may prove difficult to reconcile in the long term. In assessing the future prospects of the EMS, and the wider aim of European monetary integration, the important differences, in terms of performance as well as policy, between the main European nations should be borne in mind.

The relationship between exchange rate policy and economic performance is complicated, and the post-war record does not yield any easy conclusions about the most sensible long-term policies. The exchange rate experience of the countries with the most successful economic records has differed quite substantially. Whereas the Deutschemark and the Japanese yen have moved steadily upwards over the past three decades, the French franc has fallen heavily. In spite of this apparent divergence, all of these three rapidly expanding economies benefited, at least at some stage in their post-war history, from an exchange rate which was heavily undervalued. Thus, one tentative lesson is that although a country which wishes to pursue a policy of rapid economic growth does not necessarily need to devalue as frequently as the French did, a competitive exchange rate, at least over some period, is an important ingredient in putting the process of economic expansion on a healthy basis. On the other hand, the U.K.'s experience demonstrates that a declining currency does not, in itself, provide the basis for economic success. Following the massive international upheavals since 1973, there is today considerable scepticism about the benefits of a devaluation, and many countries are disenchanted with floating rates. Undoubtedly the effects of a competitive exchange rate can easily be nullified by domestic cost pressures. However, the historical record strongly supports the view that, with the right domestic policies, such competitiveness can help to bring about a significant once-and-for-all improvement in economic performance.

Conclusions

Bankers, businessmen and government officials in many countries have become increasingly concerned about the possible adverse repercussions of the unusually large fluctuations in interest and exchange rates which we have seen over the past few years. People in industry who have to make decisions about pricing and investment require a reasonably stable background and there can be little doubt that the build-up of major financial uncertainties has lowered business confidence and has reinforced the tendency towards a lower rate of economic growth.

The widespread disappointment with floating rates, although understandable, has probably been overstated. It is often forgotten that the present system of managed floating is not the result of an intellectual conversion on the part of central bankers, but rather a state of affairs which emerged quite gradually, largely as a result of most governments' inability to cope with the rigidities imposed by a fixed rate system. Historically, virtually all the decisions to float or adjust parities, whether upwards or downwards, were taken under the most severe pressure, and only came about after the attempts to preserve the previous exchange rate structure failed.

International monetary tensions largely arise because of basic inconsistencies between the policy targets of the major nations, and the most important role of any exchange rate system is to provide the framework which will cope most effectively with these tensions. For the foreseeable future it seems inevitable that major currencies (or currency blocs) such as the dollar, yen and Deutschemark, will continue to float independently. The main question marks concern the position within potential blocs, most particularly in Western Europe. Earlier attempts to establish a European currency bloc did not succeed, except in the very limited framework of the mini-snake. More recently, there has been the European Monetary System, established in 1979, in which the exchange rate arrangements involve all present members of the EEC, except the U.K. and Greece.

The difficulties confronting any attempts to move towards greater monetary integration in Europe are very great. However, neither the EMS nor its predecessors were ever intended to establish rigid, fixed links between the various currencies. Regular changes in the EMS parity structure have taken place and will continue to be necessary, to take account of basic economic differences between member countries.

While there is now growing awareness that governments have only limited freedom for independent action, there is still a large measure of disagreement about the precise mechanism through which exchange rate changes operate. Persistent volatility in the international financial markets has generated an acute political debate, and there is considerable disagreement in most major countries about the economic approach (usually labelled in the media as "monetarism") currently being pursued in Britain and in the United States. The recent emphasis on forceful money supply policies does not necessarily signify an abrupt break with traditional policies. It should really be seen as the latest phase in a longer-term change of approach to economic policy. In the case of the U.K., the new attitude can be traced back to the firm financial measures enforced at the time of the IMF loan (at the end of 1976) and, in the United States, to the tight monetary measures which have been introduced by the Federal Reserve Board since the end of 1978, under Paul Volcker's chairmanship.

The frequent upheavals in the foreign exchange markets can be seen as a painful but probably unavoidable manifestation of the fight against inflation. In the past, countries such as Germany and Switzerland (where inflation has been relatively low) have been able to restrain inflationary pressures through less severe policies simply because those operating in the financial markets had more confidence in their determination and ability to do so, though even in these countries there has recently been some erosion of financial confidence. However, in relatively high inflation countries, such as Britain and America, inflation has become so strongly entrenched in the economic system that altering expectations (either in the labour market or in the financial markets) is proving a very lengthy and difficult process. The fight against inflation is undoubtedly having adverse short-term consequences for economic growth and employment, but a high rate of price increases, which continues unrestrained, is likely to be even more destructive in its effects on financial stability and economic prosperity.

3. Purchasing power parity

David Kern*

Forecasting exchange rates has been a frustrating activity over recent years, with both the intellectual framework and the detailed techniques employed being the subject of considerable critical scrutiny. Although the demand for forecasting services has continued to grow, as a result of the exceptional volatility in the money markets, attempts to predict short-term currency movements with any precision have rarely been successful. One reaction to the consistent failure of numerous attempts to project market movements has been the increased popularity of technical analysis or chartism, though its record is unproven and interest in this method may turn out to be nothing more than a temporary fashion. Most people concerned with the currency exchange markets still prefer to focus on basic economic factors, particularly inflation, balance of payments and interest rates. However, there have have been frequent and rather abrupt changes in the markets' attitude on the relative importance of the factors considered to be relevant.

The relevant factors can be distinguished according to the time-horizon to which they apply. A convenient assumption, largely reflecting the experience of recent years, would be that: (a) interest rates tend to dominate short-term developments (six to 12 months); (b) the balance of payments is important over a period of two to four years; and (c) inflation differentials play a major part in determining longer-term currency trends over periods of five years or more. This approach to interpreting events in the foreign exchange markets can help to clarify some of the complex events of recent years, but more sophisticated techniques do not in themselves necessarily generate good forecasts. However powerful the analytical tools at our disposal, short-term projections will remain, for a long time to come, highly imprecise and inaccurate. An objective evaluation of basic economic factors should provide a more reliable guide to underlying exchange rate trends, but there are limitations inherent in using formal analytical techniques. The main purpose of this section is to identify some of the longer-term trends affecting currencies over the next few years.

The historical record

In spite of the apparently random nature of day-to-day fluctuations in exchange rates, market operators are interested in assessing the long-term trends indicated by the experience of various countries. A casual examination of the exchange rate history of the past three decades suggests the existence of a high degree of correlation between inflation differentials and currency movements. However, a close relationship can be identified only over very long periods, and the two variables have often moved in opposite directions over relatively short periods, e.g. months, quarters or even a few years. The relevant statistical material is presented in Exhibits 2.3.1 and 2.3.2. The exchange rate information is shown in terms of spot rates against the dollar (Exhibit 2.3.1) and on a trade-weighted basis (Exhibit 2.3.2), while inflation is defined in terms of wholesale prices, a concept more closely linked with currency movements than other measures of inflation. Various analyses have been carried out for four sub-periods, covering the years 1954 to 1981, though the presentations here concentrate on the period since 1965.

The regression analysis presented in Exhibit 2.3.1 demonstrates the existence of a remarkably close relationship between inflation differentials and currency movements. A good statistical fit does not prove the existence of a causal link, and it is unwise to use a regression line as a mechanical and rather simplistic forecasting device. However, the high degree of association between inflation differentials and exchange rate movements is not a random phenomenon, and it seems perfectly legitimate to use this relationship as one important indicator of future long-term trends.

Exhibit 2.3.2 presents the relationship between wholesale prices and trade-weighted exchange rates over three sub-periods since 1965. The countries under consideration are ranked

* The author is grateful to Steve Jones, Linda Smith, Dick Howard and Geoff Brown, members of his Section, for helpful research assistance.

Exhibit 2.3.1: Regression analysis: inflation vs. currency movements. Inflation differences and spot exchange rates against the U.S. dollar

1965–81: 18 countries

$Y = 0.49 - 1.00x$ $r^2 = 0.90$, where Y = annualized % change in spot rate of each currency against U.S. dollar.

X = ratio of annualized % change in wholesale prices in each country to annualized % change in wholesale prices in the U.S.

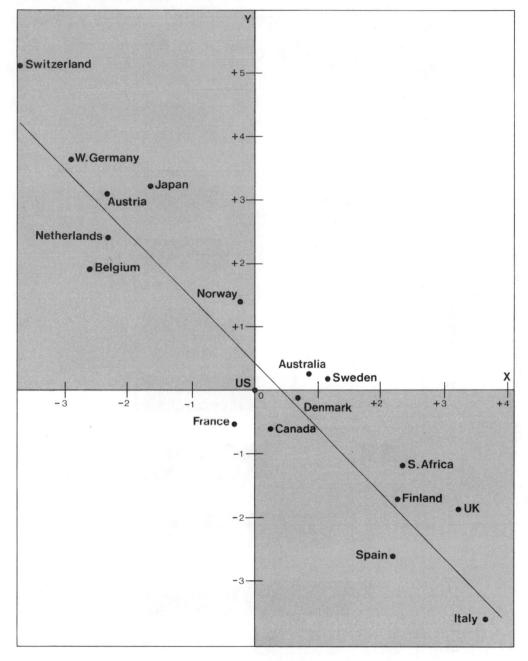

Source. National Westminster Bank, Economic Analysis, International and Statistics sections.

from left to right according to their inflation performance. A number of systematic features can be observed. In each of the periods reviewed, Italy and the U.K. had high rates of inflation and relatively weak currencies while, at the other end of the spectrum, Germany and Switzerland achieved lower rates of inflation and their currencies appreciated. However, this consistency becomes significant only when trying to assess longer-term trends rather than short-term movements.

Exhibit 2.3.2: Inflation and currency performance

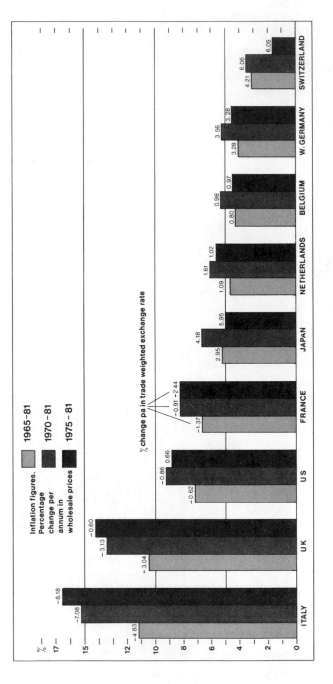

Inflation figures.
Percentage
change per
annum in
wholesale prices

1965–81
1970–81
1975–81

% change pa in trade weighted exchange rate

ITALY
−4.83
−7.08
−8.18

UK
−3.04
−3.13
−0.60

US
−0.62
−0.86
0.66

FRANCE
−1.37
−0.91 −2.44

JAPAN
2.95
4.18
5.95

NETHERLANDS
1.09
1.61
1.02

BELGIUM
0.80
0.98
0.97

W. GERMANY
3.28
3.56
3.28

SWITZERLAND
4.21
6.06
6.05

Note. Figures in brackets denote percentage change per annum in the trade-weighted index of the appropriate currency.
Source. National Westminster index: 18 country model using 1979 trade weights. Figures are calculated geometrically.

A mechanistic purchasing power parity analysis for 1981

The average 1981 exchange rate projections presented in Exhibit 2.3.3 have been calculated on the mechanistic assumption that inflation differentials (as defined by wholesale prices) have been the sole factors determining exchange rate movements in recent years. For comparison, these expected rates have been set alongside the actual average rates for 1981. This mechanistic approach has been used in the past by a few commentators, though they have usually focused on only two or three currencies. In this section, the analysis is applied simultaneously to a large number of key currencies. To overcome some of the possible biases arising from an unrepresentative base date for the analysis, we have used three different bases in the calculations — 1965, 1970 and 1975 — and the results presented in Exhibit 2.3.3 are an average of the purchasing power parity projections which each of these dates would have generated. In most cases the 1981 forecasts generated from these three different historical base dates are roughly in line with each other, but there are some small differences and these are ironed out by the averaging procedure.

Exhibit 2.3.3: A mechanistic PPP exchange rate projection for 1981

	£	US$	¥	Swfr	DM	Ffr	Bfr	Dfl	Lit
Sterling	—	1.63	434.0	3.47	3.71	7.47	51.53	3.94	1767.2
	—	(2.03)	(445.2)	(3.98)	(4.56)	(10.94)	(74.84)	(5.04)	(2288.1)
U.S. dollar	0.61	—	266.4	2.13	2.28	4.59	31.62	2.42	1084.5
	(0.49)	—	(219.8)	(1.96)	(2.25)	(5.40)	(36.95)	(2.49)	(1129.5)
Yen	2.30	3.75	—	8.01	8.55	17.21	118.72	9.07	4071.6
(×1000)	(2.25)	(4.55)	—	(8.94)	(10.25)	(24.57)	(168.13)	(11.32)	(5139.8)
Swiss franc	0.29	0.47	124.9	—	1.07	2.15	14.83	1.13	508.7
	(0.25)	(0.51)	(111.9)	—	(1.15)	(2.75)	(18.81)	(1.27)	(575.0)
Deutschemark	0.27	0.44	116.9	0.94	—	2.01	13.88	1.06	476.1
	(0.22)	(0.44)	(97.6)	(0.87)	—	(2.40)	(16.41)	(1.10)	(501.6)
French franc	1.34	2.18	581.0	4.65	4.97	—	68.97	5.27	2365.5
(×10)	(0.91)	(1.85)	(407.1)	(3.64)	(4.17)	—	(68.44)	(4.61)	(2092.2)
Belgian franc	1.94	3.16	842.3	6.74	7.20	14.50	—	7.64	3429.7
(×100)	(1.34)	(2.71)	(594.8)	(5.32)	(6.10)	(14.61)	—	(6.73)	(3057.1)
Guilder	0.25	0.41	110.3	0.88	0.94	1.90	13.09	—	449.1
	(0.20)	(0.40)	(88.4)	(0.79)	(0.91)	(2.17)	(14.86)	—	(454.2)
Lira	0.57	0.92	245.6	1.97	2.10	4.23	29.16	2.23	—
(×1000)	(0.44)	(0.89)	(194.7)	(1.74)	(1.99)	(4.78)	(32.71)	(2.20)	—

1981 forecasts are averages of the predictions from three base dates: 1965, 1970 and 1975; figures in brackets denote actual average 1981 spot rates.
Source. National Westminster Bank, Economic Analysis, International and Statistics section.

The divergences in exchange rates, expressed in terms of the percentage difference of the actual 1981 exchange rate from the projected rate, is shown in Exhibit 2.3.4. The 1981 purchasing power parity projections are not short-term forecasts of currency movements, since many factors can prevent inflation and other economic forces from being reflected immediately in actual market rates. Nevertheless, the persistence over many years of a systematic gap between expected and actual market rates indicates the need for some adjustment in the exchange rate structure.

The projections shown in Exhibit 2.3.4 support the view that sterling appears overvalued against most major currencies, the extent of this overvaluation in 1981 being, for example, 24% against the U.S. dollar and 23% against the Deutschemark. Surprisingly, sterling seems too high against the Belgian and French francs (see below). The mechanistic purchasing power parity figures should not be taken literally, because they disregard other influences on exchange rate movements (notably North Sea oil, in the case of sterling), and because of imperfections

Exhibit 2.3.4: Divergences of actual 1981 average exchange rates from mechanistic 1981 average projections

| | % overvaluation (+) or undervaluation (−) | | | | | | | | |
	£	US$	¥	Swfr	DM	Ffr	Bfr	Dfl	Lit
Sterling	—	+24.32	+2.57	+14.53	+22.91	+46.39	+45.26	+28.01	+29.48
U.S. dollar	−19.56	—	−17.50	−7.87	−1.13	+17.76	+16.84	+2.97	+4.15
Yen	−2.50	+21.21	—	+11.67	+19.83	+42.73	+41.62	+24.81	+26.24
Swiss franc	−12.69	+8.54	−10.45	—	+7.31	+27.82	+26.82	+11.77	+13.05
Deutschemark	−18.64	+1.15	−16.55	−6.81	—	+19.11	+18.18	+4.16	+5.35
French franc	−31.69	−15.08	−29.94	−21.76	−16.04	—	−0.78	−12.55	−11.55
Belgium franc	−31.16	−14.42	−29.39	−21.15	−15.39	+0.78	—	−11.87	−10.86
Guilder	−21.88	−2.89	−19.88	−10.53	−3.99	+14.36	+13.47	—	+1.14
Lira	−22.77	−3.99	−20.78	−11.54	−5.08	+13.06	+12.19	−1.13	—

Source. National Westminster Bank, Economic Analysis, International and Statistics sections.

associated with wholesale prices as an appropriate index for inflation. For example, wholesale prices do not focus exclusively on internally traded goods, as theory might require, and do not take account explicitly of other relevant indicators, such as labour costs per unit of output. While there is some disagreement about the precise extent of sterling's overvaluation, given Britain's post-war economic record, it seems plausible to conclude that the pound will weaken somewhat over the years. However, in the foreseeable future any fall in sterling is likely to be much smaller than the straight inflation comparisons indicate. Two major factors should help to strengthen the pound over the next few years: firstly, a firm monetary policy which will help to keep interest rates well above inflation for most of the time, and which will preserve financial discipline, in spite of the build-up of electoral pressures; and second, the structural improvement in Britain's balance of payments resulting from North Sea oil revenues, an improvement which seems likely to continue even if the recent slackness in the oil market persists.

The dollar's performance indicated by the PPP projections is rather mixed. The U.S. currency seems overvalued against some European currencies, undervalued against sterling and the Swiss franc, but roughly in line with the Deutschemark. More surprisingly, and rather controversially, the American currency seems undervalued in relation to the yen. Most market commentators would reject such a conclusion, and would argue that the yen should be much stronger in relation to the dollar. Since the mechanistic forecast shows the yen to be overvalued against virtually all major currencies, wholesale prices may not be a representative measure of Japan's underlying inflation, although it is difficult to see why this should be so. Japan's performance has been better on other measures such as unit labour costs, but the strong feeling in the marketplace that the yen needs to strengthen cannot be rationalized simply by using a different measure of inflation. Dealers and other market operators may have given too much weight to Japan's large trade surpluses in manufacturing goods while disregarding Japan's rather mediocre inflation performance. In the recent past, high American interest rates have been the dominant factor and the dollar has been strong against all currencies including the yen. However, continued market confidence in the yen's strength can be justified if we believe that Japan's ability to maintain a consistently above-average growth in labour productivity will be reflected in a below-average future rate of inflation and consequently a higher yen.

The French and Belgian francs emerge from the purchasing power parity calculations as particularly undervalued currencies. While the relative inflation performances of France and Belgium would suggest far stronger exchange rates for 1981, the market view of these currencies is clearly more pessimistic. Adverse sentiment about these currencies has been influenced by the underlying economic and, more recently political, problems which these countries have been experiencing. Consequently, both currencies were devalued during the first half of 1982, and their short-term prospects still seem uncertain. However, France has historically pursued a consistent policy of large, and possibly excessive, devaluations, and the present rate could, in fact, be relatively low and therefore more resilient. Fears about the inflationary implications of President Mitterrand's economic policies could prove to be exaggerated, and if the new government succeeds in tackling France's internal structural problems, there may be a case for reassessing our views of the French franc's performance.

A mechanistic PPP forecast for 1990

Having examined the PPP exchange rate projections for 1981, it is worth using the same methodology to obtain some longer-term exchange rate forecasts. This hypothetical exercise focuses on 1990. Relative rates of inflation are relevant to long-term trends; to generate the forecasts, we must first make assumptions about trends in wholesale price inflation in the countries under consideration. Such an exercise is hazardous and uncertain, and the final results can be distorted by factors other than inflation. But the results provide useful guidance about some fundamental forces. Exhibit 2.3.5 shows the specific assumptions for wholesale prices over the period to 1990 used in the calculations.

Exhibit 2.3.5: Wholesale price inflation: historical background and forecasts

	% change per annum in wholesale prices			
	1965–70	1970–75	1975–81	1981–90 (forecast)
U.K.	4.17	13.07	14.16	9.00
U.S.A.	2.71	9.65	8.98	7.80
Japan	2.17	9.40	5.02	4.70
Switzerland	1.85	5.87	1.77	4.60
W. Germany	1.35	6.24	4.59	5.00
France	2.08	9.93	8.33	11.00
Belgium	2.20	6.55	4.58	6.70
Netherlands	1.95	6.55	5.82	5.70
Italy	2.57	13.97	16.68	11.80

Source. National Westminster Bank, Economic Analysis, International and Statistics sections.

We have again applied the procedure of averaging the separate forecasts generated by the inflation trends from various base dates, and as in the previous 1981 exercise the base periods used were 1965, 1970 and 1975. The average 1990 forecasts for some of the major currencies are shown in Exhibit 2.3.6. On the basis of the inflation assumptions used, sterling looks set to depreciate against most major currencies other than the Italian lira, but the extent of its decline is fairly limited. Within the EMS structure, if the current assumptions about inflation rates prove accurate, the forecasts indicate that regular adjustment of the parity structure will be required to cope with the widely divergent trends in inflation. Thus, the Deutschemark seems likely to remain the strongest currency, while the French franc and the Italian lira are forecast to weaken quite substantially in relation to the Deutschemark.

The 1990 PPP forecasts indicate a mixed performance for the U.S. dollar — rising against currencies such as sterling, the French franc and the Italian lira, while falling against the stronger European currencies such as the Deutschemark and the Swiss franc. An intriguing point is the currency's surprisingly modest forecast fall against the Japanese yen. The divergence between market optimism about the yen and its mediocre PPP performance has already been discussed in the context of the 1981 results. It is, therefore, not surprising that the yen's rise over the period to 1990 indicated by the PPP calculations is considerably smaller than generally assumed.

The PPP results point to the broad trends in exchange rate movements which could be expected in the longer term on the basis of future inflationary differentials. Shorter-term effects resulting from the impact of, for example, high interest rates or current account imbalances (including the effects of oil), and political factors, will cause fluctuations in the exchange markets and, on occasions, will modify temporarily the basic trends. However, while

Exhibit 2.3.6: A mechanistic PPP exchange rate projection for 1990

	Sterling exchange rates		U.S. dollar exchange rates		DM exchange rates	
	Forecast 1990	Average 1981	Forecast 1990	Average 1981	Forecast 1990	Average 1981
Sterling	1.00	1.00	1.47*	2.03*	2.65**	4.56**
U.S. dollar	1.47	2.03	1.00	1.00	1.80**	2.25**
Yen	301.07	445.17	204.60	219.76	113.72	97.58
Swiss franc	2.40	3.98	1.63	1.96	0.91	0.87
Deutschemark	2.65	4.56	1.80	2.25	1.00	1.00
French franc	8.81	10.94	5.99	5.40	3.33	2.40
Belgian franc	42.50	74.84	28.89	36.95	16.05	16.41
Dutch guilder	2.99	5.04	2.03	2.49	1.13	1.10
Lira	2209.50	2288.00	1501.70	1129.50	834.56	501.50

1990 forecasts are averages of the predictions from three base dates: 1965, 1970 and 1975.
* No. of U.S. dollars per pound sterling.
** No of DM per U.S. dollar and per pound sterling.

Source. National Westminster Bank, Economic Analysis, International and Statistics sections.

recognizing the need to supplement the mechanistic PPP results with a broader assessment of other relevant factors, the results provide some understanding of future exchange rate trends.

4. Econometrics

David Wyss

Econometric models of exchange rates are a relatively recent phenomenon. Before 1971, the predominance of fixed exchange rates, with massive intervention often required by central banks, made the determination of exchange rates more of a political than economic phenomenon, at least in the short term. This change in the structure of foreign exchange markets increased substantially the volatility of exchange rates, making a forecast of exchange rates much more of a necessity for corporate planners and financial managers.

Responding to this new need, a variety of forecasting techniques have been pulled into use. Most of the forecasts fall into three main categories. First, the technical forecasts, where the future of the exchange rate is determined solely by its past, through some form of chartist or momentum forecasting technique. Second, judgemental forecasts, where attention is paid to fundamental factors as well as to trading factors, i.e. the over-sold or under-sold condition of the currency, or the likely intervention points of each central bank. Third, the econometric forecasts, where the fundamental factors — the underlying economic factors that determine exchange rates — are expressed in the form of a mathematical equation or system of equations, which can be solved on a computer.

In practice these techniques tend to blend into one another. Very few econometric forecasters will totally ignore the political factors or the recent and likely behaviour of central banks. Very few of the judgemental forecasters will not have some underlying idea of what the equation would look like, whether this is expressed in mathematical terms or simply in terms of simple rules of thumb as to what a particular interest rate or inflation change will do to the exchange rates.

Choice of techniques

The reasons for choosing the econometric technique are several. First, there is a theoretical nicety implicit in the econometric technique. It requires an explicit presentation of what we believe the underlying fundamentals are for the economy. It requires an explicit statement of the underlying assumptions in terms of economic policy and of economic performance for the currencies involved. Second, it provides a method for doing alternative simulations. This is especially important in the long run. There is not simply one possible future, or if there is, our crystal ball is not clear enough to enable us to see it with any precision. Instead, there are a variety of possible paths of exchange rates over the next few years. Which of these paths is chosen will depend on the economic policies adopted by the governments and central banks involved.

As we monitor the effect of these alternative policies on exchange rates, we can forecast a range rather than just a central point for the exchange rate. We can say that under the following optimistic assumptions about oil prices, monetary policy, and fiscal policy, the exchange rate will be A. Under more pessimistic assumptions, e.g. assuming that there is a sharp rise in oil prices, or assuming totally irrational monetary policy, the exchange rate will follow path B. This range can be important for planning purposes. For strategic planning we need to know not only a point estimate, but also an estimate of the likely variation around that central path.

The importance of the fundamental factors underlying the exchange rate becomes even more crucial in the long term. In the longer term we cannot forecast an exchange rate in isolation; we have to look at the exchange rate as part of an economic system. The actions of central banks, of administrations, of OPEC, will all change the outlook for long-term exchange rates. A corporate planner is interested not only in exchange rates. When making decisions on the siting of new plants, on sourcing of materials, on where to produce material across existing plants he needs to look at the exchange rate in the context of costs and demand in the various locations. For this purpose an econometric model is virtually a necessity. There is no other way to link automatically the performance of the exchange rates to the performance of the economies in order to provide a consistent economic outlook.

Theoretical background

Any econometric model of exchange rates has to be based on an underlying theoretical model of exchange rates. In any economic text book, the price of a commodity, whether it is the price of a currency, the price of gold or the price of wheat, depends on the supply and demand for that product. In the case of a currency, the supply and demand are affected by several factors. In the long run, it is assumed that exchange rates are determined primarily by relative prices, by what has become known as purchasing power parity. The exchange rate has to move to keep the prices of products in the various countries competitive. In the short run, however, the currencies are not primarily swung by changes in prices. Changes in prices tend to be important in the longer term, but in the short term it is the immediate changes in supply and demand, coming through either transactions or investment demand, that affect the currency.

Transactions demand can be summed up by changes in the current account deficit (or surplus) of each of the countries. The current account gives the balance between the supply and demand for funds required to complete transactions in the currencies. Exports create a demand for the currency of the exporting country to allow the payment for the goods to be made. Interest payments also create a demand for funds. The balance of these payments is the current account.

There is, however, a demand for funds for other than current transactions. Portfolio transfer is a major part of the demand for funds across countries, and portfolio investment is affected by changes in the expected earnings in each country corrected for an anticipated movement of the exchange rate.

In the model, these three factors — purchasing power parity, current account, and portfolio movements — are each summarized by a different variable. For purchasing power parity, we use the relative price. We use as a dependent variable the real exchange rate for the currency rather than the nominal exchange rate. This real exchange rate is defined as the nominal exchange rate multiplied by the ratio of prices in the home country to average foreign prices. This real exchange rate is allowed to vary by a trend, which represents the underlying change in the competitive position of a country. Some countries, such as the United States, have seen a persistent decline in their real exchange rate over recent decades, reflecting, perhaps, the fact that they have been trapped into exports for which demand has been growing more slowly. Other countries, for example Japan, have seen a general rise in their real exchange rate over the same period, reflecting the fact that their exports have been concentrated in more rapidly growing areas.

The relative inflation rate is relevant, for it allows prices to move exchange rates with a lag, rather than moving them contemporaneously. As the prices rise more rapidly, it may take some time for financial markets to adjust. As a result, the introduction of some distributed lag on the relative inflation rate allows us to introduce a lag on prices into the system.

In addition to prices, the relative current account balance enters as a determinant of the exchange rate. This current account captures the demand and supply of current funds in the market. It is only the relative balance that enters. If a change occurs which depresses all industrial country current accounts, e.g. an oil price increase, not all currencies will decline. Currencies exist only relative to one another; if they are all depressed, the exchange rate does not move.

As a proxy for changes in portfolio investment, we have used the relative real interest rate. The underlying assumption is that people will move their funds to earn the greatest possible return consistent with the expected movements of the exchange rate. We can obtain the structure of the model from two particular forms. First, we can say that people do not hedge their positions. If I move money into Deutschemarks, I will move that money only if the expected future rate allows me to earn a higher rate of return than the interest rate in the U.K. In other words, the difference in the interest rate has to be more than the expected decline in the pound against the Deutschemark. If we assume that in the long run currencies are expected to follow purchasing power parity, the expected decline in the exchange rate is equal to the difference in the expected inflation rates, so that the movement of currency is determined by the relative real interest rate, i.e. by the difference in the interest rate less the difference in the inflation rates.

This model can also be derived by an analysis of arbitrage positions. In a perfectly arbitraged model, the difference between the forward rate and the spot rate is equal to the difference in the nominal interest rates. This difference has to hold, otherwise there would be the possibility of making a certain profit by trading backwards and forwards in the currencies, i.e. by buying Deutschemarks spot, selling them forward, and investing the proceeds temporarily in bonds during the three-month interval. There are obviously enough participants in the foreign exchange market to ensure that these risk-free profits do not occur.

There is another side to the arbitrage point, however. The forward rate must be equal to the rate which is expected to prevail at that future time. In a rational expectations world, we would expect that the forward rate would be equal to the expected spot rate at that point. If we again assume that in the long run the exchange rate is determined by purchasing power parity, the forward rate will differ from the spot rate by, among other things, the inflation rate, so that the difference between the interest rates will not primarily affect the spot rate. The spot rate will move to keep the difference between the forward and spot rate equal to the difference in the interest rates.

Practical problems

Unfortunately, there are some practical problems lying between the theory of exchange rates and the real world. Although the measurement of the exchange rates themselves is pretty straightforward, many of the other variables that we would like to use in the exchange rate equation do not measure exactly what we would like them to measure. Prices, for example, are not an unambiguous measure of the price level.

There are many choices of price index to use in the econometric model of exchange rates. What we would really like is an index of the price of tradeable goods. However, there is no such index for most economies. There are several proxies that can be used, and which have been used by various econometricians. One is the consumer price index. This index has two outstanding faults. First, it includes services. Service prices do not represent purchasing power parity, because most services cannot be traded across national lines. Housing services, for example, are about 40% of service prices in the United States; the price of housing and of utilities is not a reflection of any kind of foreign trade position or foreign trade movement. Consumer prices are also affected by changes in value added taxes. For example, when the British value added tax was increased sharply in the summer of 1979, British consumer prices rose by about 6% in that one quarter. However, this did not represent any sharp decline in British competitiveness, since VAT is not charged on exports, but is charged on imports. A rising VAT rate, at least in the first analysis, should not cause any movement in foreign exchange rates.

A second index that has often been used is unit labour cost. Unit labour cost does represent a change in the cost of production in various countries and this cost of production should be reflected in a change in exchange rates. However, it is not a complete index. Changes in unit labour costs are not necessarily reflected in the price of commodities. They may be absorbed in periods of weak markets, and even though unit labour costs may go up in a country, the competitive position may not deteriorate if manufacturers elect to absorb part of the rise in cost in the form of reduced profit margins rather than reduced sales.

In our model, we have chosen to use wholesale prices as an index of the price of tradeable goods. This is not a perfect measure. Weights on wholesale prices vary substantially from country to country; the weights of the market basket of wholesale prices in Germany are not the same as in the market basket used in the United Kingdom. Wholesale prices do not consistently correct for changes in quality of goods; nor, for that matter, do any of the other price indices. The quality corrections assumed in the U.K. are not the same as the quality corrections assumed by the Bundesbank in Germany. Though we recognize the flaws inherent in the use of the wholesale price index, we feel that the wholesale price index is the best measure of the price of tradeable goods that is available.

The same data problems which are reflected in the choice of the price index are also a problem in the choice of an interest rate. Here, we would ideally like to have a direct measure of capital flows across countries, and then a model of the determination of these flows. Data on international capital flows, however, is extremely limited, and what data exists is extremely questionable. Therefore, these flows must be proxied by the determinants of the flows, i.e. by the relative earnings which are the primary cause of such flows.

There are many reasons for capital flows, as there are many types of earnings which cause such flows. If someone is trying for short-term gains, the choice of variable is fairly obvious: the difference in the short-term interest rate in the two countries. Even this has its problems. What one person can earn on short-term money is not necessarily what another person can earn. The capital markets in the various countries have a very different liquidity. Short-term loans are easy to arrange in pounds or Deutschemarks, but in lira are more subject to transaction costs.

Not everyone who moves money across national lines does so to invest in short-term bank deposits. Many people will move money to buy common stock or to invest in real assets, real estate, or for direct investment in businesses. For these types of investments, the interest rate is not really a sufficient proxy. However, on the assumption that the market within a country is arbitraged, the expected rate of return (corrected for risk) on all assets is the same. We have, thus, chosen to use the differential in the short-term interest rate as our proxy for the differential in nominal earnings on all types of assets.

Similarly, the current account balance is only a proxy for the transactions demand and supply for a particular currency. It does not include demand for funds for direct investment, nor does it include a consistent definition of tourist expenditure, although in recent years the definition of the current account balance has become more consistent within the OECD countries. The current account also includes earnings on financial assets, at least some of which are a result of exchange rate movement rather than a cause of such a movement. What we would really like is a measure of autonomous supply and demand, eliminating those components of the current account which are the effect rather than the cause of exchange rate movements. Unfortunately, the data do not provide us with any such exact measure, and the current account is the best compromise that is available readily from statistical sources.

The availability of data further restricts exchange rate forecasting. There is no point in trying to use as a determinant of exchange rates a variable which is in itself not available or forecastable.

Politics further confuse the simple world of econometric models. Econometrics by its nature assumes that the future will be a continuation of the past, that structural relations which have held in the past will continue to hold in the future. Political developments can change this assumption. The most obvious case in recent years has been the introduction of the European Monetary System in March 1979. This substantially changed the way in which currencies moved in the European community, sharply reducing the short-term volatility of these exchange rates. The specification of the econometric models had to change to reflect this change.

The most obvious way in which the structure of our (Data Resources Inc.) model changed was that exchange rates were now estimated in terms of the European Currency Unit (ECU). Forecasting in terms of the ECU allowed a very easy check on implications for movements of the parity bands and allowed us to more easily specify, or at least to more easily monitor, the way in which our forecast implied realignments of the European Monetary System.

Of course, whenever a new institutional system is introduced, we make an assumption about what the change in structure will do to the exchange rates. This had to be done after the Socialist victory in the French elections, which was assumed to substantially change the behaviour of the French franc. These judgemental adjustments must be made on top of the econometric results.

No exchange rate model can or should be run without judgemental adjustment. In the longer run, economic fundamentals tend to dominate, and the necessary adjustments tend to diminish as the time horizon is extended. In the short run, judgemental adjustments will be made for political factors, such as our judgement of how much support a central bank is willing to give its currency. If a central bank wishes to postpone a decline in the value of its currency, it has at its disposal the means for doing so, at least for a limited period of time.

Historical results

It is relatively easy to find equations to suit recent history. If we look, for example, at an equation for the Deutschemark, we find that most of the variables indicate that the real exchange rate for Germany has declined by an average of one-third of 1% per quarter. This decline is quite significant; the T-statistic is 8·7, significant at the 1% level. The interest rate differential is also quite significant, with a T-statistic of 5·2. This indicates that for every one percentage point that the German interest rate rises relative to the interest rates in the other EEC countries, the Deutschemark will rise by approximately 0·75%.

Deutschemark equation (T-statistics in parentheses)
$$\log (\text{RXECU@GY} \star \text{WPI@EEC}_{-1} / \text{WPI@GY}_{-1}) =$$

$$1.65 \; -0.0036 \; \text{TIME} \; + \; a_i \; \text{INF}_{-i} \; + \; b_i \; \text{CURACC}_{-i}$$
$$(41.1) \; (8.7)$$

$$-0.0073 \; \text{INT} \; +0.11 \; \text{DEMS} \; -0.056 \; \text{DOIL}$$
$$(5.2) \qquad\qquad (6.8) \qquad\qquad (7.1)$$

R–bar squared = 0·91
Durbin-Watson statistic = 1·75
Standard error = 0·0096
Quarterly: 1972 to 1980

$$\Sigma a_i = -3.29 \qquad\qquad \Sigma b_i = -0.22$$
$$(2.0) \qquad\qquad\qquad (2.8)$$

Where:

RXECU@GY	= Deutschemarks per ECU
WPI@EEC	= Wholesale price index, EEC average (harmonic mean)
WPI@GY	= Wholesale price index, Germany
TIME	= Time trend (1948:1 = 1)
INF	= Inflation differential, Germany less EEC
CURACC	= Current account as share of exports, Germany less EEC total
INT	= Real interest rate differential, Germany less EEC average
DEMS	= Dummy for EMS (1979:2)
DOIL	= Oil shock dummy (1973:3 to 1974)
	a and b are polynomial distributed lags of 8 quarters

In general, the interest rate differential varies in the expected manner for the currencies which are considered reserve currencies. In the cases of Germany, the United States, and the U.K., the interest rate differential is quite significant. For the currencies in which people do not normally hold large quantities of reserves, e.g. the Italian lira, the interest differential is substantially less significant.

The current account differential is also significant, although not as highly significant as the interest rate differential. The sum of the coefficients is −0·22, indicating that as the current account deficit increases by 1% of German trade, the mark will decline by 0·22%. It will take two years for the full effect of a current account deficit to appear in the exchange rate.

The inflation differential is an indication of how long it takes for a change in prices to show up in the exchange rate. The equation indicates that it takes on average about nine months for a change in prices to appear in the exchange rate. There is some over-reaction towards the middle of the period. The T-statistic is not a test of significance of prices — the price elasticity is constrained to one by the construction of the dependent variable. Rather, the T-statistic is a test for the significance of a lag. A T-statistic of two indicates that there is a 1% probability that the exchange rate adjusts completely within one quarter, and a 99% probability that the lag between a change in prices and a change in the exchange rate is longer than one quarter.

Two dummy variables have been included in the regression. The first of these is an EMS dummy — a dummy which begins with the institution of the European Monetary System. This dummy says that the European Monetary System has caused the Deutschemark to rise less than it would otherwise have risen against an average of the EMS currencies. The second dummy covers the period following the first oil price shock in 1973. During that period the Deutschemark was 5·5% stronger than the equation would otherwise suggest. The reasons for this are not completely clear. However, we have elected to handle this by introducing a dummy for the year following the first oil price shock.

The equation fits quite well over the historical period, explaining 91% of the total variance in the real exchange rate with a standard error of less than 1%. At no time during the historical interval has the equation significantly under- or over-predicted the value of the Deutschemark for more than two successive quarters. Some other equations in the model fit slightly better and some slightly worse than the equation for the Deutschemark. The standard errors are in general near 1%. There appears to be some correlation between what we would think of as the "dirtiness" of a currency's floating and the fit of the equation. Equations for those currencies whose central banks have done a significant amount of intervention generally show higher standard errors than the standard errors of the currency equations where the central banks have not intervened substantially.

The simulation properties of the system of exchange rate equations are what one would expect in the real world. A rise in a country's interest rate increases the value of its currency. An increase in the price level reduces the value of the currency, with the full effect coming only after one to two years. An increase in the external deficit similarly reduces the value of a country's currency. Reactions to a specific event depend on the position of the country. For example, an increase in oil prices increases the value of the pound relative to all the other countries, as Britain's trade balance is less affected than the trade balances of the other countries.

Forecast performance

In general, the exchange rate equations have done less well in forecasting the future than explaining the past. This seems to be a general characteristic of all models, largely because we know the institutional changes that have occurred in the past, but we do not know the institutional changes that will occur in the future. The forecasts are not constructed by simply letting the equations run by themselves. Forecasts are adjusted for what we expect to happen to institutions, and for what we expect to happen to the other variables that enter the model. The forecast depends on our judgement of likely central banks' intervention patterns and of likely political constraints upon the movements of currencies. Of course, the forecast of the exchange rates depends heavily on our forecast of the variables that enter the exchange rate equations, and in particular upon the behaviour of monetary policy in the various countries. If we assume that the central bank in Germany, for example, is going to keep a tight policy, while the Federal Reserve is going to loosen monetary policy in the United States, then we would expect the dollar to decline against the mark. Another forecaster using the same set of equations might well make the opposite assumptions on monetary policy, and get the opposite result on exchange rates.

The forecast performance has generally been better in terms of the long-run than the short-run performance. Up to a year, econometric models have not out-performed, but have done as well as, the forward market.

There is no easy way to estimate quantitatively the over-sold or under-sold position of a currency, and these positions dominate day-to-day movements. This estimate is better handled judgementally by looking at the market and by talking to the people trading on a day-to-day basis in the market. Where the econometric forecast comes into its own is in the longer run — forecasts of a year or more in length. Technical factors at this point are not as important, and any under-sold position is likely to have unwound itself well before a year has passed.

The advantages of econometric forecasting

If the models cannot guarantee us gains in short-term speculations, what good are they? There are three main reasons for using the econometric model. First, if we are going to do policy analysis, we need a structure of exchange rates which reflects the movements of economic policy. A technical forecast begs the question: what can the country do to protect its currency? The technical forecast assumes that the direction of policy is determined by the movement of the currency, or at least the direction of the policy has already been foreseen by the market and is thus evident in the past movements of the currency. Politically, we need to know what will happen if we change policies: what will happen if the central bank tightens, or if fiscal policy becomes looser. It is these questions which can be analysed by an econometric model.

Econometric models are also useful for corporate planning. In planning, we need to look at a horizon of more than a few months. If we are concerned with siting or sourcing decisions, we have to have a horizon of five or 10 years, or even longer. These decisions cannot be reversed six months from now or three months from now in the way that hedging positions can be unwound.

The econometric model provides a consistent estimate of the exchange rates within an overall economic framework, and this is also important for corporate planning. If we are building a plant, it is not important what the currency is doing in isolation. What is important is what the currency is doing in terms of the cost structure, which will determine the cost of producing from a plant in a particular country.

Of course, this consistency is also important if we are doing corporate risk analysis. Again, what is important is not just the possible error on our forecast exchange rates, but the error in the forecast of the cost of operating in country A versus country B. We may have an idea of what the likely variance in our exchange rate forecast is, and we may also have an idea of what the likely variance in our inflation forecast is. But it would be incorrect to simply add these two errors together. The errors are related. If we underestimate inflation in a country, we will overestimate the exchange rate.

5. Technical analysis

Michael R. Rosenberg

Of all the methods applied in forecasting the movement of stock, commodity, and currency values, few forecasting tools have been received so enthusiastically by the market and scorned so completely by academics as technical analysis. The technical approach has a large following, with many investors and firms taking open positions based on recommended buy and sell signals which are issued either by a mechanical trading rule or by the subjective interpretation of price formations on a bar chart. Though it is one of the oldest of forecasting tools, and has been applied for many years in the stock and commodity markets, it has only recently begun attracting a wide audience in the foreign exchange field. Its popularity in the currency arena is demonstrated by the growing number of financial institutions and advisory services now offering or proposing to offer a technical-based product.

Technical methods' performance

The profitability of technical trading rules in the stock and commodity markets has been widely investigated and the weight of evidence suggests they cannot provide their users with above-average profit opportunities. Yet, the same cannot be said for the empirical evidence on forex market behaviour. On the contrary, many researchers have concluded that a variety of technical trading rules would have provided above-average profits had they been used in the past. Moreover, in a series of studies by Stephen Goodman (Chapter 3, section 4), it was concluded that the track record of technical advisory services in the forex field was consistently superior to that of fundamental-based services.

A variety of technical models may have been profitable in the past but that does not mean they will continue to be so. However, it is interesting to ask why such trading strategies proved so remunerative.

In contrast to fundamental-based forecasts, which require independent projections of the underlying economic variables determining exchange rates, technical models generate exchange rate forecasts by extrapolating the past sequence of currency movements into the future. For example, if a currency begins to edge higher and rises above some critical value, the technical analyst will issue a buy recommendation, the presumption being that the exchange rate trend will continue upwards until a reversal (a sell recommendation) is signalled. A sell signal will be issued if, after having edged lower, the currency falls below some critical value. An investor who rigidly adheres to such rules will always be trading with and not against the trend. Since it is assumed that a trend is in existence until a reversal is signalled, an investor will jump aboard and ride for profit those exchange rate swings that are correctly predicted and he will try to quickly close positions that turn against him.

The most popular technical model is charting. Chartists examine the apparent tendency of price formations to recur on a bar chart and issue buy and sell recommendations if prices divert from their past pattern. More sophisticated extrapolation techniques, requiring less subjective interpretation of chart patterns, have been applied with the use of a computer. One popular mechanical formula is the filter rule which issues buy recommendations if exchange rates rise $x\%$ above their most recent trough and sell recommendations if exchange rates fall $x\%$ below their most recent peak.

Exhibit 2.5.1(a) illustrates the working of a filter rule. The DM/$ rate depicted falls gently during the early stages, reaching a trough at point T; then steadily climbs to a peak at point P, after which it drifts lower. An investor would be able to ride a large portion of this swing in the DM/$ rate by adhering to an $x\%$ filter rule trading strategy. For example, if a 1% filter rule is chosen, a buy $ recommendation would be issued after the DM/$ rate rises 1% above its trough at T and a sell $ recommendation after the DM/$ rate falls 1% below its peak at P. An investor who rigidly adhered to this trading strategy would buy at B and sell at S, the spread between B and S representing the profit margin per dollar invested. By varying the size of the filter, an investor would be able to capture changes in trend earlier or later. Obviously, a smaller filter

Exhibit 2.5.1: When models signal buy and sell

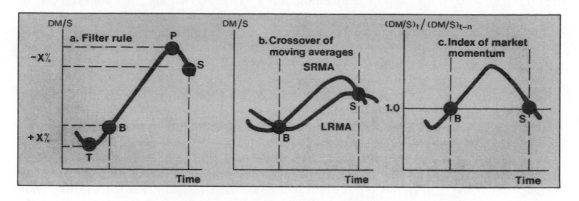

Exhibit 2.5.2: A lag trap for the investor

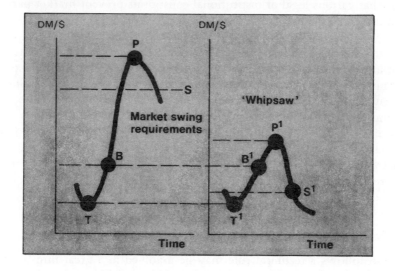

would capture the big swings earlier, but at the expense of more frequent whipsaws (see Exhibit 2.5.2) when movements in the DM/$ rate are not highly trended.

Another favourite trading rule is one based on the crossover of short and long-run moving averages. Constructed to smooth the erratic movement of daily exchange rates, an advance of the short-run average above the long-run average is seen as an indication of buying strength and vice versa.

Terms and systems

Exhibit 2.5.1(b) shows how the crossover of moving averages of the DM/$ rate can be used to project the future course of the DM/$ rate. The long-run moving average (LRMA) will always lag behind the movement in the short-run average (SRMA) because the latter series weighs the impact of recent moves of the DM/$ rate more heavily than the former. Thus, the SRMA lies below the LRMA when the $ rate is trending lower and above it when it is rising. Therefore, the crossover of the SRMA above or below the LRMA can be used as an indication of a shift in market direction. If the SRMA moves above the LRMA, it indicates that the rate is rising and vice versa. A buy $ signal would be issued at B and a sell $ signal at S. Varying the time span of the moving averages in question affects the sensitivity of the SRMA and LRMA to changes in the trend.

Yet another favourite is the momentum model which is used to predict the strength of a currency by evaluating whether it is moving up or down with rising or declining velocity. Exhibit 2.5.1(c) illustrates how an index of market momentum is used to project the future course of the DM/$ rate. A momentum index can be derived by dividing today's exchange rate

$(DM/\$)_t$ by the rate prevailing n days ago $(DM/\$)_{t-n}$. If the DM/$ rate is trending upward, then $(DM/\$)_t > (DM/\$)_{t-n}$ and the momentum index, $(DM/\$)_t/DM(\$)_{t-n}$, would exceed 1. If the DM/$ rate was trending lower, then the momentum index would be smaller than 1. Hence, as the index rises above or falls below 1, it gauges the strength or weakness in the dollar's value. As the index rises above 1, a buy $ signal is issued at point B and as it falls below 1 a sell $ signal is issued at point S. Varying the width of the $(DM/\$)_t-(DM/\$)_{t-n}$ interval, affects the sensitivity of the momentum model to fluctuations in the DM/$ rate.

Exhibit 2.5.1 shows the dependence of all technical models on the past sequence of exchange rate movements. The recommended trades of these models are shown to occur at the same point in time. (Actually, the timing of these signals may differ slightly because of differences in the mathematical properties of each model.)

Despite their growing popularity, many market participants remain sceptical of technical models. They argue that if one can devise a consistently profitable trading rule based on past currency movements, then this information will be available to all market participants, who should exploit it until the technical trading rule ceases to be profitable. If such profit opportunities are not exploited, it would suggest that the market is inefficient in processing information or that various legal or institutional constraints prevent market participants from acting on such information.

Two restrictive conditions must be satisfied for technical analysis to prove consistently profitable. First, market prices must move in trends that are readily forecastable. Second, certain legal or institutional constraints must be present which impose limits on position-taking by a sufficient number of private investors, enough to permit unexploited profit opportunities, based strictly on technical analysis, to exist.

The first condition means market prices must move in discernible trends since technical models generate forecasts by extrapolating the past price movements into the future. The duration and extent of these trends must be sustained and pronounced, to permit an investor time to recognize and profit from each swing. The larger the swing, the larger the profit. Such large swings are necessary to compensate for possibly sizeable transaction and opportunity costs.

Sustained swings overcome tardiness

An investor who follows a technical rule may be involved in a great number of trades, the number determined by the sensitivity of the technical model chosen and the volatility and variability in market prices. Not only might an investor incur sizeable transaction costs, but additional resources and time would have to be devoted to the close monitoring of price movements and the investor's outstanding positions. Relatively sustained and pronounced swings are also necessary to overcome the tardiness of reported technical signals.

Large price swings would have to occur often enough to overcome periods when market prices are not highly trended. There will be many occasions when market prices will show little overall variation. Buy and sell signals may still be issued, but the price moves are unlikely to carry far enough to yield a profit and, in many instances, may result in losses. An investor following a technical trading rule would need sufficient capital to absorb losses when false signals are issued (see Exhibit 2.5.2).

A common feature of all technical models is that the buy and sell signals are late in drawing attention to a shift in market direction. This is because technical recommendations are derived by extrapolating the past sequence of exchange rate movements into the future and therefore could only be issued after a currency has already started rising or falling. In Exhibit 2.5.1, the common recognition lag that each model shares in confirming that a shift in market direction has taken place is the distance TB(=PS). In addition to this lag the investor who subscribes to a technical advisory service must consider the length of the advisory service's reporting lag. How quickly an advisory service informs its clients that a new trend has emerged is dictated largely by the delivery system used — computer access, telex or mail. A third lag which could have an impact on the profitability of technical analysis is the reaction lag of investors in taking open positions following the issue of a buy or sell signal. Even a slight delay in investor reaction time could remove a significant profit opportunity.

When exchange rate swings are sustained and pronounced, these lags do not pose a serious threat to the profitability of most technical models. But this market swing requirement can prove to be a tall order. In markets which exhibit little overall price variation or are not highly trended, an investor who follows a technical trading rule will be vulnerable to whipsaws caused by false signals. Consider the two exchange rate series depicted in Exhibit 2.5.2. The series on the left is the same DM/$ rate depicted in Exhibit 2.5.1(a). The series on the right behaves in a similar fashion as the series on the left but its upward swing is less pronounced; the swing in the DM/$ rate from T^1 to P^1 falls short of the swing from T to P. Although the DM/$ rate swings upward following the buy $ signal at B^1, the swing fails to carry the rate far enough to yield a profit. The upward momentum loses steam early, turning down at P^1, and a sell $ signal is not triggered until the exchange rate move carries to S^1.

The spread between B^1 and S^1 represents the margin of loss per dollar invested. Hence, the buy $ recommendation at B^1 proved to be a false signal, with the investor whipsawed in the process. What this latter example demonstrates is that a technical trading rule can be correct in assessing direction 100% of the time (note that the DM/$ rate did briefly turn up after a buy $ signal was issued at B^1) but still be unprofitable.

A trading rule to minimize whipsaws

It is not necessary that exchange rates always move in large swings for technical analysis to be profitable, but that such swings should occur on a frequent enough basis to overcome those periods when currency movements are not highly trended. Since there will be many periods when market prices will exhibit little overall variation, the technical analyst's problem is to construct a trading rule which will minimize the whipsaws caused by false signals yet be sufficiently sensitive to capture a large portion of the major exchange rate swings.

Although large price swings are necessary for technical analysis to be profitable, by themselves they are not sufficient. A second condition, involving restrictions on private investor position-taking, is required. If markets are truly efficient, prices would adjust rapidly to new information, particularly information that market prices are likely to move in well-defined trends. Profit-maximizing investors would quickly capitalize on the existence of persistent price trends if they existed, and by their collective action would ensure that successive price changes were random. Thus, even if economic forces dictated large price swings, an efficient market's adjustment to this information should be so rapid that investors would not be able to consistently earn above-average profits by adhering to a trend-following trading rule.

Logically, if one is to convincingly argue that trend-following trading rules provide handsome returns, it must be proven that there are significant departures from true market efficiency. Markets will diverge from full efficiency if position-taking by a sufficient number of private investors is limited by institutional or legal restraints. For example, profit maximizing investors will be unable to quickly capitalize on persistent price trends if they are constrained by government intervention or restrictions. Even if unhindered by official constraints, key market participants might not rapidly exploit profit opportunities if self-imposed internal guidelines restrict their position-taking. If pervasive, such barriers to market efficiency would effectively reduce the speed at which the market adjusts to new information and, by so doing, contribute to the persistence of price trends.

In conjunction with fundamental forces dictating large swings in market prices, such barriers to market efficiency would provide significant profit opportunities to technical analysis. The interplay of these two forces may help explain why technical models have performed so well in the currency arena. Since 1973, exchange rates have tended to move in relatively large swings, in response to divergent monetary policies and external shocks (particularly those on the oil front), as well as to dramatic policy reversals, errors and failures. While other markets have also shown large swings in prices, the forex market appears to be unique in that institutional and legal restraints have limited the manoeuvrability of the key players to take full advantage of the evident trend in foreign exchange rates. For a variety of reasons, many forex market participants have been unwilling or unable to take open positions and exploit profitable opportunities.

The key private sector players in the foreign exchange market are commercial banks and multinational corporations. Although individual institutions have different attitudes towards foreign exchange risk, most banks and firms have internal guidelines which restrict the amount of net positions taken. For example, commercial banks generally place internal restrictions on their dealers' net positions which can be carried over from one day to the next. In several countries, limits on bank positions are imposed by the monetary authorities.

Multinational corporations also have internal policies restricting position-taking in different currencies. The general attitude of most firms is that they are not in the business of foreign exchange as such, but only in their particular product or service line. Multinational companies are more interested in minimizing their exposure to foreign exchange risk than in maximizing foreign exchange profits and, in many instances, will not take open positions even when there are profit opportunities. Also many governments seek to restrain potential speculation against (or in favour of) their currencies by imposing restrictions and authorization requirements on multinational firms' leading and lagging and borrowing and lending.

The net effect of these guidelines and regulations has been to slow the foreign exchange market's adjustment to new information. Adding to this slow adjustment process is the impact of central bank intervention. When a fundamental correction in a currency's value is called for, intervention will merely slow the adjustment of the exchange rate to its new equilibrium level. If intervention is pervasive, trends in currency movements will become evident.

It is clear that economic forces can drive currency values sharply higher or lower and that institutional and market forces can act to slow the adjustment from one equilibrium level to another. This would explain the empirical findings that a variety of technical models would have yielded above average profits had they been used in the past. It also explains why technical forecasts have provided higher average returns than fundamental-based forecasts.

The swings in exchange rates during the floating rate period generally have been larger than expected, frequently overshooting the apparent intrinsic equilibrium levels of purchasing power parity, balance of payments and monetary models of exchange rate determination. When exchange rates do overshoot such levels, fundamental model forecasts will prematurely recommend that positions be reversed as the model's intrinsic equilibrium level is breached. Technical analysis, on the other hand, has a distinct advantage over fundamental-based models when price swings are unexpectedly great. Technical models are designed to keep an investor trading with and not against the trend. An investor adhering to a trend-following trading rule would jump aboard and ride each exchange rate swing and would cling to this position until a reversal was signalled, even if the path that the currency took was not realistic.

Whether technical analysis will continue to be as profitable is a difficult question. There is a growing convergence of economic policies and government philosophies among the major industrialized nations, which could suggest less variability of exchange rates in the 1980s. In addition, the greater sophistication of corporate treasurers and private investors, as well as the recent growth in technical advisory services, suggest a more competitive and efficient foreign exchange market. Such factors lead one to conclude that the profits from technical analysis will be harder to come by. However, shocks such as sharp rises in oil prices, leading to significant wealth transfers, may contribute to dramatic shifts in portfolio preference, producing sharp movements in exchange rates.

The threat of increased protectionism and government controls on capital movements still exists. Policy goals among the major industrialized nations may be converging, but implementation could prove to be extraordinarily difficult.

6. Interest rates

David Morrison

During the past few years, it has often appeared that interest rates have been the dominant influence on exchange rates. Clearly, if this influence is stable or predictable then we have a most useful tool to help us with our currency forecasts. This section attempts to answer the following questions:

1. Is there a reasonably stable relationship between nominal short-term interest rate differentials and changes in the major currencies' cross-rates?
2. Is the relationship between nominal long-term interest rate differentials and changes in the major cross-rates superior to that of short rates and currency changes?
3. Questions (1) and (2) again but using real interest rate differentials (i.e. nominal yield gaps adjusted for inflation differences).

Short–term interest rates (nominal) and exchange rates

We have chosen to concentrate on the U.S. $, Deutschemark, yen and sterling and their corresponding money market rates over the period 1978–82. The choice of currencies represents the core or only currency in their respective blocs. Thus, any conclusions which hold for a core currency *vis-à-vis* the remaining core currencies will tend also to hold for satellite currencies (e.g. if we can establish any link between U.S./German interest rate differentials and the DM/$ rate it will tend to hold for U.S./Dutch interest rate differentials and the Dfl/$ rate, etc.).

Exhibits 2.6.1(a)–(c) show the level, in basis points,* of U.S./German, U.S./Japanese and U.S./U.K. short-term interest rate differentials from 1978Q1–82Q4 together with the contemporaneous percentage change in the corresponding exchange rate (quarter on previous quarter). The short-term interest rates used were: United States: Federal funds; Germany: call money; Japan: call money; U.K.: T–bill rate. Both the interest rates and the exchange rates are quarterly averages. In the graphs, the interest rate differentials are expressed as U.S. minus the foreign country.

DM/dollar axis

Exhibit 2.6.1(a) shows the results for the pivotal DM/$ rate. It can be seen that there does not appear to be any stable relationship between changes in the Federal funds/call money interest rate gap and the contemporaneous change in the DM/$ rate. Throughout 1978, for example, the rate gap in favour of the United States increased each quarter but was accompanied by a cumulative decline of the dollar against the German currency. By contrast, from 1980Q4 to 1981Q3 a nominal interest rate gap of over 550 basis points per quarter in favour of the dollar was accompanied by an appreciation of the dollar against the DM which averaged 8·3% per quarter.

Yen/$ and $/£

Exhibit 2.6.1(b) shows the results for the yen/$ rate. The same conclusion holds. There does not appear to be any easily predictable relationship between U.S./Japanese short-term interest rate differentials and the yen/$ rate. Indeed, over the 16 quarters considered, the yen appreciated against the dollar in eight of them and depreciated in eight, but the United States had an interest rate advantage for 15 out of the 16 quarterly periods (which averaged 543 basis points per quarter). Even during 1981 and early 1982, when there appeared to be a link between the DM/$ rate and U.S./German interest rates, there were two quarters of yen appreciation and two of depreciation despite a U.S. yield advantage of between 700–1,100 basis points per quarter. There is some evidence, however, particularly during 1980/81, that sudden changes in the size of the differential had correspondingly swift changes in the DM/$ and Y/$ rates in the expected direction.

---

* 100 basis points = 1 percentage point.

Exhibit 2.6.1: Interest rate differentials, 1978Q1–82Q2

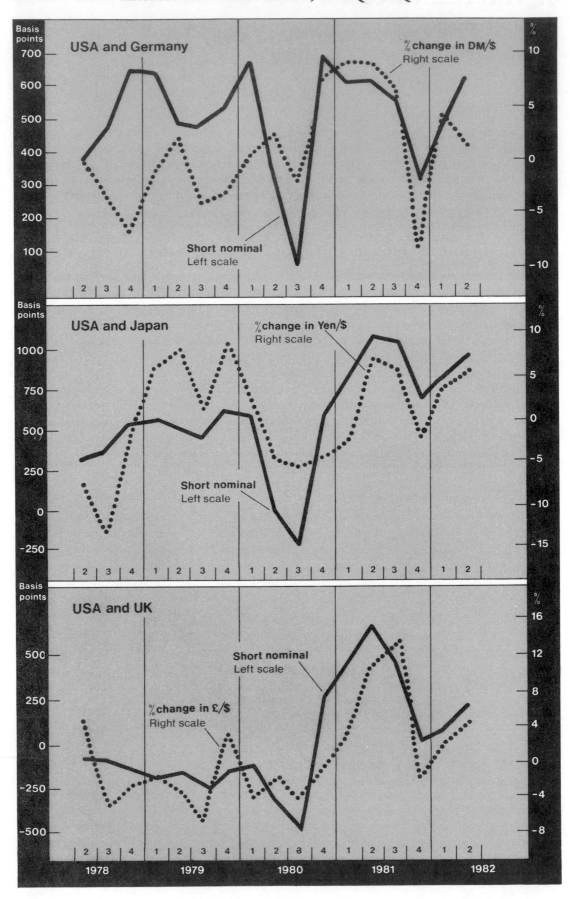

Exhibit 2.6.2: Interest rate differentials on long-term government bonds

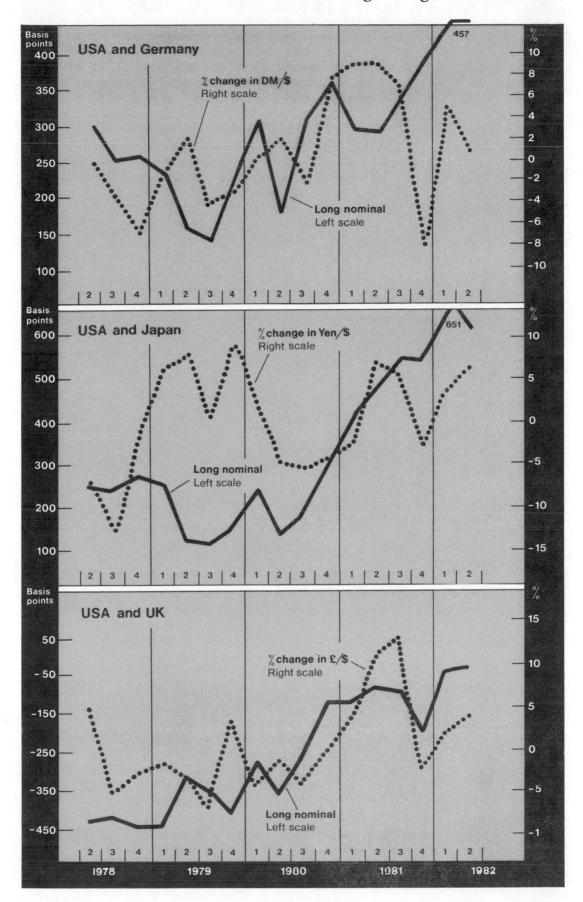

Exhibit 2.6.1(c) shows the results for the £/$ rate. Interestingly, there does appear to be some evidence of a fairly stable positive link between the £/$ rate and U.K./U.S. interest rate differentials. Between 1978Q2 and 1980Q3, the U.K. had an interest rate advantage and sterling appreciated against the dollar in eight of the 10 quarters. Then, during 1981, when the interest rate advantage switched to $ assets, the U.S. currency rose against sterling. Furthermore, there appears to be a magnitude link as well as a directional one, in that, on balance, the larger the interest rate gap, the larger the change in the £/$ rate. This has continued to hold into 1982.

Long-term interest rates (nominal)

Exhibits 2.6.2(a)–(c) show the level in basis points of the interest rate differential on long-term government bonds between the United States and each of Germany, Japan and the U.K. and the contemporaneous change in the corresponding exchange rates (quarter on previous quarter).

Using long rates instead of short rates does nothing to improve the link between U.S./German or U.S./Japanese yields and their respective exchange rates. Regarding U.S./U.K. long bond yield differentials and the £/$ rate, the link is noticeably less robust than with short rates — with 1981 being the key period supporting this view.

Short-term interest rates (real)

Exhibits 2.6.3(a)–(c) show the level of the real interest rate differential in basis points between U.S. short rates and those in Germany, Japan and the U.K. plotted against the contemporaneous exchange rate changes. The real rates were calculated by subtracting the inflation differential (using retail/consumer prices, quarter on previous quarter annualized) from the interest rate differential between the two currencies under consideration.

DM/U.S. dollar

Over most of the 1978–81 period, the rise in U.S. consumer prices has been much higher than that in Germany; so much so that for 11 of the 16 quarters the nominal interest rate gap in favour of the United States has been insufficient to offset the inflation differential. However, in the quarters when the real interest rate gap was either in favour of the United States or fell below a 100 basis points advantage to Germany, the U.S. currency was normally either stable or rising (except in 1978Q4). Although by no means robust, the link between U.S./German real short-term interest rate differentials and changes in the DM/$ rate seems to be stronger than the nominal link.

Yen/U.S. dollar and U.S. dollar/£

Exhibit 2.6.3(b) shows that the relationship between real U.S./Japanese interest rate differentials and the Y/$ rate still appears to be random. By contrast, Exhibit 2.6.3(c) shows that the link between U.S./U.K. real short-term interest rate gaps and the £/$ rate is fairly strong.

Long-term interest rates (real)

Exhibit 2.6.4(a)–(c) shows the relationship between real long-term interest rate differentials between the United States and Germany, Japan and the U.K. plotted against the contemporaneous exchange rate changes. The results add little to those that have been mentioned above.

Assessment

Although this note is only a brief comment on interest rate/exchange rate links, several points of importance seem to have emerged.

1. Taking the 1978–81 period as a whole, it does not appear that accurate interest rate forecasts (in itself an awesome task) would necessarily have led to accurate exchange rate forecasts. However, during the 1980/82 period results would certainly have been better.

Exhibit 2.6.3: Real interest rate differentials

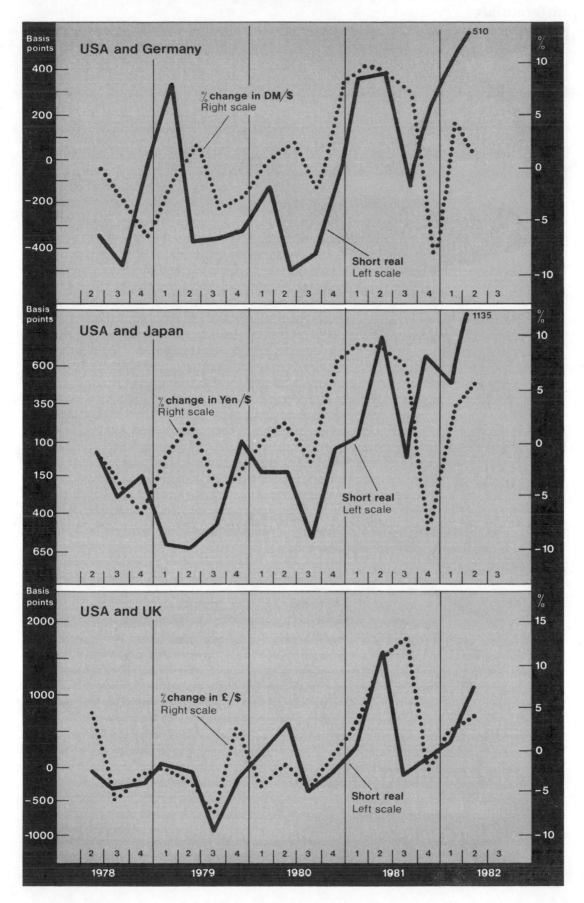

85

Exhibit 2.6.4: Relationship between real long-term interest rate differentials

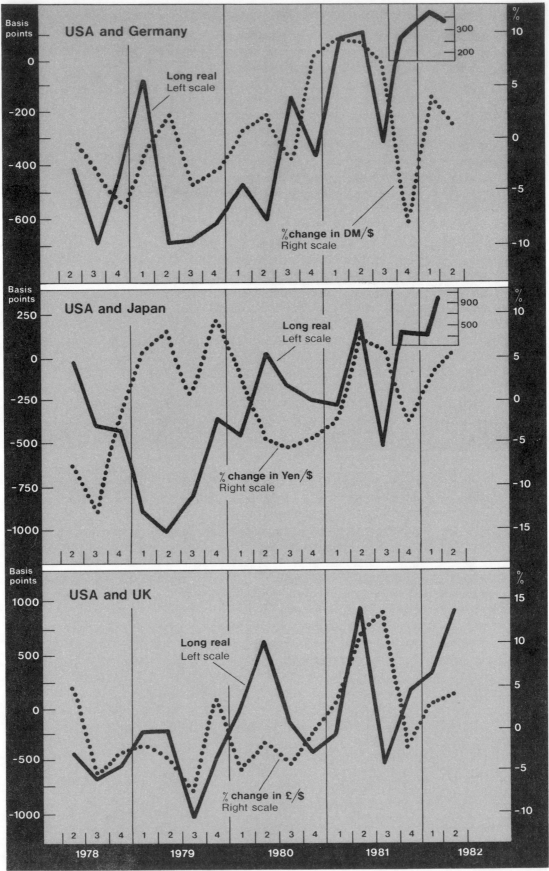

2. Having said that, the link between short-term interest rate differentials (nominal and real) in the United States and U.K. appeared to have a fairly close relationship with changes in the £/$ rate. Also, the link between U.S./German real short-term interest rate differentials and the DM/$ rate was quite close, especially when a certain "critical level" of the differential was reached.
3. The yen/$, U.S./Japanese interest rate relationship seems to be random.
4. Short-term currency movements are more likely to be influenced by short-term interest rates than long-term interest rates.

The inability to find a generally stable relationship between interest rate changes and exchange rate changes should not be surprising. First, economic theory remains unsure about whether the relationship should be positive or negative. Secondly, all serious students of, and participants in, the foreign exchange markets understand that expectations are often the key to short-term currency changes and expectations are not influenced solely by interest rates (see The Bank of England *Quarterly Bulletin*, Dec. 1981, pp. 489–509, for a rigorous analysis supporting this contention).

Finally, it is worth pointing out that in many of the examples between 1978 and 1981 where interest rate differentials and exchange rates appeared to be negatively related or unrelated, a good case could have been made for the influence of current account divergences. This is particularly true during 1978, a period of advantageous U.S. yield gaps for the U.S. dollar but of a disadvantageous U.S. trade performance. Even during 1981/82, when many foreign exchange commentators appeared to be mesmerized by interest rate changes, divergencies in current accounts supported the currency changes implied by differential yields.

Thus, for 1982, while we contine to expect interest rate gyrations to play a major role in the determination of foreign exchange values, expectations will also be influenced by other factors, especially current account swings. Interest rates and current accounts, taken together, may remain supportive of the U.S. dollar during 1982H1, but by 1982H2, the absence of trade support for the dollar and no increase in the U.S./competitors yield gap should see the U.S. currency fall.

7. Long-term forecasting

Brinsley Best

It appears reasonable to suggest that in the longer term (say five years) relative inflation rates, or, more precisely, shifts in the relative prices at which goods are being offered, are adjusted through variations in the exchange rate, and the evolution of exchange rate forecasts from analysis of such trends is feasible. At least three factors of different durability appear to be superimposed on these long-term trends: political factors; current account balances; and interest rate differentials.

Five years ago, the political situation in Italy appeared to be causing currency analysts the most concern. Its place was long ago taken by other phenomena such as Poland, socialism in France and "Reaganomics" in the United States. These will no doubt be replaced by new events in their turn. The market's concern with political factors appears to be not so much about the events themselves, but about their possible consequences for the world economy in general and the main currencies concerned by the event in particular.

Taking Poland as an example: fear appeared less centred on whether the Soviet Union might or might not invade Poland, but on the consequences which any action in that area might have for Polish debt or for western exports, particularly those of Germany, to the Communist bloc.

Under these circumstances, the Deutschemark and its associated currencies fell far more than might be indicated by a technical comparison of interest rate differentials, current account balances, inflation rates or other factors. In this case, as in others, the market appears to take a defensive line in evaluating a currency. Its logic may well be: what would the value of the Deutschemark be if Poland could not pay its debts and if Germany's trade with the East were blocked? It is possible to move from this assumption to calculate the amount by which the Deutschemark would have to be devalued in order to compensate for the worst case.

The duration over which political factors can affect currencies might be considerable, as witnessed by the Polish crisis. They may therefore be included as a factor in long-term exchange rate analysis. An interesting case for the future is in the post-1984 period for the United Kingdom. Each of the possible alternative governments may have a radically different economic policy with a corresponding impact on the exchange rate. These possibilities and their consequences should be analysed in their totality before coming to any medium-term conclusion about the pound.

Logically, analysis of current account balances should be brought in at this point. This is because political discussions made in the present can seriously affect current account balances in a future period. For example:

— High current expenditure combined with unchecked inflation can result in disproportionately high levels of imports. The extent varies from country to country but it appears particularly important in France, Italy and the United States.
— A consistent medium to long-term energy policy can significantly reduce demand for energy imports. Without such a policy, French current account deficits could be much worse.

Since fixed exchange rates were abandoned, most major trading nations whose currencies are also widely quoted have run a series of current account surpluses and deficits. Countries with significant surpluses in recent memory have frequently run a series of important deficits, e.g. the United Kingdom from 1973 to 1976, the United States in 1977–78, Japan in 1973–75 and again in 1979–80. The opposite has also been true. Germany ran a string of surpluses from 1966 to 1978 without interruption. Italy generated large surpluses in the 1960s and again in 1977–79. The French current account was in surplus for seven years out of the last 15 and as recently as 1978–79.

On a currency-by-currency basis, the foreign exchange market does not appear to have reacted to these surpluses or deficits except when they are considered excessive. This means that the market can tolerate levels of surpluses or deficits to an extent to which it has been accustomed. The threshold can be set at the average historical proportion of surplus or the average proportion of deficit to GNP over the long term. Once this threshold is significantly or consistently exceeded, the market moves to counteract it. If in deficit, the market undervalues the currency. This tends to encourage exports and restore balance or an acceptable deficit. Uncharacteristic surpluses tend to push the currency up, cutting back the potential for further surplus. Experience of such movements is plentiful; for example:

> United States — fall of dollar in 1977–79.
> United Kingdom — fall of sterling in 1967–78 and again in 1974–76. Rise of sterling and anticipation of further rises on account of oil exports in 1979–80.
> Germany — rise of Deutschemark in 1973/74 and again in 1978; fall in 1980/81.
> France — rise of franc in 1978, fall in 1969, 1974, 1976 and 1982.
> Italy — rise of lira in 1971/72 and in 1978/79; fall of lira in 1974/76 and again in 1980/81.
> Japan — rise of yen in 1977/78; fall in 1974/75 and again in 1980.
> Canada — rise of Canadian dollar in 1970/72; fall in 1976/78.

The influence of short-term interest rate differentials on exchange rates has only become evident in the late 1970s. The increase in their importance can be linked directly to the growing tendency of monetary targets to be used as guidelines for management of certain economies, particularly the United States and the United Kingdom. Their role in Germany and Switzerland and the resultant impact on foreign exchange markets should also not be ignored.

Prior to the rise of monetarism, high interest rates were usually employed to defend currencies weakened by high inflation and current account deficits. Since 1980, high interest rates have on occasion gone hand in hand with declining inflation and current account surpluses (e.g. the United States and the United Kingdom). This has provided investors with the opportunity for high current earnings combined with currency appreciation potential, at least over the short-term. This tendency has also led to the use of real as well as nominal interest rates as a basis for international comparisons.

Despite the increased importance of interest rate differentials over short-term variations in exchange rates, there are serious reasons to doubt their direct reference for medium- to long-term variations. Among possible reasons for this assumption, two are prominent:

> — the extremely short-term nature of interest rate variations and their relative unpredictability;
> — the breakdown of the interest rate/exchange rate relationship itself in 1981/82.

The lead role in setting interest rates, which in turn affect exchange rates, is at present with the United States. Money supply figures, announced at the end of each week, fall either above or below target. This is taken by the banks as evidence of whether policies are working and as an indicator of confidence in the future. Interest rates are adjusted accordingly and the gap between U.S. dollar rates and those for other currencies widens or narrows, thus influencing their exchange rates. If the movements are serious enough, other countries may also be forced to adjust their interest rates. In this way, a pattern of very short-term movements, themselves difficult to measure, has become a determinant of exchange rates which have longer term consequences.

During 1980, interest rate differentials in the Euro-markets provided a near perfect explanation of the way in which currencies moved against one another. This proved particularly true for movements against the U.S. dollar. This assumption applied whether one wished to examine values on a day-to-day, week-to-week, month-to-month, or quarter-to-quarter basis. There were also some underlying long-term trends such as the secular rise of the pound.

In early 1981, this logic fell to pieces. Even though the interest rate gap between the U.S. dollar and the Deutschemark, Swiss franc, pound and other currencies stabilized or narrowed as these countries pushed up their rates to close the gap widening between them and the dollar, their exchange rates continued to plummet. The experience of the DM/$ rate, shown in Exhibit 2.7.1, is the most illustrative. Similar patterns exist for the Swiss franc against the dollar and against the DM.

In logical terms, it is difficult to make a direct connection between movements in short-term interest rates and long-term exchange rate forecasts. It is certainly not feasible to use five-year forecasts of interest rates for this purpose. Indirectly, however, short-term interest rate movements appear of vital significance for long-term developments if they artificially raise or

Exhibit 2.7.1: DM/U.S. dollar interest rate differential

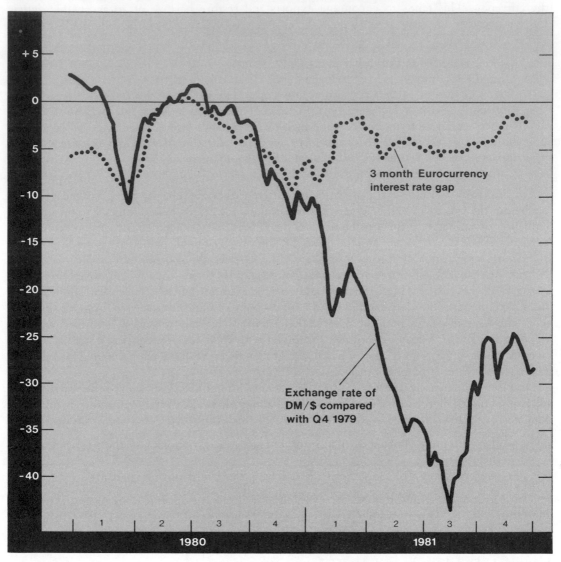

depress the value of a currency beyond levels compatible with other fundamental parameters such as cost inflation and relative current account positions. Thus, if high short-term interest rates push up the value of a currency which is already strong on the basis of the other two factors, this can only undermine the position of that currency in the long run by reducing export potential and creating wider domestic market for cheap imports. The United States is the main example of this phenomenon in 1981/82.

Combined influence of all technical factors in 1981

While a detailed statistical analysis of the interrelationships between all the technical factors mentioned above is outside the scope of this section, it is possible to devise a simple ranking and weighting system, as shown in Exhibit 2.7.2.

The combined total of the relative effects of each of these factors bears a very close resemblance to the actual performance of each of the currencies concerned during the last quarter of 1981. Alternative weightings can easily be devised. The system is self-correcting. So, if all current accounts are in surplus, the impact on all countries will be equal and their relative ranking will be unaltered. Thus, any factor becomes important only when there are wide differences in this factor between the main countries.

It is convenient to organize all the preceding factors into a hierarchical system when making exchange rate forecasts. For the short term (i.e. one year or less), interest rate differentials, both

Exhibit 2.7.2: Combined influence of technical factors on exchange rates in 1981Q4

Country	Inflation	Interest rate differential	Real interest rate	Current account	Total
France	− −	+ +	0	− −	− −
Germany	+	−	+	0	+
U.K.	−	+	0	+	+
Switzerland	+	−	+	+	+ +
U.S.A.	+	+	+	+	+ + + +

current and real, play a significant role. However, shifts in exchange rates caused by these factors take place around long-term trends generated by international competitiveness in the marketplace. Political factors and the performance of the current account provide a link between the short-term and the long-term.

Longer-term trends

The rest of this section analyses longer-term trends in international competitive positions and the role of exchange rate movements in this context. Comparisons have been made on variations in export prices[1] which approximate more closely to conditions in the world marketplace than domestic wholesale prices or the purchasing power parity concept.

Until the first oil crisis, export prices varied considerably from domestic prices, often being well above or well below. This resulted from pressures on capacity use. When export demand rose above normal working capacity, export prices which traditionally rose more slowly than domestic prices began to rise much faster. Since the mid-1970s, capacity pressures have not been a factor in export price changes. Instead, energy price increases have had a much more direct feed-back to export prices than to domestic prices in general. Looking ahead to forecasting, some clear hypothesis on shifts in the business cycle on the national and world plane are therefore necessary. A view must be taken on the likelihood of a return to pressures on capacity in a recovery situation and on the future of energy prices. Straight trend projections will not do.

The perfect model

Comparing shifts in export prices means comparing competitiveness in the international marketplace. Were the market for manufacturers to operate under perfect competition, it would be reasonable to expect that, if nation A's export prices remain constant in relation to the average of those of its competitors, then that nation's share of total trade will remain constant. Conversely, if nation A's prices rise or fall in relation to the average of those of competing states, then its market share should fall or rise appropriately.

In practice, this is not the case, as Exhibits 2.7.3 and 2.7.4 indicate. For example, Germany's share of world trade continued to rise up to 1977 even though German export prices were rising faster than world export prices from 1969 onwards. Since the 1967 devaluation of sterling, U.K. export prices slackened relative to world prices up to 1976. Despite this, the U.K.'s share of world trade continued to fall drastically. However, the sharp rises in prices since then have actually been accompanied by an increase in the U.K. share of world trade up to 1980. Most other countries lie somewhere between these extremes. In no case is there a common direct link between relative export price movements and each country's share of world trade.

This evident difference between countries underlines the relatively low importance of changes in currency parities in apportioning shares of world trade. Export price shifts, even after

---

[1] In practice, export unit values (as defined by the IMF) have been used for this updated analysis rather than export prices, EUV data being more widely comparable. For ease of comparison, EUVs will be referred to as export prices without capitals.

Exhibit 2.7.3: National shares of world* exports by value

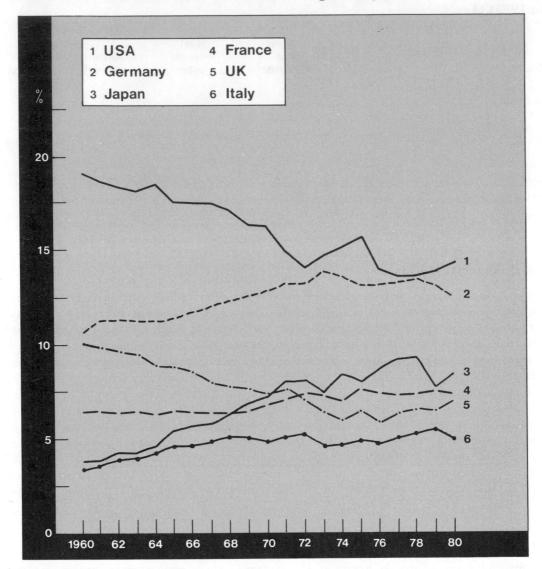

1 USA	4 France
2 Germany	5 UK
3 Japan	6 Italy

* Excludes OPEC and U.K. oil exports.
Source. *International Financial Statistics,* IMF.

adjustments for exchange rate changes, are not the sole determinants of success or failure in holding or penetrating world markets. An ever-rising proportion of the major industrial nations' exports is composed of capital equipment, sophisticated vehicles and specialized products. For such goods factors other than price are of high importance. These include: technical sophistication of the product; uniqueness (e.g. video cassette players); reliability; after-sales service; compatibility with existing equipment; and delivery delays. In other words, the potential buyer of such equipment is interested in the gain in productivity which its acquisition will bring to his operations.

The widely different reactions of various countries' share of export markets to price variations lead to the conclusion that there must be some difference in the quality of each nation's goods, the mix of products sold and the conditions under which they are supplied which explains shifts in trade not explicable by price alone. This variation we have termed the product factor.

The product factor

The causes for each country's success or failure in gaining a share of world exports can be attributed to product factors and price factors.

Exhibit 2.7.4: National export price movements relative to world export prices

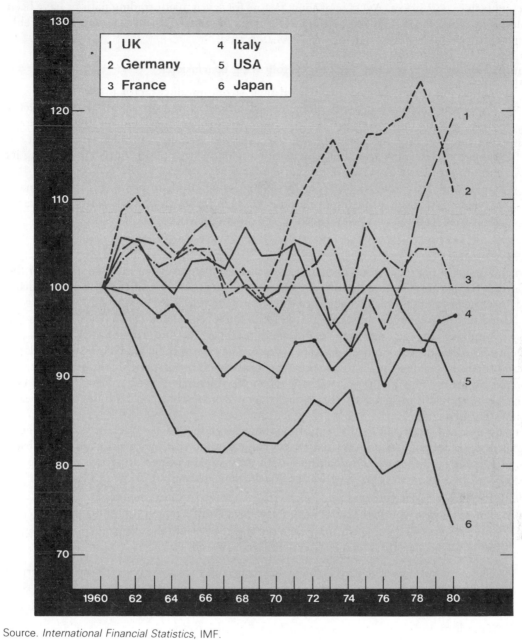

1	UK	4	Italy
2	Germany	5	USA
3	France	6	Japan

Source. *International Financial Statistics*, IMF.

Exhibit 2.7.5: Changes in non-price or product factors, 1975–80

Country	Product factor		Impact of product factor on volume of exports (% per annum)	
	1960–75	1960–80	1960–75	1960–80
France	0.09	0.09	1.16	1.21
Germany	0.16	0.16	1.22	1.27
United Kingdom	−0.30	−0.21	−4.65	−3.00
Italy	0.05	0.02	0.98	0.50
United States	−0.34	−0.35	−2.17	−2.48
Japan	0.34	0.27	4.19	4.23

Source. Best & Associés.

The product factor of a country can be defined as the annual percentage change in the proportion of world trade in current prices held by that country which cannot be explained by movements in export prices. Average product factors for seven major trading nations have been calculated for the period 1960–80 and are set out in Exhibit 2.7.5, along with comparable product factors established earlier for the 1960–75 period.

Comparison of the two series leads to the following conclusions:

— France and Germany have maintained their strong product factor profile.
— The strong negative product factor of the United Kingdom is still a serious factor limiting trade opportunities, but it has been seriously reduced since 1975.
— The negative product factor of the United States is getting worse. This means that the United States, unlike the United Kingdom, is not yet making progress in adapting its export profile to world market requirements.
— Japan and Italy may be marginally losing some of their positive product factor advantages. This is a much more serious problem for Italy, which has little advantage, than for Japan which is way ahead of the other countries.

Price factors

Up to and including 1975, floating exchange rates had been applicable in most countries for the last third of the period. Floating had also led most currencies to move either up or down. Sharp cyclical variations and complete changes of direction were relatively unknown.

This situation has changed drastically since 1975. Sharply declining currencies, such as the pound, completely changed direction, as did the U.S. dollar. By contrast, the continued rise of the Deutschemark and yen has been put into reverse. The French franc has frequently oscillated back and forth. Reflecting these movements, the steady gains or losses of shares of world trade registered by most countries up to 1975 have given way themselves to sharp fluctuations. It is thus no longer possible to speak of a steady price factor which has been behind the trend of each country's performance.

Instead, national shares of world export markets have tended to react in a much more complex way, reflecting not only relative price changes in the year concerned, but going back year-by-year for several years. This contrasts with the one-year lagged impact of relative price changes identified five years ago. Key features of the new analysis are shown in Exhibit 2.7.6, the main points of which are:

— The extension of the impact of price factors backwards over a full range of three years (i.e., A_t, A_{t-1} and A_{t-2}), starting with the current year. In the earlier analysis, only the previous year's price changes (A_{t-1}) were considered.

— The continual positive impact of price changes in the *current* year. Note that current year price changes had no impact on U.S. or Italian exports.

— Some significant changes in non-price factors, notably an improvement for the United Kingdom and deteriorations for the U.S.A. and Japan.

On price factors, it can be concluded that national price increases which rise faster than world price increases can have a negative impact on a country's share of world trade between one and two years after these increases take place. However, in the year when the relative price rises actually take place, the effect may be beneficial.

Conversely, if such a country's export price falls relative to other countries, the positive effect of this action will not be felt until one or two years later. The immediate effect of a fall in the value of a currency can, therefore, be a catastrophic loss of potential earnings. This is clear proof of the classic J-curve effect. The U.K. experience provides an illustration of this effect. Exhibit 2.7.7 relates changes in relative price of the United Kingdom's merchandise exports, excluding oil, to its share of world trade, also excluding oil. Four periods can be identified:

— 1966–69: In this period of falling relative prices and a devaluing pound, world trade share nevertheless continued to fall dramatically.
— 1970–72: A rising pound and even faster rising prices temporarily stopped the decline in world trade share.

94

Exhibit 2.7.6: Equations linking relative export price movements and share of world merchandise exports (excluding oil)*

	S = % share of world merchandise[1] exports in year (t)	A = relative export price movements in year (t), (t−1) and (t−2)	T = time in years (1970 = 0)	R²
France	$S = 5.757\,A_t - 2.827\,A_{t-1} - 4.007\,A_{t-2} + 0.090\,T + 7.909$			0.930
Germany	$S = 6.409\,A_t - 3.408\,A_{t-1} - 6.703\,A_{t-2} + 0.158\,T + 15.845$			0.834
United Kingdom[2]	$S = 8.823\,A_t - 2.542\,A_{t-1} + 2.251\,A_{t-2} - 0.206\,T + 0.868$			0.978
Italy	$S = -3.610\,A_{t-1} - 6.047\,A_{t-2} + 0.024\,T + 14.268$			0.815
United States	$S = -8.116\,A_{t-1} - 9.417\,A_{t-2} - 0.353\,T + 34.019$			0.935
Japan	$S = 10.786\,A_t - 11.095\,A_{t-1} + 0.272\,T + 7.285$			0.949
Switzerland	$S = 1.300\,A_t - 0.449\,A_{t-1} - 0.004\,T + 1.142$			0.619

*Based on observations over the period 1961–80.
[1] Excluding OPEC.
[2] Excludes United Kingdom oil exports.
A = national export price series in $ (1975 = 100) ÷ (world—OPEC) export price series in $ (1975 = 100).

Source. Best & Associés.

Exhibit 2.7.7: U.K. export unit value, world trade share and exchange rate, 1960–80

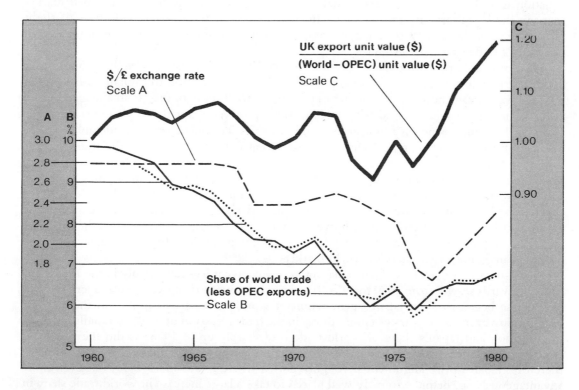

Source. *International Financial Statistics*, IMF.

— 1973–75: The price rises of 1971–72 aggravated the effect of this new period of falling relative prices. As a result, trade share was lost faster than ever before. It is probable that some markets were permanently lost in this period. Only at the end of the period did slightly rising relative prices, combined with an apparent acceleration of the pound's decline, manage to slow the decline in world trade share.

— 1976–80: A sustained period of relative price increases and increasing share of world trade.

This paradoxical situation of rising prices bringing relative success and falling prices bringing failure can be attributed to:

— the sequence in which the price changes took place;
— the United Kingdom's presence in a large number of traditional sectors early in the period;
— the possibility that the United Kingdom now has in its mix of manufactured exports a higher proportion of goods which are less dependent on price competitivity.

Experiences in other large trading nations have been somewhat different. In the United States, the world trade share fell rapidly in the 1960s, despite relatively stable prices. This experience parallels that of the United Kingdom. From then onwards, periods of price rises and falls followed, with delayed impact on the U.S. share of trade. Thus, a period of rising prices in 1969–71 was followed by another, of declining trade share in 1970–72. This was followed by a period of falling prices up to 1973, which, with lagged effect, brought boosted trade in 1975–76. During the latter period, new price rises again eroded any stabilization of the U.S. trade share, which dropped again substantially from 15·5% in 1975 to 14% or less in the 1977–80 period. Recovery potential for U.S. exports in 1981–82 was already latent in 1979 and 1980, but in 1981–82, new rises in the dollar were already compromising the situation for 1982.

In Germany, the years up to 1973 represented boom conditions in which the Deutschemark export prices and world trade share all rose together. In 1973–76, relative prices rose only slightly, as did the Deutschemark and the world trade share. In the two years up to 1980, German export prices declined, despite continued appreciation of the Deutschemark. Paradoxically, Germany's world trade share fell. Yet, this fits the pattern of the world trade share equation in Exhibit 2.7.5, indicating that Germany could probably have maintained market share in the short-term by raising prices further. However, the turn-around effect of slight relative price declines in 1980–82 is now taking hold and this should lead to significant rises in Germany's trade share in 1982–83.

France was able to gain a share of world markets rapidly in the late 1960s through price decreases, largely by devaluation. This put France in a good position to capitalize on the long 1968–73 world trade boom, enabling her to raise prices to the peak of the boom and gain a share at the same time, having started from a competitive position. Over the 1973–78 period, trade share has been increasing on a long-term trend line basis, but fluctuating considerably, largely because of the wide swings in exchange rates. Recent falls in the value of the franc may be detrimental to France in the immediate short term but, as in Germany, should prepare the way for quite sharp increases in world trade share in the future, despite high inflation.

Italian world trade experience in the 1960s was even more startling than the French, and also characterized by falling relative prices, but without any significant change in the parity of the lira up to 1975. From 1970 onwards, however, Italian export prices have been tending to edge upwards, despite wide swings, and this has slowed down considerably the rate at which the country can gain a larger share of world markets.

Finally, the case of Japan is of particular interest. Relative prices fell sharply in the 1960s, but edged upwards slowly from 1970 to 1974, largely as a result of a rising yen. An accelerating rate of increase began to slow Japan's penetration of world markets perceptibly in the 1972–75 period. However, three years of falling prices in the trade recession up to 1976 rapidly reversed this position and Japan's share of world trade rose sharply up to 1978, as did the yen. This effectively cut Japan's share of trade in 1979/80, despite a drop in the value of the yen. In 1981/82 therefore, Japan's price alignment is roughly poised where it was in 1975/76, but even more advantageously so, being extremely well placed to take a large increase in world trade share in any recovery, even on the back of a rising yen.

The sequence of yen parity and world trade cycle movement is that the yen tends to stagnate in a world trade recession and leap ahead in a boom.

Imports and the current account

Rising world trade share is not necessarily a panacea for a weak currency. The case of France illustrates this point. Although endowed with a strong product factor and relatively competitive prices, the range of French exports is quite narrow. Rapid export growth, when combined with domestic expansion (as is usually the case) leads to even more rapid increases in imports. This tends to reduce the scope for current account surpluses, even creating deficits and thus weakening the currency.

Several other countries are also affected negatively by this phenomenon, particularly Italy and the United States. By contrast, Germany, Japan and, to a lesser extent, the United Kingdom, do not suffer to the same extent.

Conclusions

Over the short term, interest rate differentials have a considerable immediate effect on exchange rates. However, as the time horizon is lengthened, traces of these effects become lost when combined with current account balances and relative price movements in determining exchange rates. Over the longer term, i.e. five years, relative price movements and current account balances tend to dominate the outlook for exchange rates.

8. Composite forecasts

Richard M. Levich

Foreign exchange rates continue to be volatile, by most standards and for most major currencies. In response to these market conditions, a large number of foreign exchange advisory services have started up or expanded their operations within the foreign exchange forecasting industry. Descriptive characteristics such as forecasting techniques, currencies and horizons vary greatly among the services, as do their costs and forecasting performance. From the viewpoint of the corporate treasurer, the availability of many professional advisers may be welcome, but it raises several questions.

First, how should the treasurer select a forecasting service, and second, how should he monitor the performance of the chosen service? Performance evaluation in financial markets has always presented complex issues. In another section of this book (Chapter 3, section 3), it is argued that some common statistical measures of performance (e.g. average forecast error or average squared forecast error) might give misleading results. An alternative measure of forecasting expertise is proposed — the percentage of correct forecasts — and applied to a sample of 13 forecasting services over the period 1977–80. Results suggested that several services had achieved track records too good to be explained by chance alone.

Does it follow that if one forecasting service is good, then two or more services combined may produce still better forecasts? This general question of the techniques and benefits for pooling various sources of information is the topic of this section. It is an important question for the treasurer who considers subscribing to two or more services, or the treasurer who already hears many forecasts (e.g. from many bank currency analysts) and wonders how to make the best use of this information. Intuitively, the treasurer might adopt a rule of thumb that attaches a large weight to forecasters who have a good track record, and a small weight to others. This section outlines a formal procedure for combining the forecasts from alternative advisory services. The initial empirical tests strongly suggest that this old idea offers a useful approach for improving forecasting performance.

Lessons from efficient markets

The degree of sophistication in trading and communications technology has shown remarkable advancement in the foreign exchange market. The efficiency of this market, in terms of volume and speed of transactions, represents a remarkable application of physical and human resources. Alternatively, the word efficiency is used in connection with the ability of market participants to process information and to make market prices fairly reflect this information. The conclusion that the foreign exchange market is efficient in this latter sense (i.e. that foreign exchange rates fairly reflect available information) is more controversial.[1]

Certainly, the foreign exchange markets possess characteristics that work in favour of efficiency — there are thousands of participants who can trade billions of dollars of liquid funds at extremely small transaction costs. The image of a foreign exchange trader is that of a person who processes information continuously and is anxious to trade for even the slightest expected profit.

On the other hand, the foreign exchange market is subjected periodically to central bank intervention which is not based on predictable economic factors. It is often argued that this influence reduces market efficiency. Furthermore, while foreign exchange traders are active in the spot market, the volume of forward trading is relatively small and the willingness of investors to hold open forward positions is likewise small. Corporate policy which requires every forward contract to be linked to an underlying actual business transaction is an example of one rule that limits forward trading. The implication is that treasurers may have formed reasonably accurate expectations of the future spot rate, but for any of several reasons (e.g. corporate policies restrict his trading, the treasurer's risk aversion restricts his trading, the

---

[1] A more detailed discussion of foreign exchange market efficiency is presented in Richard M. Levich, "Further Results on the Efficiency of Markets for Foreign Exchange," in *Managed Exchange Rate Flexibility: The Recent Experience*, Federal Reserve Bank of Boston, Conference Series No. 20, 1978.

treasurer commands limited capital and so his trading is small) these expectations are not fully reflected in the forward exchange rate.

In these examples of market inefficiency, the investor cannot look to current exchange rates for an accurate guide to the future. Market inefficiency provides a sufficient incentive for investors to consider foreign exchange advisory services and other information sources. The argument for using several advisory services is based on a subtle variation of this market inefficiency scenario.[2] Suppose that the information required to predict the future spot rate (S_{t+n}) is spread across 12 corporate treasurers. If these treasurers were completely free to buy and sell forward contracts, they would set the forward rate (F_t) equal to their consensus forecast of the future spot rate ($\hat{S}_{t+n}$) which, on average, would equal the future spot rate (S_{t+n}). However, in the real world, these treasurers are constrained in various ways — one is highly risk averse, another is not very confident in his own forecast, a third follows a corporate policy which limits forward positions, and a fourth represents a small company which cannot buy or sell many forward contracts. As a result, the forward market represents the collective wisdom of these treasurers, weighted by their dollar votes in the market, not necessarily in a way that establishes $F_t = S_{t+n}$. Composite forecasting is based on the notion that some weighted average of the raw information in these forecasters may produce a forecast better than F_t.

Techniques for composite forecasting

As a purely statistical matter, it has long been recognized that combining two forecasts whose errors are weakly correlated should improve forecasting accuracy. This is analogous to the notion in regression analysis that including additional independent variables often helps to increase the explanatory power of the regression equation. The composite forecasting approach builds on this principle. If two forecasts, $\hat{S}_1$ and $\hat{S}_2$, capture or reflect different information, it will be possible to construct a new, composite forecast that is superior to either forecast individually. One way to construct the composite forecast is through a linear regression,

$$\hat{S}_c = w_1 \hat{S}_1 + w_2 \hat{S}_2. \qquad (1)$$

If we define superior to mean minimum variance forecasters, then w_1 and w_2 are ordinary least squares regression coefficients; w_1 and w_2 are estimated from historical forecast data, so we must assume that these weights remain applicable in a true forecast period. Expression (1) can easily be extended to a case where there are more than two forecasters.

The theoretical foundations of composite forecasting rest on two key points.[3] First, we assume that different forecasters possess different information and different forecasting abilities. Market prices reflect this information only to the extent that investors have actually bought or sold foreign exchange based on these forecasts. The composite approach seeks to combine available information in a more efficient manner.

Second, the risk diversification principle suggests that single securities are risky while diversified portfolios earn the market rate of return at minimum risk. By analogy, a portfolio of forecasters reduces the risk of large forecast errors and improves forecasting accuracy relative to the record of an individual forecaster. This point is illustrated in Exhibit 2.8.1. The average and standard deviation of several individual forecast errors are plotted as S_1, S_2, etc. The line S_c represents the possible composite forecasts that might be formed with different weighted combinations of individual forecast. One particular composite forecast, S^*, has a risk factor lower than any individual forecast and the lowest risk of any composite forecast. An alternative forecast, S^{**}, reduces the average forecast error to zero by adjusting S^* by its forecasting bias.

Empirical methodology and results

In one study of composite forecasts based on 11 professional forecasting services,[4] the research design first analysed an in-sample period to estimate a set of weights and then applied these

[2] These concepts are discussed in Stephen Figlewski, "Market 'Efficiency' in a Market with Heterogeneous Expectations," *Journal of Political Economy*, August 1978, pp. 581–97.

[3] These ideas are rigorously developed in Stephen Figlewski, "Optimal Price Forecasting Using Survey Data," Mimeographed, New York University, 1980. The statistics in Exhibit 2.8.2 reflect joint research with Stephen Figlewski.

[4] Richard M. Levich, "Maximizing the Return on Forex Services," *Euromoney Currency Report*, February 11, 1981, p. 3.

Exhibit 2.8.1: Illustrating the potential gains from composite forecasting over individual forecasts

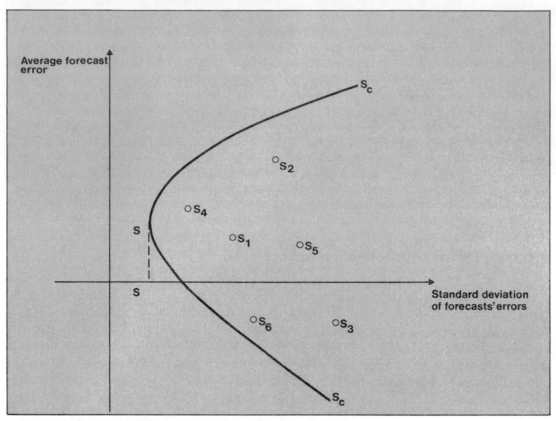

Key: S_1, S_2, etc.: Individual forecasters.
S_c: Composite forecasts formed by various weighted combinations of individuals.
S*: Composite forecast with smallest standard deviation.
S**: Same as S* but adjusted for forecasting bias so that average error is zero while maintaining low standard deviation.

Exhibit 2.8.2: Composite forecasts: post–sample results using the diagonal model

Currency	Percentage correct one-month horizon	Percentage correct three-month horizon
Canadian dollar	70.0*	76.7*
U.K. sterling	66.7*	43.3
Belgian franc	73.3*	83.3*
French franc	73.3*	80.0*
Deutschemark	80.6*	90.3*
Lira	77.4*	71.0*
Guilder	86.7*	83.3*
Swiss franc	70.0*	60.0
Yen	51.6	32.3
Average	72.2*	68.9*

Notes. A composite forecast is based on up to 11 advisory service forecasts and the forward rate. Individual forecasts made during a two-week interval are combined with the forward rate quoted on Friday at the end of the interval. All models adjusted for in-sample bias except Canadian dollar, one-month horizon.

The sample periods are as follows:
One-month horizon: "in-sample" 115 two-week intervals from 11.1.1974 to 9.6.1978.
　　　　　　　　　"post-sample" 33 two-week intervals from 21.7.1978 to 28.9.1979.
Three-month horizon: "in-sample" 110 two-week intervals from 11.1.1974 to 31.3.1978.
　　　　　　　　　"post-sample" 33 two-week intervals from 21.7.1978 to 28.9.1979.

* Probability of this track record if the composite forecast were only guessing the direction of exchange rate movement is less than 5%.

100

estimated weights in a separate post-sample period. Three composite models were analysed: (1) the mean — a simple arithmetic average of available forecasts; (2) the diagonal — which weights individual forecasts inversely proportional to their total forecast error variance; and (3) the single index — which forms a portfolio of forecasts that is unbiased with minimum error variance.

The results for the diagonal model are summarized in Exhibit 2.8.2. The post-sample period extended from July 21, 1978, to Sept. 28, 1979, and covered a period which was difficult to forecast. The results suggest that, except for sterling and yen, the percentage correct statistics are substantially greater than 50%. Compared to earlier studies, these results suggest that the composite forecasts are generally more accurate and more reliable than the best individual forecasts.

A study by Bilson (1981) uses composite forecasting to exploit diversification gains in three directions — across currencies, across horizons and across forecasting services.[5] Bilson notes that exchange rate changes are imperfectly correlated across currencies and horizons, and exchange rate forecasts from various services are also imperfectly correlated. Each dimension represents an avenue to diversify away the risks of forecast errors. Bilson's study examines five currencies, three horizons and two forecasts (i.e. the current spot rate, S_t, and the current forward rate, F_t). His results offer strong evidence that the composite technique, combined with a portfolio currency exposure management system, can lead to significant profits.

Performance evaluation in a composite model

The performance of each forecaster is usually measured separately. However, the traditional concept of economic value would imply that we measure the marginal contribution of a forecast to optimal decision-making. Evaluation procedures that focus on forecasters individually may not measure their true economic value. For example, a composite forecast based on the current spot rate and the current forward rate

$$S_c = w_1 S_t + w_2 F_t \qquad (2)$$

may represent an optimal forecast based on public information.

If a professional advisor were called in, we would include his forecast, $S_{professional}$, and arrive at a new composite forecast like

$$S_c^1 = w_1 S_t + w_2 F_t + w_3 S_{professional} \qquad (3)$$

Only if w_3 is non-zero and the new forecast increases our profits would we conclude that the professional adviser adds value. A professional forecast may rate well by itself, but in the context of (3), the new forecast might add very little. On the other hand, a poor individual forecast might be significant in the context of (3) if it reflects information not captured in the other forecasts. This makes the point that a forecast will be valuable if it brings new information that can be incorporated with existing forecasts.

Summary and conclusions

As volatility in the foreign exchange market continues, the potential for large gains and losses remains high. The demand for expert advice and advisory service forecasts in this setting is not surprising. However, if the foreign exchange market is efficient, then the information in these forecasts is already captured in market prices and it would not make sense to pay for forecasts. Our discussion suggested that when market prices poorly reflect available information, a composite forecasting approach which seeks a better combination of available information may improve forecasting performance. Several techniques for producing composite forecasts have been described briefly. The empirical evidence from two studies suggests that the composite approach can lead to results that are substantially better than individual forecasts. Since many corporate treasurers now receive diverse information on exchange rates, the composite approach may offer assistance in making the most use of this information.

---

[5] John F. O. Bilson, "The 'Speculative Efficiency' Hypothesis," *Journal of Business*, July 1981, pp. 435–51.

9. In-house forecasting

Jeffrey Mizrahi

The volatility of world currency movements is likely to continue. How should the businessman respond? Do you react passively and allow your business to be affected by matters outside your control? Or do you try to anticipate, rather than respond to, currency trends?

Before deciding whether to forecast currencies in-house, you need to define the currency exposure facing your organization. For an organization with relatively small currency exposure, probably all that is needed is for one senior financial officer to devote part of his time to currency forecasting with the aid of currency consultants or currency forecasters he can identify with and understand.

The senior financial manager entrusted with this responsibility must be aware that the purpose of forecasting currencies is to help asset or liability management and to establish a framework within which day-to-day cash management is carried out. For short-term liabilities the forward exchange rate provides its own forecast. A company can hedge through the forward market. The objective of forecasting is to be on the right side of the forward rates. This puts the emphasis on short-term forecasting techniques. For longer-term asset management, fundamental trends are of more importance.

The senior financial manager responsible for currency forecasting also needs to understand the basic approach used by the currency consultants or forecasters. He should realize that the central forecasts provided by outside advisers are subject to margins of error on either side. He should be aware of the upside and downside potential in currency forecasts, and relate these to his firm's needs and requirements.

The cost of outside advice for a company with limited currency exposure would probably vary from a very modest annual sum (a subscription to one of the international forecast publications) to a five-figure sum for a tailor-made service.

An organization with large currency exposure should consider setting up its in-house currency forecasting service. This enables it to plug in its own assumptions as they affect currency movements, rather than rely on outsiders' views of the world. Too often individuals and organizations use currency forecasts without understanding that forecasts are only as good as the basic assumptions supporting them. Forecasting is an art, not a science.

Foreign exchange markets shift in their attitudes towards economic and market influences. Differing emphasis is placed on particular economic factors. In the early and mid-1970s emphasis was put on inflation differentials as currency determinants; in the late 1970s relative monetary growth became more fashionable as a currency indicator. In 1980, it was the turn of nominal and real interest rates, and recent evidence suggests that relative current account performance is having a significant impact on market judgement. No matter how irrational these factors may appear, they have to be allowed for in currency forecasting. A special effort has to be made to detect changes in market fashions and trends that dominate market psychology.

To keep it effective and practical, an in-house service should be headed by the foreign exchange or treasury manager, and all the firm's currency management should be centralized under him unless the company's subsidiaries are self-financing profit centres. Reporting to the foreign exchange or treasury manager would be the company economist, a senior foreign exchange dealer and a senior line manager exposed to currency risk. It is important that the man heading the currency unit should report to the board of the company (or himself be on the board) and that currency forecasting be part of overall cash and/or asset management. A currency liaison or steering committee should be established to allow for regular surveillance of past and expected currency movements. Responsibilities for certain key currencies should be assigned to specific individuals, although the committee should work as a team and be kept as small as possible.

Currency forecasts should be undertaken over periods ranging from one to 12 months and, if needed, up to five years. The economist's job would be to evaluate the most likely currency trend based on central assumptions, and allow for deviations from trend based on alternative assumptions, ascribing probabilities to alternative outcomes. He would also explore the sensitivity of his projections to external shocks. For instance, he should consider the currency implications of a deterioration in east–west relations, involving military escalation in Europe or the Middle East, of debt defaults, of increased global protectionism and of a worldwide deflationary shakeout. The best conceived currency forecast may be upset by these and other external shocks.

In undertaking this work, the company economist should intially consider fundamental economic trends within each country and the country's policy, as a long-term guide to the strength of its currency. Attention should be focused on three key variables:

i. relative inflation (consumer prices);
ii. relative balance of payments (on current account);
iii. relative money supply growth (M2).

As shown in Exhibits 2.9.1 and 2.9.2, there has been a fairly close correlation between these trends and the U.S. dollar's medium- and longer-term variation against the Deutschemark and yen. However, although these charts appear impressive, the individual readings only represent quarterly averages. In the prevailing era of severe exchange rate volatility, currencies can, and often do, fluctuate very significantly during the course of a quarter. Further, to be able to rely on the historic equation as a forecasting tool implies forecasting correctly the inputs.

However, there are at least two groups of variables which overlay the influence of fundamentals and national policies. First come structural factors that influence the balance of payments on current account, irrespective of fundamentals. By far the most important are such non-price-responsive current account factors as North Sea oil and gas, which have boosted the current account position of The Netherlands for eight or nine years and the U.K. during the last

Exhibit 2.9.1: Deutschemark/U.S. dollar exchange rate

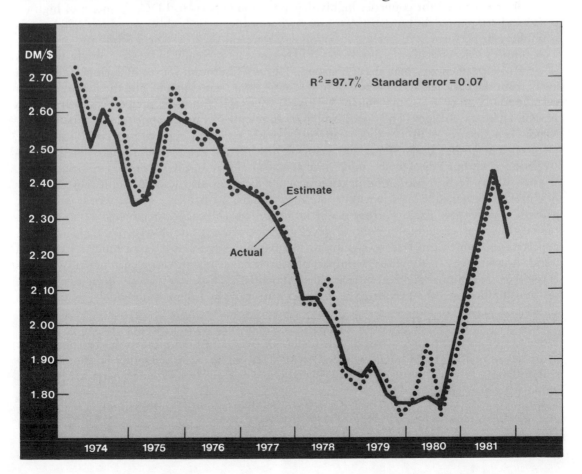

Exhibit 2.9.2: Yen/U.S. dollar exchange rate

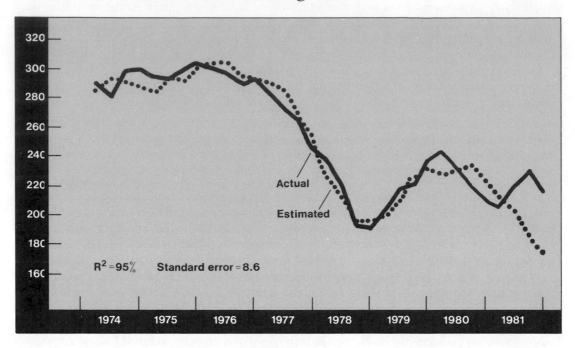

three and a half years. Other non-price-sensitive current account influences include product design, service back-up and speed of delivery, which have tended to benefit Japan and Switzerland.

The structure of exports is an important guide to balance of payments strength. Opportunities will be restricted for countries highly dependent on exports to LDCs in an era of high oil prices and crippling debt burdens. A country whose exports are highly geared to capital goods is unlikely to perform well in the prevailing environment of slow world economic growth.

A country's dependence on imported oil may cause its currency to be structurally weak, as self-sufficiency in energy may make it strong. This is a significant source of currency deviation away from the basic trend. So is any shift in reserve asset arrangements, and the deployment of surplus funds away from the dollar. Relatively small shifts in asset preferences will lead to sizeable currency changes. These are likely to be augmented by private portfolio diversification. Major beneficiaries will be those currencies with growing reserve currency roles (the Deutschemark, the Swiss franc, the yen and the French franc) and relative energy self-sufficiency (sterling, the Dutch guilder, the Canadian dollar and the Norwegian krone).

Then come cyclical economic developments, which can also lead to significant currency fluctuations either side of long-term currency trends, particularly when world economic growth is desynchronized. Further major influences on currency movements are short-term capital flows, precipitated by political developments, interest rate divergencies and currency expectations, which can lead to significant fluctuations either side of a currency's long-term trend. A useful way to allow for the impact of short-term capital flows on currency movements is to focus on nominal and real interest rate differentials. There has recently been a very close relationship between the performance of major currencies and these differentials, as shown in Exhibits 2.9.3–2.9.6.

However, cross exchange rates, whether nominal or real, do not provide the entire picture. When considering whether a currency is under- or overvalued, I find it useful to consider its prospects in relation to its trade-weighted value. This can be expressed either in nominal or in real (inflation-adjusted) terms. Real trade-weighted exchange rates provide a particularly useful guide as to how cheap or dear a currency is.

At present, the major currency blocs are the dollar bloc and the Deutschemark bloc. Sterling and the yen are not members of any world currency zone, but rather independent floaters. In currency forecasting, attention may at first be restricted to these four. But then one has to allow for the fact that, periodically, satellite currencies realign themselves against their bloc leader.

Exhibit 2.9.3: Deutschemark/U.S. dollar: exchange rate and nominal interest differential

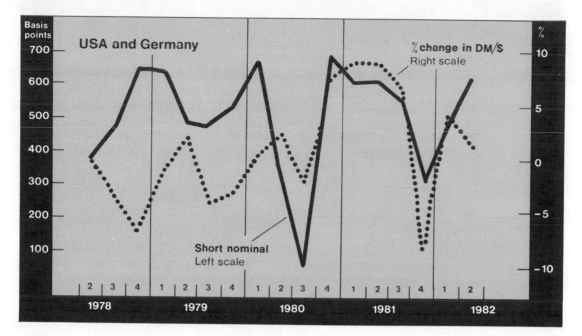

Within the Deutschemark bloc, realignments take place every 18 to 24 months. In between, exchange rates remain relatively fixed. This tends to reduce risk and encourages financial managers to put their money into high interest, high inflation countries in that bloc (the Dutch guilder, say, or the French franc) in the hope of returning to the Deutschemark just before a realignment. Movements within the dollar bloc tend to be more volatile.

As a final cross-check, it is useful to consider what the currency charts (such as moving averages, point and figure, patterns, momentum, line and bar, etc.) are telling us, irrespective of fundamentals, policy stances, structural/cyclical considerations and capital flows. Such charts can have a significant influence on day-to-day currency movements. These charts, together

Exhibit 2.9.4: Deutschemark/U.S. dollar real interest rate differential

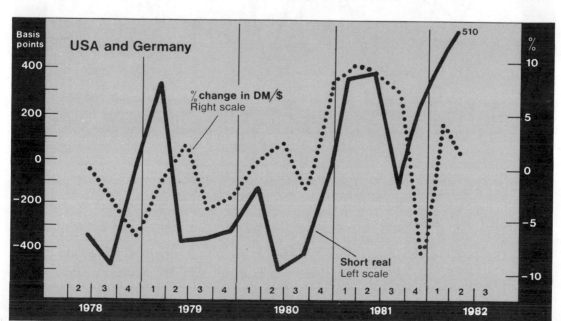

105

Exhibit 2.9.5: Sterling/U.S. dollar real interest rate differential

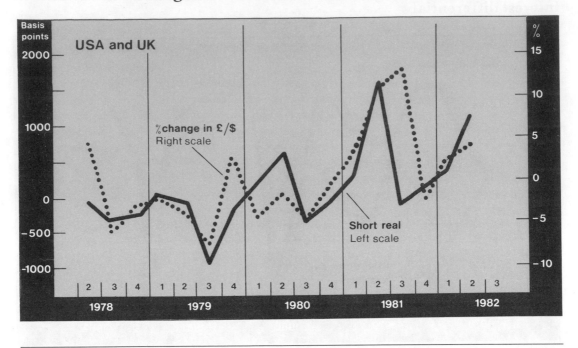

Exhibit 2.9.6: Yen/U.S. dollar real interest rate differential

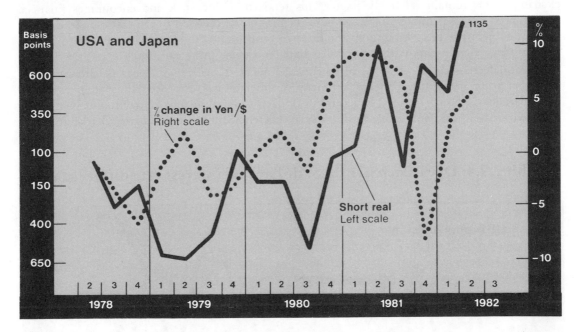

with nominal and real interest rate differentials, may help the timing of your action (or inaction) in foreign exchange markets. In terms of longer-term trends, you should rely more on relative fundamentals and policy stances.

The above approach should allow a firm's steering committee to evaluate the risk/reward trade-off in currency forecasting. It should be the committee's job (not the economist's) to make the judgement about how much risk to assume in relation to currency forecasts.

A further responsibility of the currency committee is to measure the performance of the forecasts. A number of measuring rods could be used including the spot currency rate, the forward rate and the comparison between the spot currency rate and selling forward.

To be completely successful, an in-house forecasting system should improve both the unmanaged spot rate and the technique of hedging by selling forward. However, most firms would be happy with just beating the spot rate and doing better, on average, than the forward rate. This ought to be achievable under the system I have outlined.

CHAPTER THREE
Using foreign exchange markets and forecasts

1. Understanding foreign exchange trading

Adam Ruck

International trade in goods and services is worth some $10 billion for every working day. Direct investment flows account for another few hundred millions. Yet trading volume in the world's foreign exchange markets is over $200 billion a day. So about 95% of foreign exchange is not direct commercial business but trading between market makers — the foreign exchange dealers of the world's international banks.

The world's foreign exchange markets span the globe, so that for at least 23 hours a day currencies are being bought and sold, and prices are moving somewhere. When a London dealer opens up in the morning he does not start dealing at the previous day's closing prices, but simply works on rates in the Far Eastern markets. Now that rates move sharply overnight, a London dealer cannot be complacent about the positions left open from one day to the next. He may insist on a call from Chicago at eight or nine in the evening, a call from Singapore at one or two in the morning, and another at about six, to keep in touch, and if necessary adjust his position. Volume varies substantially according to market conditions, and according to the time of day. The market is deepest, or most liquid, early in the European afternoon when the world's largest dealing centres — London, New York, Frankfurt and Chicago — are all open together. This is the best time to ensure the smooth execution of a very large order. The market is at its thinnest when West Coast U.S. dealers are hanging up their phones for one day and Hong Kong is preparing to open its lines for the next; this may make it easier for central banks or aggressive position-takers to move the market and influence sentiment in their favour.

Apart from a few recently developed currency futures markets, there is no physical marketplace. Dealers communicate directly with each other by telephone and real time VDU screens, and indirectly via foreign exchange brokers, who act as agents matching buyers and sellers for a brokerage fee.

A market maker in a currency will nearly always quote a selling and a buying price. Prices move as in other two-way markets because dealers who are keen to buy try to attract sellers by quoting a higher price than other market makers, and those keen to sell quote lower prices; if a dealer is asked why the DM is going down, his answer will be: "More sellers than buyers".

Dealers quote their selling price first (for the $/£ rate the selling rate for dollars); this means the lower number. Dealers are in such a rush they abbreviate as much as possible — a price will not be spelt out more than anyone who is well informed about the going market rate will need. So a rate of 2·1010/20 might be called "ten twenty on ten" or simply "ten twenty". Round numbers in hundreds of points are "the figure" — 2·0990/00 would be "ninety the figure" or "ninety the figure ten"; 2·1100/10 would be "figure ten".

If the market rate as quoted by a broker for the DM/$ is 2·1010/15, a dealer who wants to buy

Exhibit 3.1.1: The jargon

Dealers talk to each other in their own language; they are usually prepared to talk to customers in English. Understanding their jargon is as much a matter of curiosity as it is of importance. Some of the market terminology is technical, and not peculiar to the foreign exchange markets. Most of it is just slang and abbreviations to save time. Here is a selective list of terms:

Cable: The spot $/£ exchange rate, once upon a time cabled from London to New York. When the Irish punt severed its sterling parity the $/I£ rate was immediately christened "the wire".

Paris: French franc. "What's your spot Paris?"

Stocky: Swedish krona.

Oslo: Norwegian krone.

Copey: Danish krone.

Brussels: Belgian franc.

Scud: Portuguese escudo.

Ozzi, or A$: Australian dollar.

Five: (e.g. "I sell you five") Five million dollars, or pounds in the $/£ market. Standard amounts in the London market are £1–3 million for $/£, $3–5 million in the major European currencies.

Give: Sell.

Take: Buy.

Yours: I sell.

Mine: I buy. Yours and mine are frowned upon by the Bank of England. (You might say to a bank "yours at ten," and he could say, "OK, I'll take 20 million".)

Tom next: The interest rate for deposits from tomorrow to the next day, used for calculating the exchange rate for settlement the day before spot value date, and swaps.

Depo: Deposit.

Week fixed: One week deposit.

Spot a week: A one week swap, equivalent to a one week deposit. Similarly, Tom next a week, spot a month, etc.

Lay off, reverse, get out, unwind: Match a position by selling what has just been bought and *vice versa*.

Buba: Bundesbank.

Which way are you?: Are you a buyer or a seller? Because a dealer's major concern is to find out what's going on in the market, and because he's most vulnerable when the whole market knows which way he is, there is frequently a large element of bluff in prices dealers quote each other.

He hit me at ten: He dealt at my price of ten (e.g. 2·9910).

Full up: Exposed to the limit, so unable to deal. Usually applies to a bank's exposure to a particular counterparty.

Point: 0·0001.

Pip: 0·00001. Occasionally points are confusingly referred to as pips.

DM might adjust his quotation to 2·1008/13, making his selling price (2·1008) uncompetitive and his buying price (2·1013) competitive. If an ill-informed dealer or customer chooses to buy DM at 2·1008, he can still replenish his DM position by buying in the market at the lower cost of 2·1010. If he is reluctant to deal at all for any reason, he might quote 2·1008/17, making both sides of his quotation uncompetitive. The difference between the dealer's selling (always on the left) and buying price is the spread but not, in a world of floating exchange rates, his profit, which comes from capital gain on successful position taking. Because dealers do not have to rely entirely on their turn to make money out of dealing, and although risks are higher in floating currencies, spreads are very narrow — DM0·0005 or "5 points" is typical in the DM/$ market, making a spread of about 0·025%. From the example it is clear that when no dealers want to deal — ahead of important news, or on a Friday afternoon when their positions have been squared for the weekend — spreads widen. Unless prices are moving very sharply in one direction, high trading volume will be accompanied by narrow spreads, because with so much liquidity in the market a dealer can be confident that whatever position he takes he can reverse immediately, so his risk is small. If a price is moving fast a dealer cannot be sure that the market rate he bases his quotation on will last more than a few seconds so his risk is greater. In a thin market he may have to wait for some time before he can get out of any position; again his risk is greater, so he quotes a wider spread. Naturally spreads on minor currencies are wider than on the majors.

A case of heavy trading volume but little movement occurs when a currency is under heavy pressure but being held at a certain level by a central bank. If, for example, the Bank of England

110

is determined to stop the pound falling below $2·0150, its pose indicates that it is a big seller of dollars at that level. No market maker will bid for dollars at a rate higher than $2·0150, because he can buy them more cheaply from the bank. But with a guaranteed way out of pounds at $2·0150 (maximum liquidity) market makers will compete for pounds at the narrowest of margins below $2·0150. A dealer might quote a price of $2·0149/50 instead of a more normal five-point spread. He can still make $100 on £1 million.

Nearly all foreign exchange deals take the form of purchases or sales of a currency against the dollar. In the past dealing between different centres was complicated by differing conventions of pricing; a DM/$ rate of two in Germany might be quoted 0·50 in New York. Now the use of "dollar terms" — the unit price of a dollar — has become universal for all major currencies except sterling (and the Irish £), which is quoted in sterling terms — the dollar price of a pound. So a $/£ trader's selling price is the price at which he sells dollars not pounds, although, increasingly this is changing. Terms can have more than merely technical significance, given the psychological importance of round numbers, which may induce central banks to defend them. When the Canadian $ was losing value in 1977/78, speculation centred on whether it would fall through the 90 (US¢) level. If the same decline were taking place now the important barrier would be (Can$) 1·10, or roughly US¢91. In the last few years the use of US$ terms for the Canadian $ has gained increasingly wide acceptance in the marketplace; but many economists still think in terms of US¢ per Can$ and it remains the one major trading currency whose pricing is confused.

Although almost all deals between market makers (interbank) feature the dollar, there is considerable commercial demand for cross rates, for example DM/£. Any bank which makes a market in both currencies will quote a cross rate on demand, based on its current quotations for both DM/$ and $/£. The spread on the cross rate will be the product of both other spreads, for the bank will have to do two interbank deals to reverse its position. So if a bank quotes DM/$2·1020/30 and $/£2·2340/45 its DM/£ quotation will be 4·6958/92. A few banks specialize in making a book in certain cross rates — French banks may deal directly in Ffr/DM for example — and may be able to offer finer quotations than those that work through the dollar.

Spot and forward

The current exchange rate, the rate at which at least two-thirds of all foreign exchange transactions are carried out, is the spot rate. Spot rate deals are for value two business days after the dealing date, so if a dealer buys $1 million spot for DM on Monday he must transfer DM to his counterparty's German account on Wednesday, and he will receive $1 million in his U.S. account on Wednesday.

Holidays can be confusing. The only dates which are not eligible value dates are holidays in either country in which settlement of the deal must take place. The place of dealing is not affected. Take the example of Friday, May 1, 1981, a German holiday, and Monday, May 4, a U.K. holiday;

	Dealing date	Centre	Value date
DM/$ deals			
	Wed., April 29	all	Mon., May 4
	Thurs., April 30	Frankfurt	Tues., May 5
	Thurs., April 30	London/NY	Probably May 5, but could be May 4
	Fri., May 1	London/NY	Tues., May 5
$/£ deals			
	Thurs., April 4	all	Tues., May 5
	Fri., May 1	London	Wed., May 6
	Fri., May 1	NY	Probably Wed., May 6, but could be May 5
	Mon., May 4	NY/Frankfurt	Wed., May 6

A DM/£ quotation on Thursday will have to be for value on Tuesday, so there will have to be an adjustment to the DM/$ element of the quotation to allow for the extra day's interest.

If two centres are quoting different spot value dates for the same exchange rate, the prices will be different. A London dealer who rings Frankfurt will expect to deal for Frankfurt's value date, unless he specifies to the contrary.

The treasurer who has to repay a DM loan, or pay for a DM-denominated import in three months time may wish to cover his exchange risk. He can buy DM spot and deposit them for three months, or he can use the foreign exchange forward market, agreeing a price today for the purchase of DM in three months time. Either way, the result will be approximately the same in a free market system, for the forward market is essentially a deposit market with the forward price for DM against the dollar being determined in this case by the difference between the yield on three months DM and $ deposits. So if the spot rate is DM2·1000 and the three-month deposit rates are 10% a year for dollars and 8% a year for DM (yielding 2½% and 2% respectively) the three-month DM/$ should be

$$\frac{2 \cdot 1 \times 1 \cdot 02}{1 \times 1 \cdot 025} = 2 \cdot 0898$$

At this rate any U.S. investor in DM deposits who sells the full maturing proceeds forward finds that the total return is the same as that available on a dollar deposit, and vice versa. If the forward price is out of line with the interest rate differential for any length of time, flows of funds one way across the exchanges bring prices back into equilibrium. Taking advantage of anomalies is called arbitrage.

Forward exchange rates are determined by interest rates not consensus forecasts, although expectations certainly influence forward rates by bringing about interest rate changes and spot rate changes. Assume that in the case above someone in the market expects the DM/$ rate to be DM2·00 in three months time, and therefore offers to buy at DM2·05. At this price it will now be extremely attractive for anyone considering a dollar deposit to invest instead in a "covered DM deposit". So with $1 million the comparison is $ dep: $1 million at 2·5% yields $1,025,000. Covered DM dep (arbitrage): buy DM2,100,000 spot, deposit at 2% to yield DM2,142,000, sold forward at 2·05, to yield $1,044,878 — a risk-free 4·5% return on the dollars. This kind of anomaly would not occur but if it did it would not last because (a), everyone would buy DM spot, driving up the spot rate, (b), the drain of dollar liquidity would drive up dollar deposit rates and (c), the oversupply of DM would depress DM deposit rates, all of which would narrow the difference between the spot and forward rates, known as the DM's forward premium, since the currency with the lower interest rates always trades at a higher price forward than spot. The difference between the spot and forward price of a higher interest rate currency is known as a forward discount. If in the same example the forward rate was the

---

Exhibit 3.1.2: Dealing with the limits

Banks' dealing rooms operate under internally and externally imposed limits. A bank will have a limit to its overall exposure to all currencies, to each individual currency, to each and all currencies spot, to each and all forward.

Overnight limits are much smaller than the maximum exposure permitted at any moment during the day, partly because overnight limits tend to be those imposed or "advised" by central banks, but mainly because a position can be reversed in seconds during the day, while the only thing a dealer can do to control his position overnight is place a "limit order" (to buy or sell a currency should it reach a certain level), or ask for midnight phone calls. Internal limits may depend on the experience of each dealer; it is not untypical that if a chief dealer is out of the office, the overall limits are halved. Banks also impose limits on their exposure to individual counterparties to control default risk, in the same way that bank clients have overdraft limits. A forward deal is a loan by both parties, which reduces the default risk, but a bank is still exposed to the risk that if a counterparty fails to honour a forward contract it will have to match its new position (short of DM if it had bought them forward) at a loss in the market. That the risk of total default has to be considered is illustrated by the celebrated Herstatt closure. The German bank was closed early in the afternoon in Germany, after maturing DM had been paid into its account, but before it could pay dollars maturing the same day into its counterparties' accounts in the U.S.

equilibrium rate of DM2·0898 and market makers suddenly came to a unanimous view that the spot rate would move to DM2·00 over the period, there would be no advantage in covered deposits, but straight DM deposits could be expected to show a profit as the rate moved up. So the same flows of funds would affect the spot exchange rate and interest rates until the forward rate came into line with expectations.

Forward prices

Dealers usually quote forward prices for multiples of one month, in most major currencies out to one year. Forward prices further into the future can be quoted, as long as there are adequate deposit markets. The market gets increasingly thin beyond three months, and spreads tend to widen. Some minor currencies have no practical forward market beyond three or six months.

Dealers do not quote the outright forward selling and buying rates but the forward premium or discount in points (0·0001), which is known as the swap rate. So if the DM/$ spot rate is DM2·0995/05 and the outright 12-month forward rate is DM2·0230/65, the dealer quotes 765/740. This is not an untypical spread for a 12-month swap, wider than the spot spread because of the thinner market. Being based on deposit rates, forward prices could in theory be much wider (and may be for distant dates, or in very thin markets), reflecting the bank's bid/offer spread for deposits in both currencies, for if a dealer sells DM forward against dollars, he is borrowing DM and lending dollars. This is rarely the case in, say, the DM/$ market because banks are competing for business.

Swap rates are frequently expressed in percentage terms. This is correctly worked out by dividing the swap or the spot by the outright rate. Dividing the swap by the spot rate could lead to discounts of over 100% (which are as impossible as devaluations of over 100%), and understates premiums. Because $/£ is quoted the wrong way round, the swap is the dollar's forward premium or discount. To work out sterling's forward discount or premium, the swap is divided by the spot. In the DM/$ example given the calculation (dealer's selling rate) is

$$\frac{0·0765}{2·0230} = 0·0378 = 3·78\%.$$

This is the absolute premium; to annualize it, the rate should be multiplied by 360 and divided by the actual number of days in the period. This is necessary even for a 12-month rate for the period is unlikely to be 360 days long. Assuming this is a 367-day "year", the DM's annualized premium, often expressed as the cost of buying DM forward, is

$$\frac{0·0765 \times 360}{2·0230 \times 367} = 3·71\% \text{ pa.}$$

It is often assumed that the equilibrium forward rate is a premium or discount numerically equal to the interest differential in basis points, i.e. that if DM deposits pay 15% and $ deposits pay 19%, the DM should trade at a 4% forward premium. That this is not the case can be shown by working through the cash flow of a covered DM deposit, taking the above interest rates (DM deposit 15%, dollar deposit 19%) and the following exchange rates:

Spot: DM/$:2·0795/05
Swap: 805/795 (4·02%/3·97%)
Outright: 1·9990/2·0010

A U.S. investor with $1 million executes the following transactions simultaneously:

Purchase: DM2,079,500 spot
Invest: DM2,079,500 @ 15% to yield DM2,391,425
Sell: DM2,391,425 forward @ 2·0010 to yield $1,195,115

giving a return of 19·51% on his dollars. Even assuming, as this does, that he has been charged the spot dealing spread, which reduces his effective premium to

$$\frac{2·0795}{2·0010} - 1·0392 \text{ or } 3·92\%$$

113

this premium has outweighed the 400 basis point interest differential. The reason for this is that he has sold the DM interest forward at a premium, as well as the principal. The premium on the interest is $0.0392 \times 0.15 = 0.00588$, an extra 0.588%. The total return on his covered deposit is $15\% + 3.92\% + 0.588\% = 19.51\%$. To take account of this the interest differential can be more usefully expressed for comparative purposes

$$\frac{119}{115} = 1.0348$$

indicating a differential of 3.48%, which is what the equilibrium forward premium for the DM would be. Doing the same sums with DM/$ rates of 2.0700/05 (spot) and 700/690 (swap), a premium of around $3\frac{1}{2}\%$, shows no arbitrage opportunity in covered deposits to either U.S. or German investors.

Forward value dates

The value date is, wherever possible, the same date in the month as the spot value date however many months forward. If the date in the future month is not eligible the value date is postponed to the next eligible day, unless this would involve breaking into a new month, in which case the value date is moved backwards. Thus, when the spot value date is May 31, the one month forward value date is not July 1, but June 30. Because value dates are pushed forward up to but not beyond the end of the month there tends to be an accumulation of rollover maturities at the month end, which can affect prices. If a bank lends 10-year money at a varying interest rate, fixed according to the three-month deposit rate, the bank will match its interest rate risk by bidding for a succession of three-month deposits, of which the maturity value dates will gradually approach the month end.

Foreign exchange months vary in length much more than calendar ones, from about 26 days (say Jan. 31 to Feb. 26) to as many as 35 (March 1 to April 5 if Easter intervenes). This makes it important to be aware of exactly how many days a forward contract covers when calculating what the price ought to be or what the quoted swap rate represents in terms of percentage a year. This also applies to calculating interest on deposits.

Exhibit 3.1.3: Understanding brokers

Brokers act as agents marrying buyers and sellers, nearly always banks, and are a particular feature of the London market because until 1979 all London to London interbank deals has to be done through the broking system. Now London banks can contact each other directly, but brokers still play an important role passing on information. Because there are over 300 banks operating in the London market, with each one dealing regularly with only about a dozen others, there are also very good reasons for dealers to use brokers.

Since direct dealing was introduced, interbank volume is reckoned to have trebled, and the brokers' share of the market to have declined to about 50%. So their actual turnover and brokerage income has gone up. Brokerage is the fee a bank pays a broker for a deal, varying from currency to currency. A $/£ deal is the cheapest, at £9 per £1 million, a DM/$ deal costs £12 per £1 million. A peseta/$ deal might cost £60 per $1 million.

Although brokers theoretically don't act as principals, they can be stuck with one half of a marriage if the other pulls out. Bank A might let a broker know that he's in principle a seller at 10, so the broker might agree to sell to Bank B at 10. Bank A might then say he's just sold to someone else, or he can't deal with Bank B because he's full up to his limit. Usually Bank B will agree to forget it, but if the rate is moving against the broker Bank B may insist, especially if he has already laid off his deal at a profit. So the broker is in effect a principal and has to cover his position. Most brokers have friendly dealers who are prepared to help out or "wash" these kind of deals, perhaps even accepting the broker's loss which will be repaid over time, by the broker's passing him deals which suit his book.

As a *quid pro quo* for direct interbank dealing brokers were given the right to deal direct with commercial customers. Hardly any business is done this way, partly because there is little awareness of brokers outside the market, mainly because they stand to lose much more business than they gain by taking a bank's favourite corporate customer.

It is possible to deal for value somewhere in between the usual units of months forward. Dealers work out prices on interest earning days and might quote a wider spread for the inconvenience of having odd-dated exchange on their books. It is also possible to deal for the day before the spot value date and in some currencies for settlement on the dealing day. This depends on time discrepancy and local clearing practice. It is not possible to deal in yen in London for settlement today, as Tokyo's banking today is over. It is very rarely possible to deal in European currencies for value today because of early clearing requirements, but same-day dealing is possible between London and North America and between Canada and the U.S. Prices for these dates are in a sense backward rates, and are worked out on the basis of overnight and Tom/next (Tomorrow/next day) deposit rates. So a low interest rate currency trades at a discount. It is the possibility of dealing for value earlier than the spot value date that enables dealers to carry a spot position over from one day to the next.

Swaps

A currency's forward discount or premium in points is called the swap rate because most forward dealing does not take the form of outright purchases and sales of currencies, but of dealers' swapping a spot position for a forward position without any change in their overall exposure to a currency. In this kind of transaction, when a dealer sells DM spot and repurchases them forward from the same counterparty, the spot rate used is immaterial, and the banks will use the same rate for the spot deal and as the base of the forward deal (because neither party is assuming an exchange risk, the spread is unnecessary). The only rate that matters is the swap.

Why do a swap? Not to make money out of the movement of the spot rate. Anyone who is confident in a 12-month forecast of the spot rate which is out of line with the forward rate should do an outright forward deal. Dealers do not normally do this because they are not in business to take positions for a capital gain in 12 months, but to make money on positions from day to day. If they locked up all their positions to their limits and sat on them for months they would be idle and speculative, and the market would be illiquid. When a dealer takes a view on the movement of the exchange rate it is a short-term view and he takes a spot position. In contrast to a spot deal a swap enables a dealer to take an interest rate position, since the relationship of spot to forward rate depends on interest rates. Doing a swap in this sense is like buying a Treasury bill, with the difference that this will show a profit or a loss during the course of its life depending on the development of interest rates in one country, whereas the profitability of a swap depends on their movement in two. If DM interest rates decline, or U.S. interest rates rise, or both, the forward premium on the DM will increase, so a dealer who has done a swap selling DM spot and buying them forward will make a profit.

One very good reason for doing a swap rather than an outright deal is that, other things being equal, interest rate movements push the spot rate up when they push the swap down, and vice versa: in this case falling DM rates and/or rising U.S. rates depress the DM spot but "strengthen" the DM swap rate, partly because they encourage swaps which involve selling DM spot, partly because they enhance the yield attraction of dollars relative to the DM. Another case for doing a swap might be the expectation of falling U.K. interest rates lending strength to U.K. gilts, but depressing the pound: a U.S. investor could participate in the gilt market without the exchange risk, by selling pounds forward. The aim in this case is not to make a profit on the swap rate — it would be likely to make a loss — but to strip £ out of gilts.

Swaps do not have to consist of simultaneous spot and forward deals. It is equally possible to establish an interest rate exposure or to cover an exchange rate exposure for a particular period in the future: if a dealer expects DM interest rates to fall, but not for three months (or expects the DM to strengthen, but not for three months), he might sell DM three months forward and buy six months forward. Again the spot rate used as a base for the transactions is immaterial. If the three-months swap is 80/70 and the six-months swap 160/140, the transaction would be done at a rate of 160 − 70 = 90.

These examples show that the forward market can be used differently by two operators with the same view of the future: assuming DM interest rates are going to fall and weaken the DM, a treasurer with DM assets might conduct an outright forward sale of DM. A dealer would do a swap buying forward DM.

Exhibit 3.1.4: A few don'ts in the foreign exchange world

There are a few "don'ts" when dealing with dealers:

Don't ask a dealer for a buying price for a currency if you want to buy it. Your buying is his selling price, unless you want to buy sterling.

Don't expect a dealer to deal on a price you have requested "for indication".

Don't expect a dealer to deal on a dealing price he quoted you 10 minutes ago.

Don't expect a dealer to deal at the rates shown on the screen, which are for indication only. Apart from a few cases of influential market makers trying to manipulate the market by showing phoney rates on the screen, dealers try to keep their dealing rates as close as possible to what they're displaying. But naturally when prices are moving fast the screen can show rates that no longer apply. A dealer will always look after his position before he looks after his screen.

Don't expect a dealer always to be competitive; at any time he will be more interested in buying or selling and will quote accordingly. Any one with a moderate amount of exchange business will find that looking around for the best rates in the market is time profitably spent. Two points on $1 million is DM200. The best way to avoid ringing dealers in a state of ignorance about the going market rate and to save precious time while the markets move, is to have a screen, giving access to all major dealers' rates at the touch of a few keys. When executing a cross rate deal (e.g. DM/£), it may be cheaper to split the operation into two, and look for the finest DM/$ and the finest $/£ quotations. They will rarely come from the same bank. Naturally your anxiety to secure the finest possible rate may be tempered by a particularly strong relationship with a bank. If a dealer gains your respect and saves you large sums by giving advice about timing, this will outweigh the odd point on his quotations. A dealer might well save you two or 300 points by telling you to postpone a deal for 24 hours. It would be churlish then to give the business to another bank offering you a better rate. And naïve to think that the first dealer wouldn't hear about it.

Again depending on the degree of confidence established, you may or may not insist on a two-way price (sell and buy) before saying which way you are. Provided you're well informed about the market rate there's no need to be scared of an uncompetitive quotation. Take your custom elsewhere. Many of the largest commercial users of the exchange markets know their dealers well enough to ring up and say "I've got DM50 million to sell. Do it at best."

Don't try to execute a large order when the markets are thin, late on a Friday afternoon or in the European afternoon of a U.S. holiday.

Always take the trouble to confirm details as soon as the dealer says "done" however rushed both of you may be. "I buy from you $1 million at DM2·1095, value 29 March. I pay DM2,109,500 to ABC Bank Frankfurt account DEF Bank London, you pay $1 million to XYZ Bank New York account International Widgets Limited."

When doing a swap don't pay the dealer's spot rate spread. The same rate should be used as the base of both sides of the swap. So a dealer quoting a competitive swap price, regardless of his spot or his outright, should get the business.

Don't expect a dealer's quoted price to be good for amounts of less than $1 million in the major currencies.

Don't use the same bank for all currencies; they specialize, especially in the minor currencies. For cross rate deals it may well make sense to look abroad for the best rate. A bank in Brussels would be a logical source for a Bfr/DM quotation, a bank in Vienna for Asch/DM.

A swap rate is a premium if the bigger number comes first (for the $/£ rate a premium on the dollar), and has to be subtracted from the spot rate. If the smaller number comes first (e.g. 200/250) the swap is a discount. In nearly all cases 200 means 0·02, but on a few "light" currencies, such as the lira, swap rates are usually abbreviated — a swap of 15/20 would be more likely to indicate a forward discount of 15 than 0·0015 lira per dollar. Getting the decimal place right is easily checked provided the approximate interest rate differential is known. Currencies which attract similar interest rates will trade close to par (the spot rate) in the forward market, and a dealer may offer to sell a currency at a premium and buy it at a discount. He might quote a swap of "minus ten plus twenty" or "ten twenty around par".

2. A trader's approach

Claude Tygier

The dramatic expansion of the foreign exchange markets is illustrated by two surveys taken by the Federal Reserve Bank of New York, in 1975 and 1979. In both instances, between 75 and 90 banks operating in the United States were asked to report their foreign exchange activities over a period of one month. It was found that the daily turnover had more than tripled, although the various types of activities remained the same on a percentage basis. The total membership of the Association Cambiste Internationale, the umbrella group of national foreign exchange dealer associations, was approximately 5,000 in about 10 countries in 1975; present membership is in excess of 12,000 in more than 25 countries. In the United States alone, there are about 1,000 members. In addition, a large parallel market has expanded in Chicago, with the growth of the IMM.

The foreign exchange market has grown from a group of centres to a truly integrated global market, where the only remaining barriers are time differences and local regulations. This integration is the result of improving technology and the need for protection in ever-changing market environments. The electronic revolution of the 1970s has enabled dealers to have at their disposal the best in computer and communication technologies. Calculations require only fractions of seconds. Programmable calculators provide instant analyses of interest rate changes, spot fluctuations, and any technical factors which affect dealing. Reuters and Telerate screens provide a wealth of instant information on all financial markets throughout the world; Dow Jones and Reuters flash news instantaneously; and even rumours spread through the markets in minutes. The advent of efficient telephone communications has relegated the telex to the role of auxiliary instrument. Direct lines between the branch networks of the giant banking institutions are the norm rather than the exception, and the North American and European markets now function practically as one market while their trading hours overlap.

The concept of dealing around the clock has arisen for two reasons. The first occurred in the 1970s, when some countries applied restraints on spot positions taken by their local banks. These institutions decided to get around some of the regulations by switching their positions to their foreign branches. However, these positions had to be monitored during off hours, and senior dealers started doing business at home, many of them installing news services and monitor screens there to follow overseas markets more closely. Round-the-clock dealing, switching of positions and overnight orders have provided some markets — especially in the Far East — with extra liquidity, allowing for a smoother transition between the close of one market and the opening of the next. At present, there is still a hiatus of approximately four hours between the close of the New York market and the opening of the Far East markets.

How dealers assess the market

The measure of success for dealers is in correctly evaluating market movements and acting accordingly. Only experience can properly synthesize all the pieces of information and all the factors that make markets move. All market participants have at their disposal a wealth of data, which can confuse as often as it can enlighten. Dealers must sift rapidly through this information and decide what is significant and what is not. On a more intangible note, they must guage the mood of the market, to determine whether it will be influenced by certain developments or not. Dealers are strategists who pit themselves against market forces which can easily change. At times, certain news will have a disproportionate importance, while other news will be disregarded, i.e. the psychology of the market will determine the reactions. Certain things, however, never change. The dynamics of spot movements, the war of nerves played between large dealing rooms, the appearance — and subsequent disappearance — of financial institutions which assume a high profile in the markets, are all elements which experienced dealers know how to work with.

Market liquidity

The single most important factor determining short-term movements is the market's liquidity. The inter-bank market, although very large, constitutes a zero sum game when other participants do not intervene. Banks, no matter what their size, have limits, both during the day and overnight. Any open position is eventually closed, hopefully at a profit. The markets acquire an extra dimension with the appearance of participants who need to take or close positions. Customers need to buy or sell currencies to settle transactions, not to make a profit, and their business adds liquidity to the market. Institutions or individuals who buy or sell currencies which they do not really need are simply an extension of the inter-bank market, and more often than not add an element of instability.

The banks themselves operate on a three-tier system. First, the large money centre banks constitute the core of the market. They are market makers, and are prepared to deal — on a reciprocal basis — for large amounts with their counterparts. They have the largest number of customers, and are more apt to detect or precipitate movements, because they are more attuned to market forces. Second, there are the smaller market makers whose limits are not so large, and who take smaller positions. Their far greater number compensates for the fact that they cannot move the markets in the way the larger banks do. The third tier is composed of banks who may take positions and who may have clients, but who do not actively participate in the markets. In the United States, the IMM has contributed to this third tier in a major way.

Which indicators dealers watch

In an age when communications are instantaneous, it is presumed that everyone in the market knows what is happening or what may happen. Any advance knowledge is quickly disseminated. Dealers and clients stay in close touch with their own economists and with other financial markets. Dealers, however, measure the news against market expectation, and then carefully weigh the reaction. Ten years ago, market participants used to react to news instantly. Nowadays, the element of anticipation is so important that reaction to expected news can be the opposite of conventional wisdom. Timing has therefore become more important than speed of response.

Dealers must be discriminating in assessing news, whether political, financial or economic, and know what will be taken seriously by the market. Since all markets have essentially a sheeplike attitude, dealers concentrate on what the rest of the market pays attention to; they also bear in mind that moods and trends can change rapidly. This is why they are also apt to change their minds quickly.

Two major factors influence exchange rates — and hence the market: patterns of international trade, and capital flows. In recent years, interest differentials between major countries have been prime determinants in movements of capital. In the past three years, both the U.S. dollar and the British pound have been in demand largely because of their high levels of interest rates. However, political considerations have recently assumed a greater importance for capital flows. The Deutschemark suffered from the unrest in Poland, and the advent of a socialist government in France dealt its currency a grave blow. The importance of short-term capital flows is underscored by the attention paid to current account statistics, rather than trade figures.

In recent years, there has been renewed interest in technical analysis — momentum, moving averages and charts. This trend, common in commodity markets, developed in the IMM, and has now spread through the financial markets. Awareness of this type of information is important, if only because it has a large following.

How dealers relate to clients

The client–dealer relationship is a delicate one, involving a great deal of mutual trust. At first sight, dealer and client interests do not coincide. The dealer's first responsibility is to his organization, and to secure a profit for it; the client's aim is to secure the best possible price for his transaction. This is why clients will shop, i.e. call several banks at the same time, and select the most competitive price they can obtain. For a dealer, there is no advantage in making a price to a client, beyond the fact that the client will deal on that price. At a given moment, it may or may not suit the dealer's position.

Some clients insist on being made markets, that is two-way prices. However, this type of approach implies mistrust. Furthermore, dealers normally make markets on a reciprocal basis. Ultimately, the prices and service to the client will be determined by the bank's attitude to such relationships, and the attitude of the dealers. It will also depend on the market itself, on existing positions, and on knowledge of the client.

A good relationship between clients and dealers assures the client that his interests will be looked after in a professional manner, and the dealer that the transaction will be executed profitably. The dealer also acquires extra knowledge by dealing for a customer. Large orders can be particularly important. Dealers prefer orders which they can execute in their own way, thereby combining their own dealing with the client transaction. In the interest of the client, a large order must be so executed that it will not upset the market, and will provide a competitive price for the deal. Clients try to avoid a high profile in the market, and correctly insist on confidentiality. They must also be confident that their dealers have the capacity to operate in large amounts without assuming an unduly high posture, and that they will use, but not abuse, the insider knowledge which they have acquired through their orders. Dealers must also be rewarded for the services they perform, especially when markets are erratic and orders large.

Doing business with clients requires more than simply making prices. Screens do not provide clients with information on the mood and trends of the market, and only dealers can give this extra knowledge to their clients. The timing of a given order can be of crucial importance, and certain deals may dramatically affect the liquidity of the market.

Management of a dealing room

To the outsider, dealing rooms are a study in mayhem. Desks are clustered with machinery, telephones, calculators and screens. There is constant shouting of prices and a rapid jargon which is unintelligible to the untrained ear. In reality, a dealing room operates in a rigidly disciplined manner, under the supervision of the chief dealer. The chief dealer is responsible for the performance of his team, and his skills as manager are of prime importance for a smooth operation. The chief dealer co-ordinates strategies, provides directives and leadership. He is the link between his team and management, and has the responsibility of ensuring that the needs of his dealers are attended to, and that morale remains high.

Dealers function most efficiently as a team, even though their respective tasks may be quite diversified. The responsibilities of each dealer are delineated according to his skill and experience, although within this framework, he operates with a degree of autonomy. The most exacting constraints are those which dealers impose on themselves; outside supervision must be subtle. The spirit of teamwork is important for the dissemination of information within the dealing room, and for dealing itself, especially when cross positions are taken. A good dealing room promotes people from within, and in time gives dealers to the market, rather than taking from the market.

The trading limits provided to the dealing room reflect the attitude of the institution to dealing, its goals and its functions. The limits, qualitatively as well as quantitatively, will be a function of the size of the bank and its relative importance in the market. However, the dealing room must be provided with parameters which allow it to function efficiently to achieve the goals set by management. But there must be limits, to protect the institution and prevent overtrading. The limits should be exceeded only with the knowledge and approval of management.

There are a variety of trading limits which can be imposed for control purposes, and procedures depend on the institution. The two broad categories of limits involve spot dealing and forward dealing; but the most basic limits have to do with the banks' total exposure in a given currency. Banks have an overall foreign currency limit, which comprises the maximum foreign exchange net commitments. This limit can be on a daily basis — during the dealing session — or on an overnight basis. The total limit can be denominated in the indigenous currency, or in foreign currencies. Within this overall limit, there can be subdivisions by foreign currency dealt. For instance, a bank can have maximum limits of $10 million in dollar/Deutschemarks and $5 million in dollar/Swiss francs, but an overall limit of $12 million. Spot limits may include the maximum size which can be dealt with a counterpart in one day. Forward limits control not only the size of permitted positions, but also the gaps between positions, i.e. three months vs. six months.

In recent years, interest rate movements have been extremely volatile, and the interest risk has grown. For this reason, forward limits have generally been tightened. Other limits are imposed on the dealing room, but these are credit rather than dealing limits. Such limits were considerably tightened after the Herstatt Bank collapse of 1974, and tend to be more strictly controlled whenever there are rumours of difficulties within the banking world.

The organization of a dealing room depends on its size and its activities. The smallest organizations deal only in one or two currencies, and may engage only in spot activities. It is more useful, therefore, to analyse the functioning of a large dealing room which engages in a multitude of activities.

The first differentiation is between dealing and advising clients. The corporate desk acts as a liaison between dealers and the clients. It obtains the prices from the dealers and advises them that the deal is done. It also provides information to the dealers on what clients may have to do.

The dealing desk may be divided either by currencies, or by the type of dealing — spot or forward. In the first case, senior dealers will have overall responsibility for one or several currencies which tend to behave in a group — for instance some of the EMS currencies — and supervise other dealers who will maintain spot and/or forward positions within the group of currencies dealt. Support is provided by junior dealers or position clerks who keep track of the deals done, and who man the communications. Even in a large dealing room, one or two major currencies will usually be dealt exclusively by senior dealers. These are the currencies in which the organization is most active. On the other hand, junior dealers who are just starting are given exotics — currencies which are not too actively traded. Some large rooms tend to separate spot and forward dealings, but the intricate relationship between spot and forward movements makes such systems more difficult to operate efficiently.

The professional dealing room operates under a well-defined chain of command, where responsibilities are clearly established and assumed. Each member of that team, from the chief dealer to the junior position clerk, must feel that he is an integral part of it, sharing in the good as well as the bad times.

3. Evaluating the performance of the forecasters

Richard M. Levich[*]

The growing volume of international transactions helps to intensify the demand for foreign exchange forecasts and financial advice. With over eight years of floating exchange rates, many advisory services have accumulated a lengthy history of forecasts. It is therefore appropriate to pose some basic questions — Have exchange rate forecasts been very accurate? Could exchange rate forecasts have been used to improve currency exposure management? In the broadest sense, is there evidence that professional advisory services have demonstrated forecasting expertise?

The purpose of this section is to present a study of professional foreign exchange forecasters that addresses these questions. The study includes 12 services, nine currencies, four horizons and 48 separate monthly forecasts, generating over 11,000 individual forecasts for analysis.

What we really want to know is: Do the foreign exchange rate forecasters beat the market? This is a difficult question to answer because there is not a universally accepted measure of the market's consensus forecast of the future spot exchange rate. Therefore, in this study, our focus is on a related question: Do the foreign exchange rate forecasters beat the forward rate? Under certain assumptions that are fairly plausible, it is theoretically correct to use the forward rate as the best representation of exchange rate expectations. We will argue this case shortly. Our objective — to check if forecasters beat the market — implies performance evaluation. This is always a tricky subject and the evaluation of forecasters is no exception. Several alternative performance measures will be proposed and computed.

Based on the evidence in hand, the simple answers to our questions are: No, exchange rate forecasts have not been as accurate as the forward rate prediction. Even so: Yes, exchange rate forecasts were very often on the correct side of the forward rate, therefore offering correct hedging or speculative advice. In this sense, the record of several forecasters is too good to be the result of guessing, and we conclude that the industry has demonstrated forecasting expertise.

Some of the most impressive performances from our study are summarized in Exhibit 3.3.1. The first point worth noting is that 10 of our 13 sample advisory services appear in the Exhibit; most of the services have had at least one moment of glory. Second, it appears that more forecasters have been successful with the DM than with other currencies. But the most tantalizing question is: Who is best? The data do not permit a clean answer to this question (see Exhibit 3.3.1 for the explanation). Even though comparisons across services are difficult and require further sticky assumptions, our evidence clearly shows that several forecasters have performed remarkably well. In alphabetical order: Business International, Conti Currency, Predex Forecast and Wharton achieved statistically significant results for several individual currencies and significant overall performance for at least one horizon. Multinational Computer Models also recorded many high percentage correct track records; however, most were not statistically significant because of small sample sizes.

We have presented answers to several questions, but so far we have glossed over many of the loaded phrases in our questions. How should we measure accuracy? What is a fair way to measure a track record? How impressive must a track record be before we conclude that the track record is the result of expertise? The remainder of this article explores these theoretical and methodological issues, and then presents the results of our empirical tests.

The big issues

How we structure an empirical test of forecasting expertise and how we interpret the results depends on a few key issues:

— What is the market's estimate of the future spot exchange rate?
— Does the foreign exchange market efficiently reflect available information?
— What is a reliable indicator of forecasting performance?

---

[*] The author has no involvement with any of the professional services discussed in this section.

121

Exhibit 3.3.1: Leading track records among advisory services (percentage correct forecasts)

Horizon	Deutschemark		Canadian dollar		Pound sterling		Japanese yen		All currencies	
One-month	Predex	65–B	C.M.B.	69–A	Conti	65–B	Phillips	71	Conti	61·24–C
	BI	65–B	Conti	63–B	D.R.I.	61	Conti	63–B	BI	58·82–C
	Conti	63–B							Predex	57·64–B
	D.R.I.	61							Wharton	57·58
	M.C.M.	60								
Three-month	Wharton	82	Wharton	82	Wharton	64	Phillips	100	Wharton	71·72–B
	M.C.M.	73	C.M.B.	81–A	C.M.B.	63			Predex	61·11–B
	Phillips	71			Predex, ST	60				
	Predex	65								
Six-month	Wharton	90	Wharton	70	Predex, ST	69	Phillips	86	Predex	63·12–A
	M.C.M.	79	BI	67	Predex	60	Murenbeeld	66	Wharton	62·22
	Predex	77–A							M.C.M.	61·11
	Phillips	71							Predex, ST	60·15
12-month	M.C.M.	88	Wharton	75	Predex, ST	83	Phillips	100	Predex	68·83–A
	Wharton	75			M.C.M.	75	Murenbeeld	67	M.C.M.	65·28
	Predex	71			Predex	71	D.R.I.	65	Wharton	63·39
	Predex, ST	65							Predex, ST	60·87

Note. The data do not permit clean comparisons between services for two reasons.

1. All forecasters have not been monitored over the same time period.

Take, for example, Wharton's 57·58% overall track record versus Conti Currency's 61·24% at the one-month horizon. The Wharton sample reflects 11 forecasts (on nine currencies) from 1980 while the Conti Currency record is based on 43 forecasts (also on nine currencies) from the period 1977–80. Conti Currency's record is statistically significant which might lead us to conclude that it is superior. But the two sample periods are so different, this would be comparing apples and oranges.

Even more dramatic are the 12-month Japanese yen results. The record for Phillips and Drew reflects two observations while the Murenbeeld record is based on 36 observations. Readers should refer to Exhibit 3.3.2 for an indication of the maximum sample sizes for each advisory service.

2. The probability of correct advice by a forecaster is estimated subject to error.

Take the overall track records of Predex (63%), Wharton (62%), Multinational Computer Models (61%) and Predex Short-Term (60%) at the six-month horizon. These results are so close together that, statistically, we could not reject the hypothesis that they are identical.

Entries are included in this table if the percentage correct track record exceeds 60% or if the track record is statistically significant at the 10% level. Entries are marked A, B, or C to indicate statistical significance at the 10%, 5% or 1% levels, respectively. If an entry is not footnoted, there is at least a 10% probability that the track record is the result of chance.

What exchange rate is the market expecting?

We often hear statements such as: "the market's belief that the dollar will remain strong . . .", "the market's view that the central bank will intervene if sterling reaches $1·60 . . .", or "the market's expectation that the Mexican peso will have a substantial devaluation soon . . .". Where do we observe the market's exchange rate expectations, and how do we quantify them?

One of the most commonly expressed beliefs about the foreign exchange market is that the forward rate does not reflect exchange rate expectations; rather it is felt that the forward rate simply reflects the interest differential between Eurocurrency interest rates. This is easy to understand. To verify this belief, we need only observe the forward premium (say, $/DM) and two interest rates (Euro-$ and Euro-DM) at the same moment. Casual observation and formal research concludes that the forward premium is nearly always established to eliminate covered arbitrage profits (i.e. the Interest Rate Parity Theorem).[1] To test whether the forward rate reflects exchange rate expectations, we would have to compare today's three-month forward rate with the spot rate three months hence. This establishes one datum. We would require many similar observations before we could begin to observe any empirical regularities between

---

[1] See Jacob A. Frenkel and Richard M. Levich, "Transaction Costs and Interest Arbitrage: Tranquil Versus Turbulent Periods," *Journal of Political Economy* 86, No. 6 (November/December 1977); pp. 1209–26.

today's forward rate and the future spot exchange rate (i.e. unbiased forward rate prediction). It is unlikely that very many foreign exchange traders have made these calculations.[2]

In theory, the Interest Rate Parity Theorem and unbiased forward rate prediction are not incompatible. Under restrictive but not implausible assumptions, both relationships hold simultaneously.[3] Therefore, it is correct to assume that the forward exchange rate reflects exchange rate expectations. Unfortunately, the relationship may not be perfect. The forward rate may reflect several factors including:

(1) Exchange rate expectations, $E(S_{t+n})$

(2) Risk premium for exchange rate risk, RP_t

(3) Role of transaction costs, TC_t

(4) Role of government intervention, GI_t

(5) Random error term, U_t

so that,

$$F_{t,3} = E(S_{t+3}) + RP_t + TC_t + GI_t + U_t. \tag{1}$$

Equation (1) indeed illustrates that today's three-month forward rate reflects exchange rate expectations, but the forward rate also may capture other effects. Only if these other variables offer zero contribution will there be an exact correspondence between the forward rate and exchange rate expectations.

The role of a risk premium may be illustrated easily using an analogy based on the term structure of interest rates. If we consider only interest rate expectations, an upward-sloping term structure signals that the market expects short-term interest rates to rise in the future. Suppose, however, that investors require a liquidity premium before they are willing to hold a longer-term bond. In this case, the upward-sloping yield curve reflects positive liquidity premiums rather than rising interest rate expectations. To deduce the market's interest rate expectations, analysts must adjust the implied forward interest rate for the liquidity premium.

Liquidity premia are, of course, perfectly consistent with a well-functioning, efficient bond market. There are logical reasons why investors might demand and be paid liquidity premia. The example serves to illustrate that even though the term structure of interest rates reflects interest rate expectations, liquidity premia make it more difficult to isolate the implied market interest rate expectations.

Similarly, market exchange rate expectations are not directly observable. Open foreign exchange positions involve risk and the market may pay a premium to people who maintain these positions. Consider the following example.[4] Suppose all market participants expect the $/DM rate will be $0·50 in three months. Suppose that all of today's transactions (i.e. both demand and supply) for three-month forward contracts have cleared the market, except for a DM 10 million remittance by a German subsidiary to its U.S. parent. In order to complete its sale of DM, the German subsidiary must induce someone who is happy with their $, DM portfolio mix to part with dollars and accept DM 10 million. How can they provide this inducement? Simple — if the German subsidiary is willing to accept only $0·49/DM they may

[2] The academic studies on this issue have led to mixed results. The forward rate appears to be an unbiased predictor of the future spot rate but the relationship between the forward premium and the future exchange rate change is very weak. See Richard M. Levich, "Are Forward Exchange Rates Unbiased Predictors of Future Spot Rates?" *Columbia Journal of World Business* 14, No. 4 (Winter 1979), pp. 49–61.

[3] Under certainty, both IRPT and unbiased forward rate prediction hold if exchange rates are determined so that purchasing power parity holds and interest rates reflect anticipated inflation (the Fisher effect). With uncertainty, both relationships will hold if forward speculators are risk-neutral. For details, see Ian H. Giddy, "An Integrated Theory of Exchange Rate Equilibrium," *Journal of Financial and Quantitative Analysis* (December 1976), pp. 883–92, and John F. O. Bilson, "Rational Expectations and the Exchange Rate," in J. Frenkel and H. Johnson (eds.) *The Economics of Exchange Rates*, Addison-Wesley, 1978.

[4] Solnik refers to the impact of this imbalance of private capital flows as "hedging pressure" (Bruno H. Solnik, *European Capital Markets*, D. C. Heath, 1973). A foreign exchange risk premium can also be modelled around the excess supply of official government debt. See, Jeffrey A. Frankel, "The Diversifiability of Exchange Risk," *Journal of International Economics* 9, No. 3 (August 1979), pp. 379–93, and Michael P. Dooley and Peter Isard, "Capital Controls, Political Risk and Deviations from Interest-Rate Parity," *Journal of Political Economy* 88, No. 2 (April 1980), pp. 370–84.

induce someone to supply dollars ($4,900,000 in this case). Even though the forward rate is $0·49/DM, the market still maintains its expectation that the spot rate will be $0·50 in three months. The German subsidiary has simply paid a $0·01/DM premium to reduce its risks. Foreign exchange analysts must now adjust the observed forward rate ($0·49/DM) by the risk premium in order to deduce the market's exchange rate expectations.

Paying a premium to reduce foreign exchange risks and demanding a premium to hold them are, of course, perfectly consistent with (but not required for) rational investor behaviour and market efficiency. In practice, the risk premium term in equation (1) may be zero if there is little net foreign exchange risk to be held or if the marginal foreign exchange participant is risk neutral.

What are the implications of this issue? Indeed the implications are major.

I. If the forward rate reflects a risk-premium, or terms in equation (1) other than exchange rate expectations, then we expect an advisory service forecast to outperform the forward rate.

II. If the forward rate reflects a risk-premium, then profits earned by following advisory service forecasts may represent only the fair return for taking on exchange risk, rather than an excess return for exploiting unusual forecasting expertise.

Empirical evidence on the existence and stability of an exchange risk premium remains sketchy.[5] Therefore, our tests of advisory service forecasts vis-à-vis the forward rate admit the possibility that the forecasters ought to beat the forward rate, because the forward rate is not a pure reflection of exchange rate expectations. Evidence that a professional forecast beats the forward rate will be inconclusive with respect to the market efficiency hypothesis, and it may not be very surprising to people who believe that the forward rate has proved, on occasion, to be a very bad forecaster.

Is the foreign exchange market efficient?

Suppose for the moment that the forward rate is the pure reflection of exchange rate expectations, i.e. the terms RP, TC, and GI in equation (1) are zero. Does it follow that the forward rate will be a good forecaster, i.e. one with errors that are serially uncorrelated and average to zero? The answer depends on the efficiency of the foreign exchange market. If the market is efficient so that the forward rate quickly and fully reflects available information (and remember, we have assumed that risk premium terms are zero) then the forward rate will be a good forecaster.[6]

Market efficiency is an empirical question. The evidence from the stock market suggests a high degree of efficiency. However, research on the stock market confirms that market insiders earn excess return and investors who purchase information may expect an extra (fair) return for their expenditure on information.

Tests of the foreign exchange market have generally failed to reject the efficient market hypothesis, but these tests are difficult to formulate and interpret.[7] Interestingly, departures from market efficiency have been blamed on both too much and too little speculation. Journalists often portray foreign exchange rates as too volatile. Excessive speculation, it is argued, leads to exchange rate overshooting, and so forward rates will be poor predictors of

[5] For an empirical test that rejects the risk premium hypothesis, see Jeffrey A. Frankel, "A Test of the Existence of the Risk Premium in the Foreign Exchange Market vs. the Hypothesis of Perfect Substitutability," *International Finance Discussion Papers*, No. 149, Federal Reserve System, August 1979.

[6] The forward rate may not be the "best" predictor because the available information has been combined according to "dollar votes" in the market place, rather than a formula that makes the best use of the information. This view is elaborated in Stephen Figlewski, "Market 'Efficiency' in a Market with Heterogeneous Expectations," *Journal of Political Economy* 86, No. 4 (August 1978), pp. 581–97.

[7] The literature of foreign exchange market efficiency is reviewed in Richard M. Levich, "Further Results on the Efficiency of Markets for Foreign Exchange," in *Managed Exchange-Rate Flexibility: The Recent Experience*, Federal Reserve Bank of Boston, Conference Series No. 20, 1978.

future spot rates.[8] Ronald McKinnon argued that the move from Bretton Woods to managed floating in 1973 left the foreign exchange market with too little speculative capital. As a consequence, exchange speculators did not have the risk capital to stabilize rates and push forward rates toward the expected future spot rate.[9] Michael Rosenberg has argued that technical forecast rules often generate profits for the same reason — the speculative capital of banks and multinational corporations is relatively small and not sufficient to eliminate expected profits from open positions.[10]

What are the implications of this issue?

I. If the foreign exchange market is efficient and the forward rate does not contain a risk premium, then the forward rate represents the consensus market forecast, and it is the appropriate standard for comparisons against advisory service forecasts.

The forward rate will be an appealing forecaster in this case because it reflects the collective wisdom of thousands of well-informed, profit-seeking investors, it is updated continuously to reflect new information and it is free.

II. If the foreign exchange market is not efficient, then we expect advisory service forecasts to outperform the forward rate. Investors should earn a profit for their superior information. The profit may or may not compensate them for the cost of the advisory service.

How should we measure forecasting performance?

The analysis of forecasting performance is clearly an important issue. But unfortunately, two seemingly straightforward statistical tests can easily lead to misleading conclusions.[11]

The first approach concentrates on the forecast error defined as

$$\text{Forecast error} = \text{Predicted exchange rate} - \text{Actual exchange rate} \qquad (2)$$

One desirable property of a forecast is that its forecasts errors be small. However, even this simple criterion needs qualification. For example, assume that today's forward rate is $2·00 and two alternative forecasts of the future spot rate are S1 = $1·99 and S2 = $2·08. If the actual spot rate turns out to be $2·02, the forecast error associated with S1 (−$0·03) is smaller than the forecast error associated with S2 (+$0·06). However, forecast S2 is superior because it leads investors to take long and profitable positions in sterling — i.e. forecast S2 leads to a correct decision.

As a further qualification, suppose that a third forecast, S3 = $2·14, also exists. Even though its forecast error is +$0·12, it does not follow that this forecast is twice as bad as forecast S2. If, for example, the firm is remitting a dividend to its U.S. parent and the firm is considering an all-or-nothing hedging decision, it will make the same decision using either S2 or S3 as a guide, and so there is no additional cost associated with S3's larger forecast error. On the other hand, forecast S3 may be more than twice as bad as forecast S2. If the firm is considering investing a variable amount in U.K. bonds, based on the substantial appreciation predicted by S3, the firm may invest 10 times as much in the U.K. as it would based on forecast S2. As a consequence, the firm foregoes other profitable investments. These opportunity costs of using S3 may exceed twice the costs of using S2.

Therefore, we conclude that there is no simple and unique relationship between the magnitude of forecast errors and the cost of forecast errors for investors. The implication of this statement is that there is no unique statistic for evaluating or ranking forecasters that will be

---

[8] A discussion of exchange rate overshooting appears in Richard M. Levich, "Overshooting in the Foreign Exchange Market," Group of Thirty Occasional Papers No. 5, New York, 1981.
[9] See Ronald I. McKinnon, *Money in International Exchange*, Oxford University Press, New York, 1979, pp. 155–62.
[10] Michael R. Rosenberg, Chapter 2, section 5.
[11] This section is based on Richard M. Levich, "Analyzing the Accuracy of Foreign Exchange Advisory Services: Theory and Evidence," in R. Levich and C. Wihlborg (eds), *Exchange Risk and Exposure*, D. C. Heath, 1980.

correct for all investors. An all–or–nothing hedger will only be concerned that the forecast tells the correct direction, regardless of the magnitude of the forecast error. Investors who feel that exchange gains and losses are proportional to the forecast error will rank forecasters on the basis of mean absolute errors. Investors who feel that exchange gains and losses are proportional to the squared forecast error will rank forecasters on the basis of mean squared error. It is an empirical question whether these criteria will rank forecasters in similar order.

The second common approach for evaluating forecasting performance is to calculate the stream of returns that an investor could earn by following the forecast. We would conclude that the advisory service has expertise and that the forecasts are useful if the stream of investment returns (adjusting for risk) is high relative to alternative investments. Again, this straightforward evaluation procedure raises several difficult questions.

First, how does an investor translate a set of forecasts into a set of investment decisions? The investor recognizes that forecasts are seldom perfect. If the forward rate stands at $2·00, the investor may not be willing to buy forward contracts unless the forecast is $2·02, $2·06 or perhaps higher. Furthermore, the investor is free to increase the number of forward contracts he purchases as his expected profits, and the confidence in those profits, increases. These issues are often handled by assuming that the investor uses the forecast to determine a lump-sum investment rather than an investment which increases with the expected returns predicted by the forecast or which decreases with the expected variance of returns.

The second difficult question is how we should measure the risk associated with currency investment. This calculation is necessary so that we can determine if the return on currency investment is high relative to the risk incurred. As we noted earlier, the measurement of the risk factor in forward contracts is somewhat controversial.

Examining the stream of speculative returns is prone to one further difficulty. Most extreme speculative returns result from large unanticipated exchange rate movements that were not predicted accurately by the advisory service and cannot be expected to recur in the future. For example, a 10% annual return following one service could be the result of a big move in one currency (15%) and losses in most other currencies. This situation would not suggest general forecasting expertise and furthermore, we could not be confident of a large exchange rate move to produce similar profits in the next period.

Instead of these two techniques, we propose a method that ignores the magnitude of forecast errors and calculates the fraction of periods in which the forecast correctly predicts only the direction of exchange rate movement. In our earlier example, S2 and S3 were correct relative to the forward rate while S1 was incorrect. If the fraction of correct forecasts is unusually high, then we can conclude that the advisory service has forecasting expertise.

A numerical example will help to illustrate the above procedure. In a sample of 100 observations (n), suppose there are 60 correct forecasts (r), or a 60% track record. Is this an unusually good track record or is it simply the result of a sequence of lucky guesses? The question is analogous to another basic statistics problem: If a fair coin is tossed 100 times, what is the probability that it will land on heads 60 or more times. The answer is, this event would occur with roughly 2·3% probability.[12] In this case, we would probably reject the notion that a fairly rare event happened, i.e. the forecaster guessed correctly on 60 of 100 trials. Instead, we would lean towards the view that the forecaster has some special expertise and that his probability of a correct forecast in the future is closer to 60%.

To summarize, we have drawn a distinction between correct forecasts (those that correctly predict the direction of change relative to the forward rate), and accurate forecasts. We have noted earlier that many exchange rate changes are very large and most are unanticipated by the market. Therefore, including these as large forecast errors may bias (upwards) our estimate of forecasting inaccuracy and our estimate of the potential for profits. In this sense, calculating the 'percentage correct forecast' may offer us a more useful and robust measure of forecasting expertise.

---

[12] To make the calculation we compute $Z = (r/n - 0·5)/\sqrt{0·25/n}$ which equals 2·0 in this example. The area under the standard normal curve to the right of 2·0 equals 0·023.

Data description and general methodology

Early in 1981, *Euromoney* invited more than 30 advisory services to participate in an analysis of their foreign exchange forecasts from the period 1977–80.[13] We received data from 13 advisory services. This represents 12 companies including Predex, which supplied two separate forecast series. The foreign exchange consulting services of all of the major banks were invited to participate but none accepted. Summary information on the sample services is presented in Exhibit 3.3.2. Six services forecast using econometric techniques, five services follow a judgmental approach and one service combines a basic purchasing power parity model with judgment. Predex's short-term forecasts are generated from a technical model.

Each advisory service supplied a copy of their forecasts for nine major currencies. These currencies were chosen because data on forward rates is available for comparison. Since the formats of these forecasts are not similar, several adjustments were required. For example, several services produce a quarterly average forecast. These figures were recorded as a point forecast for the mid-point of the quarter. Several services provide an end-of-quarter or end-of-period forecast. In this case we simply recorded the origin date and horizon date for each forecast. (The origin date is the date on which a subscriber could receive and act on a forecast. The services are trying to predict the exchange rate to be realized on the horizon date.) Wharton reports a sequence of end-of-month forecasts for the next 24 months. Our procedure was to record only the one-, three-, six- and 12-month ahead forecasts.

The final database includes a record of the origin date and the horizon date for every forecast. With this information, we construct a set of implied one-, three-, six- and 12-month ahead forecasts at each origin date for each advisory service. We do this so that the forecasts are compatible with available forward rate quotations. Our procedure to construct these forecasts uses linear interpolation.

In summary, our procedure is to compute the one-, three-, six- and 12-month ahead forecasts on each origin date for each advisory service. In many cases these data transformations do not alter the original information provided by the service. But in at least two cases (Exchange Rate Outlook which reports only a one-year-ahead forecast, and Predex whose short-term forecasts extend to only three months) it is not clear that the forecasts were intended for use at other horizons.[14] One could argue that these techniques for transforming the various forecasts into a common format may violate a forecaster's exchange rate predictions. But a customer who received an advisor's forecast and had to apply it immediately to a one-, three-, six- or 12-month decision might make very similar calculations.

Five services (Chase Econometrics, Citibank-Economics Department, Conti Currency, M. Murenbeeld and Predex Forecast) produced forecasts throughout the entire sample period. Track record comparisons among these five services are therefore appropriate. The remaining services began their careers at various times after January 1977, and so their results are based on different time periods. How this will effect the results is unclear. For example, the percentage of correct forecasts by Wharton is generally greater than 50% but their service began only in 1980. On the one hand, it would be correct to argue that Wharton's track record is, statistically speaking, less significant because it is based on relatively few observations. On the other hand, one might also argue that Wharton's track record is enhanced in economic significance because their forecasts are concentrated in 1980, a year with extremely high exchange rate volatility.

Once we have recorded the forward rates ($F_{t,n}$) and the forecasts ($\hat{S}_{t,n}$) for each origin date and the future spot exchange rate (S_{t+n}), our methodology follows easily.[15] For each currency and advisory service, we calculate the percentage forecast error as:

$$E_{t,n} = (S_{t+n} - \hat{S}_{t,n})/S_{t+n} \qquad (3)$$

---

[13] We did not actively solicit technical or momentum services. For an analysis of these forecasting techniques, see Stephen H. Goodman, next section.

[14] Multinational Computer Models, Inc. markets a short-term forecast which would be intended for the one-month horizon, but we were not aware of this until our statistical analysis was completed.

[15] Our source for forward rate and spot rates is the Harris Bank *Weekly Review*.

Exhibit 3.3.2: Summary information on the advisory services

Name	Sample dates	Number of observations	Frequency	Type of forecast	Horizons	Methodology	Price (dollars)
1. Business International	Mar. 1978–Dec. 1980	34	12/year	Quarterly average	6 quarters	Econometric	980
2. Chase Econometrics	Jan. 1977–Dec. 1980	48	12/year	Quarterly average	8 quarters	Econometric	12,000
3. Chase Manhattan Bank Economics Department	Nov. 1977–Nov. 1979	16	sporadic	End-of-period	1, 3, 6, 12 months	Judgmental	Free
4. Citibank — Economics Department	Jan. 1977–Dec. 1980	35	9–10/year	Quarterly average	4 quarters	Judgmental	Free
5. Conti Currency	Jan. 1977–Dec. 1980	43	11/year	End-of-quarter	4 quarters	Judgmental	12,500–25,000
6. Data Resources	Aug. 1977–Nov. 1980	28	9–11/year	Quarterly average	6 quarters	Econometric	4,100–23,700
7. Exchange Rate Outlook	Nov. 1978–Dec. 1980	26	12/year	End-of-period	1 year ahead	Judgmental	350
8. Multinational Computer Models, Inc.	Oct. 1979–Dec. 1980	15	12/year	End-of-period	3, 6, 9, 12 months ahead	Real 'PPP' model plus judgment	1,000+
9. M. Murenbeeld and Associates	Jan. 1977–Dec. 1980	43	12/year	End-of-period	3, 12 months ahead	Econometric with judgment added	2,000
10. Phillips and Drew	Mar. 1980–Sept. 1980	7	12/year	End-of-period	Mid-year and year end	Judgmental	n.a.
11. Predex — Forecast	Jan. 1977–Dec. 1980	48	12/year	Quarterly average	6 quarters	Econometric	12,000+
12. Predex — Short Term Forecast	July 1978–Dec. 1980	30	12/year	Monthly average	1, 2, 3, months ahead	Technical	5,000 + 6,000 for trading signals
13. Wharton Econometric Forecasting Associates	Jan. 1980–Dec. 1980	11	11/year	Monthly average	24 months ahead	Econometric	25,000

where n may equal one, three, six or 12 months. The speculative return on an open position is

$$P_{t,n} = W_t \, (S_{t+n} - F_{t,n})/F_{t,n} \tag{4}$$

$$\text{where } W_t = \begin{cases} +1 \text{ if } \hat{S}_{t,n} > F_{t,n} \text{ and we buy forward contracts} \\ -1 \text{ if } \hat{S}_{t,n} < F_{t,n} \text{ and we sell forward contracts.} \end{cases}$$

A variation on this calculation would set $W_t = +1$ or -1 only if $\hat{S}_{t,n}$ were greater (less) than $F_{t,n}$ by some predetermined amount, say 0·5%. Forecasts within the 0·5% bound might be indicating no exchange rate change and so no action is required. The calculated returns in (4) can be added across time periods and currencies.

A forecast is correct if both $\hat{S}_{t,n}$ and S_{t+n} are on the same side of the forward rate. The fraction

$$p = r \text{ (correct forecasts)}/n \text{ (total forecasts)}$$

estimates the probability of correct advice in any period. We want to infer whether this probability is greater than one-half. Formally, we are testing the null hypothesis

$$H_0 : p = 0.5 \text{ (advisory service has no expertise)}$$

versus an alternative hypothesis

$$H_1 : p > 0.5 \text{ (there is forecasting expertise)}$$

Using the normal probability curve, we can calculate p1, a measure of our confidence that p is greater than 0·5. Small values of p1 suggest that it is unlikely that the track record was achieved by chance alone.

Empirical results

We first present a statistic that measures forecasting accuracy relative to the forward rate. For each currency and advisory service, we computed the mean absolute forecast error divided by the mean absolute forecast error of the forward rate. Values of this ratio less than 1·0 suggest that the advisory service is more accurate than the forward rate forecast. Exhibit 3.3.3 summarizes this ratio of the mean absolute forecast errors for the entire sample period. Overall, the data suggest that these 13 advisory services have not forecast as accurately as the forward rate.

At the 12-month horizon, only 33% of the entries are less than 1·0. This figure falls to 24% at the three-month horizon. Wharton is an exception to this result with 75% of their entries less than 1·0. Other concentrations of forecasts that were more accurate than the forward rate are Conti Currency at the one-month horizon, Multinational Computer Models at horizons greater than three months, and Predex Forecast at the 12-month horizon. Even these services had difficulty making consistently accurate forecasts for the Japanese yen. But Phillips and Drew was more accurate than the yen forward rates, albeit for a small number of forecasts.

To keep perspective, it should be noted that 70% of the entries in Exhibit 3.3.3 are between 0·75 and 1·25. If the forward rate's average absolute forecast error is 4%, our data suggest that most average absolute errors are in the 3–5% range. For many purposes, this may not be a substantial difference.

Earlier we stressed the distinction between accurate forecasts and correct forecasts. Data on the percentage of correct forecasts over the entire sample period are summarized in Exhibit 3.3.4. One way to analyse the Exhibit is to count the number of track records greater than 70% (there are 67 or roughly 16%) or greater than 60% (there are 129 or 31%). Intuitively, this number seems like a high concentration of respectable track records. It certainly imparts an opposite impression of forecasting ability than we had from Exhibit 3.3.3. We can also observe that most of the high track records among our sample are concentrated in the econometric services. For econometric services, 47 of 212 track records (or 22%) are greater than 70%, and 91 of 212 (or 43%) exceed 60%. In this sample it also appears that services based on more complex econometric models (Chase Econometrics, D.R.I. and Wharton) did not consistently outperform other econometric models.

The track records alone do not tell the whole story of Exhibit 3.3.4. We must account for the number of independent observations in each track record to measure its statistical significance.

129

Exhibit 3.3.3: Mean absolute error/mean absolute forward error

One-month horizon   Services   Percentage

Currency	1	2	3	4	5	6	7	8	9	10	11	12	13	<1·0
Can $	1·20	1·03	1·03	1·32	0·90	1·06	n.a.	1·06	1·07	1·05	1·16	1·66	1·14	
£	1·01	1·11	1·15	1·44	0·89	0·95	1·03	1·05	1·09	1·30	0·99	1·11	1·13	
Bfr	1·20	1·0	n.a.	1·19	0·99	n.a.	n.a.	0·96	1·07	n.a.	1·09	1·05	0·87	
Ffr	0·89	0·96	1·18	1·31	1·06	n.a.	0·99	0·97	1·03	1·13	1·00	1·20	0·84	$\frac{30}{104} = 28\cdot8\%$
DM	0·95	1·02	1·24	1·11	0·99	1·08	1·02	0·96	1·09	1·12	1·07	1·10	0·80	
Lit	0·96	0·94	1·20	1·20	0·90	n.a.	1·02	1·00	0·95	1·03	1·35	1·24	0·96	
Dfl	1·16	1·01	n.a.	1·19	0·93	n.a.	n.a.	1·02	1·07	1·28	1·04	1·06	0·82	
Swfr	0·92	n.a.	1·07	1·16	0·99	n.a.	n.a.	0·95	1·11	1·10	0·98	1·05	0·87	
¥	1·39	0·98	1·20	1·26	0·94	1·38	1·07	1·09	1·01	0·86	1·27	1·32	1·27	

Three-month horizon

Currency	1	2	3	4	5	6	7	8	9	10	11	12	13	
Can $	1·29	1·13	1·00	1·59	0·99	1·08	n.a.	1·47	1·17	1·03	1·47	1·74	0·80	
£	1·11	1·24	0·91	1·44	1·09	0·98	1·05	1·09	1·27	1·69	1·03	1·22	1·01	
Bfr	0·95	1·07	n.a.	1·33	1·17	n.a.	n.a.	0·99	1·21	n.a.	1·06	1·01	0·77	
Ffr	0·91	0·98	1·02	1·43	1·27	n.a.	0·98	0·92	1·00	0·96	1·03	1·16	0·70	$\frac{25}{104} = 24\cdot0\%$
DM	1·08	1·13	1·07	1·28	1·19	1·35	1·06	0·83	1·19	1·07	1·13	1·04	0·76	
Lit	1·07	0·91	1·09	1·45	1·14	n.a.	1·12	1·12	1·00	1·17	1·64	1·54	0·93	
Dfl	0·80	1·10	n.a.	1·41	1·06	n.a.	n.a.	0·91	1·26	1·26	1·10	1·01	0·81	
Swfr	1·01	n.a.	1·08	1·21	1·32	n.a.	n.a.	0·86	1·06	1·04	1·04	0·94	0·63	
¥	1·42	1·05	1·02	1·23	1·08	1·45	1·09	1·24	0·94	0·47	1·31	1·30	1·79	

Six-month horizon

Currency	1	2	3	4	5	6	7	8	9	10	11	12	13	
Can $	1·40	1·34	1·05	2·06	1·20	1·24	n.a.	2·21	1·48	1·82	1·48	2·65	0·63	
£	1·38	1·33	1·28	1·56	1·02	1·04	1·20	0·99	1·36	1·28	1·02	1·39	0·97	
Bfr	1·22	1·13	n.a.	1·32	1·14	n.a.	n.a.	1·05	1·24	n.a.	0·86	1·05	0·93	
Ffr	1·10	1·02	1·21	1·35	1·23	n.a.	0·98	1·03	0·91	0·78	1·00	1·19	0·94	$\frac{30}{104} = 28\cdot8\%$
DM	1·30	1·14	1·28	1·22	1·17	1·45	1·08	0·79	1·12	0·94	0·85	0·93	0·83	
Lit	1·24	0·99	1·39	1·61	1·09	n.a.	1·14	1·21	0·93	1·15	1·52	2·00	0·93	
Dfl	1·06	1·12	n.a.	1·39	1·09	n.a.	n.a.	0·94	1·18	0·85	0·93	0·98	0·92	
Swfr	1·12	n.a.	1·20	1·16	1·14	n.a.	n.a.	0·78	1·11	0·91	0·87	0·81	0·65	
¥	1·33	1·01	0·97	1·03	1·14	1·05	1·02	1·49	0·87	0·39	1·13	1·29	1·57	

12-month horizon

Currency	1	2	3	4	5	6	7	8	9	10	11	12	13	
Can $	2·35	1·16	1·44	2·16	1·32	1·53	n.a.	3·40	1·95	3·63	1·48	5·47	0·61	
£	1·59	1·27	1·28	1·62	1·23	1·16	1·40	0·89	1·31	1·05	0·85	1·03	1·44	
Bfr	1·47	1·03	n.a.	1·37	1·33	n.a.	n.a.	0·80	1·23	n.a.	0·78	1·40	0·90	
Ffr	1·41	0·92	1·29	1·51	1·19	n.a.	0·88	0·91	0·80	0·91	0·98	1·77	0·88	$\frac{34}{104} = 32\cdot7\%$
DM	1·54	1·11	2·16	1·38	1·43	1·26	1·03	0·82	1·17	1·09	0·76	1·16	0·91	
Lit	1·30	0·94	1·28	1·58	1·12	n.a.	0·97	0·99	0·65	1·12	1·13	2·41	1·04	
Dfl	1·24	1·06	n.a.	1·37	1·35	n.a.	n.a.	0·77	1·13	0·89	0·80	1·31	0·91	
Swfr	1·32	n.a.	1·39	0·99	1·17	n.a.	n.a.	0·66	0·96	1·17	0·79	0·94	0·85	
¥	1·48	1·01	1·13	0·97	1·08	0·70	1·17	1·60	0·77	0·77	1·22	1·42	1·75	

n.a. = Data not available or not applicable.

For example, Phillips and Drew's 100% track record on 12-month yen is based on only two forecasts that could be followed to completion. When there is no forecasting expertise, the probability of two correct forecasts out of two attempts is 25%, the same as the probability of tossing heads two times in a row with a fair coin. After this calculation, we would probably not feel that the 100% track record demonstrates significant evidence for expertise; the track record could have happened easily by chance.

On the other hand, consider Business International's track record for the one-month Belgian franc, 73·5% correct. This is based on 34 observations. The chance that they might achieve 25 or more correct forecasts (73·5% of 34) by simply guessing is less than 1% — highly significant evidence favouring expertise in this case. The entries in Exhibit 3.3.4 are marked with the

Exhibit 3.3.4: Percentage correct forecasts

One-month horizon

Currency	1	2	3	4	5	6	Services 7	8	9	10	11	12	13
Can $	56	44	69 (A)	54	63 (B)	57	n.a.	53	33	29	46	43	64
£	59	44	31	20	65 (B)	61	35	33	44	29	48	53	45
Bfr	74 (C)	42	n.a.	49	60 (A)	n.a.	n.a.	60	40	n.a.	63 (B)	47	55
Ffr	59	56	56	37	53	n.a.	58	60	56	43	69 (C)	47	64
DM	65 (B)	42	31	37	63 (B)	61	50	60	40	29	65 (B)	57	55
Lit	50	54	31	46	65 (B)	n.a.	54	47	56	57	71 (C)	57	73 (A)
Dfl	62 (A)	44	n.a.	37	60 (A)	n.a.	n.a.	53	44	29	67 (B)	50	64
Swr	56	n.a.	38	34	58	n.a.	n.a.	60	47	43	54	43	64
¥	50	56	44	49	63 (B)	43	38	53	49	71	38	53	36

Three-month horizon

Currency	1	2	3	4	5	6	7	8	9	10	11	12	13
Can $	56	46	81 (A)	34	58	54	n.a.	27	42	43	48	37	82
£	44	33	63	23	44	50	31	53	44	43	54	60	64
Bfr	62	48	n.a.	31	37	n.a.	n.a.	60	40	n.a.	65	47	82
Ffr	59	52	38	31	44	n.a.	54	67	65	57	81 (C)	63	91 (A)
DM	59	44	44	34	42	43	46	73	47	71	65	57	82
Lit	50	60	31	34	58	n.a.	50	33	56	29	77 (B)	50	55
Dfl	65	50	n.a.	34	49	n.a.	n.a.	67	47	43	65	53	91 (A)
Swfr	59	n.a.	25	43	42	n.a.	n.a.	93 (B)	53	71	65	73 (B)	82
¥	41	46	25	34	53	50	35	40	51	100	31	40	18

Six-month horizon

Currency	1	2	3	4	5	6	7	8	9	10	11	12	13
Can $	67	35	50	32	56	57	n.a.	21	32	14	34	48	70
£	30	20	31	15	51	43	16	36	32	29	60	69	50
Bfr	55	35	n.a.	41	37	n.a.	n.a.	79	41	n.a.	66	62	50
Ffr	55	52	50	47	30	n.a.	72	86	73	86	83 (B)	76	70
DM	45	35	38	38	42	50	48	79	54	71	77 (A)	55	90
Lit	27	61	31	32	56	n.a.	48	64	49	43	66	55	50
Dfl	61	41	n.a.	47	35	n.a.	n.a.	71	61	71	62	59	60
Swfr	55	n.a.	31	44	47	n.a.	n.a.	86	63	71	70	76	100 (A)
¥	24	41	38	41	42	54	52	29	66	86	51	41	20

12-month horizon

Currency	1	2	3	4	5	6	7	8	9	10	11	12	13
Can $	56	46	31	30	51	52	n.a.	13	22	0	41	39	75
£	11	20	0	3	30	35	11	75	33	50	71	83	50
Bfr	41	49	n.a.	33	19	n.a.	n.a.	88	42	n.a.	73	61	75
Ffr	41	76	13	30	27	n.a.	74	88	61	100	88 (A)	78	75
DM	44	44	6	47	22	48	53	88	53	50	71	61	75
Lit	19	59	13	23	30	n.a.	58	38	64	0	71	61	50
Dfl	48	51	n.a.	40	16	n.a.	n.a.	100	61	100	73	61	75
Swfr	41	n.a.	31	53	46	n.a.	n.a.	100	72	0	78	78	100
¥	37	51	19	50	46	65	42	0	67	100	54	26	0

n.a. = Data not available or not applicable.

Summary:	Significance level	Expected number of significant entries	Actual number of significant entries
	10% (A)	42	28
	5% (B)	21	17
	1% (C)	4	4

---

letters (A), (B), and (C) to indicate the statistical significance of each track record — 10%, 5% and 1% respectively. All of the marked entries could be considered statistically significant. The entries marked (c) are the most unusual and significant.

Taken as a whole, do the entries in Exhibit 3.3.4 show statistically significant results in favour of forecasting expertise? Return for a moment to a coin-tossing experiment. The probability of three successive heads (or three successive tails) is 1/8 when tossing a fair coin. Chances are good that if we had eight monkeys, each tossing a fair coin three times, then one of the monkeys would toss three straight heads. The message is that, with many monkeys, the chances of observing an extreme outcome improve, even though everyone plays with a fair coin. In our case, Exhibit 3.3.4 represents many forecasters who predicted many currencies. Of the 416 live cells in the Exhibit we expect that 10% (or 42) will be significant at the 10% level, even though none of the forecasters had expertise. Similarly, we expect to find 21 entries that are significant at the 5% level and four entries that are significant at the 1% level, even if the forecasters have no special expertise to make correct forecasts. The actual number of entries that are significant at the 10%, 5% and 1% levels is 28, 17 and four respectively — within the range expected under the null hypothesis. Therefore, as a group, these forecasters did not display statistically significant expertise.

However, the significant track records appear to be concentrated among a few services — Predex Forecast (with 10 significant entries), Conti Currency (with seven), Wharton (with four), and Business International (with three). As we noted before, several advisory services (Multinational Computer Models, M. Murenbeeld, Phillips and Drew, and Predex Short-Term) have many high-percentage track records, but these are based on too few independent observations to be statistically significant. Only more independent observations will make clear whether these track records are the result of true expertise or random chance.

One way to increase the number of observations and, therefore, to increase the efficiency of our search for expertise, is to pool together the track records from several currencies by a single forecaster. However, we must be careful to pool only independent forecasts. Five currencies (Canadian dollar, British pound, Deutschemark, Swiss franc and Japanese yen) move relatively independently of each other over the sample period. Four other currencies (Belgian franc, French franc, Italian lira and Dutch guilder) are linked to the DM via the European Monetary System, but these linkages (especially for the French franc and the Italian lira) have been relatively weak recently. Therefore, even though an advisor forecasts nine currencies, it is conservative to assume that only one-half of these forecasts are independent. The significance levels reported in Exhibit 3.3.5 incorporate this assumption.

Exhibit 3.3.5 reports the percentage of correct forecasts for each advisory service pooling across all currencies. Conti Currency recorded the best overall track record at the one-month horizon, 61·24%. Based on 387 total forecasts (43 forecasts on nine currencies) or only one-half that number (assuming some degree of dependence between currency forecasts), this result is highly significant and unusual. Several other overall one-month track records are high and statistically significant — Business International (58·82%), Predex Forecast (57·64%) and Wharton (57·58%). Our adjustment for dependent forecasts, as expected, reduces the significance level of each track record, but the results for Conti Currency, Business International and Predex Forecast remain statistically significant.

At the three-month horizon, Wharton records the best overall track record, 71·72%, and it is statistically significant even though it is based on a shorter time period. Predex Forecast's 61·11% three-month overall track record is also highly significant. Several other track records exceed 50%, but they are drawn from too few observations to indicate statistical significance.

At the six-month and 12-month horizon, Predex Forecast, Wharton, Multinational Computer Models and Predex Short-Term achieved overall track records in excess of 60%. However, the results for Predex Forecast are statistically significant because they are based on a larger sample of observations.

Some anticipated questions and conclusions

1. Do these results prove that the foreign exchange market is inefficient?

No, they do not. The reason is because the forward rate may contain a risk premium. If so, exchange rate forecasters ought to be able to forecast better than the forward rate. The profits earned by speculators who follow these forecasts may represent only a fair return for the extra foreign exchange risk incurred.

2. Do the results prove that the forecasters beat the forward rate?

The results clearly show that many services have a record of percentage correct forecasts that is not easily explained by chance. For users who face hedge everything/hedge nothing decisions

Exhibit 3.3.5: Percentage correct forecasts for each advisory service pooled across currencies

One-month	1	2	3	4	5	6	7	8	9	10	11	12	13
Percent correct	58·82	47·66	42·86	40·32	61·24	55·35	46·92	53·33	45·22	41·07	57·64	50·00	57·58
Nobs (independent)	306	384	112	315	387	112	130	135	387	56	432	270	99
Significance level	0·10 (C)	n.a.	n.a.	n.a.	0·00 (C)	12·85	n.a.	21·94	n.a.	n.a.	0·07 (C)	n.a.	6·58 (A)
Nobs (half dep.)	153	192	56	158	194	56	65	68	194	28	216	135	50
Significance level	1·45 (B)	n.a.	n.a.	n.a.	0·09 (C)	21·14	n.a.	29·27	n.a.	n.a.	1·24 (B)	n.a.	14·44

Three-month	1	2	3	4	5	6	7	8	9	10	11	12	13
Percent correct	54·90	47·39	43·75	33·34	47·55	49·11	43·08	57·04	49·35	57·14	61·11	53·33	71·72
Nobs (independent)	306	384	112	315	387	112	130	135	387	56	432	270	99
Significance level	16·11	n.a.	n.a.	n.a.	n.a.	n.a.	n.a.	17·26	n.a.	27·22	0·38 (C)	26·35	0·63 (C)
Nobs (half dep.)	153	192	56	154	194	56	65	68	194	28	216	135	50
Significance level	24·20	n.a.	n.a.	n.a.	n.a.	n.a.	n.a.	25·46	n.a.	33·41	2·97 (B)	32·74	4·11 (B)

Six-month	1	2	3	4	5	6	7	8	9	10	11	12	13
Percent correct	46·47	39·94	38·39	37·58	43·93	50·89	47·20	61·11	52·30	58·93	63·12	60·15	62·22
Nobs (independent)	297	368	112	306	387	112	125	126	369	56	423	261	90
Significance level	n.a.	n.a.	n.a.	n.a.	n.a.	46·98	n.a.	15·43	35·95	29·61	1·41 (B)	9·15 (A)	17·19
Nobs (half dep.)	148	184	56	153	194	56	62	63	184	28	212	130	45
Significance level	n.a.	n.a.	n.a.	n.a.	n.a.	47·86	n.a.	24·11	40·04	36·05	6·03 (A)	17·60	25·89

12-month	1	2	3	4	5	6	7	8	9	10	11	12	13
Percent correct	37·45	49·39	16·07	34·44	31·83	50·00	47·37	65·28	52·78	50·00	68·03	60·87	63·89
Nobs (independent)	243	328	112	270	333	92	95	72	324	16	369	207	36
Significance level	n.a.	n.a.	n.a.	n.a.	n.a.	50·00	n.a.	22·71	38·64	50·00	1·96 (B)	18·50	31·52
Nobs (half dep.)	122	164	56	135	166	46	48	36	162	8	184	103	18
Significance level	n.a.	n.a.	n.a.	n.a.	n.a.	50·00	n.a.	29·83	42·06	50·00	7·23 (A)	26·93	39·06

n.a. = not applicable. Percent correct is below 50%.

Summary:	Significance level	Expected number of significant entries	Actual number (independent)	Actual number (half-dependent)
	10% (A)	5·2	9	7
	5% (B)	2·6	7	5
	1% (C)	0·5	5	1

---

and who can tolerate the risk associated with open positions, our results suggest that forecasts can help to improve exposure management performance.

3. The testing procedures are unfair to the advisory services. The forecasts of the different services are by nature different and not comparable. Clients realize that forecasts are not always up-to-date and they always phone for current advice. It is unrealistic to assume that clients always follow all advice and hold positions until maturity. Some positions will be liquidated early.

A user is forced to compare diverse forecasts. He is forced to extract information from a quarterly average forecast or an end-of-year forecast and make a decision today concerning his foreign exchange positions. The methods we have used do not introduce any obvious bias into the results.

We assume that the forecasts we have analysed constitute a representative sample of the forecasters advice on any day. The advice which is printed should be as good as the advice that is given over the phone. It may be the case that speculators follow a forecaster's advice on a three-month position and then reverse the position with one month remaining. The advice to reverse a position must be correct and timely (i.e. ahead of forward rate adjustments) if the reversal is to be profitable.

4. Advisory services hire and fire people and change their forecasting equations. Will an advisor's past track record be a helpful guide for the future?

We cannot know for sure. In the monkey example, the fact that one monkey tosses three straight heads does not improve the chances for tossing three more heads the next time out; the monkey still holds a fair coin. The foreign exchange forecasters in this study have compiled many good track records — for individual currencies (Exhibit 3.3.4), about the same number to be expected by chance, but when pooled across currencies for each service (Exhibit 3.3.5), too many high track records to be expected by chance.

One interpretation of the latter result is that forecasting expertise is an attribute of the advisory service — and therefore it should persist over time. The past may not be a good predictor of the future, but historic forecasts are all that we have available for concrete analysis. The efficient market hypothesis suggests that if forecasts convey useful information, speculators will purchase forecasts and use them until the information in the forecast is reflected in market prices, rendering the forecasts worthless. While these events may have been in process over the last several years, the data suggest that a significant number of forecasters were able to provide useful information concerning the position of the future spot exchange rate relative to today's forward rate.

4. Evaluating the performance of the technical analysts

Stephen Goodman

Two surveys, carried out from January 1976 to June 1978 and January 1976 to December 1979 (*Euromoney*, December 1978 and September 1980) on the potential contribution to foreign currency management by technical and econometric foreign exchange rate forecasting services, concluded that all the technical foreign exchange rate forecasting services did far better than any econometric service.

In updating this evaluation, through to December 1980, we examine three technical services with long track records and strong performance histories. They are Brian Marber's chartist forecasts; the Stoll Momentum System, and the technical services provided by Waldner & Co.

The results of one econometric-oriented service, Predex, the econometric service with the longest and best forecasting record, are also included to provide one standard for comparison. The Predex service is largely a planning and longer-term forecasting tool and should not be judged primarily in terms of data presented here, reflecting solely its contribution to an active foreign currency management programme. The relatively poor — albeit still positive — performance of this service is recognized by the Predex organization, and they are now also offering a technical service.

Return on capital at risk is the most relevant performance measure for a speculator, portfolio investor, or a multi-currency borrower, and it is the best single measure of overall forecasting performance. It is calculated assuming the user of a service blindly buys a currency three months forward (and closes any outstanding forward sale) whenever a service gives a buy signal, and sells a currency three months forward whenever the service gives a sell signal. If there is no change in signal during the three-month period of the contract, the contract is rolled over at maturity.

Return on selective hedging

Calculated in this manner — which explicitly recognizes each currency's forward premium or discount — return on capital at risk for the speculator or the investor is equal to the incremental return above the U.S. dollar interest rate on the total open position (the capital at risk) in a currency. The actual return on capital employed for the speculator would be substantially larger, depending on the margin requirement. It would be 20 times larger, for example, where there is a 5% margin requirement. For the multi-currency borrower, the return on capital at risk is equal to the savings compared with the case in which all borrowings are U.S. dollar denominated.

Return on selective hedging is probably the most relevant performance measure for a corporate treasurer who has some flexibility in managing his company's foreign currency exposure. It is calculated assuming, in the case where there is a natural short position, that the user simply buys the currency three months forward to the extent of his short position whenever a service gives a buy signal, but closes any outstanding forward purchase and remains uncovered whenever the service gives a sell signal. The return on selective hedging is simply equal to the sum of the return in following only a service's buy recommendations in the case of the natural short position (or only the service's sell recommendations in the case of the natural long position) and the return on the underlying short (or long) position.

The evaluation is undertaken on the basis of New York opening spot and forward exchange rates. It is assumed any action is taken at the prices on the trading day following the receipt of a definite signal from the forecasting service. In the case of Brian Marber's forecasts, the date assigned to a signal may be somewhat subjective as the recommended action may vary with the time frame and aggressiveness of the user.

Measures used in evaluating services

The return on capital at risk for the full period January 1977 to December 1980 using the three technical services, the arithmetic average for these services and the returns using Predex and following a passive buy-and-hold strategy are shown in Exhibit 3.4.1.

Users of the three technical services did remarkably well during the January 1977 to December 1980 period. The return on capital at risk following the services' buy and sell signals averaged, for the three services and six currencies, 12·1% annually before transactions cost. This compares with a 3·4% average annual return following a buy-and-hold strategy. An investor using the technical services to decide when to denominate an asset in a particular currency or in the U.S. dollar would have earned 20·6% annually during the period (the 12·1% average annual gain on the forward contracts — the incremental return — and the 8·5% average return on a risk-free U.S. dollar-denominated asset). A multi-currency borrower would have avoided an interest charge of over 10% annually in the case of U.S. dollar-denominated debt and, instead, would show significant interest earnings. The return on capital employed for a speculator using the technical services averaged a phenomenal 239% annually during the period, assuming a margin requirement of 5% and transactions costs of 0·5% per turnover. Following the technical services' recommendations would have led, however, to intermittent periods with considerable losses for some currencies, periods that might dishearten, if not bankrupt many individual speculators. The largest loss for any technical service or currency on a single buy or sell signal and its subsequent reversal was 2·4 times the initial 5% margin, and the largest stream of losses was 2·9 times the initial margin.

The overall results using each of the three services (and the four newer technical services, for which full results are not presented here) are quite similar, as are the results for each of the currencies individually except for the Swiss franc and to a lesser extent, sterling. The Stoll Momentum System offered the best overall performance for the full period with an average annual return on capital at risk of 14·1% including the Canadian dollar and French franc, and 17·2% excluding these currencies. To achieve these results required an average of only 4·4 turnovers or transactions in each currency annually.

Exhibit 3.4.1: Return on capital at risk, January 1977–December 1980

Currency	Brian Marber	Stoll Momentum System	Waldner & Co.	Arithmetic average† for technical	Predex	Buy and hold
				(% per annum)		
Canadian dollar	n.a.	5·3	6·6	6·0	−0·3	−4·0
transactions p.a.		4	8	6	3	—
French franc	n.a.	10·7	9·2	10·0	5·3	3·6
transactions p.a.		5	14	9	3	—
Deutschemark	14·6*	13·6	12·6	13·6	6·5	0·7
transactions p.a.	4	5	13	7	4	—
Yen	12·8*	18·5	17·6	16·3	−11·3	6·7
transactions p.a.	3	5	7	5	4	—
Swiss franc	16·0*	21·2	7·9	15·0	9·6	1·9
transactions p.a.	3	5	14	7	4	—
Sterling	12·5	15·4	8·4	12·1	2·9	11·6
transactions p.a.	4	4	10	6	5	—
Arithmetic average:						
All trans-	—	14·1	10·4	12·1	2·1	3·4
actions p.a.	3·3	4·4	11·0	6·7	3·6	—
Excluding Canadian						
and French	14·0	17·2	11·6	14·3	1·9	5·2

* From start of service, approximately January 1978, to December 1980 only.
† Arithmetic average represents vertical average.
  n.a. Indicates not available for a sufficiently long period to permit a meaningful comparative evaluation.

Results vary

A user following Brian Marber's buy and sell signals had an average annual return on capital at risk of 14·0% excluding the Canadian dollar and French franc (two currencies which this service did not forecast for a sufficiently long period to allow a meaningful comparison). A user of Waldner & Co. averaged a 10·4% annual return on capital at risk including the Canadian dollar and French franc, and 11·6% excluding these currencies. Waldner's overall results are hurt by a relatively weak performance for the French franc and, to a lesser extent, sterling.

Users of the Predex econometric service had a positive return on capital at risk during the January 1977 to December 1980 period — averaging 2·1% annually — but a return smaller than that realized by users of any of the technical services and below that obtained by following a passive buy-and-hold strategy. These findings are consistent with the results found in two independent studies which showed that on the average, econometric and judgmental forecasting services did not out-perform a passive buy-and-hold strategy, although some services, such as Predex, did show some predictive ability. In the case of one currency and one service (the Swiss franc and Waldner & Co.) the results using Predex were better than a technical service.

The technical services have the best average performance for the Japanese yen and the poorest performance for the Canadian dollar and, to a lesser extent, the French franc — currencies which are less volatile and prone to political sentiment. For each currency, including the Canadian dollar and French franc, however, the results using any of the technical services are superior to following a passive buy-and-hold strategy. Predex does poorly — with negative returns on capital at risk — for the Japanese yen and Canadian dollar, and yields a lower return than following a passive buy-and-hold strategy for the Japanese yen and sterling.

Users of the technical services did as well during 1980 as they had from January 1977 to December 1980 (Exhibit 3.4.2). The return on capital at risk following the services averaged 11·7% during the latest year, compared to a 12·1% return for the full period.

Exhibit 3.4.2: Return on capital at risk 1977 to 1980, compared with 1980 arithmetic average for technical services

Currency	Jan. 1977– Dec. 1980*	Jan. 1980– Dec. 1980
	(% per annum)	
Canadian dollar	6·0	0·8
French franc	10·0	15·1
Deutschemark	13·6	18·6
Yen	16·3	11·0
Swiss franc	15·0	15·2
Sterling	12·1	9·2
Arithmetic average: all	12·1	11·7
By service		
Brian Marber	14·0	9·7
Stoll Momentum System	14·1	11·3
Waldner & Co.	10·4	14·1

* Excludes Brian Marber for Canadian dollar and French franc. For Deutschemark, yen and Swiss franc, the Brian Marber data are from January 1978 to December 1980 only.

A comparable performance was achieved by these services during 1980 despite their wider acceptance and use and the entry of additional competing technical services. The contribution during 1980 of the technical services to a foreign currency management further undermines the sceptics who argue that exchange markets are efficient and that the technical services cannot remain consistently profitable.

Waldner & Co. had the best overall performance during 1980, offering an average return on capital at risk of 14·1%. A user of the Stoll Momentum System would have done almost as well, and a user following Brian Marber only slightly worse.

The return on selectively hedging a natural short position or a natural long position using the three technical services, the arithmetic average for these services, and the returns using Predex

Exhibit 3.4.3: Long or short return on selective hedging, January 1977–December 1980

Currency	Brian Marber	Stoll Momentum System	Waldner & Co.	Arithmetic average† for technical (% per annum)	Predex	Always cover
Natural short position						
Canadian dollar	n.a.	4·9	5·6	5·3	2·3	0·1
% of time buying		31	54	43	67	—
French franc	n.a.	4·4	4·2	4·3	2·8	1·1
% of time buying		52	59	56	65	—
Deutschemark	1·3	2·0	1·7	1·7	−0·8	−4·4
% of time buying	57	54	59	57	48	—
Yen	−2·2	3·2	2·8	1·3	−12·2	−2·7
% of time buying	26	59	63	49	57	—
Swiss franc	−2·3	2·5	−4·1	−1·3	−1·4	−7·2
% of time buying	58	55	48	54	36	—
Sterling	3·7	5·0	1·7	3·5	−0·8	3·1
% of time buying	71	69	58	66	48	—
Arithmetic average:						
All	—	3·7	2·0	2·5	−1·7	−1·7
% of time buying	53	53	57	54	54	—
Excluding Canadian and French	0·1	3·2	0·5	1·3	−3·8	−2·8
Natural long position						
Canadian dollar	n.a.	0·4	1·1	0·8	−2·5	−0·1
% of time selling		69	46	58	33	—
French franc	n.a.	6·3	4·9	5·6	2·5	−1·1
% of time selling		48	41	45	35	—
Deutschemark	13·2	11·6	10·9	11·9	7·3	4·4
% of time selling	43	46	41	43	52	—
Yen	15·0	15·4	14·8	15·1	0·9	2·7
% of time selling	74	41	37	51	43	—
Swiss franc	18·2	18·7	12·0	16·3	11·0	7·2
% of time selling	42	45	52	46	64	—
Sterling	8·9	10·4	6·7	8·7	3·7	−3·1
% of time selling	29	31	42	34	52	—
Arithmetic average:						
All	—	10·5	8·4	9·7	3·8	1·7
% of time selling	47	47	43	46	46	—
Excluding Canadian and French	13·8	14·0	11·1	13·0	5·7	2·8

and following a passive strategy of always covering a natural position are shown in Exhibit 3.4.3.

Naturally short

The corporate treasurer who, in a natural short position in the Canadian dollar, the major European currencies and the Japanese yen (and long the U.S. dollar) during the January 1977 to December 1980 period, had difficulty achieving a very profitable performance regardless of the service or strategy he chose to follow, which reflected the general weakening of the U.S. dollar against most major currencies during much of the period. He would have done much better, however, than the treasurer whose evaluation ended in 1979, because in that period (as shown in the September 1980 *Euromoney* article), it was extremely difficult to avoid an actual loss when starting from a natural short position, regardless of the forecasting service or strategy followed.

Return on selective hedging for technical users

The return on selective hedging for users of the three technical services when starting from a natural short position, averaged 2·5% annually for the six currencies during the full period. This return is made up of a 7·8% average annual cash gain on forward contracts in following the technical services the 54% of the time they recommended to cover a natural short position by buying a currency forward, and a 5·3% average annual loss on the underlying natural short position. It compares with a 1·7% average annual loss following a passive strategy of always covering (representing the average annual forward premium during the period) and a 1·7% average annual loss using Predex. The comparable results excluding the Canadian dollar and French franc are an average annual return of 1·3% for users of the technical services, an average annual loss of 2·8% for an always cover strategy, and an average annual loss of 3·8% using Predex.

For users starting from a natural short position, the Stoll Momentum System offered the best performance during the period, with an average annual return of 3·7%. Waldner & Co. offered the second-best performance and Brian Marber had the poorest performance of the technical services, but the returns on selectively hedging a natural short position using Marber were still far better than those achieved following a passive always cover strategy, or those using Predex.

Naturally long

The corporate treasurer who was naturally long in most major foreign currencies and short in the U.S. dollar during the full period was in the enviable position of showing positive results regardless of the service or strategy he used. The return on selective hedging for users of the technical services when starting from a natural long position, averaged 9·7% annually for the six currencies, made up of a 4·4% average annual gain on forward contracts the 46% of the time the services recommended to sell a currency and a 5·3% average annual gain on the underlying natural long position. The 9·7% average annual return for the three technical services compares with a 1·7% average annual gain following a passive always cover strategy and a 3·8% average annual gain following Predex.

The Stoll Momentum System again offered the best performance during the period with Brian Marber now second and Waldner & Co. third, but the returns on selective hedging using Waldner were still superior to those achieved following a passive strategy, or those achieved using Predex.

The performance evaluations have so far dealt only with the potential contribution of one or another foreign exchange rate forecasting service to a foreign currency management programme. They suggest that the speculator, the portfolio investor, the multi-currency borrower, and the corporate treasurer who is selectively hedging either a natural short or a natural long position, may wish to employ and actively rely on a technical foreign exchange rate forecasting service. But should the user subscribe to and rely on only one forecasting service, or should he hedge his forecasting bet and subscribe to a number of services on the grounds that the additional services may add incrementally to performance? Similarly, should he take advantage of the additional information the technical services often provide in terms of their confidence in the forecasts, information now generally not systematically used by most forecast consumers?

How to get the best results

The question is whether a substantially better performance can be achieved by combining the forecasts from more than one technical service or by using the additional information on forecast confidence that the services often provide.

Combining forecasts

The contribution of two technical services in combination, Brian Marber and the Stoll Momentum System, with different approaches to technical forecasting, are evaluated in terms of the time adjusted return on capital at risk and the annual return on capital at risk. It is assumed for both that the user buys a currency three months forward (and closes any outstanding forward sale) whenever a second service confirms a buy signal of the first, and sells a currency three months forward whenever the second service confirms a sell signal of the first. Whenever the signals of the two services are in conflict, it is assumed the user closes any outstanding forward contract and stays out of the market.

For the time-adjusted return on capital at risk, probably the most useful performance measure for a speculator and the best single measure of overall forecasting performance, the time the user is out of the market, is excluded from the evaluation and the returns for the in-market period are annualized. The actual return on capital employed for the speculator would be substantially larger — 20 times larger than the time-adjusted return where there is a 5% margin requirement. For the annual return on capital at risk, probably the most relevant performance measure for the portfolio investor or multi-currency borrower, the period the user is out of the market is included in the evaluation, but with a zero incremental return.

The time-adjusted and annual returns on capital at risk for the full period January 1977 to December 1980 using Brian Marber and the Stoll Momentum System in combination are shown in the second column of Exhibit 3.4.4. (Other service combinations were also evaluated with quite similar results, but the full findings are not presented here.) The results when using the Stoll Momentum System in isolation are included in the first column of Exhibit 3.4.4 to provide one standard for comparison.

Users that combined the forecasts of Brian Marber and the Stoll Momentum System did remarkably well. The time-adjusted return on capital at risk during the full period, excluding the Canadian dollar and French franc, averaged 19·6% annually before transactions costs; this compares with 17·2% average annual return using the Stoll Momentum System in isolation and a 5·2% average annual return for a passive buy-and-hold strategy. Equally significant, the risk ratio, the ratio of weekly returns to the standard deviation of the returns, was also substantially improved, increasing from 0·65 to 0·73. For each currency, the combined services outperformed the Stroll Momentum System in isolation, with the largest improvements for the Deutschemark and sterling.

On average, the two services agreed 80% of the time; thus, a user of the combined services was in the market 80% of the time and was out of the market the remaining 20% of the time. Including the period the user is out of the market in the evaluation, but with a zero incremental return, results in an average return on capital at risk for the combined services are below that for the Stoll Momentum System.

Forecast confidence

The Stoll Momentum System includes continuous data on the service's confidence in the forecasts. When the service has less confidence in a forecast, because the relative rates of change for the currency are approaching momentum levels that have historically been associated with turning points, the buy or sell signal will be accompanied by an explicit cover recommendation. Similar, albeit less specific, signals are generally provided by the other technical services to reflect their confidence in the forecasts.

The contribution of the additional information that the Stoll Momentum System includes in terms of the service's confidence in the forecasts is assessed in detail. The additional information on forecast confidence is evaluated in terms of both the time-adjusted return on capital at risk and the annual return on capital at risk. It is assumed for both measures that the user buys a currency three months forward (and closes any outstanding forward sale) whenever the service gives an uncovered buy signal, and sells a currency three months forward whenever the service gives an uncovered sell signal. Whenever the service gives a cover signal (which indicates less confidence in the forecast) it is assumed that the user closes any outstanding forward contract and stays out of the market. For the time-adjusted return on capital at risk, the time the user is out of the market is excluded from the evaluation; for the annual return on capital at risk this period is included in the evaluation, but with a zero incremental return.

The time-adjusted and annual returns on capital at risk for the full period January 1977 to December 1980, using the additional information that the Stoll Momentum System includes on forecast confidence, are shown in the third column of Exhibit 3.4.4. (Using the additional information that Brian Marber and Waldner & Co. also provide on their confidence in the forecasts yields similar, though smaller, improvements in performance, but the full findings are not presented here.) The results of using the forecast confidence information for the Stoll Momentum System in combination with the forecasts of Brian Marber are shown in the fourth column of Exhibit 3.4.4.

Users who took advantage of the forecast confidence information for the Stoll Momentum System had spectacular results. The time-adjusted return on capital at risk averaged 22·2%

Exhibit 3.4.4: Time-adjusted return on capital at risk, January 1977–December 1980

Currency	Stoll Momentum System	Brian Marber & Stoll Momentum	Stoll confidence-adjusted	Marber & Stoll confidence-adjusted
		(% per annum)		
Canadian dollar	5·3	n.a.	8·0	n.a.
% in market	100		80	
risk ratio	0·6		0·7	
annual return	5·3		6·4	
French franc	10·7	n.a.	19·3	n.a.
% in market	100		56	
risk ratio	0·6		0·9	
annual return	10·7		10·7	
Deutschemark	13·6	16·0	21·1	23·7
% in markct	100	84	73	66
risk ratio	0·7	0·8	0·8	0·9
annual return	13·6	13·5	15·4	15·5
Yen	18·5	20·7	29·6	31·2
% in market	100	77	78	62
risk ratio	0·6	0·7	0·8	1·0
annual return	18·5	15·9	23·0	19·4
Swiss franc	21·2	23·3	30·9	31·4
% in market	100	83	68	59
risk ratio	0·7	0·7	0·8	0·8
annual return	21·2	19·4	20·9	18·6
Sterling	15·4	18·5	24·5	25·9
% in market	100	76	60	47
risk ratio	0·7	0·7	0·9	0·9
annual return	15·4	14·0	14·7	12·0
Arithmetic average:				
All:	14·1	—	22·2	—
% in market	100	80	69	58
risk ratio	0·65	0·73	0·82	0·93
annual return	14·1	—	15·2	—
Excluding Canadian and French	17·2	19·6	26·5	28·1

annually during the January 1977 to December 1980 period including the Canadian dollar and French franc; this compares with a 14·1% average annual return using the Stoll Momentum System without taking account of the cover signals, and a 3·4% average annual return for a passive buy–and–hold strategy. The risk ratio also improved substantially, increasing from 0·65 to 0·82. Using the forecast confidence information substantially improved the results for every currency.

The Stoll Momentum System on the average provided forecasts in which the service had confidence 69% of the time; thus a user who took advantage of this additional information was in the market 69% of the time and out of the market the remaining 31% of the time. Including the period the user is out of the market in the evaluation results in an average annual return on capital at risk of 15·2%, which is still above the comparable return when using the Stoll Momentum System without taking account of the additional information. The results using the forecast confidence information were superior, as measured by the annual return on capital at risk, for the Canadian dollar, Deutschemark and Japanese yen, and inferior for the Swiss franc and sterling.

The results using the forecast confidence information for the Stoll Momentum System in combination with the forecasts of Brian Marber are even more spectacular. The time-adjusted return on capital at risk averages 28·1% annually during the full period excluding the Canadian dollar and French franc. The user of the confidence-adjusted Stoll Momentum System forecasts in combination with the forecasts of Brian Marber was in the market only 58% of the time, however. He was out of the market the 42% of the time either the signals of the two services were in conflict or the Stoll Momentum System gave a cover signal. Including the period the user is out of the market in the evaluation results in an average annual return on capital at risk which is below that achieved using the forecast confidence information for the Stoll Momentum System but without combining services.

The results confirm again the substantial contribution the technical foreign exchange rates forecasting services can make to foreign currency management. The three technical services assessed in detail and the newer technical services, for which full results are not presented, all allow the user to do remarkably well. The results using these services were far superior to those achieved following any passive or naive strategy or following the recommendations of the Predex econometric service. Moreover, the evaluations indicate even stronger performance can be achieved by combining the forecasts from more than one technical service.

To exploit fully the forecasts provided by the technical services, particularly the potentially more rewarding composite forecasts generated by combining services and the forecasts derived using the additional information on forecast confidence, requires a systematic analytical framework. One such framework, derived in part from modern portfolio theory, would explicitly recognize that it may be appropriate to buy or sell forward a particular currency in one period with one set of forecasts and confidences, while in other periods it may be appropriate to stay out of the market for that currency and seek to achieve nearly the same foreign currency management objectives working through a combination of other currencies. This portfolio approach to forecasting and to foreign currency management is the subject of further research still in progress — research with extremely promising initial results.

5. Corporate uses of forecasts

Jeffrey C. Donahue

While there is considerable debate over whether foreign exchange rates can be accurately projected either econometrically or judgementally, most companies engaged in overseas business have a need for forecasts. The use of forecasts underscores an awareness that foreign exchange gains and losses are an essential element of doing business abroad which directly impact a company's earnings, cash flow and equity and which therefore must be factored into the expected rate of return on foreign business as opposed to domestic business.

Some companies, however, continue to avoid the complexities of foreign exchange forecasting, usually under the rationale of, "We're in the business of manufacturing and exporting widgets and not of buying and selling foreign currencies". Many of these companies instead often adopt policies of doing nothing, or of hedging all of their exposures all the time. While such policies may have merit under limited circumstances, most multinational companies have moved or are moving towards a more sophisticated approach to foreign exchange risk involving the use of foreign exchange forecasts.

Four distinct requirements for foreign exchange rate forecasts can be identified within a multinational corporation, each of which encompasses a different format and frequency of issue: strategic planning; budgeting; exposure management; and cash management. These requirements and types of forecasts are discussed below, using Multinational Company as an ideal hypothetical setting.

Strategic planning forecasts

Strategic foreign exchange forecasts are incorporated into Multinational's five-year international strategic plan. The plan, which is updated annually to include another year within its five-year horizon, delineates Multinational's international strategies, key strategic programmes, and financial objectives, all of which are undertaken within a foreign exchange environment. As part of its annual strategic plan review, Multinational therefore evaluates its existing overseas subsidiaries in the light of the projected foreign exchange outlook. For example, in order for Multinational to compensate for projected continuing exchange losses on a net asset position in a given foreign subsidiary, it may choose to adjust that subsidiary's pricing policy, product mix, asset and liability structure, or capital structure, or may even choose to withdraw from the country in question. The strategic foreign exchange forecasts are issued yearly just prior to Multinational's planning period, and are projections of average annual exchange rates for the following five years. The forecasts are based on both short- and long-run determinants of exchange rate movements and thereby consider a wide range of economic, financial, and political variables.

Budget forecasts

Budget foreign exchange forecasts are incorporated into Multinational's annual operating budgets for its overseas subsidiaries. The budgets encompass monthly projections of foreign subsidiary income and expenses, assets and liabilities, profit or loss, and other financial and operating factors. Although Multinational's foreign subsidiary management performance is evaluated in local currency terms, monitoring of actual versus budgeted performance in dollar terms is a critical component of effective management control. The budget foreign exchange forecasts are issued monthly, and are projections of end-of-month exchange rates for the following 12 months.

Exposure management forecasts

Multinational's exposure management foreign exchange forecasts are issued (and revised) quarterly, and are end-of-quarter projections for four quarters. Unlike the strategic and budget forecasts, the exposure management forecasts are formulated on a low/most likely/high basis, a

143

flexible format conducive to statistical analysis of the risk-return trade-off inherent in exposure management. The forecasts are presented to and reviewed by Multinational's corporate foreign exchange strategy committee, chaired by the vice-president, finance. Hedging and other risk-averting exposure management actions are based on the forecasts (which emphasize shorter-run determinants of exchange rate behaviour) in the light of hedge costs, projected operational results, taxes, and other exposure, income, and cash flow factors. The manager, international finance, co-ordinates the company's current exposure management strategy, subject to the weekly review of the foreign exchange strategy committee. Multinational's exposure management strategy fundamentally emphasizes exposure minimization through asset and liability management, but the impact of exchange fluctuations on occasion has generated the need for forward contracts and probably will continue to do so in the foreseeable future. Asset, liability, and capital adjustments undertaken as part of exposure management clearly overlap with those undertaken for strategic reasons.

Cash management forecasts

Multinational's foreign exchange forecasts for cash management purposes tend to be compatible with its exposure management forecasts in format and frequency of issue. However, management of the cash embodied in short-dated transactions, e.g. trade payables, dividends, royalties, and service fees, often requires considerably greater flexibility in responding to volatile currency movements than implied in a quarterly low/most likely/high forecast. Indeed, a very short-term trader's perspective of exchange rate movements is useful. In accordance with its policy of flexible aggressiveness, Multinational will pyramid forward contracts on top of transactions to protect cash flows. In this regard the protective strategy differs somewhat from that of exposure management, wherein the corporation tends to be in and out of the forward market less frequently. Multinational can also use domestic or Eurocurrency investments/borrowings to protect the cash embodied in transactions.

Dynamic forecasting

Principally because of differences in frequency of issue, the four types of forecasts are not always in agreement in terms of timing and magnitude of exchange rate movements; this is especially the case with the exposure and cash management forecasts against the other two. Some disagreement is inevitable and, given this constraint, Multinational recognizes that only the exposure and cash management forecasts have a truly dynamic nature. Since the company's international reporting systems are computerized, however, gains and losses can be reprojected with revised currency forecasts. Similarly, Multinational can project at any time its gains or losses on outstanding forward contracts and other protective measures. Special foreign exchange rate forecasts are also periodically needed, generally for use in new country market analysis or refinancing proposals.

Multinational's foreign exchange rate forecasts are prepared internally and are largely judgemental. The company also subscribes to an external foreign exchange counselling and forecasting service in order to enhance its perspectives on exchange rate trends and exposure management. It has reviewed econometric foreign exchange projections, but has not been comfortable with them because of the plethora of exchange-rate determining variables which cannot be readily econometrically specified (if at all) and which therefore detract from the accuracy of the econometric forecasts. However, it does find them to be useful benchmarks around which to hang its own judgemental forecasts. In discussing foreign exchange forecasts and exposure management strategies with its banks, Multinational benefits from their total immersion in the foreign exchange business.

Conclusions

Several important conclusions can be drawn from Multinational's experience in using foreign exchange rate forecasts. First, as noted above, a passive attitude towards foreign exchange matters is not consistent with an overall aggressive business philosophy, and, indeed, can prove expensive. Foreign exchange is a cost of doing business abroad which management should attempt to minimize (or conceivably turn into profit, depending on corporate policy) through something more than hedging all of its exposures all of the time. Accordingly, maintenance of an internal awareness of foreign exchange trends and prospects (possibly to include internal exchange rate forecasting) and management of foreign exchange exposures cannot be undertaken on a part-time basis. Foreign exchange exposure management, like any facet of business management, requires effective planning, implementation, and control which contributes to the company's ability to weather currency crises. Well-informed outside contacts and a high degree of feedback between staff and operational personnel in the international area also contribute to good exposure management.

6. Using currency forecasts at ICI

J. A. Donaldson

Most corporations are willing to accept that foreign exchange forecasting is a problem they could do without. Why, then, do companies which trade internationally find it so necessary to essay the virtually impossible despite the fact that there is a sophisticated market in which they can obtain full cover of their exposures? There are three areas of business on which exchange rate forecasting impacts. The first is the commercial area.

Contract currency

Depending on the nature of the business, this choice may have to be made either in isolation at the time of quotation or in negotiation at the time of contract. In some cases it may be dictated by market practice or, indeed, by precedent. Whether predetermined or freely selected, the currency of contract is a very material factor in the pricing equation.

To this end it is necessary that sales staff and buyers, involved in taking these decisions, are appropriately equipped to do so. Regardless of who is to manage the subsequent exposure it is essential that they understand the implications of their actions and have some ready means of evaluating the various options.

One possibility is to use the spot and forward exchange rates published daily. Even in today's extremely volatile market, these should be sufficiently up to date as far as rate information is concerned. There are two limitations. First, the use of forward market rates constrains negotiating flexibility; in a negotiation there is a need to probe and to respond when it appears that an advantage can be obtained. The negotiator who has a "feel" for the way in which exchange rates are likely to move, and the confidence and authority to act thereon, may be able to make a better deal for his company. Second, a similar advantage can be obtained if the negotiator has an understanding of how the exposure he is contemplating accepting will fit into his company's total transaction exposure position; the knowledge, for example, that a match is available may enable him to shade his price in a specific currency.

Accordingly, it makes sense to stimulate a regular dialogue between those accepting exposures and those managing them, since the company's exchange rate forecasts are relevant for both purposes. Constant communication will be impracticable, but the facility to consult on major items should not be difficult to arrange. This can be backed up by routine circulation of company forecasts that need not, and probably should not, be too specific; what is required is an indication of the trend and of the bracket within which the particular exchange rate is expected to lie within a given time scale.

Planning

Planning is the second business area on which the company's exchange rate forecasts will have a direct impact. They will do so for two main reasons. Central to any company's planning activity will be its long-term cash forecast which will almost certainly be prepared on a cash and profit reconciliation basis. The normal route is to estimate realizations, possibly by reference to some economic statistical forecast, and convert this to a profit on the basis of an assumed margin which can in turn be converted to cash flow. The degree of sophistication will vary. But the direct impact of exchange rate movements on imported raw materials and export sales is obvious; there may well also be a secondary impact if the movement is such as to encourage or discourage foreign competition in the domestic market, as textile companies have illustrated in recent years.

Planning is a long-term matter. For this purpose forecasts may be required for five years or more. While it might be argued that the long-term relationship between differential inflation rates, on the one hand, and exchange rate movements, on the other, would make such forecasts relatively more accurate, experience does not bear this out. In practice, U.K. companies would probably have been more successful in their planning over the past decade had they made the assumption that exchange rates would not move at all. This, however, must be seen in the

146

context that long-term movements in exchange rates of continental currencies have been much more logical. The solution seems to be to try to identify as realistically as possible the upside and downside potential and to plan within that framework, retaining the maximum flexibility to change strategy should the need arise.

The other area of planning for which exchange rate forecasts are required is in the evaluation of investment proposals. Rate movements can affect the capital cost of the investment itself but, more important, can completely alter the economics of the project in one or more of three circumstances: if the new plant is dependent on imported raw materials, manufactures a product which has to be sold overseas or, thirdly, competes with an imported product. Again, the only solution seems to be to have regard to the potential extremes. But this will not help greatly in evaluating competing projects which are subject to different exchange risks.

Exposure management

In exposure management, the third area in which forecasting is essential, the period for which forecasts have to be made is much less extended; how much depends on the particular exposure. The U.K.'s Exposure Draft 27 on accounting for foreign exchange transactions, although yet to be confirmed as a standard, has greatly clarified the position as regards translation exposure management. It has been generally accepted among Treasury staff for some time now that there is no economic exposure associated with self-financing overseas investments; the reflection of this view in the net investment concept adopted in ED 27 means that happily there will probably not now be a conflict between economic and accounting exposure. This means that long-term borrowings are the only translation exposures which will require positive management. There will be differing views on the approach to be taken. At one extreme, it will be argued that, having been matched against investments, they should be totally ignored. At the other, it will be argued that reduced cost is the only justification for foreign borrowings and that day-to-day management of the risk is necessary to minimize the all-up cost.

Straightforward transaction exposure management requires forecasting related to the nature of the transactions and the policy adopted in managing them. With the suspension of U.K. exchange control regulations, an opportunity for exploiting an ability to forecast very short-term exchange rate movements has now opened up in the third area of exposure management: liquidity management.

Surplus liquidity no longer has to be held solely in domestic sterling. It was advantageous to do so during 1980; equally it was unnecessarily expensive to borrow sterling, especially on a short-term basis. A U.K. company which had the courage to have all its short-term borrowings in 1980 denominated in Swiss francs would almost certainly have a negative funding cost in that year, and those who then cried for lower interest rates were suffering from self-inflicted wounds. However, in 1981 the position turned right round and there was a long period during which sterling was the cheapest currency to borrow. Thus, the risks in liquidity exposure management are large, so no company should attempt it unless it has a competent team which is in a position to monitor the open position at all times. But with competent forecasting and the careful use of portfolio theory the risks can be contained and the rewards found can be prodigious.

7. A multinational's approach to forecasting and forecasters

Richard Hunt

It is widely accepted that the foreign exchange market acts irrationally and unpredictably, and that it conducts flirtatious affairs with certain published data. Most of the market activists who, in the autumn of 1981, made solemn pronouncements about the importance of the Fed funds' rate had no idea in the summer of that year that such a rate existed — let alone what it was. Another example is market reaction to money supply figures. In the past, if the United States published figures indicating a growth in money supply, it was interpreted as bad news for the dollar, a forewarning of inflation, and accordingly a few points were docked off dollar trading levels. Today, a growing money supply has an immediately beneficial effect on the exchange rate, the rationale being that interest rates will remain high, in an attempt to control the money supply. The high yields will create a demand for dollars from investors looking for a home for surplus funds.

Any economist could refute this, but fundamental economic thinking is far removed from the marketplace, where the rules are different. The market has to be seen as it is, rather than how we should like it to be, or even how we think it should be.

So, how should a multinational, which by definition is already in the foreign exchange market, set about protecting itself from losses caused by market fluctuations?

The centralization of all aspects of foreign exchange seems a necessary starting point, and London because of its geographic location is an ideal place. London is the largest and most sophisticated market and from London it is possible to trade in all markets, from the Far East to the West Coast of the United States. In terms of transaction exposure all subsidiary companies with foreign currency commitments that might produce a net income effect should provide a monthly statement broken down by currency. When consolidated, this produces the net worldwide transaction exposure of the corporation. Larger subsidiaries might be required also to produce a forecast position for one month out, making it possible to trade the position in advance. Smaller subsidiaries might only be required to produce such data quarterly. For economic exposure, every contract under negotiation should be reviewed before it is signed to determine the potential foreign currency exposure, and a system devised that permits regular reviews of this exposure in the light of exchange rate movements.

Having determined the exposure, what protective approach should be adopted? Not all currency exposure can be protected in the foreign exchange market because forward markets do not exist for certain Middle Eastern or South American currencies. In other instances cover is available but at prohibitive cost. Mexico is a good example of this with cover costs for the company with a natural long position against the dollar at 60%. Only if the peso devalues by more than 60% over a year is cover a sound proposition. The forecast inflation rate differential for 1982 between Mexico (50%) and the United States (7%) is only ·43%, so it is least disadvantageous to remain exposed.

Any approach to forecasting exchange rates must recognize the different time horizons, and the differing skills available within these horizons. For example, a chartist is not the person to ask about likely exchange rates in 1985 — although he might have an opinion. And avoid an economist if next Monday's dollar/sterling spot rate is required.

There are three time horizons:

— Long-term (over one year): to provide the overall perspective of the major currencies from an economic standpoint.
— Medium-term (three to 12 months): to formulate, from the long term, foreign exchange and interest-rate strategies for exposure management.
— Short-term (less than three months): to take advantage of the peaks and troughs occasioned by unforeseeable events which cause temporary aberrations in exchange rate direction.

Long term

In the long run, the economic performance of any country will be reflected in the exchange rate. Any company considering a long-term borrowing in Deutschemarks, for instance, should consider the future performance of the German economy. In fact, any long-term commitment in a foreign country needs continual review by fundamental economic analysis. For example, it may be considered unwise to be short of Deutschemarks during 1982/83, because that currency will probably strengthen against the dollar as the large German current account deficit reduces, whereas the U.S. balance is expected to swing into deficit. But should cover be effected now or later? In most currencies, it is not easy to trade forward beyond 12 months.

An economist independent of banking loyalties is likely to provide a dispassionate long-term view of economic and political trends and projections. Bank economists are likely to be more market oriented.

Medium term

Within our London treasury team, the medium term is the time-frame in which most corporations trade, particularly those with balance sheet exposures. Economic forecasts will be matched against published data and interpreted into exchange rate forecasts. Certain economic prognostications will have been either accelerated or postponed, but this need not necessarily change the long-term view, although it might if there has been an unexpected change of government.

To predict accurately a specific exchange rate for a specific day is virtually impossible. It is pure luck to forecast, to within a few points, the dollar/sterling spot rate for one year out — although a trend may be discerned.

Within Occidental's London treasury team we run a fun competition each year in which forecasts are required, on October 1, of the dollar/sterling spot rate at December 31. This competition has been won once by our insurance manager who claims to know nothing about foreign exchange beyond his annual trip to the bank for his foreign holiday requirements, and on other occasions by a secretary. The secretary displaying the most consistent accuracy over the years has always taken the October 1 spot rate as her year-end number. And on one occasion our treasurer came a close second; instead of being sophisticated, he took as his forecast the December 31 outright forward rate as quoted on October 1.

Medium-term forecasting results in an abundance of literature, much of it from the banks. To read it all is impractical; but to read differing opinions maintains a balanced viewpoint. Forecasting services also produce regular publications, with exchange rate forecasts for regular market trading periods or quarter ends.

The emphasis should be on market analysis, developments and interpretative commentary. These opinions can then be used to test in-house ideas on trading opportunities and exposure management.

Short term

In the short-term period (up to 90 days) data can be provided by selected bankers, technical analysts, and traders — both those who run their operation in the traditional "seat of the pants" way, and those who trade their rooms on chartist information. Together with a dash of gut feel, this should hopefully allow some advantages to be taken of market activity resulting from the unpredictable events which cause a temporary contradiction to the exchange rate direction indicated by the previously considered data. Trading strategies should take into account loss-limiting and profit-taking targets, to prevent a position running out of control. Such targets can be flexible and should be under constant revision.

Conclusion

Each forecaster should be used in his most effective time period. Do not expect an economist to excel when asked if a position should be traded now or after lunch. Even a trader will not always give the right answer but his market experience should give him a head start. To trade or not to trade rests in the final analysis with the corporation. All forecasters and advisers should be viewed simply as assistants in a decision; their expertise and knowledge can never be a blind substitute for corporate decision-making. Corporate foreign exchange policy should be determined at senior corporate level, after close consultation with forecasters, because market conditions change rapidly and policies may need revision in the light of such changes.

8. Bank uses of forecasts

Gary Schlossberg

The squeeze on lending spreads and heightened volatility in world financial and foreign exchange markets have prompted Euro-banks to focus more heavily on liability management to maintain loan profitability. By September 1981, syndicated lending terms still were nearly 60% below their level of early 1976, according to *Euromoney*'s index of market conditions. Moreover, spreads on loans to top-quality borrowers continue to fall short of the return needed to increase banks' capital/asset ratios. At the same time, monthly fluctuations of several percentage points in Eurodollar interest rates are no longer uncommon, and the U.S. currency continues to respond with large swings in the foreign exchange markets. In dealing with this environment, Euro-banks can generate funding income in several ways. They include (1) a mismatching of asset/liability maturities, (2) a mismatching of currencies, (3) a shift toward lower-cost Euro-CDs in loan financing, and (4) a shift to funding sources in the U.S., where domestic interest rates generally have been below inter-bank rates in the Eurodollar market since the spring of 1980.

Maturity and currency mismatching

Given the recent volatility in financial and currency markets, and the historically large spread between dollar and most non-dollar interest rates, maturity and currency mismatching offer, perhaps, the greatest opportunities for funding gains (and losses) in the Euro-markets. Banks generally attempt to match funding maturities with Euro-loan rollover periods (normally three or six months), particularly during periods of interest rate instability. But as financial intermediaries, banks normally borrow short and lend long on a net basis, transforming short-term deposits into longer-term loans (thereby creating liquidity in the process). The extent to which banks short fund depends on interest rate movements. Banks will seek to stretch the average maturity of net liabilities if interest rates are expected to move higher, thereby locking in at current yields before their borrowing costs increase. On the other hand, the average maturity of net liabilities will be shortened if interest rates are expected to move lower, permitting banks greater flexibility in reducing funding costs as rates decline.

How Euro-banks have adjusted their short-funding to interest rate movements is illustrated in Exhibit 3.8.1. The line graph plots movements in the three-month Eurodollar rate between January 1978 and November 1981, using the left scale. Short funding, defined here as net Euro-liabilities of less than three months as a percent of total Euro-claims, is plotted through August 1981 as a bar chart using the right scale. The liability data published by the Bank of England cover only London-based Euro-banks.

The Exhibit shows that, as expected, changes in the degree of short-funding generally have varied inversely with movements in Eurodollar rates, particularly since early 1979. For example, the drop in interest rates during the first half of 1979 was accompanied by an increase in short funding between February and May of that year. And rising interest rates during the second half of 1979 coincided with a fairly sizeable drop in the share of net short-term liabilities among Euro-banks between May and November. A somewhat similar, though less pronounced pattern seems to have developed over the course of 1980 and early 1981. However, it does appear that changes in Euro-banks' short-term liabilities often lag, rather than lead, major swings in interest rates. Unfortunately, the sensitivity of short-funding adjustments to interest rate changes is difficult to measure accurately because bank liability data are available only quarterly. But if Euro-banks have been slow in reacting to interest rate swings, then this limits the potential funding gains from sudden interest rate declines, or it leaves banks vulnerable to a sudden run-up of rates.

Large interest rate differences and the dollar's recovery in the foreign exchange markets also have increased the scope for currency mismatching. By borrowing relatively low-cost Deutschemarks and Swiss francs, for example, banks can earn funding profits amounting to several percentage points if these liabilities are converted into higher-yielding dollar assets. During 1977–80, for example, yields on three-month Eurodollars averaged nearly 450 basis points higher than rates on Euro-DM deposits of comparable maturity. Currency mismatching was not attractive through much of 1977–78, when banks would have risked substantial capital losses as the dollar steadily declined in the currency markets. However, the dollar's firming trend since that time has provided Euro-banks with the opportunity to expand substantially their net liabilities in Euro-marks and Euro-Swiss francs since mid-1979. Net Euro-mark and

Exhibit 3.8.1: Short funding and the interest rate cycle in the London Euro-market

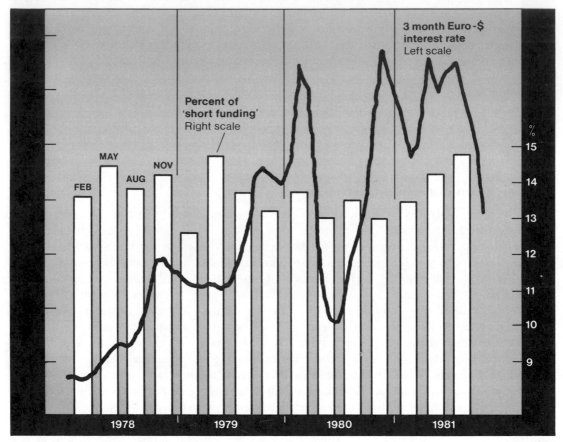

[1] Net Euro-liabilities of less than three months as a percent of total Euro-claims.
Source. Bank of England, *Quarterly Bulletin*; Data Resources, Inc.

Exhibit 3.8.2: Euro-banks' net positions in Deutschemarks and Swiss francs, and indicators of currency-mismatching profitability

	Net assets (+)/liabilities (−) of Euro-banks		Six-month % change against the dollar[1]		Three-month Euro-interest rates[2]		
	Deutsche-marks	Swiss francs	Deutsche-marks	Swiss francs	Deutsche-marks	Swiss francs	U.S. dollars
	($ billion)				(%)		
1977 June	+1·3	+1·1	1·0	−0·4	4·45	2·90	5·45
Dec	+1·7	+0·9	11·1	23·0	3·93	2·58	6·77
1978 June	+2·2	−1·1	1·4	7·6	3·32	0·99	7·68
Dec.	+4·3	0·0	13·5	14·7	3·64	0·74	10·01
1979 June	+0·2	−0·8	−1·1	−2·5	4·89	0·87	10·87
Dec.	−3·5	−2·0	6·7	5·1	7·88	2·96	13·32
1980 June	−3·2	−3·0	−1·5	−2·6	9·25	6·09	14·63
Dec.	−2·4	−2·0	−10·3	−7·9	9·10	5·78	13·74
1981 June	+5·5	−4·0	−17·2	−13·9	11·90	8·43	17·39

[1] End of period compared to end of period six months earlier.
[2] Six-month average ending in the month indicated in Exhibit.
Source. BIS, *International Banking Developments*.

Swiss franc balances among banks in the European sector of the market did shift from a net asset to a net liability position in 1979 — about the time that the dollar was strengthening in the currency markets (see Exhibit 3.8.2). Foreign branches of German banks accounted for much of the shift, indicating that a portion of these funds may also have been used to fund domestic lending in Germany. (Something similar also may have happened in Switzerland.) But the timing of the increase in net DM and Swiss franc liabilities suggests that a portion of the increase may have been converted for use in making Eurodollar loans as well. In fact, the dollar's appreciation during much of the past two years has also provided banks engaged in currency mismatching with potential capital gains as the deposits mature.

The growing use of Euro-CDs

Even if Euro-banks wish to minimize maturity and currency mismatching, profitability can be bolstered by issuing Euro-certificates of deposit (Euro-CDs) and by borrowing in the U.S. money markets. Because they are negotiable, interest rates on Euro-CDs are lower than rates on Eurodollar time deposits — the principal funding instrument in the Euro-market and the base lending rate for most Euro-loans. Those larger banks capable of issuing Euro-CDs can fix rates below those on time deposits because the secondary CD market provides the investor with a more liquid investment (permitting liquidation before maturity) and with potential capital gains should interest rates decline. During the 12 months ending November 1981, the interest rate spread between three-month Eurodollar deposits and Euro-CDs of a similar maturity ranged from 27 basis points (in November 1980) to nearly 80 basis points (in October 1981), averaging about 50 basis points during the period.

Euro-CD issuance by London-based banks has picked up considerably since December 1980. After ranging from $44–50 billion in 1980, outstanding Euro-CDs jumped to $74 billion by November 1981. This increase boosted their share of total Euro-liabilities in the London market from less than 11% at the start of the year to a peak of over 13½% in August — the highest percentage since the Bank of England began publishing the data regularly in January 1977. Two factors which may have accounted for much of the rise were (a) interest arbitrage opportunities between relatively low-cost Euro-CDs and the returns on inter-bank deposits, and (b) the surge in Libor-based borrowing by U.S. corporations throughout 1981.

Encouraged by stepped-up merger and acquisition activity in the U.S. and by an attractively large spread between the higher U.S. prime rate and Libor, lending by U.S. bank's foreign branches to U.S. entities peaked at $13 billion in late November 1981. This was triple the outstandings as of the end of 1980. As indicated in Exhibit 3.8.2, U.S. banks were encouraged to fund a portion of this increase with Euro-CDs, because interest rates on these liabilities (which are not subject to U.S. reserve requirements if the funds are used offshore) have been below effective (reserve-adjusted) interest rates on CDs issued in the U.S. The two previous jumps in Euro-CD issuance, during July–November 1979 and January–March 1980, were also accompanied by strong U.S. loan demand. But in each of those instances, the Euro-CDs issued by U.S. banks were used to fund domestic lending, partly because U.S. corporate loan demand remained at home.

Exhibit 3.8.3: Euro–CD issuance and selected Euro–bank funding costs

| | Euro-dollar CDs | | Interest rates | | | |
| | | | | | Three-month effective CDs[1] | |
	Amount	% of total Euro-liabilities	Three-month Euro-CDs	Three-month Euro-deposits	Domestic	Eurodollar
	($ bn)				(%)	
Dec. 1979	43·3	11·7	14·36	14·68	14·68	15·68
Dec. 1980	49·0	10·8	19·16	19·54	19·57	20·00
Mar. 1981	55·8	11·2	15·02	15·54	15·14	15·68
June 1981	66·1	13·0	17·49	18·00	17·87	18·26
Sept. 1981	69·7	13·2	17·31	17·92	17·64	18·05
Nov. 1981	74·0	13·3	12·91	13·56	13·18	13·46

[1] Assumes (a) a 0·5% FDIC premium and (b) a reserve requirement of 8% in December 1979, 3·75% during December 1980 to August 1981, and 3·625% beginning September 1981.

Funding at home vs. funding abroad

Although relatively low Euro–CD rates have encouraged foreign branches of U.S. banks to fund a portion of their Euro-lending offshore, funding from sources in the U.S. offers an important means of bolstering Euro-profitability as well. The inter–bank Eurodollar market still represents the principal funding vehicle for banks wishing to finance loans offshore, but the domestic CD market provides an important alternative when Euro-interest rates move above effective borrowing costs in the United States. As indicated in Exhibit 3.8.4, foreign branches of U.S. banks usually increase net borrowing from (or reduce net lending to) their U.S. parents when Eurodollar deposit rates rise above borrowing costs in the U.S. Those branches shifted from a position as a net lender to a net borrower of funds from their U.S. parents in the second quarter of 1980, when the effective rate on domestic CDs moved below Eurodollar interest rates. Such liabilities increased $6 billion, or 45%, in the first four months of 1981, before declining through August in response to a squeeze on Euro vs. domestic interest rate spreads.

Exhibit 3.8.4: Borrowing costs and the flow of funds between U.S. banks and their foreign branches

Interest rate difference between three-month Eurodollar deposits and effective three-month CDs in the U.S.

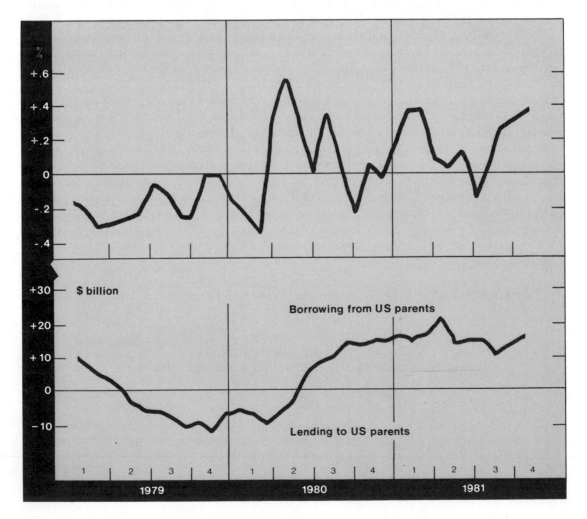

154

9. Use of forecasts in constructing a portfolio

John F. O. Bilson★

The currency management programme discussed in this section is not for the FX manager who, because of personal preferences or corporate policy, is constrained to hedge all foreign cash flows. Nor is it intended for those whose self-esteem is of a sufficient magnitude to justify open FX positions independently of professional advice. It is, however, for those managers who believe that a properly managed FX exposure programme may be both a source of profit and a method of diversifying risk from other operations. This audience will recognize that the creation and continuation of the programme is a difficult and expensive activity.

It is useful to think of the management programme as a machine which converts inputs of information into an output of positions in forward or futures markets. The informational inputs include the initial exposures, a set of forecasts, and an estimate of the co-variance matrix of the forecast errors. The co-variance matrix embodies both an estimate of the probable size of the forecast error for each currency and a measure of the correlation between the forecast errors. Given the corporation's tolerance for risk and desire for return, this information set determines a unique position in the forward exchange market. The problem, then, is to build the machine which creates this unique position from the set of informational inputs.

The construction is a two-stage process. In the first stage, the available forecasts are evaluated and a composite or consensus forecast is created. In addition, the variance of the forecast errors and the correlations between the forecast errors are estimated. It is then possible to estimate the risk and return associated with the addition of a particular forward position to the existing portfolio. In the second stage, the optimal portfolio of open positions is estimated. In estimating the optimal portfolio, it is important to take account of transactions costs. Portfolio management programmes which ignore transactions costs are liable to take extreme spread positions with whip-saw trading patterns.

Evaluating the forecasts

Early attempts at the evaluation of forecasting services typically relied on a horserace approach in which each forecast was compared with the market forecast embodied in the forward rate.[1] The evaluation procedures employed by Levich and Goodman are appropriate if the purpose of the evaluation is to choose the one best service for foreign exchange forecasting. The problem with the approach is that most FX managers do not want to rely on one service and, from the perspective of financial theory, they are correct in this preference.

A perspective from portfolio theory may be appropriate here. If a brokerage house touted an investment system in which they picked the best stock each quarter and invested all of the funds under management in that stock, they would be laughed out of the market for ignoring the benefits of diversification. At the other end of the scale, there are a number of index funds which buy a wide range of stocks so that the return approximates the return on the market. When we construct the portfolio of forecasts, should we choose the one best service, or should we choose an index fund of forecasts? The evidence appears to suggest that the index fund approach is likely to be both safer and more profitable than the best-service approach.

On the basis of an evaluation of the forecasts of Brian Marber and the Stoll Momentum System for four currencies — Deutschemark, yen, Swiss franc and sterling — over the period

★ I am grateful to Dr. Charles Ramond of Predex Corporation for providing me with the data used in this study. The views expressed are solely the responsibility of the author and are not necessarily the views of the sponsoring organizations. Phillipe Jorion helped to develop the computer programmes used in the simulations.

[1] In section 3 of this chapter, the evaluation statistics include the mean absolute error ratio — the mean absolute error of the forecast divided by the mean absolute error of the forward rate — and the per cent correct statistic — the per cent of the trials in which the service predicted the correct open position. In section 4, the preferred statistic was the return on capital at risk from blindly following the advice of a particular service.

155

from January 1977 to December 1980, Goodman estimated the following returns on capital at risk for the individual services and some combinations.

Service	Return	Risk
	(% p.a.)	
Marber	14·0	n.a.
Stoll Momentum	17·2	0·65
Stoll Momentum (confidence-adjusted)	26·5	0·82
Marber and Stoll Momentum (confidence-adjusted)	28·1	0·93

A manager following Brian Marber's buy/sell signals blindly would have made a return on capital of 14% per annum over the sample period. The Stoll System provides both buy/sell signals and confidence-adjusted buy/sell signals which allow for the manager to be out of the market in periods of low confidence. The confidence-adjusted system, a combination of two inputs, offers a return which is higher than the simple system and a more preferable risk ratio. However, one can do even better by trading only when both the Marber and the Stoll Momentum System with confidence adjustment agree with each other. The combined system offers an *ex post* return of 28·1% per year and a risk ratio of 0·93.

Another simple form of composite forecasting involves the use of econometric forecasts to "confirm" technical or judgemental forecasts. The Technecon forecast marketed by Predex Corporation (see also section 3) and the combined forecasts provided by David Morrison (see Chapter 2.6) are examples of this approach. In the Predex Technecon approach, a buy/sell signal is generated on a daily basis by a momentum model, but the signal is only acted upon if it is confirmed by the Predex short-term econometric forecast. The return on capital at risk and the value of the largest loss as a percentage of the dollar value of the contract are statistics that may be used to evaluate the incremental return from the confirmed signals. These statistics are based upon the operation of the Technecon system over the period from July 1980 to March 1982.

Currency	Technical	Technecon
Yen — return (% p.a.)	17·81	12·29
— loss (%)	3·68	3·68
Deutschemark — return (% p.a.)	10·34	17·96
— loss (%)	5·97	2·76
Sterling — return (% p.a.)	4·73	8·83
— loss (%)	9·37	9·37
Can $ — return (% p.a.)	−2·42	−0·88
— loss (%)	6·73	5·00
Average — return (% p.a.)	7·61	9·52
— loss (%)	6·43	5·20

Source. Predex Technecon Forecast, March 1982.

Although these results are not as decisive as those reported by Goodman, they do suggest that the confirmed forecasts generally offer both a higher rate of return and a smaller maximum loss than the technical system by itself. A currency manager would have been unambiguously better off in terms of both risk and reward if he or she had employed the confirmed forecast in three of the four currencies studied. It is only in the case of the yen that the pure technical system had a superior rate of return.

While the results reported by Goodman and Predex Corporation suggest that combined forecasts are superior to individual forecasts, the extent of the use of combined forecasts in these exercises is very limited. There are two approaches to a more general composite forecast. The first, which is close to the index fund approach in finance theory, is simply to take an unweighted average of all available forecasts in order to arrive at a composite. Although this approach may be correct when there are a large number of assets available in the market, it will generally not be correct when one has only a small number of services to choose between and when some information is available about the forecasting expertise of the different services. Hence, in setting up our composite forecast, we adopt a modified portfolio approach: an attempt is made to include a variety of different forecasts, but the weights in the portfolio are chosen on the basis of an evaluation of past forecasting performance.

Before proceeding to the construction of the composite, it is useful to begin with a description of the types of forecasts that should be considered in the analysis. At the present time, there are five different types of forecasts available in the market. These are:

1. Forward exchange rates: the favourite son of the efficient market men.
2. Spot exchange rates: included for the benefit of random walkers.
3. Technical or momentum forecasts: chartists, technicians, and others who use past prices to predict future prices.
4. Econometric or fundamental forecasts: economic models relating prices to underlying economic variables.
5. Judgemental forecasts: informal synthesis of all of the above.

The five types of forecast should be considered as the industries in the forecasting economy. Within each industry, there are a number of firms producing a similar product. The degree of similarity in the product depends to a great extent on the consensus on the techniques. It appears, for example, that technical forecasters have arrived at a similar set of technical forecasting techniques. Goodman reports, for example, that Marber and Stoll Momentum System agree in their buy/sell signals approximately 80% of the time. Within the econometric and judgemental categories, on the other hand, there is likely to be a greater diversity of technique and opinion. These considerations are important in the selection of the composite forecast, since they suggest that one or two technical services may be sufficient to represent that industry whereas a a larger number of econometric or judgemental services should be considered.

The forward and spot exchange rates are themselves included in the forecasting portfolio. The aim of the composite forecast is to find the best forecast of the future spot rate and any help that may be garnered from current market prices is welcome. This philosophy is quite different from the horse-race methodology in which the forecasts are compared with the forward rate, and the results of the evaluation are often quite different.[2] A forecast may do well in combination with the forward and spot rates when it does badly in a one-on-one confrontation with the forward rate. The spot rates are included because of the recent evidence that exchange rates do tend to evolve as a random walk.[3] If the spot rate does follow a random walk, the best forecast of any future spot rate is the current spot rate.

The first step in the evaluation is to collect as many of the past forecasts as are available. This is both a frustrating and time-consuming process. Although all forecasting services have the same objective, there is very little consistency in the information provided by them. Forecasts may be the end of period or period averages, point forecasts or buy/sell signals, they may be delivered daily by telex or monthly through the mail. It is, in fact, the difficulty involved in creating a set of comparable forecasts which is the main barrier to the more widespread use of composite forecasts. However, if some government commission required all forecasting services to provide a set of forecasts at the end of each month which applied to the end of the next month, a consensus on the appropriate value for the exchange rate would rapidly appear.

In the absence of this revolutionary step, the advantage of the Predex forecasts is that they do provide both an econometric and a technical forecast and that these forecasts are provided at the end of each month for a reasonable period of time. The econometric forecasts are taken from the published bulletins of the Corporation, while the technical forecasts are based upon a system implemented in July 1980.

---

[2] For evidence on this point, see John F. O. Bilson, "The Evaluation and Use of Foreign Exchange Forecasting Services," in Richard J. Herring (ed.), *Managing Foreign Exchange Risk*, Cambridge University Press, forthcoming.

[3] Evidence on the importance of the spot rate as a forecast of the future spot rate is presented in John F. O. Bilson, "The 'Speculative Efficiency' Hypothesis" *Journal of Business*, July 1981.

The technical system used by Predex is a variation of the momentum/oscillator model: when a short-term moving average crosses a longer-term moving average from below, a buy signal is generated. When the short term crosses the longer term from above, a sell signal is generated.[4] These buy/sell signals are transmitted to clients on the day the signal is generated. The econometric forecasts, in contrast, are end-of-period point estimates generated at the end of each month. This, then, is a good example of the problems involved in constructing composite forecasts: we have a daily series of buy/sell signals which we must combine with a monthly series of point estimates.

The econometric forecasts are provided for both three- and six-month maturities, and it would be useful to consider a model which allows for both cross currency and cross maturity spreading. This complicates the evaluation phase, however, since it implies that the forecast horizons are different for the different maturities. There is, however, a way out of this problem. If we are willing to assume that the manager has a three-month planning horizon, the evaluation can be based on the assumption that the contracts are closed out at the end of three months. For example, suppose that we enter a six-month forward contract to buy sterling at $2·00. At the end of three months, we realize the gains or losses by writing a three-month forward contract to sell sterling at the three-month forward rate in three months time. The profit or loss on the transaction will depend upon the difference between the six-month forward rate today and the three-month forward rate in three months time. In other words, we can consider today's six-month forward rate as a forecast of the three-month forward rate in three months time.

Leaving aside the technical forecasts for the moment, we have three-point forecasts of the future spot rate: today's spot rate, S_t, today's three-month forward rate, $F3_t$, and today's three-month Predex forecast, $P3_t$. We want to construct a weighted average composite forecast of the form:

$$S_{t+3} = w_1 S_t + w_2 F3_t + w_3 P3_t.$$

The similar weighted average for the six-month market is the following:

$$F3_{t+3} = w_1 F3_t + w_2 F6_t + w_3 P6_t.$$

On the assumption that we will close out our six-month contracts in three months time, the price that we are trying to forecast in the second equation is the three-month forward rate. The random walk forecast for the future three-month forward rate is the three-month forward rate today; to the random walker, the best forecast of any future price is its current price.

We modify these weighted averages by introducing two considerations. First, we want the shares of our three informational assets in the portfolio to sum to unity in order to prevent a continued drift in the post-estimation period. Second, our real interest is in predicting the market bias rather than the future prices themselves. Hence, we set the weight on the market forecast, w_2, equal to $1 - w_1 - w_3$ and restate the equations in the following form:

$$S_{t+3} - F3_t = w_1 [S_t - F3_t] + w_3 [P3_t - F3_t]$$
$$F3_{t+3} - F6_t = w_1 [F3_t - F6_t] + w_3 [P6_t - F6_t]$$

The dependent variables in these equations are now the profit per unit of foreign currency purchased.

The next step is to combine these combined econometric forecasts with the technical momentum signals — which poses a problem. The econometric forecasts are provided at the end of each month, whereas the technical forecasts are generated on a daily basis. In addition, the value of a technical signal declines rapidly with a delay in acting upon it. Goodman reports that if signals are acted upon five days after they are generated, approximately 50% of the value of the signal is lost. There will typically be a small number of signals given on the day when the econometric forecasts are generated, and an approach which includes the long/short position recommended by the technical service will underestimate the value of the service by ignoring the timing consideration. Hence we require a way of employing the technical service which is compatible with the econometric evaluation procedures.

---

[4] For a more extended description of the Predex technical system, see Charles Ramond, "Momentum Trading Produces Profitable Currency Trades," *Commodities Magazine*, July 1981, and "The Econometrics Debate: A Forecaster Replies," *Euromoney*, November 1981.

One solution to this problem is to include the value of the momentum series itself rather than the buy/sell signals generated by the system. A more sophisticated approach is to include both the level of the series and its change over some recent period. An example may illustrate how this system works. Suppose that the momentum — a short-term moving average divided by a longer-term moving average — is high. This implies that the exchange rate has recently increased relative to a longer run trend. Given the tendency of exchange rates to overshoot, there will be a tendency for the forecast of the future exchange rate to fall when momentum is high. On the other hand, if the momentum series is increasing, particularly from a low base, then this will suggest an increase in the forecast of the future spot rate.

This procedure differs from the way that technical analysts typically use momentum series. The standard method generates buy/sell signals on the basis of the cross-overs in the momentum, whereas this econometric procedure uses the level and the change in the momentum directly. Consequently, we cannot use the results reported below to evaluate the technical forecasting services because we are not using those services in the manner suggested by them. It is, however, interesting to investigate if this alternative procedure also works.

The final equations, then, are of the following form.

$$S_{t+1} - F3_t = w_1 [S_t - F3_t] + w_3 [P3_t - F3_t] + w_4 M_t + w_5 DM_t + u_t$$
$$F3_{t+1} - F6_t = w_1 [F3_t - F6_t] + w_3 [P6_t - F6_t] + w_4 M_t + w_5 DM_t + v_t$$

In these extended equations, M represents the value of the momentum and DM represents the change in the momentum from the previous month. We expect the addition coefficients, w_4 and w_5, to be negative and positive respectively.

In Exhibit 3.9.1, estimates of the weights are provided based upon three regression techniques. The first procedure simply estimates the equations for each currency and maturity independently. The numbers reported in the Exhibit are the average values of the estimated weights and the average standard errors. The standard errors are quite large, so that the simple regression procedure does not yield a very precise estimate of the shares of the different forecasts in the portfolio. In addition, there is a tendency for the weights to be large. In the composite econometric forecast, for example, the estimates suggest giving a weight of 170% to the spot rate, 18% to the Predex econometric forecast, and −88% to the forward rate. Since the weights on the momentum signals are also larger than from the other procedures, the simple regression model would tend to result in a very active portfolio management strategy. For both of these reasons, the simple regression procedures are not recommended.

The second estimation procedure constrains the weights to be the same for all currencies and maturities. The advantage of this approach is that the ratio of the number of weights to be estimated to the number of observations is increased. This results in more precise estimates of

Exhibit 3.9.1: Shares in the forecasting portfolio

Estimation procedure	Spot rate	Forward rate	Predex econometric	Predex momentum	Change in momentum
Separate estimates	1·70 (1·17)	−0·88 —	0·18 (0·19)	−1·60 (0·90)	0·58 (0·51)
Pooled estimates	0·96 (0·17)	−0·15 —	0·19 (0·05)	−0·93 (0·15)	0·37 (0·08)
Pooled estimates (Zellner)	0·76 (0·04)	0·23 —	0·01 (0·02)	−0·80 (0·19)	0·37 (0·11)

Note. The composite forecast is a weighted average of the five forecasts included in the Exhibit. The estimates are estimates of the shares in the composite forecast for three different estimation procedures. The statistics in parentheses beneath the estimates are standard errors which provide a measure of the precision of the estimate. Since the weight on the forward rate is derived as a residual from the spot and Predex econometric forecasts, its standard error is not reported. In general, one should prefer estimates with small standard errors and with small estimates for all forecasts other than the forward rate. On the basis of both criteria, the Zellner estimates are to be preferred. The technical details behind these estimation procedures are available from the author.

the weights, as can be seen from the smaller standard errors. A further gain in efficiency may be had by taking account of the cross-correlation in the forecast errors through the use of the "seemingly unrelated regression" procedure.[5] The Zellner estimates are presented in the third line of Exhibit 3.9.1. Of the three procedures, the Zellner procedure is to be preferred because it offers both the most precise estimates of the weights, as measured by the standard errors, and the most conservative management strategy. In other words, for any set of values of the forecasts, the Zellner procedure will predict the smallest expected profit from an open strategy. This procedure, then, is most likely to avoid disappointments in actual outcomes.

The three procedures used for estimating the weights are only a sample of the range of possible approaches that could be used to estimate the shares in the forecasting portfolio. However, any of the other possible efficient approaches should yield similar results. My suggestion would be to choose the set of estimates which both take account of the full information set and which result in a conservative management strategy. Of the procedures presented in Exhibit 3.9.1, the Zellner estimates are clearly superior on both grounds.

The other information that we obtain from the estimation stage are estimates of the variance of the forecast errors and of the correlations in the forecast errors across currencies and maturities. Over the 90-day horizon, the standard deviation of the forecast errors for most of the currencies is between 5–6%, the one exception being the Canadian dollar for which the standard deviation is around 2%. The other general empirical regularity is the high degree of correlation in the forecast errors across the maturity spectrum. We are forecasting the spot rate in three months time and the three-month forward rate in three months time. As one would expect, the errors in the two forecasts are correlated very highly. The correlations range from 94% to 98%.

The correlations across currencies are presented in Exhibit 3.9.2. Certain expected patterns emerge from the Exhibit. The Deutschemark and the French franc are highly correlated, but the Canadian dollar is almost uncorrelated with the yen. The portfolio theory consequently suggests that it is risk-reducing to take offsetting positions in the Deutschemark and the French franc, while any combination of Canadian dollars and yen may be considered. In selecting the portfolio, it is necessary to take account of both the variance of the forecast errors and the correlations across currencies and maturities.

There is no reason to believe that either the variance of the forecast errors or the correlations will remain constant over time. The high correlation between the Deutschemark and the French franc could, for example, be drastically reduced if the EMS broke up. When the principles discussed here are applied, additional techniques are introduced to provide an updated forecast of the elements of the co-variance matrix on a timely basis. For the moment, however, the constant co-variance matrix will do for illustrative purposes.

Exhibit 3.9.2: Correlations among forecast errors

	Can $	Ffr	DM	£	¥
Can $	1·00	0·25	0·28	0·15	0·02
Ffr		1·00	0·88	0·36	0·49
DM			1·00	0·51	0·32
£				1·00	0·30
¥					1·00

Note. The statistics reported are the correlations between the forecast errors for the spot rates. The correlations for the forecast errors of the three-month forward rates are very similar.

Selecting the portfolio

Although based on standard portfolio theory, the procedures which are used to select the portfolio of positions are complicated by a number of factors, the most important of which is the need to take account of transactions costs. In conventional portfolio theory, there are

---

[5] Developed by Arnold Zellner.

typically a large number of alternative assets whose returns are not highly correlated. In the currency case, we have a small number of positions and we have very high correlations across the maturity spectrum. The usual procedure for selecting the portfolio is to tell the computer to choose the positions which will maximize the return for some given level of risk. If transactions costs are ignored, the computer will respond to this request by choosing some enormous maturity spreads. It will say, for example, to buy Can\$ 600 million in the three-month market and sell Can\$ 599·999 million in the six-month market to make an almost certain profit of \$35. The algorithms developed for this project impose a transactions cost of \$0·001 per dollar of currency purchased or sold. This figure is broadly consistent with published estimates of bid/ask spreads on the inter-bank market and with commission costs on the IMM currency futures market.

In selecting the position, the portfolio programme chooses between spreads across currencies, spreads across maturities, and outright speculative positions. It evaluates the incremental risk and incremental return from all such positions and selects the options which maximize the safety of the entire portfolio. The objective is not to make a profit on every trade, and in fact losses are expected to be made on certain positions which are chosen to diversify the risk of other profitable positions. The principles of portfolio selection suggest that diversification is the key to reducing the risk of an open position.

We have already made use of this principle in creating the portfolio of forecasts. The portfolio selection procedure also makes use of it in choosing the positions at each point in time. There is, however, yet a third level of diversification: diversification across time. The potential for profit relative to risk is not constant. It will change with the forecasts and with the revised estimates of the co-variance matrix. It will clearly be better to attempt to make money when conditions are good rather than when conditions for profitable trades are limited. A full currency management programme consequently requires that we specify a timing mechanism which will complement the portfolio selection procedure.

Before describing this mechanism, a word about specialization. Financial markets are full of specialists. Among forecasters, there are econometricians, technical traders, judgemental forecasters and chartists. Among portfolio managers, we have stock pickers and market timing specialists, arbitragers, spreaders, and outright speculators. While each of these specialists touts his or her own technique, the principles of diversification suggest that a combination is generally less risky than a specialized position. All that the currency management programme is doing is to combine all of the elements of financial advice in a logical and consistent way. The model allows for a combination of forecasts, for a variety of open positions, and for timing the participation in the market.

For the timing mechanism, we specify that the dimension of the position taken on a given day is related to the average target profit through the safety ratios. The safety ratio, also known as the Sharpe ratio, is the expected profit on the position divided by the standard deviation of the expected profit. If we denote the ratio by the letter s, then the entry function is defined by the relationship:

$$\text{Expected profit at time } t = (s^2/\bar{s}^2) \text{ target profit}$$

where $\bar{s}$ is the average value of the safety ratio, and the target profit is the amount that the manager would like to make when the safety ratio is equal to the average value. For example, suppose we had a safety ratio of 0·5. If target profit was set equal to \$1, then roughly 68% of the outcomes would lie between a loss of \$1 and a profit of \$3; 95% of the observations would lie between a loss of \$3 and a profit of \$5. These numbers may be multiplied by any number to scale your position up or down. With this safety ratio, a target profit of \$100,000 would lead to 68% of the outcomes being expected to lie between −\$100,000 and \$300,000.

If we stay with this example, now consider the case in which the safety ratio on a given day was actually 0·75. The scale factor, $s^2/\bar{s}^2$, would then be 2·25 so that target profit for the day would be set at \$225,000. If the safety ratio fell to 0·25, then the scale factor would be 0·25, and the target profit would be set at \$25,000. This entry function minimizes the variance of profit for any given level of target profit over a number of transactions. The entry function, then, completes the diversification of the portfolio.

An example

Suppose that you wanted to make $1 million through the placement of four positions. To spread the example out over the sample period, I assume that the four positions are taken in January of 1978, 1979, 1980 and 1981 and that they are all held for one quarter. The first step in creating the portfolio is to estimate the implied forward rate bias for each currency and maturity. From this information, in conjunction with the estimated co-variance matrix, the safety ratio for each portfolio can be estimated. These ratios are presented in Exhibit 3.9.3. Despite the fact that our calculations include transactions costs, the ratios are comparable to the average safety ratio over a large number of trades for individual technical services as estimated by Goodman. Using the strategy outlined above, the safety ratio for the four portfolios is 1·705. If the distribution of outcomes is normal, the probability that we will make a loss on four positions is less than 5%. This probability refers to the probability that profits *net* of transactions costs will be less than zero. The safety ratio could be further increased by being content to make our million dollars over a larger number of transactions, but millionaires — certainly prospective millionaires — typically feel that impatience is a virtue.

Exhibit 3.9.3: The timing decision

Date	Safety ratio	Target profit
Jan. 1978	0·82	480
Jan. 1979	0·38	100
Jan. 1980	0·45	150
Jan. 1981	0·61	270
Total	1·70	1,000

Note. Target profit is expressed in $'000. The total safety ratio is the safety ratio for the portfolio, which is not the same as the sum of the individual safety ratios.

There is a good deal of variability in the safety ratios of the four portfolios. The first portfolio, with a safety ratio of 0·816, provides the best gamble, and hence the timing rule sets the target profit for this portfolio at $480,000, almost half of the total anticipated profit. One-quarter of the profit allocation goes to the fourth portfolio, and the two intermediate portfolios pick up the change.

The four portfolios are presented in Exhibits 3.9.4, 3.9.5, 3.9.6 and 3.9.7. The reason for the high safety ratio of the first portfolio is fairly easy to see. The composite forecast predicted an upward bias in the French franc and a downward bias in the Deutschemark, hence the portfolio model attempts to make most of its target profit through a series of spreads across the two currencies. Further short positions in sterling yield an overall long position in the European currencies of $5·776 million. This position is then hedged by a $5·888 million short position in the yen. The open position in dollars for this portfolio is consequently very small. When we look at the actual profits column, it is evident that this was a portfolio that did not work. Because of the substantial losses on the Deutschemark and yen positions, the realized profit was only $84,000, and $45,000 of this sum must pay for the transactions costs, thus yielding a net profit of roughly $40,000. Compared to the anticipated profit of $480,000, this result is disappointing.

The second portfolio, for January 1979, offers two excellent examples of cross-maturity spreads. In the Canadian dollar, we take a $42 million long position in the three-month market offset by a $34 million short position in the six-month market. In the yen, a $49 million short in the three-month market is offset by a $31 million long in the six-month market. These maturity spreads may be considered as bets on the future course of international interest rate differentials, since the difference between the spot and three-month forward rates in three months time is primarily determined by interest rate differentials. In addition to the maturity spreads, the model again engages in a spread position between the French franc and the Deutschemark. Including sterling, the overall long position on the continentals is offset by a net short position

162

Exhibit 3.9.4: Portfolio 1: January 1978

Currency maturity	Position	Expected profit	Actual profit
		(US $ thousand)	
Can $: 3-month	−257	0·4	9·1
Can $: 6-month	−485	0·9	18·2
Ffr: 3-month	11,602	102·4	612·6
Ffr: 6-month	10,455	106·3	715·1
DM: 3-month	−5,413	67·0	−272·8
DM: 6-month	−10,201	133·1	−497·8
£: 3-month	−659	16·0	12·7
£: 6-month	−8	0·2	0·2
¥: 3-month	−5,888	98·6	−511·7
¥: 6-month	−9	0·1	−0·8
Total		525·0	84·8
Transactions costs		45·0	45·0
Net profit		480·0	39·8

in yen and a net long in Canadian dollars. *Ex post*, the second portfolio performed very well indeed. Both of the cross-maturity spreads were profitable, and the currency spread between the French franc and the Deutschemark also came out ahead. As a result, the realized net profit of $369,700 exceeded the target level of $100,000. After the second portfolio, total realized profits were $409,500 compared to target profits of $580,000.

Exhibit 3.9.5: Portfolio 2: January 1979

Currency maturity	Position	Expected profit	Actual profit
		(US $ thousand)	
Can $: 3-month	5,780	5·4	142·8
Can $: 6-month	−4,730	3·5	−90·8
Ffr: 3-month	4,343	−32·9	−183·3
Ffr: 6-month	2,780	−21·4	−125·4
DM: 3-month	−2,113	36·7	108·6
DM: 6-month	−5,182	92·4	304·7
£: 3-month	955	−7·4	16·1
£: 6-month	102	−0·8	1·5
¥: 3-month	−6,849	113·7	733·5
¥: 6-month	4,239	−51·8	−500·2
Total		138·0	407·7
Transactions costs		38·0	38·0
Net profit		100·0	369·7

The third portfolio illustrates an outright speculative position. Apart from some small spreads in the continentals and the yen, the model attempts to make almost all of the target profit from a position in sterling. Realized profits of $119,400 are a little short of the target level of $150,100, and hence the cumulative realized profits slip further behind the target level. There is, however, little reason for complaint since the first three trades have netted $528,900, and we have yet to have a losing portfolio.

The fourth portfolio returns to spread positions. Six-month French francs are set against three-month Deutschemarks and a maturity spread is taken in the yen. The big action, however, is again in sterling where we find a rare combination of a downward bias in the three-month forecast and an upward bias in the six-month market. Such opportunities are not to be missed, and the model takes an $18 million spread between the three- and six-month markets. In a champagne and caviar conclusion to the event, all of the positions work, and a net profit of $482,000 is realized.

Over all of the positions, our budding millionaire would have netted $1·011 million, and in this game, being that close is good enough. After paying the transactions costs, there was

Exhibit 3.9.6: Portfolio 3: January 1980

Currency maturity	Position	Expected profit	Actual profit
		(US $ thousand)	
Can $: 3-month	3	0	0
Can $: 6-month	0	0	0
Ffr: 3-month	132	−0·7	−13·5
Ffr: 6-month	2,108	−9·5	−191·2
DM: 3-month	0	0	0·0
DM: 6-month	−1,311	19·7	151·0
£: 3-month	−11,808	328·3	297·6
£: 6-month	6,772	−165·2	−97·5
¥: 3-month	−239	1·4	12·8
¥: 6-month	297	−1·2	−17·1
Total		172·8	142·1
Transactions costs		22·7	22·7
Net profit		150·1	119·4

still a profit to be made from each individual position. This is not to say that there were not any surprises since, in fact, the accuracy with which the profit for each individual position was predicted was poor. To understand why the final outcome was predicted with reasonable accuracy, an analogy with a roulette wheel may be helpful. In roulette, the house cannot forecast the return on any single turn of the wheel with great accuracy, but if the wheel is spun a sufficient number of times, the return to the house becomes reasonably certain since the law of large numbers lends a hand. The same principle applies in the speculative strategy outlined above. Like the house, the composite forecasts allow the manager to perceive the small biases present in the market. If these biases are accurately estimated, the risk can be reduced by playing the game a large number of times. To make the $1 million, 40 positions were taken. Although this is not a large set, it is sufficient to allow for a good deal of cancellation of errors and hence to reduce the variance of the forecast of the average return.

Exhibit 3.9.7: Portfolio 4: January 1981

Currency maturity	Position	Expected profit	Actual profit
		(US $ thousand)	
Can $: 3-month	1,135	−2·4	4·9
Can $: 6-month	−3	0	0
Ffr: 3-month	−598	9·1	57·1
Ffr: 6-month	6,080	−26·9	−551·5
DM: 3-month	−5,404	103·1	669·6
DM: 6-month	628	−6·4	−72·4
£: 3-month	−18,359	57·1	464·5
£: 6-month	18,888	122·4	272·7
¥: 3-month	6,560	127·7	350·9
¥: 6-month	4,343	−51·7	−250·2
Total		332·0	544·9
Transactions costs		62·0	62·0
Net profit		270·0	482·9

Is the story wrong in some basic way? There are two reasons why these results may be too optimistic. First, the portfolios were selected from within the sample period and there is no guarantee that these results will continue to hold in a post-sample period. Second, the momentum forecasts which were used in the composite forecasting equation are also in-sample. For these reasons, the worth of the portfolio approach should be judged on the basis of its logic, rather than its performance in the experiment outlined above. The model absorbs and synthesizes a number of different forecasting techniques and speculative strategies into a general computer-based model. And those who believe that computers will never be able to trade currencies probably also believed that computers would never be able to play chess.

10. Using currency forecasting to reduce borrowing costs

Stanley C. Waldner

It is cost effective to borrow in a foreign currency whenever the interest rate differential favours the foreign rate. No minimum difference is required for this strategy to be applicable — just a differential, i.e. the U.S. dollar rate must be higher than the Eurocurrency rate.

This is a substantial departure from the positions taken nearly two years ago in an article[1] which advocated a strategy referred to as the 4% rule. Under the provisions of that strategy, it was essential that the Eurocurrency in which the borrowing was considered be cheaper by four or more percentage points than the Eurodollar. If this were the case, the borrower could expect, based on use of dyna-line[2] models, to reduce his borrowing cost by two to five percentage points below the existing Eurodollar cost.

Early research

Exhibit 3.10.1 is a comparison of 12-month Eurocurrency rates for the dates indicated. It shows that, in accordance with the 4% rule, borrowings in the Deutschemark, Swiss franc, or yen would not have been permissible in either 1976 or 1977 because the 4% criterion was not met. It also shows that for both 1978 and 1979, a 4% differential did exist — the Eurodollar borrowing cost was 4% greater than that of either the mark, franc, or yen. Thus, using the borrowing strategy was appropriate.

Exhibit 3.10.1: Comparison of 12–month Eurocurrency rates

	Eurodollar	Euro-DM	Euro-Swiss franc	Euro-yen
		(%)		
1976	7·1875	4·8125	4·0625	7·6125
1977	5·5000	4·7500	2·4375	6·1250
1978	7·6250	3·0625	2·0000	3·2500
1979	12·0000	3·8750	0·6250	2·5000

Source. Harris Bank, Jan. 2, 1976, Jan. 7, 1977, Dec. 30, 1977, Dec. 29, 1978.

Exhibit 3.10.2 shows net borrowing costs, employing the 4% rule. It shows that interest expense for 1978 was reduced from the 7·6250% Eurodollar rate to the 4·9788% Euro–DM rate, and for 1979 from 12·0000% to 6·1113%, a saving of 2·6462% (7·6250% less 4·9788%) and 5·8887% (12·0000% less 6·1113%), respectively. For the Swiss franc, the savings were 2·3478% (7·6250% less 5·2772%) and 3·2498% (12·0000% less 8·7502%), respectively. For the yen, the savings were 6·0500% (7·6250% less 1·5750%) and 21·1760% (12·0000% less −9·1760%), respectively. To borrowers weary of high U.S. dollar rates, the 4% rule offered some reprieve, contributing directly to the bottom line. Further, it offered practitioners of the strategy indirect

Exhibit 3.10.2: Net borrowing costs, employing the 4% rule

	Eurodollar	Euro-DM	Euro-Swiss franc	Euro-yen
		(%)		
1976	7·1875	n.a.*	n.a.*	n.a.*
1977	5·5000	n.a.*	n.a.*	n.a.*
1978	7·6250	4·9788	5·2772	1·5750
1979	12·0000	6·1113	8·7502	(9·1760)*

* A borrowing was not appropriate in accordance with the 4% rule.

---

[1] Stanley C. Waldner, "How to Borrow in a Foreign Currency," *Euromoney*, June 1980.
[2] Technical foreign exchange management models upon which Waldner & Company bases its strategies.

improvement in performance: the cost of money savings could have been employed by them to reduce the cost of their end products, thereby making them more competitive in the marketplace.

Recent developments

Since the original article was written, we have expanded the data base over which the 4% rule is operative, i.e. October 1977 through December 1981, four and a quarter years, as opposed to two years. At the same time we have enhanced our exposure management models, which now employ more complex analyses. As a result, we can deal effectively with a Eurocurrency borrowing without the safety net of a 4% buffer, given any margin of premium in the Eurodollar rate. This is demonstrated in Exhibit 3.10.3, which shows strategy performance from June 30, 1977, through December 31, 1981. The Exhibit reflects data based on a strategy related not only to the 4% rule, but to a 2% rule, and a 0% rule, as well. The borrowing performance is shown by currency — DM, Swfr, and ¥ (columns 6, 7, and 8) — under "effective net interest rate". These columns show how well a total borrowing in a single currency would have fared. Under the heading Net average rate (column 9) the figures are based upon an equal fraction of the borrower's liability being distributed in each of the currencies which met the 4% differential test — a third of the funds borrowed in each currency if all three currencies meet the test; one-half, if only two; all, if only one. In my judgement, this is the preferable borrowing approach in that diversification of the debt generates a more uniform cost than single source borrowing. Correspondingly, the data relative to the 2% and the 0% rules are shown as a composite figure under the heading "Net average rate" in columns 11 and 13, respectively.

The effective net interest rate

The effective net interest rate is a function of two factors: (1) the interest rate differential between the Eurodollar rate and the Eurocurrency in which the borrowing is completed; and (2) the efficiency with which the foreign exchange exposure is managed. When a potential offshore borrower is considering where to place the borrowing, he lacks sufficient insight on how volatile each of the currencies is likely to be during the period of the borrowing, and how effectively the exposure can be managed. Therefore, the borrower is unable to make a sound judgement based solely on the size of the interest rate difference — the exposure management function could ultimately prove to be the major determinant in the makeup of the effective net interest rate figure.

As an example, see Exhibit 3.10.3, line 12: the rates — US$18·0625% (column 2), DM 10·3750% (column 3), Swfr 7·4375% (column 4), and ¥13·4375% (column 5). Given a US$/Swfr differential of 10·6250% (18·0625% less 7·4375%), greater than either the US$/DM, at 7·6875% (18·0625% − 10·3750%) or the US$/¥, at 4·6250% (18·0625% − 13·4375%), we might suppose that Swfr would also show the smallest effective net interest rate. However, this is not the case. The smallest is DM at 6·18% (column 6), exceeded by ¥ at 9·67% (column 8), and, finally, Swfr at 12·82% (column 7). This shows the extent to which adverse exposure management can influence the effective net interest rate figure. Since the exposure management factor for a specific currency — a function of future development — cannot be judged with the same assurance as can the interest rate differential, portfolio diversification has been found to be the answer.

For additional emphasis, take as a further example the value for DM at 9·1250 (column 3, line 15) and compare it with that of Swfr at 5·4375 (column 4, line 15) and ¥ at 8·7500 (column 5, line 15). Given these relative Eurocurrency interest rates, with DM highest, ¥ second highest, and Swfr lowest, one could hardly have guessed that the effective net interest rate order would be DM at −2·21% (column 6), a reduction from the Euro-rate of 11·34 percentage points, followed by Swfr, at 3·32 (column 7), a reduction of 2·12 percentage points and ¥ at 11·60 (column 8), an increase of 2·85 percentage points. Although an examination of the Exhibits will show that the exposure management function performed by the models is consistently good, there are isolated instances of poor performance. In any event, by distributing the borrowing among the three currencies, the impact of unusual foreign exchange volatility during the period of the transaction is minimized, and the ultimate results more stable.

166

Exhibit 3.10.3: Net borrowing costs, using 4%, 2% and 0% rules*

	(1) Period	12-month Eurocurrency rates[1]				Effective net interest rate			4% rule		2% rule		0% rule	
		(2) US $	(3) DM	(4) Swfr	(5) ¥	(6) DM	(7) Swfr	(8) ¥	(9) Net average rate	(10) Improvement over Euro-dollar rate	(11) Net average rate	(12) Improvement over Euro-dollar rate	(13) Net average rate	(14) Improvement over Euro-dollar rate
(1)	30. 6.77–30. 6.78	6.3750	4.3125	3.8125	6.2500	5.07[3]	3.51[3]	−9.21[2,3]	0.00	0.00	4.29	2.09	5.93	0.45
(2)	30. 9.77–29. 9.78	7.0625	4.1250	2.9375	5.0625	6.96[3]	6.80	10.52[3]	6.80	0.26	8.09	−1.03	8.09	−1.03
(3)	30.12.77–29.12.78	7.6250	3.0625	2.0000	3.2500	3.86	4.48	4.56	4.30	3.32	4.30	3.32	4.30	3.32
(4)	31. 3.78–30. 3.79	8.0000	3.3125	1.2500	3.5625	3.02	4.56	0.69	2.76	5.24	2.76	5.24	2.76	5.24
(5)	30. 6.78–29. 6.79	9.2500	3.6875	2.1875	4.1250	3.11	7.15	−3.08[4]	2.39	6.86	2.39	6.86	2.39	6.86
(6)	29. 9.78–28. 9.79	9.8125	3.8125	1.3125	3.1875	4.07	6.20	−8.10[4]	0.73	9.09	0.73	9.09	0.73	9.09
(7)	29.12.78–31.12.79	12.0000	3.8750	0.6250	2.5000	5.35	9.35	−13.03[4]	0.56	11.44	0.56	11.44	0.56	11.44
(8)	30. 3.79–31. 3.80	10.6875	5.5000	1.3750	5.8125	−7.20[4]	−2.95[4]	−10.10[4]	−6.75[4]	17.44	−6.75[4]	17.44	−6.75[4]	17.44
(9)	29. 6.79–30. 6.80	10.2500	6.8125	2.3750	6.1250	3.02[3]	9.44	−8.64[4]	0.40	9.85	1.28	8.97	1.28	8.97
(10)	28. 9.79–30. 9.80	12.3750	7.5625	2.4375	6.9375	0.59	4.87	−4.91[4]	0.18	12.19	0.18	12.19	0.18	12.19
(11)	31.12.79–31.12.80	13.0000	8.3125	5.6250	7.6250	−3.52[4]	0.46	3.93	0.29	12.71	0.29	12.71	0.29	12.71
(12)	31. 3.80–31. 3.81	18.0625	10.3750	7.4375	13.4375	6.18	12.82	9.67	9.56	8.51	9.56	8.51	9.56	8.51
(13)	30. 6.80–30. 6.81	9.9375	8.3125	5.3125	9.2500	−12.65[2,3,4]	−4.84[4]	2.38[2,3]	−4.84[4]	14.78	−4.84[4]	14.78	−5.04[4]	14.97
(14)	30. 9.80–30. 9.81	13.6875	8.8125	5.8750	10.5000	−13.38[4]	−6.19[4]	8.52[3]	−9.79[4]	23.47	−3.68[4]	17.37	−3.68[4]	17.37
(15)	31.12.80–31.12.81	15.1250	9.1250	5.4375	8.7500	−2.21[4]	3.32	11.60	4.24	10.89	4.24	10.89	4.24	10.89
(16)	averages	10.8833							4.24	9.74	4.24	9.32	4.24	9.23

* Results based on models actually in place during the period.
[1] "International Money Market and Foreign Exchange Rates", Weekly Review, Harris Bank.
[2] Borrowing not appropriate with 2% rule.
[3] Borrowing not appropriate with 4% rule.
[4] Negative borrowing cost equals income from borrowing.

The most useful information in Exhibit 3.10.3 is in columns 10, 12, and 14 — Improvement over Eurodollar rate — relating to performance, employing the 4%, 2%, and 0% strategies. Other columns provide supporting information. This Exhibit is more comprehensive than Exhibit 3.10.2, where the research simply dealt with calendar years, assuming that the borrowing would take place at the turn of the year and terminate at the end of the year. Thus, we illustrated four measurable periods: 1976, 1977, 1978, and 1979.

In Exhibit 3.10.3, the 12-month unit period of measurement is maintained. We chose, however, to begin each period at the beginning of each quarter, ending it on the last working day of the corresponding fourth quarter, because we felt this approach provided a more comprehensive test of the strategy in that there are more sample periods — 15, compared with four in the earlier article. Moreover, few borrowers structure their debt on a calendar basis. Therefore, this presentation generates substantially greater credibility in that it is readily apparent to a potential borrower that the strategy is applicable to any borrowing period of a year or greater duration, without regard to when the period begins or ends. This, we feel, is an important consideration to any borrower.

Exhibit 3.10.3 is not complicated. Column 1 defines the period to which the data on the respective numbered lines apply. Columns 2 through 5 reflect U.S. dollar, mark, Swiss franc, and yen Eurocurrency rates which prevailed on the first day of the respective periods. For example, on line 3, the ¥ rate of 3·2500 (column 5) was the Euro-yen rate for December 30, 1977.

Columns 6, 7, and 8 show the effective net interest rate for mark, franc, and yen borrowings (without regard to the interest difference between the currency and the Eurodollar). These values reflect foreign currency interest cost, reduced by foreign exchange gains or increased by foreign exchange losses. Thus, column 6, line 12, shows a value for DM of 6·18. When compared with the Euro–mark rate of 10·3750 (column 3, line 12), it can be seen that effective exposure management in this instance reduced the Euro–mark rate by 4·1950 percentage points to the 6·18 shown. This issue was dealt with earlier.

The net average rate, column 9, is the average of the values under effective net interest rate (columns 6, 7 and 8) of only those currencies which satisfied the 4% rule. The test involves comparison of the Eurodollar rate (column 2) with the respective Eurocurrency rates (columns 3, 4, and 5). Similarly, columns 11 and 13 refer to the 2% and 0% rules.

Under improvement over Eurodollar rate (columns 10, 12, and 14), we are dealing with the amount by which a given strategy over or underperformed the Eurodollar rate. For example, under column 10, line 12 we find the value 8·51. This is the amount by which the strategy, employing the 4% rule, improved upon the Eurodollar rate (18·0625 − 9·56).

The 4%, 2% and 0% rules

In no instance, over the 15, 12-month periods considered, did the strategy employing the 4% rule fail to reduce borrowing costs (column 10).[3] The range of that improvement varied from a low of 0·26 (column 10, line 2) in the face of a Eurodollar rate of 7·0625 on September 30, 1977 (column 2, line 2) to a high of 23·47 (column 10, line 14) when the Eurodollar rate stood at 13·6875 on September 30, 1980 (column 2, line 14). The average improvement over the average Eurodollar rate for the 15 12-month periods was 9·74 percentage points (column 10, line 16). This compares with an average Eurodollar rate over the period of 10·88 (column 2, line 16) and results in a borrowing cost over the four-and-a-half-year period averaging 1·14% (10·88 less 9·74). By any standard of measure, this performance must be considered impressive.

Columns 11 and 12, and 13 and 14 are obtained in the same manner as columns 9 and 10 except that they show similar data in conformity with the 2% rule and 0% rule, as opposed to the 4% rule.

Column 12, relating to the strategy employing the 2% rule, is shown to have an applicability during the only period for which the 4% rule did not — the 12-month period beginning June 30, 1977. This is seen in comparing column 12, line 1 with column 10, line 1. Aside from this, the performance reflected is quite similar. In fact, results obtained with the 2% rule (column 12)

---

[3] On 30.6.77 the interest rate differential did not exceed 4%; therefore, the rule did not apply for the period 30.6.77–30.6.78.

are identical with those obtained with the 4% rule (column 10) except for the values on lines 1, 2, 9, and 14. The average of the improvement under column 12, of 9·32 percentage points (line 16) is substantially the same as the average under column 10 of 9·74 (line 16). This occurs despite an underperformance in one (line 2) of the 15 periods analysed. Because of the similarity in these results, there should be no concern in employing the strategy associated with the 2% rule.

Let us now turn to the 0% rule. Column 14, Improvement over Eurodollar rate, differs marginally from columns 10 and 12. It also shows one period (line 2) in which the strategy underperformed the Eurodollar rate. Aside from this, 0% strategy performance is identical to 4% performance except for lines 1, 9, 13, and 14 (column 10 versus 14). The average improvement under column 14 is 9·23 percentage points (line 16). This compares with 9·74 and 9·32 relating to the 4% and 2% strategies (columns 10 and 12), respectively.

The similarity of these averages shows there should be no concern about Eurodollar/Eurocurrency rate differential. Borrowings can be made consistently within the framework of the 0% strategy without undue degradation of results, or concern that the Eurodollar costs will be exceeded. This has been proven employing actual Waldner & Company dyna-line signals.

Conclusions

Our work is no more than reflective of a transformation taking place within the foreign exchange exposure management segment of the international financial community. As recently as two or three years ago, those who voluntarily incurred liabilities abroad in the cause of a routine borrowing programme were considered pioneers. Like many pioneers, they trod uncertain ground.

The technology of exposure management has now advanced substantially. Good models can effectively deal with foreign exchange exposure. Therefore, the borrower who consistently outperforms the Eurodollar rate is only being highly competitive in a competitive environment.

CHAPTER FOUR
Hedging procedures

1. Hedging techniques and costs
Robert K. Ankrom

For the major convertible currencies there are actions one can take, either through the local money market or in the international foreign exchange market, to protect against exchange loss. The actual techniques are as numerous and as imaginative as one would expect from the highly competent corps of international treasurers and bankers who work in this area. Basically, the techniques can be broken down into three general categories: forward cover in the foreign exchange market; management of balance sheet assets and liabilities; and anticipatory price planning.

Forward cover in the exchange markets

The exchange markets are quite efficient in providing forward cover for most of the major currencies for periods of up to one year, sometimes longer. The only problem is the matter of price. Weak currencies are sold at such a discount that more may be lost by hedging them in the forward market than will be lost by remaining exposed. Likewise, strong currencies may not carry sufficiently high premiums to warrant selling them to reduce a theoretical exposure. The cost of protecting in the forward markets is not simply the discount or premium at the time the forward cover is purchased but rather the difference between the forward price and the spot price at the time the forward matures — a point discussed in greater length later in this section.

This dilemma forces a treasurer to make an educated forecast or guess about the future course of the exchange market, and to relate this to the current forward price in order to come up with an estimate of the cost of a hedging policy. He also needs to look back over the past to calculate how expensively his policy has worked out, as compared to an alternative policy. The point is, however, that there is a potential cost to buying protection in the forward markets, and a treasurer needs to know that cost to assess the wisdom of continuing to buy protection.

Management of balance sheet assets and liabilities

Most techniques for reducing exposure come under the general heading of managing local currency denominated assets and liabilities. The basic objective is to balance off exposed local currency denominated assets with local liabilities, by either reducing exposed assets or substituting local liabilities for external ones.

One category of techniques involves simply changing the denomination of receivables and payables. For instance, if your customers will stand for it, you can change your billing currency from local billing to, say, dollars and reduce exposed receivables. Similarly, if your external suppliers will accept it, you can start paying them in local currency and increase your currency denominated liabilities. Both techniques are simple, probably costless, but involve the co-operation of another party who may not be willing to accept the exposure you are trying to get rid of.

Another more common approach is to take action to change the currency in which you are financing local assets. The initial problem is to obtain more local currency denominated debt, and the second is to use these funds either to reduce externally denominated debt or to pay dividends. If the funds raised through additional local borrowings were not converted and sent out of the country but merely invested in the local money market, there would be no change in the net exposure to that currency.

But in some countries the local money markets are so underdeveloped that it is impossible to obtain reasonable amounts of local funds. In others, local regulations prevent foreign subsidiaries from borrowing all the local funds they may need. These laws, which were adopted to protect less creditworthy local industries, often force the foreign subsidiary to borrow a certain minimum amount of its fund requirement outside the country.

Problems of local availability may be circumvented by arranging parallel loans or currency swaps, assuming the local authorities permit this. These opportunities arise when another local subsidiary or firm has excess local currency which it cannot remit out of the country, while at the same time it needs some external currency outside the country. Assuming you have excess external currency somewhere else in your organization, it makes sense to exchange your excess external currency for the other firm's excess local currency. The currencies are either swapped outright or a parallel loan is arranged at an interest rate differential reflecting the difference in internal interest rates between the two countries. In either case, local funds are made available where there were none in the local market, to reduce exposure.

Another technique for getting round the lack of local fund availability is to borrow in the Eurocurrency markets. Short-term Eurocurrency funds are normally available for all the major currencies. Eurocurrency loans are really nothing more than Eurodollar funds which have been swapped. The rate is the Eurodollar rate plus the forward discount or minus the forward premium for the particular currency involved. Availability is restricted by the amount of swaps available in the forward exchange market. As a hedging technique, Eurocurrency borrowing is equivalent to covering in the forward market, since there is no theoretical difference between a subsidiary borrowing Eurocurrency to fund itself, or borrowing Eurodollars with the subsequent increase in exposure being hedged in the forward market. But there may be fiscal or other practical reasons for preferring the Eurocurrency approach over the forward cover approach.

Obtaining additional locally denominated liabilities, whether in Eurocurrencies, parallel loans or local borrowings, is the necessary first step; it is by no means the last step to reduce exposure. Net exposure will be reduced only after these locally denominated funds have been converted and remitted outside the country. It is on that subject that the local authorities usually have a great deal to say. (If the funds have been borrowed to make local purchases there is no need to shift them out of the country but there was no prior exposure either.)

The techniques for remitting funds out of a country fall within the major categories of dividend declaration, external debt repayment, and advance payment of payables. The main problem is in getting local permission to do them. Local authorities of weak currency countries are normally reluctant to permit an increase in local borrowings if they know that the funds will eventually be used to make dividends or repay external loans. There may also be a ceiling on the amount of dividend that can be remitted in any one year, and an absolute prohibition against the early retirement of external debt. Speeding up the payment on payables, both public and inter-company, is generally easier to accomplish since they are normally more loosely controlled, but even then, the customs or exchange authorities may question payments if they are made before invoice due date. What this generally adds up to is that hedging through the management of assets and liabilities cannot be an overnight affair but has to be consciously planned over many months and carefully tailored to fit local regulations.

The cost of asset and liability hedging depends on the particular technique employed but in the main boils down to a difference in interest rates. Hedging by borrowing weak currencies involves additional interest expense. Balancing an exposure to a strong currency, while it may result in less interest expense, involves the giving up of a potential currency gain on the exposed position.

Hedging through pricing action

Price planning is the third major category of hedging techniques which a treasurer can use to protect against exchange loss. Pricing is not so much a method of protecting exposed assets as a way of anticipating their decline and accumulating additional profit before that decline. It is the only effective method of protection in high inflation countries where local borrowing and forward exchange cover are normally unavailable. The objective is to achieve price increases faster than the rate of inflation and in advance of the inevitable devaluation.

Operating management has to understand their role in this type of hedging, since it falls on them to achieve their sales targets at the prices necessary to protect against devaluation loss. The management reporting system has to be tailored to give management the proper incentive by setting aside a part of the current profit into a reserve to be used to offset, for management reporting purposes, the loss which will finally occur when the devaluation hits.

The obstacle to price hedging is local competition, which may not be under the same pressures to raise local prices. This can be particularly acute in the case of a company exporting into a market where there is effective local competition. There may also be local price controls which prevent the raising of prices arbitrarily; price planning will not work under all circumstances.

The cost of hedging

Calculating the cost of hedging is often done by looking at the forward rate in relation to the current spot rate. The difference between the two, the so-called forward premium or discount, is computed as a percentage of the spot rate and sometimes annualized. While the forward premium or discount is a known, easily calculable number, it is misleading as a measure of cost. The true cost is rather the difference between the forward rate and the spot rate *at the time the forward matures*.

A simple example may help to explain the difference. A bank foreign exchange trader decides to build a position in, say, sterling by buying forward. Sterling is at a discount in the forward market so the forward price is less than the spot. Did the trader make a profit when he bought? Obviously not. He will not know whether he makes a profit until he closes out his forward position. The fact that the forward rate was less than spot at the time he took the position is a past fact, but immaterial. What counts lies in the future, i.e. the rate at which he closes his position in relation to the forward rate.

Similarly, for a corporation, what counts in hedging is not the past spot rate but the spot rate which will occur on the day a foward matures. Assume that a U.S. manufacturer with a £1 million exposure wants to hedge by selling sterling forward. The current spot rate is $1·77 and the forward rate is $1·76. The one cent forward discount on £1 million works out at $10,000. This discount is what some think of as the cost of covering.

But what happens when the forward contract matures? The hedging company has contracted to deliver £1 million against $1,760,000. If the company does not have sterling, it will have to buy it at the spot rate in effect at the time the forward matures. The cash outlay the company will have to make or the cash inflow it will enjoy on the closing of the forward contract will depend on that future spot rate.

> Assume the spot rate is $1·75 or less than the forward rate of $1·76. Then to buy £1 million the company needs only $1,750,000. On closing the forward contract, the company will enjoy a cash inflow of $10,000.
>
> Assume the spot rate is $1·76 or exactly equal to the forward rate. Then there will be no cash inflow or outflow on the closing of the contract.
>
> Assume the spot rate is $1·77 or exactly equal to the spot rate at the time the forward contract was taken out. Then the company will have to find $1,770,000 in order to buy the sterling and will have an additional cash outlay of $10,000.

It is apparent that the cash outlay equals the forward discount only in the last case, where the spot rate does not change.

Now let us put this analysis in the context of the total profit effect on a company exposed to £1 million. Again, we start the period with a spot rate of $1·77 and we end at three different assumed spot rates. We assume that, in one case, the company hedges its exposures by buying sterling forward at $1·76 and, in the other case, the company leaves its position exposed. The following shows the total pre-tax profit and loss effect on the company.

End of period spot rate	Exposed position	Covered position	Cost of covering
$1·75	$(20,000)	$(10,000)	$10,000
$1·76	$(10,000)	$(10,000)	—
$1·77	—	$(10,000)	$(10,000)

The "exposed position" column indicates the loss on translation due to the spot rate changing from its beginning value of $1·77. The "covered position" column represents the translation loss, less the effect of hedging. For example, when sterling went to $1·75 from $1·77 the company lost $20,000 on translation but gained $10,000 on liquidating the forward contract, for a net loss of $10,000. The last column is the amount the company made or lost on the forward contract. It is the cost of covering for it represents how much better or worse off the company is for having covered its position.

What covering your position does is fix your loss from exposure. In the above case you would lose no more nor less than $10,000 if you covered forward. That amount is the forward discount, the difference between the forward rate and the spot rate *at the time the forward was being taken out.*

But fixing your loss is not the same as calculating the cost of having done so. That cost is the difference between what you would have booked had you done nothing, compared to what you in fact do book by hedging. It is the difference between the forward rate and the spot rate *at the time the forward matures.*

2. Forward hedging

Ian Giddy

The traditional view of the costs of hedging in the forward market in a world of floating exchange rates is that the cost of a forward hedging transaction can be calculated by considering the discount or premium as compared with the spot at the time of conclusion of the contract.

In contrast, it has been argued that the real economic cost of forward hedging can be measured only in an opportunity cost sense — that is by comparing the forward rate with the actual spot rate on the day of maturity of the contract. The advantage of this method is that it explicitly compares hedging with its alternative — purchasing or selling the foreign currency spot when the payment occurs. The problem with this approach is that it does not explicitly provide a decision-making criterion that will help determine whether or when a firm should hedge. Nor is it clear that you can directly compare the cost of a fixed-in-advance hedge with a risky open position.

The only correct way to evaluate the cost of hedging is to compare the forward rate with one's forecast of the future spot rate. If the forward discount underestimates the rate of depreciation that we expect, then we might be willing to sell the currency forward. If the forward rate overestimates the depreciation that is expected, then we would tend to rely on the spot market or even buy the foreign currency forward. The only question is under what circumstances the forward rate is likely to be consistently biased below or biased above the expected future spot rate.[1]

Kohlhagen has shed some light on this question for floating rate markets by asking whether in the long run the forward market has served as a low-cost means of hedging exchange risks.[2] He does this by examining the average difference between the 90-day forward rate and the subsequent spot rate for six countries under fixed and floating rates. His findings? That measured *ex post*, a consistently long or short position in the forward market would sometimes yield profits and sometimes losses, but in the long run these average profits or losses have not been significantly different from zero. This suggests that the forward rate is an unbiased estimator of the future spot rate.[3]

Several other authors reject the idea of hedging consistently and have sought to develop models or criteria for deciding when or when not to hedge. The best-known of these are those of Shulman,[4] who bases the decision on the expected value of a devaluation loss and a corporate risk factor; of Shapiro,[5] who applies dynamic programming techniques to a re-evaluation of the hedging decision in each time period; and of Lietaer,[6] who uses the techniques of portfolio diversification to generate an efficient set of hedging policies, each of which minimizes expected costs and maximizes protection. Other writers adopt the more general approach of maximizing the expected utility of the firm rather than minimizing variance, avoiding all risk, and so forth. The concepts and calculations involved, however, render these of dubious applicability to hedging decisions. And all these methods explicitly or implicitly require the specification of probabilities for alternative future currency values as well as an assessment of the firm's risk aversion.

---

[1] One example of a clearly biased forward rate would be in South Africa, where the government offers "cheap" forward hedging to favoured exporters.

[2] Steven W. Kohlhagen, "Evidence on the Cost of Forward Cover in a Floating System," *Euromoney*, September 1975, pp. 138–41. For more details see Kohlhagen, "The Performance of the Foreign Exchange Markets: 1971–1974," *Journal of International Business Studies*, Fall, 1975.

[3] These results are borne out by those of several other studies; see Robert Z. Aliber, "The Short Guide to Corporate International Finance", unpublished manuscript, *University of Chicago*, 1975: and Richard Levich, "Tests of Foreign Exchange Forecasting Models and Market Efficiency," *New York University, Graduate School of Business Working Paper No. 75–88*, November 1975.

[4] Robert B. Shulman, "Are Foreign Exchange Risks Measurable?" *Columbia Journal of World Business*, May–June 1970, pp. 55–60.

[5] Alan C. Shapiro, "Hedging Against Devaluations — a Management Science Approach," in C. G. Alexandrides (ed.), *International Business Systems Perspectives*, Atlanta: Georgia State University, 1972.

[6] Bernard A. Lietaer, "Managing Risks in Foreign Exchange," *Harvard Business Review*, March–April 1970, pp. 127–38.

This section argues that the cost of hedging, measured properly, is zero — but that in general the benefits from hedging are zero, too. And I shall suggest that techniques which purport to provide optimal hedging decisions in reality determine optimal speculation decisions, and that since they rely on currency forecasts they may, in a floating exchange rate environment, be decidedly sub-optimal.

Selective or consistent

Exchange risk is not the possibility of a devaluation; nor is it the possibility of suffering a loss in the translation of foreign currency accounts; nor is it even the possibility of lower reported income from foreign subsidiaries as the result of an exchange rate change. Exchange risk is concerned with fluctuations in real economic value, and therefore with future cash flows. It is the additional variability in a firm's cash flows arising from exchange rate changes.

Hedging strategy is properly concerned with how this variability may be reduced, and the costs of doing so. If forward hedging can be regarded as an insurance against exchange risk, we would expect firms to hedge transactions as consistently as they buy fire insurance. But they do not do so. Most would argue that consistent hedging is too expensive, and that it should be done selectively. That selectivity is what the management science applications listed above are all about.

The reason why hedging is done selectively is that corporate treasurers believe they can forecast devaluations more accurately than they can forecast fires. In other words, the success of a selective hedging strategy depends on the forecasting ability of the decision-maker. The first step is thus to forecast the probability of various exchange rate changes. When a currency is likely to devalue, the next step is to reduce cash and other short-term assets denominated in the weak currency, and to increase liabilities as far as possible in that currency by borrowing or selling the currency forward.

This approach has two obvious shortcomings. First, it ignores the so-called Fisher effect,[7] which says that interest rates in weak currencies tend to be high enough to compensate for devaluation losses. Second, it relies on exchange rate forecasting, which has become highly unreliable in the efficient market world of floating exchange rates where anticipations of future exchange rate changes are already reflected in spot and forward rates so that there may be no gain from forecasting.

In effect, then, selective forward hedging is not hedging; it is speculation based on a forecast. If a selective hedging strategy is to be successful, the corporate treasurer must believe that he is a superior exchange rate forecaster. And if he is, he should perhaps take advantage of his ability irrespective of hedging needs.

Balance sheet hedging

Some companies genuinely aim to reduce risk rather than speculate via a selective hedging strategy. They seek to avoid losses (and forego gains) by trying to match assets with liabilities in the same currency. For U.S. firms, this approach was encouraged by the original FASB ruling (No. 8) on translating foreign currency statements and by the U.S. Treasury department's exposure reporting requirements. By focusing on accounting translation, these concern themselves with the wrong thing, for actual gains or losses arise not from assets and liabilities themselves, but rather from the cash flows that these assets and liabilities generate.

The only reasonable approach to hedging, then, is to attempt to reduce the variability of actual cash flows from foreign operations by matching, whenever possible, each period's cash inflows with that period's cash outflows in a particular currency. This could be achieved through a careful restructuring of operations, sales and so forth, as is recommended by Shapiro and Robertson.[8] Most corporate treasurers, however, recognize that a firm cannot alter the nature of its business simply for exchange risk reasons. Hence, they sensibly do the inflow–outflow matching by appropriate structuring the currency and maturity of the firm's financial assets and liabilities rather than altering operating cash flows.

---

[7] See Ian H. Giddy, "Exchange Risk: Whose View?" unpublished working paper, *University of Chicago*, 1976.
[8] Alan C. Shapiro and Thomas S. Robertson, "Managing Foreign Exchange Risks: The Role of Marketing Strategy", *University of Pennsylvania Working Paper*, 1975.

In practical terms, this principle means that whenever a firm has cash inflows from sales in a particular foreign currency, it should seek to match those inflows by incurring contractual outflows in the same currency, either (i) by borrowing in the same currency as the firm has sales receipts, or (ii) by entering into a forward contract to sell that currency at the time the foreign currency will be received. Since interest rate parity generally prevails, the additional (or lower) cost of foreign currency debt should be equal to the forward discount (or premium) and the cost of either method will be the same.

Let us examine a typical example to illustrate how these techniques work. Under interest rate parity conditions, the borrowing cover will be equivalent to the forward cover method. I will discuss only the latter and generalize to hedging via foreign currency borrowing later. Assume a U.S. exporter expects to receive 100,000 Belgian francs three months from today as the result of an export sale. If the franc is selling at a 4% discount in the three-month forward exchange market, the exporter can fix his dollar receipts at 99% of the sales price by selling Belgian francs forward. The firm has, in effect, arranged a contractual cash outflow to match its expected cash inflow in the foreign currency, i.e. the one-shot hedge.

The value of forward hedging, from the point of view of this firm, is that the exporter has a fixed, predetermined amount of dollar cash at a future date, instead of an uncertain amount depending on the spot rate that will prevail one year hence. And by subtracting the forward discount, or adding the premium, the exporter can decide in advance whether or not the dollar receipt is sufficiently attractive to sell abroad rather than at home.

It is easy to see why such a forward contract is popularly regarded as insurance against exchange risk, and why forward hedging appears to eliminate exchange risk. However, forward hedging is not really insurance at all, and hedging does not reduce exchange risk for most firms engaged in international business.

Not insurance

The idea of insurance is that a large number of people, by pooling small premiums, share the cost of unexpected disasters. It is commonly thought that the cost of hedging is the premium necessary to avoid large exchange losses. One writer has expressed it as follows:

> Like the risk of fire, exchange risk can either be insured or the full financial consequence borne at the time the catastrophe occurs. If the exchange risk is managed, a modest loss is incurred in each accounting period: if the risk is not managed, there may be a large loss in a single period.[9]

But forward hedging cannot be regarded as insurance as we usually understand the term. With insurance, everyone benefiting from the safety of the insurance must pay some small amount, the total of which will be used to pay the person or persons who suffer a loss. For an exporter who is hedging by selling foreign currency forward, however, if the forward rate equals the expected spot rate, he can gain the safety, such as it is, without any expected cost. And if the forward rate is above the expected spot rate, he is actually getting a reward for using the safety of the forward market.

Suppose, for example, that the U.S. exporter wished to hedge export receipts in Belgian francs as described above, and that in addition a Belgian exporter receiving dollars in three months wished to hedge the franc value of his dollar receipts. The two exporters could enter into a mutually satisfactory agreement to exchange francs for dollars three months from now. As long as their currency expectations were similar, they could agree on a rate at which the francs would be sold for dollars. This is, of course, how the forward exchange market works, except that banks act as intermediaries between parties in a forward exchange contract.

Thus, both exporters benefit from the locked-in rate without either one bearing the burden of the other's risk. No insurance premium is involved since the agreed-upon forward rate will approximately equal what the parties to the contract feel will be the spot rate in three months' time. As long as the forward rate is an unbiased predictor of the future spot rate, the expected cost of hedging is zero.

---

[9] Newton H. Hoyt, Jr., "The Management of Currency Exchange Risk by the Singer Company", *Financial Management*, Spring 1972, p. 13.

This argument can be extended to the situation where the forward rate does not equal the expected future spot rate. In every such situation an upward bias on one side of the market implies a downward bias on the opposite side. Hence, one-shot exporters in one country or the other receive a positive expected return from hedging. I know of no insurance company that would similarly pay one for accepting insurance.

Not usually worthwhile

The classic one-shot example of an exporter or importer reducing risk through forward cover is hardly a realistic one. Most firms have continuing sales and costs, and therefore continuing receipts or outflows in a particular currency. For these, repeated forward hedging is of dubious value.

It is easy to see why this is so if we think of a U.S. exporter who makes monthly shipments to his Belgian customers, billing on 90-day terms. Every month in the future, he can expect to have revenues in Belgian francs. How can he reduce the variability of his revenue stream? The conventional answer would be to hedge his foreign currency receivables each time a shipment is made, by selling francs in the 90-day forward market.

But how does this help? The exporter looking ahead to his monthly franc revenues can fix today the value of the next three months' revenues, and perhaps some of the revenues for the next twelve months. For anything beyond that, however, even if he plans to use the forward market consistently, he faces exchange risk, because he does not know what forward rates will prevail when he does his future hedging operations.

For the habitual exporter or importer who plans regular foreign currency transactions indefinitely, exchanging his currency via the forward market yields just as much uncertainty as would waiting until the payment date and exchanging currency in the spot market each time. Since (a) future forward rates are just as unpredictable as are future spot rates, and (b) the forward rate appears to be on average an unbiased predictor of the spot rate so that there is no long-run expected cost or gain from using the forward market, use of forward hedging provides no more certainty (beyond the first few periods) than does waiting and simply exchanging everything in the spot market.

On the other hand, while there is no real benefit to using the forward market, there is no obvious harm in doing so either. Neither market can promise certainty for all future periods. The choice comes down to deciding (a) which market experiences fewer fluctuations, or lower variability in rates, and (b) in which market transactions costs are lower.

Transactions costs, as measured by bid–ask spreads, are almost invariably higher in forward markets than in spot markets. It is not clear why. Perhaps the markets are thinner; and, the thinner the markets, the wider the spreads.

The issue of relative variability is less clear-cut. It is not obvious what a good measure of relative variability would be, or how variability in exchange rates themselves affects variability in earnings. If all we are concerned with is comparing foreign currency receipts exchanged in the forward market as opposed to the spot market, the standard deviation of spot and forward rates seem to be a reasonable measure. For the Swiss franc, the variability of the two rates has been virtually identical. This simply means that, in general, the factors causing movements in spot rates also induce similar movements in forward rates.

Conclusion

Neither transactions costs nor variability provide a strong incentive for using forward rather than spot markets. On the other hand, there is no strong disincentive to the use of forward rates, either, since the difference in transactions costs is a very small percentage of the size of any transaction. For a habitual exporter or importer, repeated forward hedging can do little to reduce exchange risk defined as the variability of future cash flows in dollars. If covered interest arbitrage ensures that the borrowing cost differential equals the forward premium or discount, then the same conclusion holds for hedging via the money market rather than through the forward exchange market.

3. Forward contract accounting

Boris Antl, Douglas Bender and Jeffrey Donahue

Forward exchange contracts are considered foreign currency transactions under FASB 52. There are four types of forward exchange contracts, and the Statement specifies the following ways in which to dispose of gains and losses on these transactions.

1. Gains and losses on forward contracts (or other foreign currency transactions) which are designated as, and are effective as, an economic hedge of a net investment in a foreign entity are recorded directly in the translation adjustment account in shareholders' equity.

2. Gains and losses on forward contracts which hedge recorded foreign currency transactions are reported in net income.

3. Gains and losses on forward contracts which are designated as, and are effective as, a hedge of a firm foreign currency commitment are deferred and included in the measurement of the related foreign currency transaction when recorded.

4. Gains and losses on speculative forward contracts (i.e. contracts that do not hedge exposures) are reported in net income.

FASB 52 allows greater discretion in the accounting treatment of discounts and premiums on forward contracts than was the case under FASB 8. Generally, discounts and premiums on all forward contracts other than speculative contracts are to be included in income over the life of the forward contract. However, if a contract hedges a net investment, the related discount or premium *may* be included in the translation adjustment account in shareholders' equity along with the gain or the loss on the contract. Similarly, if a contract hedges a firm commitment, the related discount or premium *may* be deferred and included in the measurement of the related foreign currency transaction along with the deferred gain or loss on the contract. If a contract hedges a recorded foreign currency transaction, there is no option, and the related discount or premium must be reported in income along with the gain or loss on the contract. For speculative forward contracts, no separate accounting recognition is given to the discount or premium. The accounting for forward contract gains and losses is reviewed in greater detail below.

Hedging of transaction exposure

Transaction exposure arises whenever an entity — parent or subsidiary — has on its books assets or liabilities whose monetary value is denominated in currencies other than its own. Transaction exposures normally have a direct cash and tax impact, whereas translation exposures may not affect cash flows and/or taxes (*see* Hedging of translation exposure). Accordingly, exchange gains and losses on transaction exposures are included in income under FASB 52, whereas translation gains and losses are not. Accounting for forward contracts hedging transaction or translation exposure follows the accounting for gains and losses (and tax effects) on the underlying exposure (i.e. gains or losses on forward contracts hedging transaction exposure are included in income, whereas gains or losses on forward contracts hedging translation exposure are recorded directly in equity).

Since transaction exposure may occur at either the parent or subsidiary level, these exposures and related hedges will be accounted for in either the parent (reporting) currency or the functional currency of the foreign entity. In the example that follows, we illustrate transaction exposure and the hedging thereof at the parent company level.

The assumptions

The accounting treatment and cash impact of a foreign currency transaction exposure and an offsetting forward contract are shown in Exhibit 4.3.1, with the following assumptions:

- A U.S. multinational company books a payable of 1,666·67 foreign currency units (FC) on 31/12/X0. The payable is due on 31/12/X1. The exchange (spot) rate on 31/12/XI is FC 1·00 = $1·00. The tax rate for the U.S. parent is 40% and is assumed to apply to gains and losses on both the transaction and the forward contract.
- On December 31, 19X0, the U.S. parent projects a substantial appreciation of the foreign currency against the dollar over the next year, and buys forward FC 1,666·67 to cover its exposure on an after-tax basis for delivery on December 31, 19XI at $1·05. The exchange rate moves to FC 1·00 = $1·15 at December 31, 19X1.

The exposure and forward contract data are shown in the first column of Exhibit 4.3.1. The second column shows the results for the year 19X1.

Exhibit 4.3.1: Accounting treatment and cash impact: transaction exposure of parent

Exposure

		31/12/X0	31/12/X1
(1)	Date		
(2)	Exposure (foreign currency)	(1,666·67)	(1,666·67)
(3)	Exchange rate ($/FC)	1·00	1·15
(4)	$ equivalents	(1,666·67)	(1,916·67)
(5)	FX gain (loss) before tax		(250·00)
(6)	Tax (40%)		100·00
(7)	FX gain (loss) after tax		(150·00)

Forward contract

(8)	Amount bought	1,666·67	1,666·67
(9)	$ value of contract: lines (8) × (3)	1,666·67	1,916·67
(10)	FX gain (loss) before tax		250
(11)	Tax (40%)		(100)
(12)	FX gain (loss) after tax		150

FASB 52 gain (loss)

(13)	FX gain (loss) before tax: lines (5) + (10)		0
(14)	FX gain (loss) after tax: lines (7) + (12)		0

Income and cash impact

(15)	Premium to be amortized ($)*		(83·33)
(16)	Tax (40%)		33·33
(17)	Decrease in after-tax income		(50)
(18)	Total increase (decrease) in net income: lines (14) + (17)		(50)
(19)	Total cash flow from forward contract: lines (12) + (17)		100
(20)	Overall cash gain (loss): lines (7) + (19)		(50)

* Premium to be amortized = (spot at start of contract − forward rate) × FC amount bought = (1·00 − 1·05) × 1,666·67 = ($83·33).

Treatment

The first seven lines of the Exhibit concern the exposure data and the related foreign currency transaction gains or losses. On the forward contract data (lines 8 to 12), the foreign exchange gain or loss is computed in accordance with FASB 52.

Line 13 shows the total reported FASB 52 foreign exchange gain before tax. This is the sum of the before-tax foreign exchange loss on the net exposed liability of FC 1,666·67 and the before-tax foreign exchange gain on the forward contract. Line 14 shows the after-tax foreign exchange gain or loss, which is the reported FASB 52 foreign exchange gain net of the appropriate tax impacts of the transaction exposure and the forward contract. If the after-tax exposure is perfectly hedged, line 14 should be zero, as it is in the Exhibit.

Lines 15 to 20 identify the cash and net after-tax income implications of a foreign currency exposure and a related forward contract. The reported foreign exchange gain or loss on a hedge contract does not include the premium/discount accounting entries. A decrease of $50·00 (line 17) in after-tax income, which would occur from amortization of the premium, would not be classified as part of the foreign exchange gain or loss on the forward contract. Line 18 identifies the total decrease in after-tax income, which in this case is identical to the after-tax premium expense of $50·00.

The cash impact of hedging transactions is another consideration. Cash flows in this situation will be affected by both the transaction and the forward contract. Accordingly, as the after-tax cash loss resulting from the settlement of the liability is $150 (line 7) and the cash gain resulting from the closing of the forward contract is $100 (line 19), the overall cash loss is $50 (line 20). This cash loss is identical to the total decrease in net income (line 18), which, in turn, is identical to the after-tax premium expense (line 17). The overall cost of hedging a transaction is thus the premium/discount expense/revenue after tax.

Hedging of translation exposure

If a forward contract is designated as, and is effective as, a hedge of a net investment in a foreign entity, gains or losses should be calculated in each accounting period based on the spot exchange rates at the beginning (or inception date of the contract, if later) and end (or termination date of the contract, if earlier) of the accounting period, pursuant to paragraph 18 of FASB 52. Such gains or losses are recorded directly in the translation adjustment account in shareholders' equity, pursuant to paragraph 20a of FASB 52.[1] Before taxes, the translation adjustment on the exposed net investment position is exactly offset by the gain or loss on the forward contract if the contract is for the same amount of foreign currency units as the underlying exposure (net investment).[2] If taxes are taken into account (i.e. if the forward contract is intended to provide full after-tax protection), the amount of the forward contract may be increased to the amount of the foreign currency exposure multiplied by the reciprocal of (one minus the tax rate). This formula applies when the unrealized gain or loss on the net investment exposure is not taxed, but the gain or loss on the contract is.[3] The original discount or premium on the contract should be accounted for separately by amortization over the life of the contract; the amortization during the hedge period *may* be recorded directly in the translation adjustment account together with the other components of gain or loss on the hedged net investment position.

The assumptions

The accounting treatment, cash impact and economic implications of a net investment exposure and an offsetting hedge contract are shown in Exhibit 4.3.2 with the following assumptions:

— A U.S. multinational company has a net investment exposure of 1,000 foreign currency units (FC) on 31/12/X0 in a subsidiary in country A. This exposure remains unchanged throughout the accounting period. The spot rate on 31/12/X0 is FC 1·00 = $1·00. The tax rate for the U.S. parent is 40%.

— On December 31, 19X0, the U.S. parent projects a substantial depreciation of the foreign currency against the dollar over the next year, and sells forward FC 1,666·67 to cover its net investment exposure on an after-tax basis, for delivery on December 31, 19X1 at $·95. The exchange rate moves to FC 1·00 = $·85 at December 31, 19X1.

— The company chooses *not* to include the amortization of the discount in the translation adjustment account.

The parent's exposure data and forward contract data are shown in the first column of Exhibit 4.3.2. The second column shows the results for the year 19X1.

---

[1] Under FASB 8, gains or losses on forward contracts hedging exposed net asset or liability positions were recorded in income, as were the translation gains and losses resulting from the exposed positions.

[2] As it may not be feasible or practical to hedge in the same currency as the functional currency of the foreign entity, FASB 52 allows hedging transactions to be denominated in a currency for which the exchange rate generally moves in tandem with the exchange rate for the functional currency of the foreign entity (paragraph 130).

[3] Paragraph 24 of FASB 52 requires that any income taxes related to translation adjustments be allocated to the same separate component of equity as the translation adjustments.

Exhibit 4.3.2: Accounting treatment and cash impact: translation exposure

Net investment exposure

		31/12/X0	31/12/X1
(1)	Date		
(2)	Exposure (FC)	1,000	1,000
(3)	Exchange rates ($/FC)	1·00	0·85
(4)	$ equivalents	1,000	850
(5)	Translation adjustment before tax		(150)
(6)	Tax (0%)		0
(7)	Translation adjustment after tax		(150)

Forward contract

		31/12/X0	31/12/X1
(8)	Amount sold	(1,666·67)	(1,666·67)
(9)	$ value of contract: lines (8) × (3)	(1,666·67)	(1,416·67)
(10)	FX gain (loss) before tax		250
(11)	Tax (40%)		(100)
(12)	FX gain (loss) after tax		150

FASB 52 translation adjustment

Lines (7) + (12)	0

Income and cash impact

(13)	Discount to be amortized ($)*	(83·33)
(14)	Tax (40%)	33·33
(15)	Decrease in after-tax income	(50)
(16)	Total cash flow from forward contract: lines (12) + (15)	100
(17)	Total economic impact (implied cash flow): lines (7) + (16)	(50)

* Discount to be amortized = (forward rate – spot at start of contract) × FC amount sold = $(0·95 – 1·00) \times 1,666·67 = ($83·33)$.

Treatment

Going down the lines of data in Exhibit 4.3.2, the first seven lines concern the net investment exposure data and the related translation adjustment. Because the exchange rate is $·85 on December 31, 19X1, a translation adjustment of $150 would be charged to the translation adjustment account, reflecting the decrease in the parent's net investment translated at current exchange rates. This reduction in carrying value, as line 6 shows, is not tax deductible in the foreign country and is assumed not to reduce taxes in the United States.

On the forward contract data (lines 8 to 12), the foreign exchange gain or loss is computed in accordance with FASB 52. Line 8 identifies the amount to be sold forward if the after-tax exposure is to be fully hedged. If the after-tax exposure is perfectly hedged, the sum of lines 7 and 12 should be zero, as it is in the Exhibit.

Lines 13 to 16 identify some of the cash and net after-tax income implications of foreign currency exposures and related hedge contracts. The reported foreign exchange gain or loss on a hedge contract does not include the premium/discount accounting entries. A decrease of $50 (line 15) in after-tax income, which would occur from amortization of the discount, would not be classified as part of the foreign exchange gain or loss on the forward contract, but it could have been included in the translation adjustment account had the company so opted. The cash impact of hedging is another consideration (line 16), and the Exhibit indicates that the after-tax cash gain is $100. This gain is equal to the after-tax foreign exchange gain of $150 minus the after-tax discount expense of $50.

The only cash ramifications of a hedge of translation exposure are those arising from the forward hedge contract itself; translation gains or losses do not produce or require offsetting cash flow. This is in contrast to hedges of transaction and commitment exposure, where the underlying exposure being hedged produces (requires) cash flows which may be used for (obtained from) settlement of the forward contract. Hence, forward contracts hedging translation exposure are virtually always closed by entering into an equal and offsetting contract immediately prior to termination of the original contract.

In the above example, the parent would purchase FC 1,666·67 on, say, December 30, 19X1. Assuming the spot price had moved to FC 1·00 = $0·85, the cash received upon closing the hedge contract would be $166·67 (forward value of original contract of $1,583·34 less value of offsetting contract of $1,416·67). After taxes of 40%, the net cash gain is $100, the same amount as derived in Exhibit 4.3.2 (line 16).

Finally, the overall economic impact of hedging strategies is computed (line 17). This figure is derived by adding the after-tax translation adjustment on the exposure (i.e. the paper gain or loss) and the cash impact of hedging, under the assumption that as exchange rates change, net assets abroad are worth more or fewer dollars. To illustrate, if the Deutschemark suffered another 1923-style depreciation, net assets in that currency would be worth just a few dollars; hence, the term economic gain or loss. In this context, the economic loss with coverage (line 17) is the same as the total decrease in net income (line 15).

While the accounting for hedges of translation exposure is considerably different under FASB 52 from what it was under FASB 8 (i.e. gains or losses go to equity rather than income), the same trade-off with respect to risking cash to protect translation exposure persists. However, under FASB 52 it is fluctuations in *equity* versus cash gains and losses, whereas under FASB 8 it was fluctuations in *income* versus cash gains and losses. If a company is averse to risking cash, it should not hedge translation exposure and instead incur fluctuations in equity. Conversely, if it cannot tolerate fluctuations in equity, it must be prepared to risk cash.

Hedging of a foreign currency commitment

A forward contract is treated as a hedge of a commitment if the two conditions laid down in paragraph 21 of FASB 52 are met. The conditions are: (a) the foreign currency transaction is designated as, and is effective as, a hedge of a foreign currency commitment, and (b) the foreign currency commitment is firm.[4]

Commitment exposure generally begins at the time a purchase contract is issued or a sales contract is accepted, but accounting recognition of the commitment is delayed until the transaction date, which is the date on which the purchase or sale is recorded in the accounting records in conformity with generally accepted accounting principles. (Some commitments do not involve purchases or sales; for example, the transaction dates under a lease are the dates on which individual lease payments come due.)

Since no accounting recognition is given to the commitment or the exchange rate fluctuations during the commitment period, FASB 52 specifies that no separate recognition be given to the gain or loss on the covering forward contract during that period. Instead, any gain or loss on the forward contract is deferred (unless deferral would lead to recognizing losses in later periods) and included in the measurement of the related transaction on the transaction date. From that time (i.e. after the transaction is recorded), the covering forward contract will have to be accounted for as either a hedge of a foreign currency transaction or a speculative contract (depending on whether the transaction exposure remains or is closed by payment), with any gain or loss on the forward contract going to income, unless the contract is redesignated as, and is effective as, a hedge of a net investment in a foreign entity (*see* Hedging of translation exposure) or another foreign currency commitment.

The premium or discount on the forward contract should be accounted for separately; it must be amortized (recognized) over the life of the contract, but the portion amortizable during the commitment period may be included in the measurement of the related transaction, e.g. as an adjustment of the cost of the inventory purchased.

The assumptions

The accounting treatment, cash impact and tax implications of a foreign exchange commitment exposure and an offsetting forward contract are shown in Exhibit 4.3.3 with the following assumptions:

---

4 Under FASB 8, as amended by FASB 20, three conditions had to be met: (a) the life of the forward contract had to extend from the foreign currency commitment date to the expected transaction date or a later date, (b) the forward contract had to be denominated in the same currency as the foreign currency commitment and (c) the foreign currency commitment had to be firm and non-cancellable.

- A U.S. company commits itself on December 31, 19X0 (commitment date) to purchase inventory in foreign currency (FC) for FC 1,666·67 on June 30, 19X1 (date at which it takes delivery of the inventory and therefore the transaction date), payable on December 31, 19X1. The tax rate for the U.S. company is 40% (tax effects are discussed further below).
- Projecting an appreciation of the FC against the dollar, the company enters into a 12-month forward contract on December 31, 19X0, to buy FC 1,666·67 at $1·05.
- The exchange rate moves as follows:
  - 31/12/X0 FC 1·00 = $1·00
  - 30/6/X1 FC 1·00 = $1·05
  - 31/12/X1 FC 1·00 = $1·15.
- The company chooses *not* to include the contract premium relating to the commitment period in the measure of the dollar basis of the inventory.
- After the transaction date (June 30, 19X1), the transaction exposure remains (i.e. it is not closed by payment) and the company chooses *not* to redesignate the forward contract as a hedge of its net investment position in an FC subsidiary or another foreign currency commitment. Accordingly, the forward contract is accounted for as a hedge of a foreign currency transaction, with gains or losses on the contract after the transaction date going to income.
- Purchased inventory remains on hand through December 31, 19X1.

The exposure data and the forward contract data are shown in the first column of Exhibit 4.3.3. The remaining columns show the results for the first and second halves of 19X1 (columns two and three), and the cumulative impact of foreign exchange fluctuations on cash, income, taxes and inventory in 19X1 (column four).

Treatment

Going down the lines of data in the Exhibit, the first sub-group concerns the balance sheet exposure data (lines 1 to 7, inclusive). As the first column shows, the commitment of FC 1,666·67 is the equivalent of $1,666·67 on December 31, 19X0. On June 30, 19X1, the commitment, although unchanged in FC terms, has increased to the equivalent of $1,750·00, as the FC has appreciated in value from $1·00 to $1·05 (column 2). Since the commitment is an off-balance sheet item, no foreign exchange loss on the contractual liability would be recognized or reported by the company under U.S. accounting principles.

On June 30, 19X1 (transaction date), the inventory is delivered and an account payable of $1,750·00 (FC 1,666·67 times $1·05) is recorded in the books. When the debt comes due on December 31, 19X1, the FC payable is translated at the prevailing exchange rate of $1·15 and is the equivalent of $1,916·67. Accordingly, a foreign exchange loss (on the payable) of $166·67 ($1,916·67 minus $1,750·00) is recognized by the company, in part mitigated by a tax credit of $66·67, resulting in an after-tax loss of $100·00.

Lines 8 to 12 inclusive concern the forward contract data. As the first column shows, the amount of FC 1,666·67 purchased forward is the equivalent of $1,666·67 on December 31, 19X0. On June 30, 19X1 (column 2) the contract is worth $1,750·00 (FC 1·00 = $1·05) but no foreign exchange gain is recognized or reported, consistent with the non-recognition of the foreign exchange loss on the commitment during the first half of 19X1. (On the transaction date the unrecognized gain of $83·33 on the forward contract will be included in the dollar measure of the inventory purchased.) From July 1, 19X1, to December 31, 19X1 (i.e. after the transaction is recorded), the forward contract must be accounted for as a hedge of a foreign currency transaction as described earlier, thereby offsetting the transaction loss on the open FC liability.

Line 13 shows the total before-tax foreign exchange gain or loss reported under FASB 52. This is the sum of the before-tax foreign exchange loss on the FC liability of 1,666·67 and the before-tax foreign exchange gain on the forward contract after the transaction date. Line 14 shows the after-tax foreign exchange gain or loss, which is the reported FASB 52 foreign exchange gain or loss, net of the appropriate tax credit or expense resulting from the transaction loss on the FC liability and the forward contract gain after the transaction date (the same tax rate

Exhibit 4.3.3: Accounting treatment and cash impact: commitment exposure

Exposure

	31/12/X0	30/06/X1	31/12/X1	Cumulative for 19X1
(1) Date				
(2) Exposure (FC)	(1,666·67)	(1,666·67)	(1,666·67)	
(3) Exchange rate ($/FC)	1·00	1·05	1·15	
(4) $ equivalents	(1,666·67)	(1,750·00)	(1,916·67)	
(5) FX gain (loss) before tax			(166·67)	(166·67)
(6) Tax (40%)			66·67	66·67
(7) FX gain (loss) after tax			(100·00)	(100·00)

Forward contract

	31/12/X0	30/06/X1	31/12/X1	Cumulative for 19X1
(8) Amount bought (FC)	1,666·67	1,666·67	1,666·67	
(9) $ value of contract: lines (8) × (3)	1,666·67	1,750·00	1,916·67	
(10) FX gain (loss) before tax			166·67	166·67
(11) Tax (40%)			(66·67)	(66·67)
(12) FX gain (loss) after tax			100·00	100·00

FASB 52 gain (loss)

	31/12/X0	30/06/X1	31/12/X1	Cumulative for 19X1
(13) FX gain (loss) before tax: lines (5) + (10)			0	0
(14) FX gain (loss) after tax: lines (7) + (12)			0	0

Income and cash impact

	31/12/X0	30/06/X1	31/12/X1	Cumulative for 19X1
(15) Premium to be amortized ($)*		(41·67)	(41·66)	(83·33)
(16) Tax (40%)		16·67	16·66	33·33
(17) Decrease in after-tax income: lines (15) + (16) + (14)		(25·00)	(25·00)	(50·00)
(18) Total cash flow from forward contract, cumulative at maturity: lines (21) + (22) + (12) + (17)				100·00

Inventory

	31/12/X0	30/06/X1	31/12/X1	Cumulative for 19X1
(19) FC value		1,666·67		
(20) $ value: lines (19) × (3)		1,750·00		
(21) FX gain on forward contract during commitment period		83·33		83·33
(22) Tax (40%)		(33·33)		(33·33)
(23) Decrease in $ value of inventory		(83·33)		
(24) Book ($) value of inventory: lines (20) + (23)		1,666·67		

* Premium to be amortized = (spot at start of contract − forward rate) × FC amount bought = (1·00 − 1·05) × 1,666·67 = ($83·33).

is assumed for both transactions; see below). If the FC liability is properly hedged on an after-tax basis, line 14 should be zero, as it is in Exhibit 4.3.3.

The cash implications

Lines 15 to 18 inclusive identify some of the after-tax income and cash implications of the commitment and liability exposures and the related forward contract. The reported foreign exchange gain or loss on the forward contract does not include the premium or discount accounting entries. The decrease of $83·33 (line 15, last column) in before-tax income, which would occur from the amortization of the premium, would not be classified as part of the foreign exchange gain or loss on the forward contract. The cash impact of the forward contract is another consideration (line 18), and the Exhibit indicates that the after-tax cash gain (on the contract) is $100·00. This is the sum of the foreign exchange impact of the contract during the whole of 19X1 plus the premium cost of hedging, all net of taxes.

As a result of all the transactions, total after-tax income will decrease by $50·00 (line 17, last column), which is the sum of the after-tax gain on the forward contract after the transaction date (line 14) and the after-tax premium expense over the life of the forward contract (lines 15 and 16). Because the FC liability was perfectly hedged on an after-tax basis, the decrease in the reported after-tax income is thus equal to the after-tax premium expense.

The impact of the above transactions on the inventory is analysed in lines 19 to 24 inclusive. When the inventory is received on June 30, 19X1 (column 2), it is valued at $1,750·00, which is FC 1,666·67 translated into dollars at the June 30th exchange rate of FC 1·00 = $1·05. The dollar value of the inventory must then be adjusted to reflect the foreign exchange gain on the forward contract deferred during the commitment period, i.e. $83·33 (line 21). The book value of the inventory as of June 30, 19X1 is therefore $1,666·67 (line 24), precisely the cost (spot rate) prevailing on December 31, 19X0 when the inventory was ordered (commitment date). If the tax of $33·33 (due to the foreign exchange gain of $83·33 on the forward contract during the commitment period — line 22) is payable before the inventory is sold, a deferred tax debit will be established and be charged to income when the inventory is sold.

FASB 52 provides for after-tax hedging of a commitment, as did FASB 8, as amended by FASB 20. An after-tax hedge should be based on after-tax exposure. A commitment is most likely to be hedged in an import or export situation where only the domestic tax laws apply and the after-tax hedge (the after-tax exposure divided by one less the tax rate) will equal the before-tax exposure except when different tax rates apply to the results of the transaction and to the results of the forward contract. When a portion of a forward contract is intended to provide a hedge on an after-tax basis, a gain or loss pertaining thereto, to the extent that that portion is in excess of the related commitment (none in the case of the import or export situation described in the preceding sentence), shall be deferred and shall be offset (literally) against the related tax effects when they are recognized, i.e. that portion of the gain or loss on the forward contract is credited or charged to tax expense for accounting purposes.

The hedging calculations in the preceding paragraph are illustrated by the import example used in this section. The company commits to purchase inventory costing FC 1,666·67, establishing a before-tax commitment exposure (short) of that amount. A 40% tax rate is assumed applicable to the exchange difference on the exposure (whether it is considered for tax purposes to be an exchange gain or loss, or an adjustment of inventory cost and therefore ultimately of cost of sales), so the after-tax exposure is FC 1,000·00 (FC 1,666·67 times one less the tax rate or FC 1,666·67 times 0·60). A 40% tax rate is assumed applicable to the gain/loss on the forward contract. The after-tax hedge is, therefore, FC 1,000·00 divided by one less the tax rate or FC 1,000·00/0·60 or FC 1,666·67 and the company should enter into a forward contract to buy (go long) the latter amount if it wishes to hedge on an after-tax basis its before-tax commitment exposure of the same amount.

Simple speculation

Forward foreign exchange contracts which are neither a hedge of a net investment in a foreign entity, nor a hedge of a foreign currency transaction nor a hedge of a foreign currency commitment are treated as speculative contracts under FASB 52. Speculative contracts are the easiest to account for. The reported foreign exchange gain or loss on an outstanding speculative contract is the difference between the contract rate and the current forward rate to the maturity of the existing contract, i.e. the current market quote for a contract which would offset the existing contract for its remaining term. Premiums or discounts are not accounted for separately on this category of forward contracts.

The assumptions

The accounting treatment, cash impact and tax implications of a speculative forward contract are presented in Exhibit 4.3.4 with the following assumptions:

— Anticipating an appreciation of the foreign currency (FC) against the dollar, a U.S. company enters into a twelve-month forward contract on December 31, 19X0, to buy FC 1,666·67. The tax rate for the U.S. company is 40%.

— The exchange rates (spot and forward) move as follows:

	Spot rate	Forward rate to maturity
31/12/X0	FC 1·00 = $1·00	$1·05
31/12/X1	FC 1·00 = $1·15	$1·15

The forward contract data are shown in the first column of Exhibit 4.3.4. The second column shows the results for the year 19X1.

Exhibit 4.3.4: Accounting treatment and cash impact: speculative forward contract

Forward contract

		31/12/X0	31/12/X1
(1)	Date		
(2)	Amount bought (FC)	1,666·67	1,666·67
(3)	Fwd contact rate ($/FC)	1·05	1·05
(4)	Fwd rate to maturity ($/FC)	1·05	1·15
(5)	Value of contract if sold: lines (2) × (4) (in $)	1,750·00	1,916·67
(6)	FX gain (loss) before tax		166·67
(7)	Tax (40%)		(66·67)
(8)	FX gain (loss) after tax		100·00

Income and cash impact

		31/12/X1
(9)	Spot ($/FC)	1·15
(10)	Amount received ($): lines (9) × (2)	1,916·67
(11)	Amount paid ($): lines (3) × (2)	1,750·00
(12)	Cash gain (loss) before tax	166·67
(13)	Tax (40%)	(66·67)
(14)	Cash gain (loss) after tax	100·00

Treatment

Going down the lines of data in the Exhibit, the first subgroup concerns the income impact of the foreign exchange forward contract (lines 1 to 8). As the first column shows, the purchased amount of FC 1,666·67 is equivalent to $1,750·00, which is the amount of FC bought multiplied by the forward contract rate. This purchased amount of FC 1,666·67 can (by definition) be sold to the same maturity for $1,750·00 (line 5). Accordingly, no foreign exchange gain or loss exists as of December 31, 19X0. When the contract matures on December 31, 19X1, a foreign exchange gain of $166·67 (before tax) will be recorded in line with the movement of the forward rate from $1·05 to $1·15 (the spot rate at maturity equals the forward rate to maturity). This gain will incur a tax expense of $66·67, resulting in a net gain of $100·00 during 19X1.

Lines 9 to 14 concern the actual cash flows. The company contracted to pay $1,750·00 for FC 1,666·67 it purchased on December 31, 19X0 at $1·05 (line 11). This same amount of FC 1,666·67 concomitantly will be sold for $1,916·67 at the prevailing spot rate at maturity on December 31, 19X1, of $1·15 (line 10). The difference between the dollar amounts received ($1,916·67) and paid ($1,750·00) is the before-tax cash gain of $166·67 (line 12). A tax expense of $66·67 will reduce this gain to $100·00, which is the same amount as reported in the income statement (line 8).

Summary

As Exhibit 4.3.5 indicates, the cash impact of a forward contract is the same, regardless of how the forward contract is classified for accounting purposes under FASB 52 (line 7 of Exhibit 4.3.5). The reported income (line 8) in the four situations, however, varies as the underlying exposures or transactions vary.

In the case of covered translation exposure (i.e. hedge of a net investment), the only impact on income is the after-tax premium/discount expense; the after-tax translation adjustment on the exposure and the after-tax gain on the contract are both recorded directly in a translation adjustment account in shareholders' equity.

Exhibit 4.3.5: Cash impact of a forward contract: summary

Type of forward contract

Item	Hedge (translation)			Hedge (transaction)			Hedge (commitment)			Speculative		
	Before tax	Tax	After tax	Before tax	Tax	After tax	Before tax	Tax	After tax	Before tax	Tax	After tax
(1) Exposure loss — recorded*	(150)	0	(150)	(250)	100	(150)	(166·67)	66·67	(100)	—	—	—
(2) Exposure loss — unrecorded	—	—	—	—	—	—	(83·33)	33·33	(50)	—	—	—
(3) Forward contract gain — recorded*	250	(100)	150	250	(100)	150	166·67	(66·67)	100	166·67	(66·67)	100
(4) Forward contract gain — deferred	—	—	—	—	—	—	83·33	(33·33)	50	—	—	—
(5) FASB 52 FX gain/(loss): lines (1) + (3)*	100	(100)	0	0	0	0	0	0	0	166·67	(66·67)	100
(6) Premium/discount expense	(83·33)	33·33	(50)	(83·33)	33·33	(50)	(83·33)	33·33	(50)	—	—	—
(7) Cash impact of forward contract: lines (3) + (4) + (6)	166·67	(66·67)	100	166·67	(66·67)	100	166·67	(66·67)	100	166·67	(66·67)	100
(8) Income impact: lines (5) + (6)†	(83·33)	33·33	(50)	(83·33)	33·33	(50)	(83·33)	33·33	(50)	166·67	(66·67)	100
(9) Overall cash impact: lines (1) + (2) + (7)	16·67	(66·67)	(50)	(83·33)	33·33	(50)	(83·33)	33·33	(50)	166·67	(66·67)	100

* Recorded directly in the translation adjustment account in shareholders' equity for hedge (translation).
† Only line 6 for hedge (translation).

In the case of covered transaction exposure (i.e. hedge of a foreign currency transaction), the after-tax loss on the transaction is perfectly offset by the after-tax gain on the contract; the only impact on income is again the after-tax premium/discount expense.

In the commitment situation, the after-tax loss on the foreign currency liability is also perfectly offset by the after-tax gain on the forward contract after the end of the commitment period; an opportunity loss (not recognized for accounting purposes) on the unrecorded payable has occurred during the commitment period and the foreign exchange gain on the forward contract during that period is credited to the inventory account. Again, because of perfect after-tax hedging, both during and after the commitment period, the only impact on income is the after-tax premium/discount expense.

Finally, in the case of a speculative contract no underlying exposure exists, and the after-tax cash and income impacts are the same. In the final analysis, the key difference between the various types of forward contracts is the manner of reporting them under FASB 52.[5]

---

[5] For accounting investment of forward foreign exchange contracts under FASB-8, see *The Management of Foreign Exchange Risk*, 1st edition, edited by Richard Ensor and Boris Antl, Euromoney Publications, London 1978.

4. Corporate borrowing, tax and exchange risk

Malcolm J. Finney and Nigel Meade

One of the most likely reasons for models to be criticized is that they tend to be too sophisticated for practical purposes and are built with too ambitious an objective. There tends to be an innate fear of columns of figures purporting to provide optimal solutions which have been produced by the somewhat mysterious workings of a computer.

Here, we describe a practical approach to the corporate long-term foreign currency borrowing decision, capable of use by both companies and their advisers. In particular the methods described are designed to avoid the pitfalls of the need for excessive data requirements and to avoid the need for specific point forecasts of currency exchange rates.

Tax treatment

In a world of floating exchange rates, whenever a company borrows any currency other than the domestic currency of the country in which it is situated, there will inevitably be a currency risk. The tax treatment of any loss of profit arising on the eventual capital repayment of the borrowing will depend upon the legislation in the country of residence of the borrower. In the case of the U.K., no tax relief is currently available, but conversely no gain is taxable. In the United States, the opposite is true.

As an example, a U.K. company borrows $900,000 to purchase a capital asset in the United States. Over the duration of the loan, say, five years, assume that the interest paid (in dollars) exactly balances the dollar income generated by the asset and assume that the $/£ exchange rate appreciates from a level of $2·25 to $1·50. At the end of the five years the loan becomes repayable, but assume the asset only realized $750,000. There is thus a real loss of $150,000. However, what is the tax position? The example below sets this out:

		Exchange rate ($/£)	
Proceeds of sale	$750,000	1·50	£500,000
Cost of asset	$900,000	2·25	£400,000
Real loss	$150,000		
Taxable profit			£100,000
Tax on chargeable gain (30%)			£30,000

In other words, the company, despite having made a real loss of £100,000 (i.e. $150,000 at a $1·50/£ exchange rate) finds itself for U.K. tax purposes with a profit of £100,000 and a £30,000 tax bill. The reason for the apparent lack of tax symmetry stems from the fact that the Finance Act 1965 which introduced capital gains tax contains no reference to liabilities and none of the provisions can be construed as applying to liabilities.

Gains and losses on liabilities cannot, therefore, in any circumstances be assimilated to capital asset gains and losses. Basically, either one gets relief against trading profits or there is no relief at all.

What is more important — indeed, fundamental — is the fact that many companies have borrowed foreign currency to finance assets in the same currency in the belief that they are fully hedged. In reality, they may have been taking a very serious exchange risk indeed when tax is taken into account, i.e. the gain on the asset would be taxable but the corresponding loss on the liability would not be tax allowable.

The trade-offs from the point of view of the company are the same, regardless of the purpose for which the money is borrowed. The figures are exactly the same whatever use the borrowing is put to.

There is a simple but highly effective and practical tool which can be used as an aid in choosing the currency in which to undertake a corporate borrowing. It is not put forward as a panacea, but simply as an easy-to-use tool which can be used as an input to the corporate borrowing decision.

None of us has a crystal ball to forecast currencies, but for the corporate treasurer faced with borrowing five-year Deutschemarks or five-year Swiss francs, some assumptions as to the future must be made. What assumptions should be made and how sensitive is the final outcome to these assumptions?

For example, a U.S. corporation wishes to borrow $1 million for five years and has two alternatives. It can either borrow in its own currency at, say, 8·5% per annum or Deutschemarks at, say, 5·5% per annum. Let us assume that the initial exchange rate of the time of undertaking the borrowing is DM2·01/$1 and then examine the consequences for the company if the dollar depreciates against the Deutschemark by (a) 2% per annum over the life of the loan, and (b) 4% per annum over the life of the loan. Under (a) the DM/$ rate at the end of the five-year period would be DM1·82/$, and DM1·63/$ under (b). Exhibit 4.4.1 sets out the repayment schedules under (a) and (b) and the resultant net present values (NPV) of applying a discount rate equal to the coupon attached to the five-year dollar borrowing, i.e. 8·5% (semi-annual coupons are assumed).

Exhibit 4.4.1: Repayment schedule (a)

Loan	0	1	2	3	**Payment period (years)** 4	5	6	7	8	9	10	NPV
					(Expressed in $ equivalents)							
$	1,000	(42·5)	(42·5)	(42·5)	(42·5)	(42·5)	(42·5)	(42·5)	(42·5)	(42·5)	(1,042·5)	0
DM (a)	1,000	(27·8)	(28·1)	(28·3)	(28·6)	(28·9)	(29·2)	(29·5)	(29·7)	(30·1)	(1,134·4)	(39·9)
DM (b)	1,000	(28·0)	(28·6)	(29·2)	(29·7)	(30·3)	(30·9)	(31·5)	(32·2)	(32·8)	(1,250·1)	(46·6)

The net present value figure represents the net inflow or outflow of cash to the company discounted back to the date at which the loan was undertaken. Thus, if the Deutschemark borrowing is undertaken and the rate of depreciation of the dollar is 2% (option (a) per annum) then compared to the dollar borrowing the company would be $39,900 better off. Under (b), however, the rate of depreciation would be such as to result in the company being worse off to the extent of $46,000 (these amounts are in present-day terms).

This exercise can clearly be carried out for any number of borrowing options and the resultant net present values compared. In addition, the effect in post-tax terms can also be computed. Although such an exercise is useful, it merely serves to highlight that a problem exists. It does not provide a practical means of deciding which currency to borrow although it does give an insight to a possible solution.

What would be helpful is the break-even exchange rate on the borrowing. Basically, what this involves is calculating the rate of exchange at the end of the life of the loan, which will result in the cost to the borrower equating with that of a borrowing in his own currency. In the case of the example given, the cost attached to the Deutschemark loan would be equivalent to the cost of the dollar loan if the dollar depreciated by some 2·94% per annum over the life of the loan, implying a break-even exchange rate of DM1·74/$1 at the end of the five years. The resultant repayment schedule is given in Exhibit 4.4.2.

Exhibit 4.4.2: Repayment schedule (b)

Loan	0	1	2	3	**Payment period ($\frac{1}{2}$ years)** 4	5	6	7	8	9	10	NPV
					(Expressed in $ equivalents)							
$	1,000	(42·5)	(42·5)	(42·5)	(42·5)	(42·5)	(42·5)	(42·5)	(42·5)	(42·5)	(1,042·5)	0
DM (assuming break-even depreciation rate)	1,000	(27·9)	(28·3)	(28·7)	(29·1)	(29·6)	(30·0)	(30·4)	(30·9)	(31·3)	(1,187·8)	0

Assuming that the DM/$ exchange rate moves at 2·94% per annum over the life of the loan, then to the U.S. corporate borrower the true cost of borrowing the Deutschemarks would be 8·5% and not 5·5%, the same as the cost of the dollar borrowing.

This excercise may be repeated for a variety of currencies and rates. Part 1 of Exhibit 4.4.3 takes four interest rates in four different currencies. Part 2 illustrates the results of repeating the exercise shown in Exhibit 4.4.2. It shows, first, the spot rates of three of the currencies against the U.S. dollar (except for sterling) and second, the break-even exchange rate at the end of the period of the various loan lengths which would equate the cost of the particular currency borrowing with the cost of the U.S. dollar borrowing.

Exhibit 4.4.3: Interest rates in different currencies

		Period of loan (years)						
		1	2	3	4	5	10	15
Part 1: Euro-interest rates (% per annum)								
US $		3·00	8·00	8·25	8·25	8·50	9·00	9·25
DM		3·25	4·00	4·75	5·25	5·50	5·00	5·75
Swfr		1·50	2·25	2·50	3·25	3·25	3·75	4·00
£		8·50	8·75	9·50	10·00	10·25	11·00	15·00
Part 2: Break-even exchange rates	spot							
DM	2·01	1·92	1·86	1·81	1·79	1·74	1·44	1·21
Swfr	1·82	1·70	1·62	1·54	1·50	1·41	1·09	0·84
£	1·94	1·93	1·91	1·87	1·81	1·78	1·60	0·86

Thus, the true cost of a 10-year borrowing is 9% per annum; for a 10-year Swfr borrowing the nominal coupon attaching to such a loan is, say, 3·75%, a substantially cheaper borrowing. However, if the Swfr/$ rate appreciates from 1·83 to 1·09 over the life of the loan then the true cost of the Swfr loan will be 9% per annum and not 3·75%.

In the analysis it has been implicitly assumed that the movement of the exchange rate through time is a constant percentage. Is this realistic? If not, how does this affect the analysis?

A glance at exchange rates shows that this assumption cannot in fact be supported. The contrast between the dramatic fluctuations of actuality and the constant depreciation rate assumption needed to achieve the same result is striking. Exhibit 4.4.4 gives, as an example, more typical statistics of actual currency movements. All the changes considered are over six-month intervals, since it has been assumed that interest on any of the borrowings discussed is payable at six-monthly intervals and it is these dates that are relevant to the borrowing decision.

Exhibit 4.4.4: Typical exchange rate changes

Exchange rate	Mean depreciation (6-months) (%)	Standard deviation	Upper* limit	Lower* limit
US $/£	−1·29	6·79	12·82	−13·64
DM/$	−3·45	11·91	21·25	−23·12
DM/£	−5·71	9·08	11·81	−20·48
Swfr/$	−5·46	10·48	17·25	−23·76
Swfr/£	−7·66	6·65	6·27	−19·78

* 95% confidence limits.

In Exhibit 4.4.4 the figures show that, as a rule of thumb, about 65% of the six-monthly depreciation rates will be within one standard deviation of the mean depreciation rate and 95% will be between the upper and lower limits shown. Thus, in the case of the DM/$ rate, on average 95% of the six-monthly rates of depreciation will be between 23·12% and 21·25%. Since the exchange rates do not change at a constant rate through time and the effect on the cost of borrowing of, departures from this assumption must be examined. The highest variability occurs in the DM/$ exchange rate and so this case is examined in detail.

192

If the decision criterion of the break-even rate is to be useful, the implied cost of borrowing should be virtually the same as the coupon on the comparable dollar loan regardless of intermediate exchange movements. To test whether this is the case, the following exercise was carried out.

For each term of loan, sequences of exchange rate movements over the term were generated with the same variability as that observed historically and all terminating at the appropriate break-even rate. Using the DM/$ example, the implied cost of the Deutschemark borrowing was calculated for each sequence and 100 sequences were examined for each term of loan. As an example, Exhibit 4.4.5 shows three sequences generated for the 15-year loan as well as the constant depreciation rate. Sequence (2) is a fairly extreme outcome, producing significant differences between the implied cost of capital and the dollar coupon. Sequence (3) is an outcome where the implied cost of capital is the same as the dollar coupon. Both outcomes have the same variability as historical exchange rate movements.

Exhibit 4.4.5: Exchange rates outcome, same final rate

Exhibit 4.4.6: Implied capital cost of DM loan with variable rates

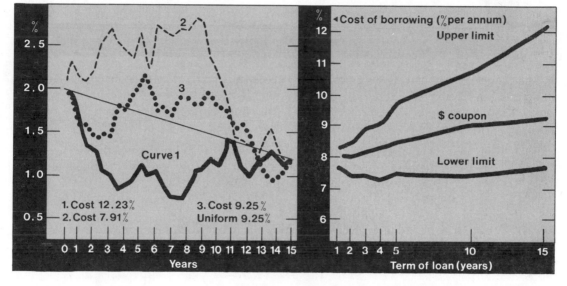

Exhibit 4.4.6 shows that the variation in the depreciation rate over the life of the loan does have a noticeable effect on the implied cost of capital and this effect increases (as would be expected) with the term of the loan. The deviations from the actual cost of capital (i.e. the dollar coupon rate) become particularly significant for terms greater than five years. Thus, for these longer terms there is a very real risk that, even if the break-even exchange rate does occur, the path taken may be such that the resultant cost of capital may be as much as 2–3% greater than expected. With this degree of uncertainty, the validity of the break-even exchange rate as a decision criterion is clearly suspect.

Having demonstrated the inadequacy of the single break-even rate as a decision criterion, it is necessary to supplement this rate with extra information to provide a more useful decision criterion. The method suggested, is to consider fairly extreme outcomes of exchange rate movements (such as sequences (1) and (2) in Exhibit 4.4.5), but which, if realized, would result in the implied cost of capital being equivalent to the dollar coupon rate. If we consider two extreme paths on either side of the constant depreciation rate, both of which lead to the equivalence of the loans as before, then we have identified a break-even range within which the loans may be equivalent. Exhibit 4.4.7 shows schematically how the range is derived. For all rates above the top of the range, it is very unlikely that the dollar loan would be cheaper than the Deutschemark loan regardless of intermediate exchange rate movements. Similarly the converse holds for rates below the bottom of the range.

Exhibit 4.4.7: Break-even between DM loan and U.S. dollar loan

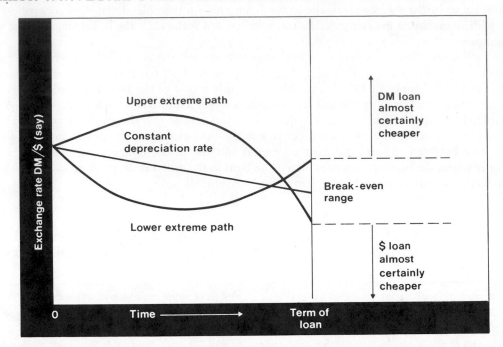

The ranges just described have been computed again for the DM/$ loans and are shown graphically in Exhibit 4.4.8. For ease of explanation, the possible end of term exchange rates are divided into four regions — A, B, C and D. The implication of the eventual end of term exchange rate falling into these regions is as follows:

A: The Deutschemark loan will be cheaper with a probability greater than 95%.
B: The Deutschemark loan will be cheaper with a probability of 95% at the upper limit decreasing to a probability of 50% at the break-even rate.
C: The dollar loan will be cheaper with a probability of 50% at the break-even rate rising to a probability of 95% at the lower limit.
D: The dollar loan will be cheaper with a probability greater than 95%.

Exhibit 4.4.8: Bounds on the equality of DM vs U.S. dollar loan

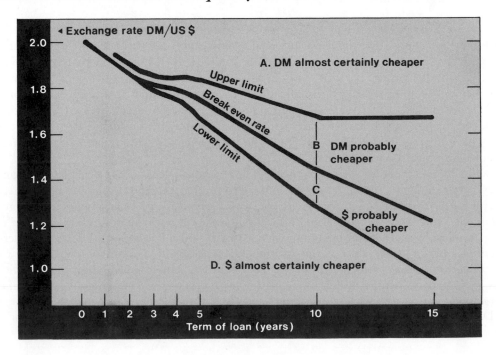

The upper and lower limit lines are dependent on the variability of the exchange rate between the currencies involved and the probabilities assigned to them. Exhibit 4.4.9 shows the upper and lower limits on exchange rates for equality between U.S. dollar loans and loans in Deutschemark, Swiss francs and sterling.

Exhibit 4.4.9: How to make an informed decision

Upper and lower limits on exchange rates (95% probability limits) for equality of DM/US $ loan, Swfr/US $ and £/US $.

| Currencies | Period of loan | | | | | | |
	1	2	3	4	5	10	15
DM/$	1·93	1·88	1·86	1·86	1·84	1·69	1·67
	1·92	1·85	1·79	1·74	1·67	1·27	0·97
Swfr/$	1·71	1·63	1·55	1·53	1·45	1·20	1·03
	1·70	1·62	1·52	1·47	1·38	1·02	0·74
$/£	1·94	1·93	1·91	1·88	1·87	1·85	1·21
	1·92	1·89	1·83	1·75	1·69	1·36	0·58

Using the information presented in Exhibits 4.4.3 and 4.4.9, the corporate treasurer can assess the implications of borrowing in a particular currency and judge whether these implications are consistent with his expectations of future exchange rates. It can thus be seen that with this type of analysis the corporate treasurer is in a position to make an informed and, through time, consistent set of decisions. These decisions are not based on single part estimates which, if in the event are different from those expected invalidate the decisions, but on realistic and probabilistic underlying assumptions.

5. Currency swaps and long-term forwards

Victoria Blake

The use of long-term currency swaps and foreign exchange contracts has mushroomed in the past two years to a point where the volume of swaps completed probably exceeds $500 million in some months. The reason lies in the infinite variety of uses of currency swaps and the vastly increased demand for the technique in the international marketplace. Traditionally, interest in currency swaps came from corporations who used them to accomplish foreign currency funding and/or hedging objectives. Today, many corporations also use the technique to generate home currency funding at attractive rates; investors employ swaps as a way to increase yields and/or diversify their portfolios, and supranationals and governments use swaps as a way to generate a currency funding in volumes not available in the ordinary market.

Historical background

The origin of the long-term currency swap can be traced to the parallel loan, a funding technique which is employed infrequently today. Under a parallel loan a parent company and a foreign subsidiary or sister company located in different countries would enter into equal but opposite loans/deposits with two affiliates of another company.

Exhibit 4.5.1: A parallel loan

U.K.

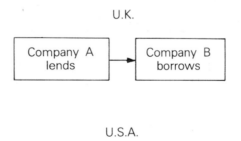

U.S.A.

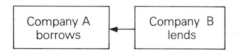

The parallel loan was conceived mainly as a means of complying with exchange control regulations which restricted the outflow of capital and/or using available cash and thereby reducing consolidated interest expense.

Parallel loans are unpopular today because it is difficult for the corporations involved to set up a legal framework which ensures a clean right of set-off between the two transactions. This means that if the borrowing entity in either country defaults, it is not certain whether the courts will allow the sister company to withhold repayment of its loan. It also forces the participating companies to make credit judgement about the other (an exercise which many corporations are reluctant to undertake). Hence the back-to-back loan was born. Under this structure, one cash surplus company deals directly with the other as both a lender and borrower and on-lends the funds to the subsidiary company.

This structure solved the set-off problem in most countries, permitted by exchange control because the end result was essentially the same as a parallel loan, and also allowed for banks to intermediate and thereby assume the credit risk of each party.

Exhibit 4.5.2: A back-to-back loan

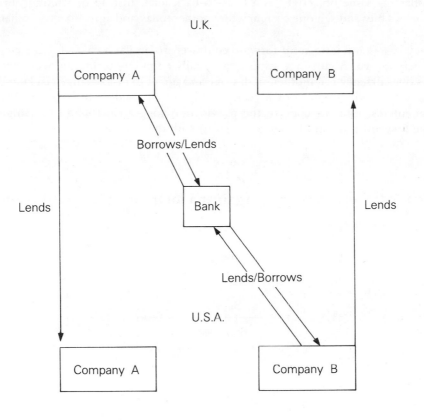

Exhibit 4.5.3: Currency swap

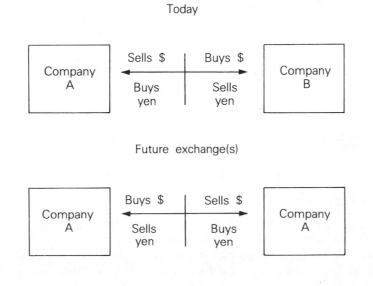

The currency swap is a technique that has long been used in the foreign exchange market and accomplishes the same objectives as a back-to-back loan. Instead of lending/borrowing, the two companies buy and sell one currency for another today and agree to a re-exchange at a later date.

Currency swaps and long-term forward contracts are similar techniques: the chief difference is one of perspective. A currency swap is essentially a funding technique whereby a borrower exchanges one currency for another on day one and agrees to re-exchange at a later date. Instead of paying and receiving interest each year, a net amount is paid by the effective "borrower" of the higher interest rate currency to the provider. A long-term foreign exchange contract is simply the forward portion of a currency swap with the spot portion omitted.

Exhibit 4.5.4: Currency swap against a long-term forward contract

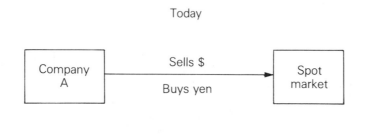

An understanding of the relationship between the long-term hedge and the currency swap provides an insight into the link between interest differentials and forward exchange rates. The following example illustrates this.

A shipping company (Company B in Exhibit 4.5.4) contracts to purchase five vessels from a Japanese shipyard financed via a 10-year export credit denominated in yen. During the delivery period, the yen weakens. As the shipping company has a dollar income stream, it wishes to lock in the cost of the yen by buying the principal plus interest due under the debt against the U.S. dollar. What should the forward rates be?

The counterparty is a U.S. corporation (Company A in Exhibit 4.5.4) seeking to obtain fixed rate funding for its Japanese subsidiary. It can raise U.S. dollars for 10 years at, say, 14·5% p.a. all-in and believes 8·5% p.a. is a fair yen borrowing cost, If the shipping company agrees to pay an average premium on the yen of approximately 6·4% p.a., then the U.S. corporation achieves its funding objectives.

Cost of swaps and forwards

As can be seen from the above example, interest rate differentials are a primary factor in determining the cost of long-term forwards and currency swaps, but there are a number of other factors which can play an important role in determining the rates. Such influences would include the availability of counterparties, exchange controls, withholding taxes and conditions in the capital markets.

Exhibit 4.5.5: A contract example

Spot $1 = Yen 230

Year	Yen	Dollars	Forward FX rates
0	+230·00	−1·0000	
1	−42·55	+0·1952	217·95
2	−40·60	+0·1965	206·53
3	−38·64	+0·1974	195·72
4	−36·69	+0·1979	185·43
5	−34·73	+0·1976	175·73
6	−32·78	+0·1968	166·55
7	−30·82	+0·1953	157·80
8	−28·87	+0·1931	149·54
9	−26·91	+0·1899	141·68
10	−24·69	+0·1839	134·27

	Yen	Dollar
	IRR = 8·5%	IRR = 14·5%

In most currencies, there is usually one side of a transaction which is in more demand than another. Understandably, the less available side can usually command a slightly more favourable rate because of scarcity value. Conversely, a company wishing to conclude a transaction quickly may have to relinquish something in the rate in order to meet its closing deadline. The lead time in actually concluding such long-term transactions, must be considered.

First, counterparties must be contacted and details provided, an analysis must be made, and the transaction must be recommended and approved, sometimes at board level. Tax and accounting problems must be resolved and documentation agreed. Unless a similar transaction has already been completed, the process can take time and a counterparty will be more inclined to proceed rapidly if the transaction being offered is especially attractive.

Exchange control regulations and conditions in the capital and exchange markets can greatly restrict the availability of counterparties for certain types of transactions. Market conditions are also an important factor. Uncertainty about the course of interest and exchange rates may cause companies to want to hedge against a possible worsening of these factors, whereas a general expectation of improving markets causes one side of the market to withdraw pending more advantageous circumstances.

Accounting and tax

Since back-to-back loans, currency swaps, and long-term forward contracts are similar transactions, the decision about which technique to use generally depends upon the accounting and tax (and, to a much lesser degree, legal) considerations which pertain. The chief concerns are the timing of the recognition of the interest expense/forward discount/premium, the ordinary or capital treatment of any foreign exchange gain or loss and the impact of withholding taxes. The treatment varies from country to country so it is best to consult a tax adviser before making a structural decision. The accounting for such transactions can also be problematic. These problems mainly relate to the hedging of interest payments due after one year and the timing of the recognition of interest expense/income.

Interest rate hedges

Interest rate hedging is another type of transaction which is being used today. With this, a borrower can effectively cover the interest rate risk involved in borrowing variable rate funds. As in a forward currency contract, a forward interest rate is fixed and any difference between this rate and the variable rate is compensated between the hedging parties. The hedge may be completed in the financial futures market or, for longer-term transaction, against counterparty companies.

Bank intermediation versus dealing direct

Most transactions are arranged with the help of a bank which, through its contacts, can locate companies with equal but opposite requirements. Once a match has been made, a company has the option to deal directly with the other company or to allow the bank to intermediate. The latter has the advantage that neither side need know the identity of the other, thereby ensuring privacy; it increases the possibility for structural mismatching thereby allowing the optimal tax and accounting treatment, and it places the credit risk with a bank so that neither side need be concerned with the creditworthiness of the other.

The question sometimes arises whether the banks intermediating a transaction actually have a counterparty or are positioning it on their own books. Given the size and maturity of most transactions, the difficulty in closing out a position and the risks incurred, most banks are reluctant to take positions. Similarly, a bank will charge more for a positioned than a matched deal, because of the greater risk.

Maturity, size and availability

Transaction maturities are typically between five and 10 years, although they may extend to 20 years. Transaction sizes are normally US$20 to $50 million equivalent, but can be as large as $150 million or as small as $5 million. In practice, transactions are less viable (both in terms of economics and management time) once they involve less than $5 million equivalent: the amount of work involved is the same, regardless of the size of the deal.

Currencies most available for such transactions are U.S. dollars, yen, sterling, Deutschemarks, French francs, Swiss francs, Canadian dollars, Dutch guilders, Australian dollars and, to a lesser degree, Scandinavian currencies, Belgian francs, Italian lire, Spanish pesetas, Saudi riyals and Kuwaiti dinars.

Theoretically, almost any currency could be swapped. However, the demand for more exotic currencies tends to be one-sided and/or exchange controls or domestic regulations tend to prohibit such transactions.

Management time spent in arranging such exotic transactions must also be considered. The potential savings gain over more conventional financings are quickly eroded by legal and advisory costs if the volume is small and the structure complicated. Small transactions in exotic currencies are normally best avoided.

6. The export finance company
David K. Slifer

An offshore export finance company can provide an additional layer of financing flexibility which may not always be available to major multinational corporations with subsidiaries in many countries. This is in addition to the tax advantages normally associated with such a vehicle.

The interest differentials between a domestic currency and a Eurocurrency often provide a profit opportunity. The export finance company also provides the vehicle for centralizing a multi-subsidiary company's currency transactions risk. Many companies do not fully appreciate the cost-saving opportunities which arise when a multinational company with multi-currency cash flows merely attempts to eliminate currency risk from its international commercial transactions. The export finance company can provide:

— flexibility — by permitting a company to use domestic or external financing, depending upon which is cheaper;
— centralization of an entire group's transactions risk on the books of a single entity;
— a clear delineation of a group's transactions and translation (consolidation) currency risks that permits easier management of both types;
— a vehicle for netting or matching a group's currency transactions.

A captive export finance company may prove profitable when serving a multi-subsidiary company with at least $50 million in cross-border turnover, either inter-company, or third party.

An export finance company is designed to manage the corporation's short-term international cash flows. It should have the authority to borrow and deposit for short periods (up to six or nine months) on a multi-currency basis. The company is not designed to provide major or long-term financing for the corporation, but to have the short-term flexibility it needs to anticipate shortages and surpluses, by currency, in the groups cash flow. Longer-term risks are best met by medium- or long-term borrowing in the country where the company has made its fixed asset investment. It is assumed that the currency risk policy of an export finance company is to minimize transactions currency risks at the lowest possible cost.

An export finance company is normally based in a country which has easy access to the external money markets. Switzerland or The Netherlands are often used as a base, not merely for their tax benefits, but because of their reputation in international banking. This does not mean, however, that the international corporate treasurer working on behalf of the export finance company could not be located in a money market centre or close to the corporation's regional headquarters. It may not be essential to form a separate company to handle the function. Many firms already have an individual on the corporate treasury staff with the operating responsibility. The separate company requires a separate set of financial statements that isolate the results.

Reinvoicing

The export finance company may either develop as a best-efforts financing vehicle, or a formal reinvoicing centre for managing currency exposure and the company's total short-term financing. On a best-efforts basis, the finance company might offer external sources of financing (by purchasing a subsidiary's receivables) when the external sources of financing provided a better rate than the domestic interest rate. The export finance treasurer merely offers alternatives to the local subsidiary treasurers who remain autonomous. For example, an export finance company whose subsidiary was exporting from the U.K. to its German subsidiary, suggested to the U.K. controller that if the U.K. controller was willing to invoice via the finance company, they would be willing to buy the receivables and finance them at 5% below the domestic sterling financing costs, with no currency risk on the books of the company. The finance company manager borrowed Euro-marks to match his receivable's maturity, and paid off the U.K. company, less the interest costs. The company thus lowered its interest cost by locking in the strength of the DM as an interest differential. The finance company had a Deutschemark borrowing matched by a DM receivable. While the company gave up any potential currency exchange gain, it had reduced its interest costs. This had a measurable impact on the group's income statement, while the treasurer of the company could not otherwise be sure that he would realize a future currency gain, nor was he certain he could otherwise isolate that gain in the group accounts. The U.K. company itself could have combined DM invoicing with a Euro-mark borrowing under current regulations, but many companies make such transactions the responsibility of a regional treasurer in an export finance company.

Below are two examples of an export finance company operating as a captive offshore factoring company.

Example I
In 19X0, ABC SpA in Italy wished to ship components to its Australian sister company for subsequent assembly, inventory and sale in Australia (see Exhibit 4.6.1). The Australian company wanted one-year credit on the imports. Italy at the time was going through high inflation, high interest rates, and credit restrictions. Financing costs were in the area of 20%, but the bankers to ABC SpA had no funds available due to the credit ceilings. ABC SpA contacted the Australian subsidiary and enquired about the availability of financing in Australia.

Exhibit 4.6.1: Using an export finance company

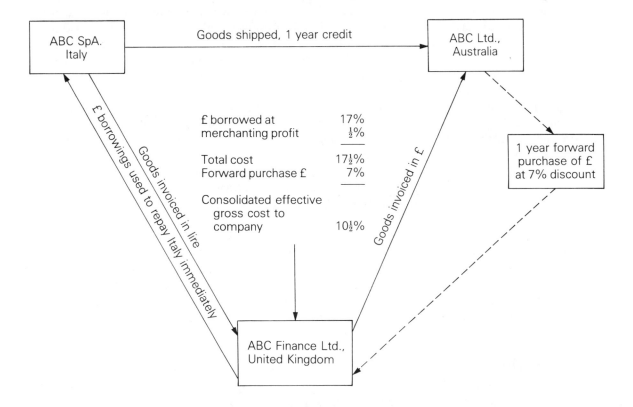

Australia was also at the time going through high inflation and high interest rates. Australian dollar financing costs were at 26%, the highest ever seen in Australia. The Australians were unhappy with the interest rate being charged at the time, so they contacted their export finance company manager. The export manager felt that if he purchased Italy's export receivables and converted Australia's liabilities to sterling, he could finance with sterling at a cost of 17%. He charged an additional ½% on the transaction which gave Australia an effective sterling cost of 17½%, and created a profit on the transaction.

With the sterling borrowings, the export finance company manager purchased lire and paid off the Italian company, relieving it of its cash bind. The export finance company then had a sterling borrowing on its books, matched by a sterling receivable from the Australian company.

The Australian company then had an exchange risk against sterling which it accepted. The Australian company purchased sterling forward one year at a discount of 7% to remove the risk. This decreased the net cost to it on the total transaction to an effective 10½%.

Example II — two years later

By 19X2, Italy was again going through a currency crisis. The company had decided, well in advance of the early 19X2 decline of the lire, to invoice all of the Italian subsidiary's exports in dollars. From an exchange point of view the Italian company was covered. However, as the 19X2 lire crisis grew, financing again became a problem. This time the Italian banks had only limited amounts of dollar funds to lend.

Again, the group's captive export finance company came to the rescue. This time a Swiss-based captive company purchased the Italian subsidiary's dollar receivables, borrowed dollars to offset the risk on the Swiss company's books and paid off the Italian subsidiary. The effect of the export finance companies during the past two years has been to keep the Italian company producing, selling and exporting due to the additional flexibility provided by the captive finance companies, and the importing companies also received the necessary financing.

The function of the finance company

The function of the finance company is to support the underlying transactions of the company it serves. Its job is not to speculate, but to reduce currency risk through prudent management, eliminating any large gains or large losses, realizing economies of scale, and an overall reduction in financing costs on the company's international trade transactions.

The operation of the company is in three main areas:

(a) matching/netting;
(b) borrowing short term in anticipation of currency inflows, or alternatively, depositing in anticipation of currency disbursements; and
(c) buying or selling currencies forward.

Netting of inter-company transactions is very popular because it is both profitable and easy to understand. By reducing the number of foreign exchange transactions, savings of up to ¼% of the amount netted is a rough rule of thumb for eliminating two foreign exchange transactions with their associated buy/sell spreads plus bank charges, if any. Some payments may be eliminated altogether. Matching, on the other hand, is the channelling of payments and receipts by currency through external currency accounts where a company has a sufficient inflow and outflow of a given currency. Since currencies have been floating, however, the ½% pales when compared to the currency risk and associated interest differentials.

The export finance company can often borrow strong currencies on the external markets at interest rates below those available to other units of the company. Where it is more advantageous to maintain borrowings in the domestic money markets, this can be continued by the local subsidiary. High interest rates can be obtained on deposits in the external market that are made in anticipation of a projected need for the currency. Both operations are done, not for speculative reasons, but merely to match a shortage or surplus in a particular currency which will be received or disbursed at some future date.

Another method of eliminating exposures is by selling or buying currencies forward. It may be the only way a company with one-way cash flows can avoid risk under exchange control regulations in many countries.

To ensure that the export finance company successfully serves the overall interests of the multinational group, the policies can best be set by a currency committee made up of financial managers of the most important subsidiaries. A suggested committee might include:
1. The parent company treasurer or assistant treasurer for international.
2. The overseas regional treasurer.
3. The local financial managers of major manufacturing or sales subsidiaries.

The committee's main function is to establish guidelines within which the export finance treasurer operates. The meetings provide a forum for a consensus of views on the direction of currency moves and the implications for the corporation's liquidity and currency risk. The parameters set by the currency committee provide a certain degree of protection to the finance company treasurer, preventing hindsight inquests by senior corporate officers on one individual's actions under changing conditions. In fact, the minutes of the meeting are the guidelines for the following month's operations.

What does the export finance company cost? There will be start-up as well as operating costs. The start-up costs include:

1. Initial capital investment.
2. Legal fees.
3. Tax adviser fees.
4. Communications equipment.

The capital investment of the firm should be sufficient to allow the company to have short-term multi-currency facilities from banks in order to consider borrowing as a method of removing exposure and financing the group's international transactions at the same time. If the export finance company is not sufficiently capitalized to obtain lines of credit on its own, then there must be an arrangement, either of parent guarantees, or the items being traded themselves must serve as collateral. The legal fees can vary all over the map, depending on the location and the quality of advice. There should be an opinion from the firm's external auditors on the tax implication of the new company. It is advisable that the company be open and above board in matters of taxation. Since most export finance companies involve some kind of reinvoicing, the operation will be subject to the close scrutiny of the tax authorities in the producing subsidiaries' countries. The group and the company must be prepared to show that the purpose of the export finance company is purely centralization of exposure management and financing of the group's external trade, rather than shifting profits to avoid taxes. A thorough investigation of all tax consequences, particularly in a reinvoicing company, is necessary to achieve a successful operation. Indeed, an export finance company using reinvoicing may remove some of the flexibility of the company.

The operating costs of the unit are a function largely of communications, personnel and space. There are export finance companies that have started up with a single person occupying a corner of a regional headquarters and using their secretarial staff part-time. A unit which is systematically reinvoicing transactions for a large multinational enterprise might consist of a treasurer, an internal foreign exchange and money dealer, an administrative assistant who could be a good secretary, and one or two accountants who may be located in the country of incorporation, rather than at the administrative headquarters.

The personnel must combine a certain knowledge of domestic and Euro-finance over a broad range of countries, with a good knowledge of the group's overall goals and activities. It is often inadvisable to take someone from the company and train him to do the exchange and money dealing, rather than hire an ex-bank dealer who may look at money *per se* as his basic commodity. The dealer of the export finance company needs to realize that he is there only to support the underlying transactions of the group he is working for. Any other policy obviously leads to speculation.

The benefits of the export finance can be summed up in one word: flexibility — the kind of flexibility which comes from (1) professional management of currency risks and cash; (2) free access to the external money markets for the total group; (3) the more efficient use of funds after interest and currency risk. Additional savings may come from the economies of scale in buying or selling foreign exchange in large amounts. These economies of scale could be as high as $\frac{1}{8}$% of the total foreign exchange trades, depending upon the location and size of a corporation's present transactions.

In addition, the company would have a new profit centre which would serve to isolate the company's efficiency in the area of currency exposure management. Isolating the commodity which all companies use to function, i.e. money, is no different from creating units of specialization in the company's sales or purchasing departments. The manufacturing subsidiaries are normally glad to have the currency shifts removed from their operating figures. The professional management found in the export finance company serves to manage the group's cash exposure and even advise on the translation exposure so that currency gains or losses at year end should either not exist, or else should provide no surprises.

7. Using SDRs

Bluford H. Putnam

Foreign exchange managers do not need anyone to tell them that their jobs have become more difficult in the last five years. The dollar's value on the exchange markets went through the floor in 1977 and 1978, only to shoot through the ceiling in 1981. U.S. interest rates have become unbelievably volatile with interest rates in Europe and Japan being affected as well.

A natural response to increases in risk and uncertainty is to diversify. Through diversification a portfolio manager can reduce the risk of the portfolio without trading away an equally large portion of the investment yield. In 1977 and 1978 when the dollar was in decline, dollar-based multinational corporations actively moved to relatively greater diversified currency positions. This trend ended when the dollar strengthened because of a reversal of U.S. inflationary policies. The Federal Reserve increasingly became the focal point for fighting inflation, and the ability of the Fed to remain anti-inflationary through the business cycle was enhanced greatly by the election of President Reagan and the support that the president gave to fighting inflation with monetary policy.

Nevertheless, while dollar strength has made life easier for some dollar-based companies, others are not suited to benefit. The sharp increase in interest rate volatility that accompanied the dollar's rise has made exposure management strategy all the more important.

Risk management strategy

When both interest rate and foreign exchange volatility are major problems, the best risk management strategy combines these elements. In doing so, there may be substantial benefits. The new SDR may offer some interesting possibilities for managing residual forex and interest rate exposure and may be a useful vehicle for both borrowers and investors.

An emerging risk management strategy in today's financial environment involves understanding the relationship between interest rate movements and foreign exchange movements. By managing both interest rate exposure and foreign exchange exposure through one strategy, there are substantial gains in risk reduction with only modest losses in yield, i.e. there are beneficial risk-return trade-offs from linking interest rate exposure management to foreign exchange exposure management.

We must develop foreign exchange and interest rate expectations in which interest rate and forex movements are specified. For example, in the spring of 1981, many analysts believed that U.S. interest rates were ready to decline and that the dollar would go through a period of weakness. But U.S. rates rose and remained high, while the dollar surged to levels not witnessed since 1976. In this instance, betting on falling interest rates and betting on a weak dollar were one bet. A multinational's failure to take this into consideration could have meant that the actual exposure of the corporation to financial uncertainties was sharply higher than senior management would have liked. Yet, if interest rate management is separate from foreign exchange management, then corporations may often find themselves underestimating the true size of the risk they are taking (see Exhibit 4.7.1).

While this may seem straightforward, the appropriate strategy depended critically on rising interest rates being associated with a strong currency. In 1977 and 1978, U.S. interest rates rose steadily, while the dollar depreciated.

The difference between 1977–78 and 1980–81 (see Exhibit 4.7.1) holds an important lesson for foreign exchange and interest rate management. Interest rate changes may reflect only one of two critical signals about the economy: (1) inflation is expected to rise, or (2) real (inflation-adjusted) expected returns are rising. The opportunity costs of holding financial assets are affected by these factors, but they have different impacts on currency behaviour. If interest rates are rising because inflation is rising, then the currency in question is likely to be weak, not strong. But, if interest rates rise to compensate investors, either for higher productivity or in this case for increased financial risk, then real (inflation-adjusted) interest rates are rising. This will cause currency appreciation since it is not associated with expectations of more inflation.

Exhibit 4.7.1: DM/US $ exchange rate and U.S. interest rates

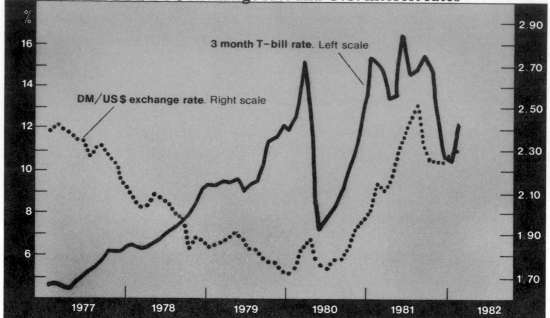

Note. All SDR interest and exchange rates are based on the current five-currency definition.

The exhibit shows that prior to October 1979 the U.S. dollar was depreciating, as U.S. interest rates increased, affecting rising U.S. inflation. After October 1979, the U.S. dollar largely appreciates as U.S. interest rates decline reflecting the Fed's anti-inflation policies.

Combining interest rate and foreign exchange exposure management requires a careful examination of the potential causes of interest rate changes. A reliable signal concerning the meaning of interest rate changes is often contained in the yield curve. When rising interest rates are associated with inverted yield curves, then monetary policy is usually anti-inflationary. Further rises in interest rates may cause currency appreciation. When interest rates rise, usually slowly, in association with a flat or positive yield curve, then monetary policy is not particularly anti-inflationary and may even be inflationary. This was the case in the United States in 1977 and into 1978. The rising interest rates in the United States were associated with future inflation and dollar weakness.

Aside from the argument for merging foreign exchange and interest risk management, there is inherent in any forex management programme some interest rate exposure. Forward foreign exchange contracts embody an interest rate assumption. Through arbitrage in the Eurocurrency markets, Eurocurrency inter-bank bid and offer rates are compared against forward exchange rates and their implicit Eurocurrency interest rates. The economic theorem, known as interest rate parity, expresses this relationship as an equality between the foreign exchange forward premium (or discount) and the Eurocurrency interest rate differential of the same maturity as the forward forex contract. Any foreign exchange forward contract embodies a view of the expected difference between the Eurocurrency interest rates on the two currencies involved in the forward contract. Therefore, a normal forex exposure management programme has implicit in it a view on interest rates. Financial managers should consider the interest rate exposure contained in their foreign exchange management programmes as part of their overall interest rate exposure.

In the context of managing interest rate and foreign exchange exposure jointly, the currency cocktail approach may have substantial merit. A properly constructed basket of currencies can provide natural offsets to swings in both interest rates and exchange rates. Depending on the portfolio of expected multi-currency cashflows involved, the currency cocktail method may provide a more useful hedge than individually tailoring a foreign exchange programme for each currency and interest rate exposure. This would not be true if perfect hedges were possible, but as all financial exposure managers know, there is no such thing as a perfect hedge. This ideal state appears in textbooks, but never on the corporate books.

206

A pre-packaged hedging tool

In a perfect world forex managers could offset all of the firm's foreign exchange exposure with forward contracts and leave the worrying to the asset and liability managers. Interest rate managers would then buy and sell financial futures and the new financial options contracts to hedge their exposure, and they too could rest easy. But cashflows are hard to predict and hedges may involve a substantial basis risk, transactions costs, and general monitoring frustrations. Moreover, hedges often affect cashflow in negative ways even though an underlying asset is gaining in value.

In our less than perfect world, there may be a very useful role for certain pre-packaged hedging tools. The SDR is such a tool. One SDR is in effect a basket of five currencies and, as such, is a diversified portfolio of currencies: dollars, Deutschemarks, sterling, yen, and French francs. On an interest rate and foreign exchange basis, the behaviour of this arbitrary basket may provide a natural hedge for many corporations exposed to international financial risks.

A common question is: why does the basket have to be arbitrary for a given corporation? Cannot the foreign exchange manager create his own basket? He can, but he cannot trade that basket to anyone else. It must first be dismantled. As the SDR market develops from its infancy, the foreign exchange manager will have the option of choosing an arbitrary basket — the SDR — that is liquid in and of itself. There are substantial transaction cost gains available. Perhaps more important is the opportunity to save the cost of constantly monitoring multi-currency positions.

It is likely that most corporations will always hedge the majority of their exposures through individual currency management, but many will involve SDRs in their management programme. There is a role for SDRs in managing residual foreign exchange and interest rate risk. Indeed, the attractiveness of the SDR as a residual risk management tool is that it automatically combines the interest rate and foreign exchange management problems.

Countries tied closely to the United States through trade and the tradition of currency stability may find that, in the current American policy environment, their own policy choices are more constrained than they would wish. As the United States takes a more stringent stance, through monetary policy, to control inflation, dollar-bloc countries must either match that policy stance or see their currencies depreciate against the dollar, while still feeling the impact in their financial sectors of volatile U.S. interest rates. For borrowers in these countries, either private or official, this means that to tap the traditional U.S. markets will place them short on dollars at just the wrong time — when interest rates are high, together with a strong dollar.

One solution is to borrow in SDRs. On the interest rate side, because the dollar is such a large component of the SDR, SDR interest rates are not low, but during the recent period they have tended to remain below dollar interest rates (see Exhibit 4.7.2). On the exchange rate side, dollar-bloc borrowers gain a pleasant surprise. As the dollar has appreciated against most dollar-bloc currencies, the dollar has appreciated by even greater proportions against currencies outside the dollar sector. Thus, such currencies as the Canadian dollar or the Mexican peso have tended to appreciate against European currencies during the period of U.S. dollar strength; and against the SDR, these currencies have appreciated as well (see Exhibit 4.7.3).

If U.S. monetary policy were to make a left turn toward significantly lower interest rates, rapid money growth, and then future inflation and a depreciating U.S. dollar, the SDR would still provide some benefits for dollar-bloc borrowers. In this case, the SDR interest rate would fall, but by something less than the fall in dollar rates. And the appreciation of dollar-bloc currencies against the dollar would tend to offset dollar-bloc weakness against other currencies. For dollar-bloc SDR borrowers, the SDR value in terms of their own currency might be surprisingly stable.

SDR provides a natural hedge

SDR investments are likely to appeal to a wide variety of multi-currency portfolio holders in a world of divergent monetary policies. When interest rates across countries show wide differentials, the potential for major exchange rate movements is also heightened. While some degree of harmony is enforced in Europe through the European Monetary System, the ability

Exhibit 4.7.2: SDR interest rates are more stable than U.S. dollar interest rates—the benefits of diversification

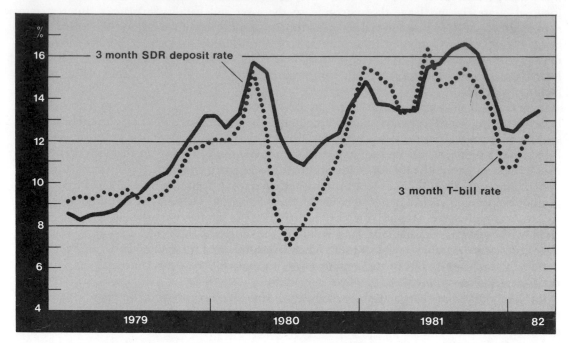

Note. All SDR interest and exchange rates are based on the current five-currency definition.

Exhibit 4.7.3: SDR/Canadian dollar exchange rate splits the difference between the U.S. dollar/Canadian dollar and DM/Canadian dollar

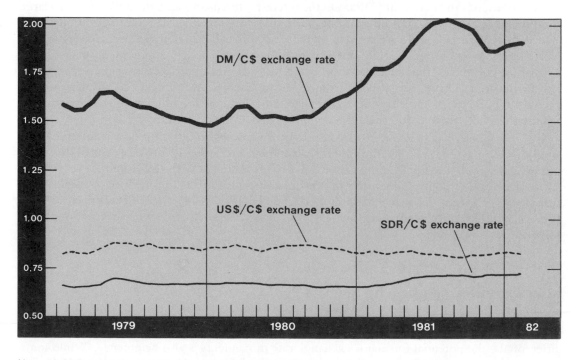

Note. All SDR interest and exchange rates are based on the current five-currency definition.

208

of a member country, say France, to take a path sharply divergent from that of Germany is still quite large. The SDR provides a natural hedge against the implications of these divergent policies.

A major hindrance to SDR investment in the past was the structure of the basket. With a multitude of currencies included, many with no capital markets of any size and no forward exchange markets, the SDR was doomed to illiquidity. But the new five-currency basket introduced in January 1981 has significant promise for liquidity. The overall liquidity of the SDR is limited by the smallest individual market of the five currencies, presently the French franc market. Even so, the French franc Euro-deposit market is sufficiently deep to allow the SDR market to have gained a small foothold.

The basic conditions that make interest rate and foreign exchange exposure management such a dangerous business are not likely to disappear in the near future. Financial managers can be expected to devise strategies to handle the combined problems of volatile interest rates and volatile exchange rates. Furthermore, managers will begin to gain an appreciation of the complexity of the interest rate/foreign exchange relationship and the necessity to consider these exposure problems as one larger problem. In this context, such management tools as pre-packaged currency cocktails, and specifically the SDR, may very well establish a small but important role.

8. Yen hedging and investment techniques

Mark Borsuk

This section provides a brief summary of the various techniques available for dealing with yen-denominated transactions, a market which is seeing increased foreign participation.

There are several reasons for the yen's increased presence abroad. First, the greater volume of yen-denominated trade which shifts the exchange risk to foreigners. Second, the marked increase in yen borrowings by non-residents. Third, the yen's increasing role as a reserve and investment currency.

Foreign exchange market

Yen trading has shown a remarkable increase in volume over the past few years, and participation worldwide has grown dramatically (see Exhibit 4.8.1).

Exhibit 4.8.1: Tokyo foreign exchange market volume

	1979	1981	% change
	($ million)		
All transactions	458·200	968·400	+111
Daily	1·800	3·900	
Third currency portion	13·200	66·400	+403
Daily	52·8	265·6	

Note. Interbank dealing reported through resident FX broker.

The movements of the yen are increasingly volatile. Leading and lagging, speculative transactions, interest rate sensitivity and portfolio shifts account for much of this instability. The impact on the exchange rate of leading and lagging by domestic participants is substantial; and trade transactions and the growing volume of capital transactions induce volatility. The impact of leading and lagging abroad also causes pressure on the rate: about 40% of export, and 3% of imports, are yen-denominated.

The growth of yen trading outside the Tokyo market, especially in such speculative centres as the IMM in Chicago, can at times dramatically exaggerate an appreciating or depreciating trend initiated by the Tokyo market. The yen is increasingly sensitive to interest rate differentials. This is largely the result of changes in the foreign exchange and capital control regulations introduced in 1980. Residents may borrow more freely from abroad and invest in foreign currency-denominated securities. The heightened sensitivity of the short-term money markets to rate trends abroad is due to the liberalization of interest rates in Japan.

Foreign government and large institutional borrowers rely on the Tokyo capital market as a source of medium- and long-term capital. Between 1979–81, they raised $5·7 billion equivalent in Samurai bonds. Portfolio shifts by non-resident investors have a powerful effect on the exchange rate, and between 1979–81, non-residents increased massively their holdings of yen-denominated securities — as did domestic investors (see Exhibit 4.8.2).

Exhibit 4.8.2: Net portfolio investments

	1979	1980	1981
		($ million)	
Non-residents			
Equities	−685	4,988	3,522
Bonds	1,741	5,330	5,771
Residents			
Equities	403	−369	240
Bonds	5,495	4,297	5,810

Note. Transactions under one year excluded, Ministry of Finance basis.

Forward exchange rates and their impact on hedging

An evolutionary change has taken place in the yen forward market: capital transactions are bringing interest rate differentials and forward prices into equilibrium. Trading rules in Tokyo require that non-bank transactions, whether done on a spot or forward basis, be supported by actual demand. This principle of actual demand has tended to exaggerate the movement of premiums and discounts. The leading and lagging of commercial receivables and payables and restrictions on Japanese bank positions can create intense pressure on the forwards — due to the large component of trade in Japan's balance of payments — moving them drastically out of line with interest rate differentials. However, with the revision in 1980 of the foreign exchange and capital control regulations and increased arbitrage transactions, the forward prices have moved closer to interest rate differentials. Nevertheless, treasurers need to be aware that forward prices and interest rate differentials remain imperfectly correlated and from time to time profitable opportunities, known as covered interest arbitrage, exist to invest, borrow and hedge transactions.

Selected hedging techniques

The techniques outlined below are ones external to the institution and should complement those techniques already being used internally for exchange risk management. These techniques may also be rapidly executed in the exchange and money markets — an important consideration when evaluating their merits.

Purchase spot and placed on deposit

On occasions, the dollar will be at a discount to the yen which makes the forward purchase of yen more expensive in dollar terms than the spot price. If the treasurer feels the cost is excessive in terms of the likely future price for settlement, the yen could be purchased spot and invested. The maturity of the investment would coincide with the maturity of the yen payable. However, a real expense would be incurred by using this hedging technique, i.e. the need to borrow a currency to convert into yen, or an opportunity loss would arise, i.e. the loss of interest income from surplus funds already earning interest in another currency.

Forward outright purchase

In this transaction, the yen would either be bought or sold for a specific date in the future, or with the option to receive or pay during a specific period. The latter transaction is called a forward option contract and is generally more expensive.

Forward outright transactions can be done for any period under one year. There is a growing market for transactions over one year but the depth of the market is limited and obtaining price quotes on a consistent basis is difficult. Nevertheless, the long-dated forward market continues to expand.

One advantage to covering forward is the ability to reverse the transaction prior to maturity, which allows the treasurer to take a view on the exchange rate. In other words, if the treasurer thought that before maturity the yen would depreciate, he might consider reversing the forward yen purchase and leave it uncovered until maturity. However, when reversing a previously covered position, the remaining premium or discount on the dollar will be included in the reversing price. If, for example, the dollar was at a discount, that portion of the remaining higher dollar cost would be recaptured. Conversely, if the dollar was at premium, that portion of the remaining reduced dollar cost would be lost.

Borrow–deposit hedge

An alternative to the forward outright purchase in the exchange market is to simultaneously borrow and deposit in the money markets. While theoretically forward rates should equal interest rate differentials, the Tokyo market is imperfectly arbitraged, and a cost savings can result from using this method. The example in Exhibit 4.8.3 compares the dollar cost of hedging a yen payable by the borrow–deposit technique and in the forward market. In the example, the dollar is at a discount and the yen payable amount has been discounted to minimize the dollar borrowing cost.

Exhibit 4.8.3: Comparative cost of hedging the yen: borrow deposit hedge and forward outright

Amount to be hedged: ¥238,900,000
Due in three months (92 days)
Spot rate: ¥238·90–00
Forward rate (three month): 507–497 (outright price 233·83–234·03)
Euro-dollar rate (three month): $14^{13}/_{16} — 14^{15}/_{16}$ p.a.
Euro-yen rate (three month): $6^7/_{16} — 6^{11}/_{16}$ p.a.

Item 1: Borrow-deposit hedge cost

$$\frac{¥238,900,000}{(1 + (0·064375)(92/360))} = \frac{¥238,900,000}{1·01645139} = ¥235,033,374·30$$

$$\frac{¥235,033,374·30}{¥238·90} = \$983,814·88$$

$$\$983,814·88 \times (1 + (0·149375)(92/360)) = \$983,814·88 \times (1·03817361) = \$1,021,370·65(A)$$

Item 2: Forward outright hedge cost

$$\frac{¥238,900,000}{¥233·83} = \$1,021,682·42 \text{ (B)}$$

Cost comparison

$$B - A = \$1,021,682·42 - \$1,021,370·65 = \$311·77$$

$311·77 represents the cost savings from a borrow-deposit hedge.

In the case of a yen receivable, the treasurer may consider selling the proceeds forward, discounting them to gain immediate access to the funds or, by borrowing yen, to hedge the asset with a liability.

Short-term investments

A treasurer may have idle yen balances, or wish to secure a higher return on surplus funds either on a covered or uncovered basis. There are a number of attractive options available in the short-term money markets. These markets are likely to grow as a result of the authorities' interest in progressively liberalizing Japan's financial markets.

The major impetus for change has been declining economic growth rates. In recognition of this, in 1975 the Bank of Japan (BoJ) initiated a policy of maintaining price stability by setting money supply growth targets (M2 + CD). This approach has led it to rely increasingly on interest rates as a tool of overall economic management. Since 1978, it has embarked upon a programme of progressively liberalizing interest rates and increasing participation in the short-term money markets. The BoJ's objective was to induce interest rate arbitrage among the various market sectors, thereby making all short-term rates responsive to supply and demand. The BoJ could thus influence macro-economic behaviour in attaining its goals. Parallel with this development was the progressive liberalization of foreign exchange and capital trans-actions.

In December 1980, the formerly restrictive foreign exchange and capital controls were significantly modified to permit, in principle, unfettered foreign currency borrowings and investments. Corporate and institutional investors have become progressively sensitive to the yield on their investments and the necessity of minimizing borrowing costs. All these factors combined have led to the expansion of the open market segment of the short-term market to the point where it now rivals the traditional inter-bank market.

There are two distinct short-term money markets in Japan: the inter-bank market and open market. Non-financial institutions are barred from participation in the inter-bank market. The inter-bank market consists of the call market where funds are exchanged for periods of one week or less. The major participants on the borrowing side are city banks and some regional banks; the lenders are mostly agricultural cooperatives, mutual and trust banks and insurance companies. Funds are raised in the bill discount market by discounting commercial promissory notes. The maturities range from one to four months and the pattern of borrowers and lenders is the same as with the call market.

The open market consists of participants in the inter-bank market, corporations and non-residents.

The *Gensaki* (repurchase) market was organized by the security brokers as a means of raising short-term funds from their bond inventories. The security firm promises the investor that, after a certain fixed period, it will repurchase the bond at a specific price. The difference between the purchase and resale price on an annualized basis equals the yield. Recently, banks doing *Gensaki* trades have been bypassing the brokers.

The certificate of deposit (CD) market was established in 1979 and gives the banks increased flexibility in funding. Original issuing maturities for CDs are between three and six months, and a secondary market has developed in repurchase trading.

Periodically, the BoJ sells government bills (*Seifu Tanki Shōken*) to the market as a means of managing liquidity. The Bank is experimenting with selling these bills at comparable money market rates. Unless the investor is a qualified international institution or central bank, interest rates on domestic deposits are considerably below equivalent money market rates.

There has also been a substantial growth in the Euro-yen market over the last few years and its size is now estimated at US$20 billion.

Rate relationships

The inter-bank market rate trend sets the overall pattern for interest rates. The call rate is generally the lowest money market rate; the bill discount, *Gensaki* and CD rates are higher. The BoJ is able to influence the call and bill discount rates directly by its liquidity draining or supplying activities, and these rates in turn influence the others. Short-term interest rates in Japan display a high degree of seasonality due to such factors as tax and bonus payments.

The *Gensaki* market is linked to the call and bill discount markets by the arbitrage activities of authorized financial institutions. In turn, the CD market is linked to these markets by the

Exhibit 4.8.4: Short-term investments

Instrument	Maturities	Market characteristics	Non-resident tax status	Minimum denomination
CD	Three to six months. Majority issued for three months.	Primary issuer may be willing to do repurchase trade. Non-residents may be able to enter secondary market in the future.	Final holder at maturity pays withholding tax.	¥500 million.
Gensaki	Most under three months.	Most highly developed secondary market. Important arbitrage instrument.	No tax on difference between purchase and resale price.	Usually in lots over ¥100 million.
Government bills (*seifu tanki shōken*)	Varying maturities around two months.	When bills available, repurchase transactions can be arranged through banks or securities firms.	No tax on difference between discounted purchase price and redemption price.	Usually in lots over ¥100 million.
Domestic deposits	At notice to fixed periods.	Rates fixed among banks. Lower than money market rates.	Withholding tax of 20% unless reduced by tax treaty. Same for CD.	No minimum amount.
Euro-yen	Week to fixed periods up to several months. Longer or shorter periods can be negotiated.	Basically in line with *gensaki*/bill discount/CD rates for similar period.	Not available in Japan.	Usually ¥100 Smaller amounts are negotiable.

fund-raising activities of the major borrowers, the city banks, and by corporations selecting investments between the CD and the *Gensaki* markets.

Euro-yen deposit rates are governed by differentials between the Euro-dollar rate plus or minus the annualized yen swap rate for the equivalent period. While this rate should approximate the domestic rate, occasionally it is possible to engage in arbitrage between the Euro-yen, *Gensaki* and CD markets.

Investment considerations

When contemplating a yen money market investment, a number of points should be considered: the relative ease of entering the market and the instrument's availability, whether the desired maturity is available and whether value dates match. No tax complications exist, and the amount to be invested conforms with market norms (see Exhibit 4.8.4).

Japan's financial system is in a period of transition which is likely to expand investment and hedging opportunities. Thus, a treasurer will need to remain abreast of changes occurring in the Japanese foreign exchange and money markets to minimize the costs associated with exposure management and to maximize the return on investments.

9. Exposure management in Australia

Graham Cocks

In September 1981, the Campbell Committee presented its final report on the Australian financial system to the government. They recommended extensive deregulation of the domestic financial system and the foreign exchange market for the Australian dollar. If implemented, these recommendations would greatly change the Australian environment for exposure management.

With the Campbell recommendations now being studied by a government task force, this section has two objectives. First, it describes the present environment for exposure management in Australia and identifies some currently available exposure management options. Second, it considers changes that might be expected to follow from the Campbell Report.

The present environment

The present environment is shaped by Australia's administered exchange rate system and extensive system of exchange controls. The two primary objectives of exchange control are:

— to conserve scarce foreign exchange resources within official hands for use in management of the foreign exchange system;

— to inhibit substantial capital flows which could cause problems for the exchange rate and for the domestic economy.

Exchange controls are also used for tax screening and to support the government's foreign investment policy.

Timing constraints are also placed on most current or revenue transactions, and residents require authorization prior to entering into contracts with non-residents involving current transactions other than trade contracts.

Multinational companies should be aware that Australian exchange control regulations have extra-territorial application for offshore subsidiaries of Australian companies. Approval for direct investment abroad is subject to the requirement that overseas subsidiaries are not used as vehicles for transactions which would not receive exchange control approval if initiated from Australia. Net earnings of overseas subsidiaries must also be declared as dividends and promptly transferred to Australia.

Exchange control is administered by the central bank, the Reserve Bank of Australia, which has wide discretion but may not grant retrospective authorities. The Bank has appointed the local trading banks as its agents, enabling them to authorize most non-capital transactions.

Current transactions

All export proceeds must be received in Australia either in a foreign currency, which must immediately be sold to a bank in Australia, or in Australian currency from a bank account in Australia of an overseas bank. Proceeds must be received in Australia as soon as practicable after payment, which may not be later than six months after exportation or earlier than one month before exportation, unless the export value of the goods does not exceed $10,000, when payment may be made up to six months before exportation.

Like all foreign currency proceeds, export proceeds may not be retained abroad, even temporarily, without Reserve Bank authority. Against specific application, the Bank may authorize retention abroad for up to a maximum of one month for the purpose of meeting within that time an exporter's approved commitments.

Imports must be paid for not later than six months after arrival of the goods, unless a longer period has been approved by the Reserve Bank as normal commercial practice. Pre-payment may be made up to one month ahead of the expected arrival date. Earlier payment may be allowed in special circumstances but not generally in advance of a firm order being placed. Proof of arrival of goods in, or their movement to, the country must be sighted by the importer's bankers.

In most cases the authority of the Reserve Bank is required before Australian residents enter into agreements which provide for non-capital payments to non-residents such as interest, dividends, service fees and royalties. Such agreements could be subject to tax screening if the overseas party is resident in one of the 18 prescribed tax havens.[1]

Payments due for services must be made within six months of their becoming contractually due. Dividends and interest must be paid within one month of becoming payable. Where no date for payment is specified, dividends must be paid within three months of declaration. Such payments may not generally be paid in advance of their due date.

Capital transactions

In general, non-residents may not raise funds in Australia. When they buy Australian assets they are expected to pay in full by inward remittance to settle the transaction.

As well as being subject to exchange control, direct investment in Australia by non-residents may be subject to examination by the Foreign Investment Review Board which advises the government in the administration of its foreign investment policy. In that case, exchange control authorization may be given subject to clearance under the government's foreign investment policy being obtained. An important element of that policy is that Australians be given the maximum opportunity to participate as fully and effectively as possible in the ownership and control of Australia's industries and natural resources.

There is no exchange control limitation on purchases of shares on Australian stock exchanges by non-residents, but each purchase of fixed interest securities by a non-resident requires the specific authority of the Reserve Bank. Apart from overseas banks, governments, central banks and other governmental agencies, non-residents are generally authorized to deposit funds at interest and make other interest-bearing investments in Australia subject to observance by the accepting institution of any borrowing controls.

Between September 1972 and June 1978, two supplementary exchange controls were applied to overseas borrowing by Australian residents. An embargo was placed on borrowings repayable within a specified period and a variable deposit requirement (VDR) was placed on borrowings longer than the embargo period. Under the VDR, a proportion of funds borrowed had to be lodged in Australian currency with the Reserve Bank as an interest-free non-assignable deposit until loan repayments were made.

At present both the embargo and the VDR are suspended (set at zero), but they could be reactivated. When they were operative the embargo period was set at six months and two years and the VDR set at 5%, 25% and $33\frac{1}{3}$%. They did not apply to borrowings to finance overseas trade on normal trade credit terms or borrowings aggregating $200,000 or less in any period of 12 months.

The government is prepared to provide longer-term assurance of freedom from future adverse changes to the controls on overseas borrowings which might prejudice forward plans for all major projects involving estimated capital expenditure of $500 million or more.

With these borrowing controls currently suspended, authority is generally given for Australian residents to borrow from non-residents, provided the overall cost payable to the non-resident lender is not excessive in relation to current interest rates appropriate to the market in which the currency is to be borrowed, and provided the length of the borrowing is commensurate with its purpose, and any proposed security arrangements are consistent with normal financial practice. Foreign currency proceeds must be brought into Australia immediately on draw-down although approval may be given to retain the proceeds overseas to meet approved commitments falling due within one month of draw-down. Retention for longer periods is subject to special consideration by the Reserve Bank.

Authority is normally given for direct investments abroad by Australian residents which involve a significant measure of Australian managerial participation in the overseas enterprise and the export of managerial or technical skills, promote Australian exports, or protect an existing Australian investment abroad. Proposals for direct investment in purely financial

---

[1] The 18 tax havens are: the Bahamas, Bermuda, British Channel Islands, British Virgin Islands, Cayman Islands, Gibraltar, Grenada, Hong Kong, the Isle of Man, Liberia, Liechtenstein, Luxembourg, Nauru, Netherlands Antilles, Panama, Solomon Islands, Switzerland and Tonga.

216

enterprises by Australian residents are more likely to be approved where the main source of loanable funds is other than Australian.

Authority for the provision of capital, in cash or kind, to an overseas venture is conditional upon any return of capital being remitted to Australia together with all net earnings, although necessary retentions for financing growth in working capital and for firmly planned future expansion are permitted. Use of the overseas enterprise is not permitted for transactions which would not be authorized directly from Australia.

Although prior exchange control approval is required for all portfolio investment overseas by Australian residents, since July 1981 there has no longer been any restriction on the amount they may invest overseas in equities and real estate. Investment in fixed interest securities in any financial year is restricted to $10,000 for individuals, $250,000 for substantial private companies and $1 million for public companies. Fixed interest investments are further restricted to securities traded on a recognized securities market overseas which have not less than one year to run to maturity at date of purchase. Investment in banks, money markets and similar short-term deposits and direct loans to non-residents are not permitted.

Guarantees

Authority may be given for the issue of guarantees in Australian or foreign currency by, or on behalf of, residents where the underlying transactions conform with exchange control policy. Guarantees in respect of obligations not connected with Australia are not generally permitted.

Non-residents are normally permitted to guarantee commercial obligations of residents in Australia provided that it is not intended that recourse under the guarantee will provide the primary cash flow for performance of the obligation, except in case of genuine default.

Bank accounts

Non-residents may conduct bank accounts in Australia to receive from and pay to Australian residents amounts due in Australian currency, and under special circumstances they may be permitted to conduct foreign currency accounts with banks in Australia. Foreign currency accounts must be funded from a foreign currency source and all non-resident accounts must normally be conducted on a credit basis.

Australian residents are only permitted to conduct foreign currency accounts with banks in Australia or overseas for such purchases meeting commercial commitments which cannot conveniently be met by individual remittances through the Australian banking system, receiving foreign currency accruals to facilitate their remittance to Australia or their use abroad for approved purposes, or paying small frequently recurring transactions. These accounts must be conducted on a credit basis and the Reserve Bank reserves the right to call for statements of account and details of transactions.

Forward exchange

Forward exchange facilities are provided to Australian residents for export and import transactions and to some related non-capital transactions by the trading banks at rates based on the A$/US$ spot and forward rates set by the Reserve Bank each day for its dealings with the banks. The Bank covers the net forward positions of the banks in U.S. dollars at these rates at the end of each day and thus bears the exchange risk generated by the imbalance of supply and demand at the rates it sets.

To reduce the potential risk to which the Reserve Bank may be exposed, non-residents and capital transactions are excluded from this market and strict eligibility conditions have been set for trade transactions. To be eligible, transactions must be based on firm underlying commercial contracts and there must be evidence of a firm amount and delivery date of currency. Furthermore, applications for forward cover must be lodged with an Australian trading bank within one week of the trader first acquiring the foreign exchange risk. Beyond one week of the risk being incurred, an otherwise eligible transaction becomes ineligible for cover on this official forward exchange market.

Given the restrictions on the officially provided forward exchange facilities, an unofficial hedge market has developed to meet unsatisfied demand for forward cover facilities. This market, in which trading banks and merchant banks act as intermediaries, has developed rapidly in recent years and rates are now publicly quoted.

The hedge market is based on the principle of mutual indemnification. Two parties with equal but opposing exposures to the same foreign currency undertake a legal agreement to indemnify each other to the extent that the exchange rate at the date of settlement differs from a predetermined level. These arrangements are not subject to exchange control regulations since settling transactions are conducted in terms of Australian dollars.

The need to settle in Australian dollars excludes non-residents from the hedge market, but all transactions by, and balance sheet exposures of, Australian residents may be covered. Although transactions are conducted in a number of foreign currencies, the market is heavily concentrated in U.S. dollars. Exposures in other foreign currencies may be covered in two steps by taking out an A$/US$ hedge contract and separately covering the resulting U.S. dollar/third currency exposure.

Authority is generally available for Australian residents to enter into forward contracts between two foreign currencies with a bank in Australia or direct with a bank overseas to cover a genuine underlying current or capital transactions and to vary the currency denomination of non-deliverable risks such as equity investments or balance sheet exposures.

Taxation

The administration of taxation and foreign exchange control are closely linked. A tax clearance may be required before exchange control approval is granted for any transaction. A tax clearance must be produced for capital transactions and most current transactions with the New Hebrides and for capital transactions with 18 other prescribed tax havens (see footnote 1, above).

Non-residents are subject to income tax by way of withholding taxes on dividends and interest, and by way of an annual assessment on other income derived from sources in Australia. There is no capital gains tax.

The general rate of withholding tax on dividends is 30%. But the rate of withholding tax on dividends is half the general rate for residents of countries with whom Australia has concluded comprehensive agreements for the avoidance of double taxation.[2]

A withholding tax at a rate of 10% of the interest is imposed upon the gross interest derived from Australia by non-residents. Major exclusions and exemptions from the tax are interest paid to non-resident superannuation funds which are exempt from tax on the interest in the country of their residence, interest paid on bearer securities issued overseas on a widely spread basis and interest paid on borrowings which support whole or substantial Australian ownership of ventures outside Australia.

Royalties earned by non-residents from Australian residents are usually taxed at a rate of 51%. However, agreements reached with 13 currencies provide for lower taxation rates on royalties earned by non-residents ranging between 10% and 25%.[3]

There are no specific provisions relating to the income tax consequences attaching to foreign exchange gains and losses. As a general rule, however, exchange gains are assessable and exchange losses deductible for income tax purposes in the year of income in which they are realized where they relate to revenue account. Gains and losses incurred on capital account are usually not assessable or deductible.

Exposure management options

The options available for managing foreign exchange exposures in any country may be conveniently divided into forward exchange transactions, financial transactions and operational changes. Each of these are limited by the Australian exchange controls outlined above.

---

[2] These are Belgium, Canada, Denmark, Japan, France, Germany, Malaysia, the Netherlands, New Zealand, Papua New Guinea, the Philippines, Singapore, Sweden, Switzerland, the U.K. and the U.S.

[3] These are 10% for Belgium, Canada, Japan, France, Germany, the Netherlands, Singapore, Sweden, Switzerland and the U.K., 15% for Malaysia and New Zealand, and 25% for the Philippines.

Conventional forward exchange facilities are available only for export and import transactions conducted by residents. Those traders which qualify should always compare the rates prevailing in the official market with those in the hedge market before covering forward.

Residents who cannot qualify for the official market must turn to the hedge market for forward cover transactions, perhaps in conjunction with the offshore forward exchange market if the exposure is denominated in a foreign currency other than the U.S. dollar. An A\$/¥ exposure, for example, can be covered by a US\$/¥ forward exchange contract executed offshore (via an Australian or overseas bank) and an A\$/US\$ hedge contract executed within Australia.

While the bulk of hedge market contracts are for normal trade credit periods, contracts have been written for as long as 10 years. Trade transactions can be covered for up to two years on the official market provided there is clear evidence of firm amounts and delivery dates.

Non-residents seeking forward cover on Australian dollars are restricted to the forward market for the Australian dollar in overseas centres such as London, New York, San Francisco and Hong Kong. The depth of these markets is restricted by the control on short-term fixed interest investments overseas by Australian residents and the ban on arbitrage between Australia and these centres.

The timing constraints on export and import payments and the repatriation of export proceeds are evidence that leading and lagging of trade payments has been widely used to manage exchange exposures in the past. Despite these controls, leading and lagging trade payments remains one of the most readily accessible options open to a trading corporation wishing to alter Australian dollar exposures.

There is relatively little scope to accelerate payments of royalties, interest, dividends and other such payments, but they may be delayed within the constraints outlined above. Extra dividends could be declared to reduce the foreign exchange exposure of a local subsidiary and the Australian dollar exposure of its parent company.

For multinational corporations with subsidiaries operating in Australia, leading and lagging of payments on inter-company account provides further scope for adjusting exposures. However, changes in inter-company indebtedness were subject to the supplementary controls on direct overseas borrowings during 1977–78.

The suspension of the embargo on short-term overseas borrowings in June 1978 created scope for Australian residents to incur short-term liabilities abroad to offset long exposures to foreign currencies. But the restriction on short-term fixed interest investment overseas and the requirement that foreign currency proceeds be immediately repatriated severely limits the ability of residents to accumulate short-term assets abroad to offset short foreign currency exposures.

Under the so-called 30-day rule, retention of foreign currency proceeds abroad for a period of up to one month to meet firm commitments due within that time may be authorized by the Reserve Bank. This limited facility is often used to retain proceeds from exports or foreign loan draw-downs overseas to meet near-term commitments and reduce currency exposures.

Many large exporting companies have developed internal hedges by borrowing overseas in the currency in which exports are denominated, usually U.S. dollars. This practice is particularly common among companies with major resource development projects which are intended primarily to service overseas markets and which cannot be financed entirely within Australia.

Non-resident multinational corporations with subsidiaries operating in Australia may reduce their Australian dollar exposures by assisting their subsidiaries to borrow locally and reduce their financial dependence on the parent company. Guarantees may be issued to local financial institutions by the parent company or its international bankers. Because they are prohibited from issuing guarantees, American banks provide standby letters of credit. These may be confirmed by Australian banks to increase their acceptability to local financial institutions.

Non-residents cannot reduce long Australian dollar exposures by borrowing directly in Australia themselves, but both Citibank and Rank reduced their Australian dollar exposures by issuing Australian dollar notes on the Euromarket. The Australian Industry Development Corporation and the Australian Resources Development Bank have also issued Australian dollar notes on the Euromarket. This enabled them to tap international sources of funds without incurring exchange risk.

An offshore export financing vehicle or reinvoicing vehicle may add considerable flexibility to corporate exposure management in the Australian environment. As well as centralizing the exposure management function, such intermediaries increase the volume of inter-company transactions and offer opportunities to avoid exchange controls.

Local mineral exporters who operate on the basis of long-term contracts frequently seek to reduce their exposure risks by inserting clauses which have the effect of distributing any gains and losses from exchange rate changes in accordance with a pre-arranged formula between the exporter and the foreign customer. An alternative approach, which is also used, is to insert a clause to provide for renegotiation of prices to take account of exchange rate changes, either at regular intervals or under certain clearly defined circumstances. These clauses may provide for arbitration in case subsequent price renegotiations break down.

The future

After a two-and-a-half-year study ending in September 1981, the Campbell Committee of Inquiry into the Australian Financial System recommended extensive decontrol of both the domestic financial system and the foreign exchange market for the Australian dollar. If their recommendations are implemented, interest rates and the exchange rate will become more market-oriented, with government policy operating through open market operations rather than direct controls.

The Committee recommended that the present administered exchange rate system should be terminated "at an early date" and that the exchange rate should thereafter be determined in the market with the authorities dealing in the market if they wish to promote a particular rate. The Committee further recommended that, apart from technical smoothing, any official intervention in the foreign exchange markets should be "relatively light, infrequent and only for short periods".

However, the Committee anticipated that it may be necessary to maintain a significant degree of official intervention in the early stages of development of the foreign exchange market. During this period, it recommended that a broadly based forward foreign exchange market, with non-resident participation and with the value of the Australian dollar being determined basically by market forces, should be allowed to develop simultaneously with the gradual freeing of the spot market.

Consistent with these developments, the Committee recommended that the present exchange control mechanism should be progressively dismantled. However, again "at an early date", the Committee recommended that the administrative basis of exchange controls should be changed to permit all foreign exchange transactions freely, except those specifically designated. That would reverse the present situation. To prepare for this change the Committee recommended that an appropriate monitoring and reporting system should be developed immediately, based on notification of transactions as they occur.

On specific controls, the Committee recommended that controls on the timing of payments for trade and services should be abolished at an early date, that embargoes on short-term borrowings should not be used, but that, during the transition period, the authorities should retain a reserve power to apply (as a last resort measure) a VDR or like instrument, which preferably had the capacity to cover flows of both debt and equity portfolio investment.

The Campbell Committee also recommended that all realized foreign exchange gains and losses in respect of borrowings should be treated as revenue items, making gains assessable and losses deductible for income tax purposes, and that hedging and forward contract costs in respect of borrowings should be deductible with any proceeds therefrom assessable.

Implementation of these recommendations would result in a much freer environment for exposure management in Australia. In particular the present restrictions on forward exchange and short-term financial transactions would be eliminated, as would the controls on the timing of foreign exchange transactions. As authorization for most transactions would be automatic, prior application for exchange control approval would be unnecessary.

Administration of the exchange rate has become more responsive to market supply and demand in recent years. If the Campbell recommendations were implemented, this trend would be extended until the exchange rate was determined largely by market forces. The exchange rate could then become more volatile, at least in trade-weighted terms.

The effect on bilateral exchange rates for the Australian dollar against the U.S. dollar and other foreign currencies may vary. Because over 70% of foreign exchange transactions in Australia are denominated in U.S. dollars, the exchange rate is currently administered to smooth fluctuations in the A$/US$ rate. As a result, fluctuations of the Australian dollar against other foreign currencies are sharper than they would be under a more market-oriented system. Whether this changes significantly in a post-Campbell reform setting would depend on the degree of market intervention by the authorities and the relative weighting given to the trade-weighted value of the Australian dollar and the A$/US$ rate by the authorities in setting their intervention objectives.

Domestic interest rates would become more volatile if the domestic financial system is deregulated in accordance with the other recommendations of the Campbell Committee.

The government has appointed a task force to report on the Campbell Report. It is likely to recommend gradual reform, with deregulation of the domestic financial system preceding decontrol of the foreign exchange market. Deregulation of the domestic financial system will be complicated by the fact that presently controlled interest rates will tend to rise as a result. These include rates applying to the politically sensitive housing industry and to small businesses as well as rates on official securities.

With the prospect of accelerating inflation threatening to put upward pressure on these and other interest rates, the government will not wish to be seen to be taking any action which will cause interest rates to rise. Therefore, the timing of the changes which are likely to flow from the Campbell Report is uncertain. But, if reform of the foreign exchange system is to be preceded by reform of the domestic financial system, it is likely to be some time before there is a major change in the environment for exposure management in Australia.

CHAPTER FIVE
Management approaches to risk

1. Applying management principles to foreign exchange exposure

David Zenoff

Mature multinational corporations are beginning to move from a technical focus to an emphasis on management in international finance. This evolution in focus is significant and provides a stimulus for reconsidering corporate approaches to foreign currency exposure management.

It is both necessary and possible to apply top management principles to international finance and foreign exchange. This reflects the effort which has gone into technical development, the importance of international business for most large companies, and the increasing awareness of top management to international business results. This section suggests some opportunities and elements for applying proven top management principles to corporate operations in a multi-currency world.

The principal management problems and issues that foreign exchange questions present are:

1. What is an appropriate definition of exposure?
2. FASB response:
   — Can we ignore translation exposure?
   — How much should be hedge translation versus transaction exposure?
3. Top management does not understand or contribute sufficiently to foreign exchange policies, difficult decisions.
4. Should we centralize or decentralize the foreign exchange function?
5. Should we use a committee approach or designate an individual for foreign exchange management responsibility?
6. Are we speculating? Should we?
7. How can we forecast currencies?
8. How can we manage without credible currency forecasts?
9. I am bogged down by past decisions; no time to improve state-of-the-art.
10. How long is this going to last?

The solutions to points 1, 2 and 6 might be considered partly technical and partly philosophical in nature. Points 3 and 9 reflect the intellectual mystique and complexity which have long been associated with international finance and foreign exchange by top management and others outside the field. Points 4 and 5 concern the application of management principles to a functional speciality — foreign exposure management. Point 7 and to some extent 8, reflect the as yet underdeveloped state-of-the-art of forecasting; and 10 reflects the exasperation and fatigue which the earlier problems and issues pose for international financial officers.

When considering the application of proven management principles to business operations in a multi-currency environment, the key starting point is to adopt a top management view of foreign exchange and the worldwide company. The existing and projected relevance to the company of foreign exchange must be explored comprehensively.

Out of such an examination should come:

(a) an accurate picture of precisely where in the company structure, and in the management cycle, there is involvement with more than the home currency;

(b) a perspective about the relative importance of foreign exchange to the company as a whole, and to the respective units of the company;

(c) an appreciation that the involvement with foreign exchange must be managed — just as the company's involvement with purchasing components, transporting goods, hiring personnel, motivating a sales force must be managed — with skill and a commitment of resources commensurate with their importance and complexity;

(d) an acknowledgement that management of foreign exchange should fit into the overall company — just as purchasing, personnel hiring, sales force management — rather than be treated as a stand-alone functional speciality.

It is important to integrate foreign exchange into the company, to ensure consistency in the management of foreign exchange, i.e. the relevance of foreign exchange to the company should be factored into capital budgeting decisions, project evaluations, financing plans, business unit planning, when basic plans and decision and strategies are formulated. If foreign exchange has significance for the corporation, foreign exchange requires of top management a long-term point of view.

For example: a long-term perspective is the key in formulating global product sourcing and marketing strategies. In a similar vein, some exposures which are considered undesirable can be eliminated before they become critical or too costly to cover. The difficult value judgements for management, such as, "Should balance sheet protection be allowed to negatively influence a company's method of doing business?" or "Should we change operations and reduce a subsidiary's efficiency to reduce net exposure?" are best dealt with in basic strategy formulation sessions, rather than in the midst of fiscal periods.

The process by which foreign exchange is managed should be consistent with the style of corporate management, the values of corporate leaders, the realities of organizational behaviour within the company, and the nature of product lines and competition. Should subsidiary managers be responsible on a local currency or dollar basis? Should we take long positions in (what we believe to be) strong currencies? What currency should be used for inter-company billing? The answers to these and other associated policy and technical decisions must be found through incorporating foreign exchange into management's basic thinking, and adopting foreign exchange management to each company's unique style and circumstances.

To ensure integration of foreign exchange into corporate management, a foreign exchange management programme should be devised, to incorporate all the principal elements in a total foreign exchange management approach.

The relevance of foreign exchange to the corporation must be clarified through discussions and interactive analysis between the international finance function and corporate management. With this factual base and perspective, top management foreign exchange ground rules can be

Exhibit 5.1.1: Foreign exchange management requirements

Foreign exchange should fit in with overall company

— strategy formulation;
— organizational structure;
— management style;
— administrative processes.

Foreign exchange should be

— factored into basic business analyses and planning;
— is not a stand-alone functional speciality.

Exhibit 5.1.2: Elements in a corporate foreign exchange programme

A corporate foreign exchange programme should include:

— top management mandate;
— ground rules;
— responsibility designation;
— expertise;
— strategy development;
— data and analysis.

established and communicated to all appropriate units. The ground rules will reflect top management values, overall corporate objectives, management style, corporate image, and the realities of the business environment.

In turn, the existence of ground rules will guide financing decisions, structuring corporate exposure management, deciding how much risk the corporation is willing to accept to improve return on capital, and determining whether or not to double hedge to reflect tax implications.

Key questions

Anyone who has been involved with foreign exchange is aware of the intellectual difficulties of formulating effective foreign exchange objectives, defining speculation and what a company's position towards it should be, determining whether or not to worry about the impact of unrealized foreign exchange losses on common stock prices and an image in the financial community. Not surprisingly, a variety of corporate responses to these issues exists.

In terms of objectives and ground rules, the following are illustrations among *Fortune 100* companies: "Prevent large FX losses"; "no FX losses"; "cover FX risks where possible — unless we decide otherwise"; "maximize dollar equivalent of foreign income"; "minimize risk of loss"; "avoid surprises"; "minimize quarter-to-quarter fluctuations".

There are no "best" universally applicable foreign exchange ground rules, although I am tempted by a framework which includes "minimizing a company's after-tax, domestic currency cost of financing". I also believe that few, if any, corporate managements have ever fully determined what constitutes speculation in this area. Hence, unless a best set of foreign exchange objectives are formulated, five other management principles provide the most appropriate guidelines:

1. Top management objectives, whatever their deficiencies, are preferable to none at all. They provide standards of reference and cornerstones for all levels of management and management decisions, and they provide the basis for consistency.
2. The foreign exchange objectives should be consistent with where the company is in time and space. If, for example, uninterrupted earnings per share growth is of paramount importance, the foreign exchange approach should be supportive.
3. Because of the importance of foreign exchange objectives in formulating an overall approach to foreign exchange management, and the considerable intellectual complexity in working in this area, substantial time and effort should be devoted to this task; and, many members of top management should be involved — including line managers and non-financial functional officers.
4. Care should be taken in adopting other companies' foreign exchange ground rules, not because they are likely to be wrong, but there are dangers in: (a) assuming that one company's overall objectives and management style are sufficiently close to another's, and (b) shortcutting the intellectual discipline and corporate interaction which are prerequisites to sorting out this complex area.
5. Foreign exchange objectives and ground rules should be rethought and modified as corporate circumstances and environmental conditions change. For example, at one point in time a company might not be able to afford a major foreign exchange loss; whereas, at other times, a company might not want to incur the cost of hedging.

Organizing for foreign exchange

When deciding how best to organize for managing in a multi-currency environment, a few basic observations stand out:

1. Organizations are best designed in response to basic business objectives, corporate circumstances, the impact of the external environment, and political realities within each company.
2. Within this broad guideline, there is evidence that at least some elements of foreign currency exposure management should be (a) centralized, and (b) appropriate for a top management committee orientation.

The principal virtue of using a committee approach to foreign exchange management is in involving many members of management in most or all aspects of the challenge. The involvement, if taken seriously, is likely to educate functional and general managers on the nature and scope of foreign currency's impact on the business and make them aware of their own responsibilities and opportunities to manage.

The involvement of managers in a foreign exchange committee can also benefit the company through the sharing of experience and judgement of top level officers. Too often, important international business strategies and decisions are left to a few specialized managers and, therefore, do not benefit from the breadth and quality of top management's wisdom. This pattern tends to carry over to the foreign exchange field.

Shortcomings associated with committees are well known. Fortunately, the use of committees for foreign exchange matters does not require that decisions be made by committee. Rather, serious effort is made by committee members to consider all relevant phases of difficult foreign exposure issues, and to provide guidance to policy- and decision-makers.

Forecasting currencies

A final element in a corporate foreign exposure management programme is the difficult matter of forecasting currencies and recognizing credible forecasts. It is important to recognize the potential variety of physical locations within a multinational corporation, and the occasions within the management cycle when currency might have an impact on the corporation.

1. Strategy formulation/ capital budgeting:
    — markets to serve;
    — sourcing patterns;
    — project evaluation.

2. Financing new investments:
    — capital structure;
    — sources of funds;
    — instruments.

3. Ongoing business financing:
    — invoicing currency;
    — terms; collections;
    — use of surplus funds;
    — inventory levels;
    — payables management;
    — where/when/amount to borrow:
        — currency;
        — cost;
        — maturity.

4. Inter-affiliate transactions:
    — terms;
    — invoicing currency;
    — pricing.

5. Subsidiary remittances:
   — amounts;
   — timing.
6. Planning, budgeting, review:
   — targets;
   — evaluation.

Each of these is likely to warrant currency forecasts, yet many companies restrict their attempts to forecast to only one or two of the management areas mentioned above, and forecasting approaches are not tailored to specific management requirements.

Some currencies can be adequately projected in response to certain corporate requirements. To ignore these possibilities could have a high opportunity cost to the firm. Likewise, the intellectual discipline of developing and reviewing forecasts, and the sensitivities that can be developed by involved corporate officers, can be valuable. Over time, the cumulative experience and sensitivity will contribute to better quality currency forecasts, to equal rating other facets of the international business environment, and to clarifying the uncertainties with which the corporation must deal. On many occasions, this discipline has prompted serious new questions about an environment and/or management's assumptions about it. Timely reassessment of corporate vulnerabilities and operating plans is then possible.

The evidence from a recent study[1] of the foreign exchange management in 107 U.S. multinational corporations reveals a growing commitment to trying to develop and work with currency forecasts. Among the 107 companies, three had no forecasts; four relied completely on externally provided forecasts; 17 monitored currencies for trends but did not prepare formal forecasts; and 83 developed formal forecasts. Among the 83 companies which developed formal currency forecasts, 40 focused on the direction of a foreign currency's movement only (usually against the dollar); 33 developed point estimates of spot rates at one or more specific future dates; nine formulated internal estimates of future spot rates (i.e. upper and lower limits to estimates); and two developed complete probability distributions. Most of these companies made or revised their forecasts on a monthly or quarterly basis.

Without attempting to suggest specific techniques of currency forecasting, the importance of management guidance, parameters, and direction to those charged with forecasting must be emphasized. Exhibit 5.1.3 provides eight key questions that might be considered by management as stimuli to guidance for foreign exchange forecasters.

To minimize currency losses and to develop new techniques for responding to the uncertainties of operating in a multi-currency world, we sometimes overlook the impact on corporate operations of other environmental changes related to a country's balance of payments weakness or strength. It is valuable to review the variety of public policy options that might be employed individually or in concert in response to balance of payments conditions (see Exhibit 5.1.4).

Exhibit 5.1.3: Foreign exchange forecasting

Eight key questions:
   — intended use?
   — who will use it?
   — what will they want to know?
   — required precision?
   — time spectrum?
   — form of answer?
   — what constitutes a "correct" answer?
   — cost of being "incorrect"?

---

[1] "Foreign Exchange Risk Management Project" headed by Prof. W. R. Folks, Jr., School of Business, University of South Carolina.

Exhibit 5.1.4: Policies and measures prescribed for correcting balance of payments deficits*

Domestic monetary policy
1. Stop increasing domestic bank assets.
2. Reduce domestic bank assets.
3. Retard domestic bank assets.
4. Raise short-term interest rates.
5. Raise long-term interest rates.
6. Allow prices to decline.

Price and income policy
7. Keep price level stable.
8. Allow wage rates to decline.
9. Keep wage rates stable.

Commercial policy
10. Raise tariffs and other import barriers.
11. Introduce or raise export subsidies.
12. Tie foreign loans to exports.

Fiscal policy
13. Increase personal income taxes.
14. Reduce business taxes (to attract foreign and domestic exportable capital).
15. Reduce government spending at home.

Foreign spending, lending, and investing
16. Reduce government spending abroad.
17. Reduce government grants abroad.
18. Reduce government lending abroad.
19. Discourage private long-term capital exports.
20. Control private long-term capital imports.
21. Encourage private long-term capital imports.
22. Discourage private short-term capital exports.
23. Encourage private short-term capital imports.
24. Control private short-term capital exports.

Exchange rate policy
25. Ration foreign exchange or prohibit certain payments.
26. Devalue the currency against foreign exchange (and gold).

The resulting influence on the business environment of the policies could be more significant to the short-, medium- or long-run success of a corporation than a change in a subsidiary's relative currency value. Hence, programmes for managing foreign exchange should be broad enough to include appropriate analysis of all government responses to balance of payments conditions.

The educational challenge

The preceeding discussion suggests the desirability of stepped-up, effective, and continuous education about foreign exchange management. The multinational corporation finance function can aim to ensure that corporate management understands as clearly as possible the international payment system, the impact of the currency variable on the business, the foreign exchange issues and policies that must be faced by management, the scope of strategies and

---

* From F. Machlup, *Real Adjustment, Compensatory Corrections, and Foreign Financing of Imbalances in International Payments*, International Finance Section, Princeton University, September 1965.

tactics available to the corporation and the trade-offs for the firm of pursuing available courses of action.

If this educational task, however difficult, is accomplished, management is likely to recognize that foreign exchange is not only a concern for the finance function, and will become more meaningfully involved in all facets of the challenge. The beneficial results are many; management can (1) contribute judgement and wisdom to the foreign exchange management process; (2) reduce the strain between line management and the finance function; (3) minimize the likelihood of formulating ineffective or incorrect policies, objectives, and decisions; (4) understand currency's impact on business operations; and (5) integrate wherever warranted currency considerations into the management process.

2. The issue of organizational structure I
R. Geoffrey Bardsley

This section begins with a discussion of the policies that a multinational corporation might use to manage the treasury functions of financing, cash management and foreign exchange. It then suggests some ways of putting these policies into effect, and concludes with an outline of the responsibilities of the head office to the operating units.

The choice of policies lies at any point on the scale between complete centralization of control and completely decentralized responsibility. Most corporations choose a point somewhere in the middle. Very few are at either extreme. Those companies with completely centralized treasury management tend to be the smaller corporations with little international experience, although some larger companies are included. And only a limited number of companies can be found at the other end of the spectrum because there are undoubted advantages in keeping some degree of centralized control over the foreign operations.

An interesting development sometimes occurs as a corporation becomes very large, especially if its overseas units do a great deal of financing. When overseas borrowings become large and complex, the need for centralized review and co-ordination may increase. This is because of the effect that such overseas financing can have on the consolidated group balance sheet and on the financing capacity of the parent company itself. Similarly, lenders to the parent company may impose constraints on the freedom of foreign subsidiaries, giving rise to the need for centralized review of overseas financing activities. Thus a company with sincere commitment to the principle of decentralized management may find itself forced into a higher degree of centralized control than it really wants.

Differences of environment

International treasury management is complicated by differences of time, distance and culture. Distance causes delay; it takes longer to get from London to Johannesburg than it does from London to Birmingham. International communications are slower and often less reliable than in the domestic environment.

Time differences are a major factor and a considerable nuisance. There are, in addition, the problems of language, custom and tradition, not to speak of accounting practices that vary from country to country. Each national money market also has its distinctive mechanisms: overdrafts are standard in London but unknown in New York; Japanese banks require high compensating balances but make it up in the interest rate; and so on.

Government and central bank regulation of credit markets, and particularly of access to those markets by foreign-controlled corporations, is a familiar story to company treasurers in Paris, Tokyo and many other financial centres. But it may take a lot to convince the chairman of a large U.S. multinational that his foreign subsidiaries cannot always operate freely in their local money markets, because there tend to be very few such regulations in the United States, at least in the short-term markets. Exchange control, of course, is a continuous nightmare for the international treasurer. Finally, perhaps the most troublesome problem of all are exchange fluctuations — probably the biggest single cause of insomnia and premature ageing in the profession.

There are many differences between domestic and international treasury management. How should the international treasurer at the head office organize to cope with these differences?

Policies for treasury management

Looking at the two extremes of complete centralization and complete decentralization, and assuming that the company is both substantial and experienced in international operations, I suggest a mixture or blend of these two extremes. Centralized co-ordination expresses the concept that is advocated here. Under this management concept of centralized co-ordination, overseas treasury managers are responsible for a large share of normal day-to-day decisions. On some matters, however, the subsidiary is required to consult with the head office. Finally, some decisions are reserved to the head office itself.

230

A delicate balance is involved. Centralized co-ordination is almost always desirable. It ensures the best use of the group's global cash resources and worldwide credit capacity. In some areas of the business, it is a virtual necessity. On the other hand, too much centralization kills local initiative and may cause costly delays. If overseas managers are forced to refer every decision to head office, the corporation pays a high price because the local manager eventually loses his interest, involvement and initiative. There is a great deal to be said for leaving the largest possible degree of decision-making at the local level. After all, only the local manager really knows and understands the day-to-day workings of his national money market.

There are additional arguments in favour of decentralized decision-making when the foreign company is less than 100%-owned. The presence of a minority partner, or of public shareholders, must be taken into account.

To put these concepts into practice, three things are needed. First, an organization must be set up. Second, the head office and the subsidiary must agree which decisions have to be referred to headquarters. Finally, a monitoring system should be established.

Organization, responsibilities and monitoring system

The organization can vary widely, depending on the size and sophistication of the operating units. A large subsidiary can justify a sophisticated treasury organization which would be an expensive luxury in a small company. The same expertise can, however, be made available to the smaller units through a regional treasury headquarters responsible for several companies in a particular geographical area.

Within the subsidiary's treasury organization, the local treasurer will normally report, either directly or through various layers of management, to the chief executive of his own company. He will, however, have a strong functional responsibility to the international treasurer of the parent company. Which decisions must be referred to the head office, and which can be delegated to the subsidiary, depends on the competence of the overseas treasury managers and the management philosophy of the parent company.

The bigger and more mature the corporation, the less it will insist on reserving the entire decision-making process to the head office. But there are some decisions that almost all companies will require to be approved at the centre: for example, changes in a subsidiary's capital structure, acquisition of real estate, borrowing above a certain level, acquisitions of other companies and major changes in banking relationships.

A few decisions should always be taken at the head office level. These include the hedging of foreign currency exposures, because only at the centre can a complete evaluation be made of the impact of these exposures. Dividend policy is also a prerogative of the parent company, although the subsidiaries have the right and the duty to draw the parent's attention to any tax, legal or financing factors that may influence a dividend decision. Finally, the issuance of parent guarantees of subsidiary debt is obviously a matter for head office decision.

On the other hand, certain decisions are best left to the discretion of overseas management. The more expert the management, the more leeway it can and should be given. Local management should be authorized to borrow and repay money within the limits of approved credit facilities. It is often possible to delegate considerable authority to overseas management to negotiate new borrowings, particularly of a short-term nature. In general, the head office should seek ways to delegate more responsibility to overseas management, even at the price of being less than completely informed about what is going on at any particular moment.

Exhibit 5.2.1 gives a list of rules and procedures for borrowing from third parties as an example of a control mechanism over financing activities of foreign subsidiaries. This list of rules, modified to fit individual circumstances, has been found useful by some corporations.

As all managements know, the mere establishment of rules does not guarantee that they will be obeyed. A strong-minded overseas manager will sometimes test his head office by ignoring the rules, and if there is no monitoring system he may well find that he can do this with impunity. One fairly simple monitoring device is to require the subsidiary's board of directors to approve actions which, under the company's internal rules, require head office clearance. Head office reads the minutes of the subsidiary's board meetings and is able to pick up any instances where authorities have been exceeded.

Reports by the subsidiary to the head office provide a simple means by which central

Exhibit 5.2.1: Rules and procedures for borrowing from third parties

1. Subsidiary management may take the following borrowing actions without prior reference to head office:

   (a) Borrow any amount under a credit facility or term loan agreement whose establishment has received prior head office concurrence.

   (b) Establish short-term borrowing arrangements (defined as credit facilities permitting repeated borrowings each of which may not exceed 180 days) with local banks or other local lenders in an aggregate amount not to exceed $10 million equivalent, and borrow under such credit arrangements.

2. The following borrowing actions require prior head office concurrence:

   (a) Any short-term borrowing arrangement of the type described in 1(b) above that exceeds $10 million or which causes the aggregate amount of such borrowing arrangements, i.e. arrangements that have not received prior head office concurrence, to exceed $10 million.

   (b) Any borrowing arrangement under which the subsidiary is permitted to borrow funds having a maturity of over one year.

   (c) Any borrowing arrangement under which the subsidiary is required to provide collateral, or to accept any limitations on its freedom of action, or to give any undertaking with respect to the maintenance of any level of assets or liabilities or of any balance sheet or other ratios.

   (d) Any borrowing in the public markets, whether short-term or long-term.

   (e) Any borrowing in a currency other than the subsidiary's national currency unless a forward exchange contract is taken out in the subsidiary's name at the time of the borrowing so that the obligation for both principal and interest is effectively denominated in the national currency.

   (f) Any borrowing from a lender resident outside the subsidiary's own country.

3. The head office concurrences described above may be given by any one of the following:

   senior vice president, finance;
   treasurer;
   assistant treasurer.

   Such concurrences should normally be requested and given in writing. Any concurrences given orally are to be confirmed in writing.

4. The subsidiary will submit a monthly report of borrowing to head office treasury.

---

management can monitor the activities of the subsidiary. Reports should be kept to a minimum. Provided there is frequent consultation between overseas management and head office, few formal reports should be necessary. A periodic statement of cash, borrowings and short-term investments, including interest rates and maturity dates, is essential once the overseas subsidiary's finances have progressed beyond infancy. There should also be statements and forecasts of foreign exchange exposures and cash forecasts for as far ahead as can be reasonably seen.

Visits, in both directions, are essential for both monitoring and informational purposes. In today's rapidly moving money markets, such visits should be frequent. Moreover, the personal contacts they provide are the only way of building the mutual trust and confidence that is vital to the success of a multinational treasury function. International travel tends to be an early victim of budget cutbacks, but a price is almost always paid when communications are reduced.

Head office responsibilities

Because the head office sits at the centre of a worldwide spider's web of operations, it must respond promptly to requests for guidance or approval from overseas subsidiaries. There is no point in having a head office if it takes 10 days to answer every urgent request from across the ocean.

The head office must be familiar with the operations of the overseas subsidiaries and with overseas money markets and financial mechanisms. Members of the head office treasurer's department must travel overseas and meet foreign bankers and other financial experts. They must also keep in touch with overseas developments through sources in their home country.

Overseas management must be given clear rules to work by. If a mistake is made or an opportunity missed because local management did not understand its responsibility, the fault is almost certainly that of head office which failed to communicate its wishes. Given competent subsidiary management and an atmosphere of trust, one can expect local management to exercise a great deal of initiative and judgement. But it is unfair to expect local management to operate in a vacuum, and it is in the interests of both sides that clear rules be established.

International treasury management is a complex art. Although the basic principles are the same as those of domestic treasury management, they are enormously complicated by the interplay of different currencies, tax laws, exchange controls, investment regulations, government intervention and national custom. The suggestions made in this section constitute only a very broad outline of a management philosophy. Each company will arrive at its own philosophy as the result of experience, and will fashion its internal procedures to fit that philosophy.

3. The issue of organizational structure II
Alan Clements

Most people imagine that multinationals are organized as Christopher Tugendhat has described in his *The Multinationals*: "The most striking characteristic of the modern multinational company is its central direction. However large it may be, and however many subsidiaries it may have scattered across the globe, all its operations are co-ordinated from the centre." This is not the case in the field of finance. Some time ago, Lee Remmers pointed out that the financial structure of multinationals can be either group orientated, i.e. centralized, or subsidiary orientated, i.e. decentralized, and what we are really considering is whether, in real life, multinationals tend towards one or the other of these organizational patterns.

In Section 2, Geoffrey Bardsley considers the context of a homogeneous group, in which most of the units are 100%-owned, or nearly so. This means that the choice between centralization and decentralization is a real one, i.e. the centre could opt for complete centralization of decisions, somewhat on the lines depicted by Tugendhat, if it so wished, but it has not. It follows also that centralized co-ordination is not something forced on the group by external factors, such as the existence of powerful partners, considerable minorities in some subsidiaries, or even pressure from foreign governments, but rather something which has been deliberately chosen in preference to complete centralization. The reason suggested by Bardsley is that centralization would kill initiative, and thus in the long run prove to be sub-optimal. The message is clear — multinationals can be rational enough to choose a type of organization which many of their critics implicitly believe that they automatically reject, namely one in which much more independence is accorded to the separate enterprises than is commonly supposed.

In many cases the situation is really much more complex than the relatively homogeneous type of group pictured above. In many groups a number of subsidiaries are not 100%-owned. Some may be partnerships or joint ventures with other companies, others may have substantial parts of their equity owned by the local public, or even the local government. In addition, part of the total investment portfolio of the group may consist of associated company investments, where the possibility of control by the parent is even more remote. Complex groups like this reflect a real tug between centralized co-ordination, and enforced decentralization. The objectives of the finance function remain precisely the same as in other groups — in the short term, the maintenance of solvency and even liquidity, to be able to cope with departures from plan, and achievement of protection against inflation, currency changes, and so on; and in the long term, formulation of distribution and gearing policies which will produce a satisfactory growth in earnings per share. But these objectives have to be achieved in a complex organizational environment, and, moreover, in one which is subject to change as expansion proceeds sometimes through the addition of wholly-owned subsidiaries, and sometimes through the addition of subsidiaries in which one becomes involved with minorities, partners, and so on.

The typical situation which emerges is, I believe, something like this. There is a solid core, or heartland, of the group, consisting of wholly-owned operations — sometimes branches, or divisions, sometimes subsidiaries. In addition, there is a substantial element of the group consisting of semi-independent subsidiaries, with considerable public minorities in their equities, and of joint ventures with other companies, and so on. In the case of the solid core of the group, in theory complete control and centralization of financial operations is possible, even though some subsidiaries are located at the other end of the world.

Golden mean

In practice, there is usually an attempt at achieving the golden mean of centralized co-ordination. A good deal of mobility and flexibility is possible in the pursuit of the short-term objectives of solvency, liquidity, and avoidance of undue risk. In the longer term, desirable group capital structures, distribution policies, and so on, can be achieved by control over local borrowing by subsidiaries, centralized financing operations and general oversight over cash flows to the centre. As for the rest of the group, the semi-independent part, achievement of even the golden mean is not really possible. Subsidiaries are likely to experience problems which cannot be resolved by normal methods, and which may disrupt any general plan for the group as a whole. They may, for example, quite legitimately wish to pursue borrowing policies which do not fit in with the plans of the centre. They may be forced to contemplate equity operations which create difficulties for the parent at that particular time. The cash which flows from them to the centre is either almost entirely in the form of dividends, and outside the centre's ability to control, or, as in the case of joint ventures, is subject to considerable variation and fluctuation.

There should, however, be a close and continuing dialogue between the centre and the subsidiaries involved. Financial officers in the latter will come to understand and appreciate the policies, plans and problems of the group as a whole, and in the long run, solutions will be possible which will mean that while the aspirations of the subsidiaries will still be met, overall group objectives will not be jeopardized. Once the complex, and possibly difficult, dialogues with the semi-independent subsidiaries are over, their programmes settled and their financing plans agreed on, the total group picture can be pieced together and kept under review, on a continuing basis.

Gearing

It is also possible to imagine a group in which the solid core of wholly-owned operations is reduced to a minimum. Complete control, financially, by the centre — the holding company — is lost, and problems hinted at above emerge. Gearing for the group as a whole becomes more difficult, as subsidiaries pursue their own policies; optimum financing, in the sense of the use of the right markets at the right time, becomes more of a dream and less of a reality; the parent's distribution policy, dependent on flows from the subsidiaries, is increasingly subject to risk; difficulties emerge in the field of equity, as different companies in the group use paper to raise cash, or acquire other businesses; and, in the short term, solvency is exposed to danger as flexibility and mobility between different parts of the group are lost. Such a situation exists in some groups already, and may become the general pattern for the future. A number of forces, such as nationalism, worker participation, or full involvement of local interests, are pushing multinationals in this direction, and this may be the only way in which these trends can be reconciled with the benefits which still flow from size and cross-border involvements.

What are the problems of the treasurer in this type of group? I believe they take on new, more complex, dimensions than those already described. He will be less involved in actually raising finance, managing cash, etc., and more concerned in advising. He will have to point out how the plans of particular subsidiaries react on the parent through their results in terms of gearing, distributions to the centre, and liquidity; he will be constantly concerned with the reliability of projected flows to the centre, and with implications for the parent of the investments proposed by subsidiaries; and with possibilities of divestment by the parent as a solution to the problems seen at the centre. Above all, as the group tends to become more complex and as the possibility of achieving even centralized co-ordination in finance becomes more remote, he will become increasingly involved in deciding on the extent to which this can be permitted to take place without complete loss of financial viability.

Conclusions

1. The popular version of the financial organization of multinationals — much as depicted by Christopher Tugendhat — is misleading. Even in the case of groups consisting almost entirely of wholly-owned operations, it is much more likely to correspond to Bardsley's centralized co-ordination.

2. But in many other cases the situation is even more complex, and is likely to emerge as a mixture of centralized co-ordination (in that part of the group which is wholly-owned) and of dialogue, and co-operation by agreement (in that part which is semi-independent).

3. In other groups, as wholly-owned operations and investments become the exception, the problems of safeguarding solvency, the parent's distribution policy, and the group capital

structure in an environment where even centralized co-ordination is not possible, become overriding. In this situation, in one sense, the treasury function would become more powerful since many investment and divestment decisions will be based solely on financial considerations — decisions which can be taken only at the centre, and not by the subsidiaries themselves. Before the extreme of a pure holding company organization, concerned only with portfolio type decisions, is reached, the treasurer will probably point out the desirability of retaining at least some measure of wholly-owned operations, if only as an aid in maintaining solvency.

The organization will be nothing like the simplistic picture — of totally centralized operations — which exists in the popular imagination.

4. The issue of organizational structure III

Friedrich W. Meierjohann

The pendulum has swung back and forth during the last 10 years on the subject of the centralization of the currency exposure management in a multinational corporation. In the early 1970s, everybody seemed to be in agreement that centralization of the exposure management function was vital for successful hedging. The announcement of FASB-8 in 1975 produced further advocates of this view.

At about the same time, first signs of a counter-movement became visible. The emphasis in many corporations moved back from the hedging of the balance sheet to the overall cash flow. Many U.S. companies explained to their shareholders why they did not believe in the hedging of the FASB-8 accounting exposure, and others referred to offsets between balance sheet translation losses and favourable cash flow effects, both caused by the same exchange rate movements. Many centralized exposure management programmes which had not produced the expected results were dismantled.

During the past few years, less rigid and more balanced approaches have emerged, with the management of the cash flows at the individual operating units and the hedgings of the translation exposure at some central level, as the main focus.

The basic decision

The discussion for or against a centralized currency exposure management system has several dimensions which are often confused.

Centralization or decentralization as such does not produce superior results. It is the quality of the management decisions which makes the difference. However, well-structured centralized systems have inherent advantages, which look very convincing:

— The hedging decisions are taken on the basis of awareness of the worldwide currency exposure of the total company.
— The timing of currency conversions is not dictated by the due dates of receivables and payables.
— Minimization of cross-conversions, i.e. situations in which one operating unit buys one currency which another unit has to sell at the same time.
— Better prices on conversions, deposits and borrowings due to pooling.
— Policy issues, such as the potential conflict between the hedging of translation versus cash flow exposure, can be resolved more easily above the level of the operating units.
— Most companies allocate only limited resources to the currency management function. Centralized currency exposure management schemes tend to provide an expertise in currency management at the central level which usually is not available at the operating unit level under decentralized solutions.

There are also many arguments for decentralization, such as the involvement of more management levels in the hedging decisions, and the fact that these decisions are taken in the environment of the financial markets of the individual foreign currencies, but these advantages can hardly outweigh the disadvantages of decentralization.

Centralized currency exposure management requires centralization of the exposure itself. Some companies have, however, tried to design a centralized hedging programme for a decentralized exposure. Centralized management of a decentralized exposure can take two forms: the central hedging unit, in its own name and for its own account, can hedge positions which it does not have and which are the positions of the various operating units of the company; or it can provide guidance or issue hedging instructions to the operating units. A variation, which combines elements of these two systems, is the hedging by the advisory unit for the account of the operating units. All three approaches have serious weaknesses.

If a specific unit, which may be the parent company, or one of its domestic or foreign subsidiaries, takes the hedging positions on its books but does not have the exposure against which the hedging positions were taken, the taxation position may be unfavourable. Losses on the hedging positions which were intended to protect regular income of affiliates could be classified as capital losses which — in some countries — can only be compensated with capital gains of the same or a similar type. If no such gains exist, the company may not have any tax benefit at all on the losses which were caused by these hedging positions. In other cases, the authorities may rule that such losses cannot be tax deductible since they were not incurred in the course of the regular business operations. The tax authorities could even argue that the hedging of exposure of other entities of the company represents a service on behalf of those other entities, for which it must be compensated by the parent company or the other entities. If such compensation is not provided, the rules for deemed dividends could be applied.

The possible consequences of the second concept are equally unpleasant. Under this concept, the company's management issues hedging recommendations or instructions to the individual operating units. The majority of the corporations, which operate under this concept, have chosen a regional structure.

This gives rise to operating and tax complications. The most serious problem is the delay in the execution of a hedging operation which the advisory unit considers necessary. It may take hours and even days to convince the financial manager of an operating subsidiary of the need for a hedging transaction, and his execution may involve a price which the advisory unit would not have accepted. When the advisory unit wants to reverse a hedging position, it could mean taking a loss of some size.

To overcome such communication difficulties, some companies have chosen a variation of this scheme: their advisory unit acts on behalf of, and for, the account of the operating units which have the exposures. However, the authorities of the country in which the advisory unit is a resident for tax purposes may attempt to tax the income, which the activities of the advisory group have generated for the operating units, under the mind-and-management principle. Since credits for such taxes often cannot be claimed at any other level within the worldwide company, the corporation could pay dearly for an unsophisticated operation. Some companies have responded by formalizing communication flow between the advisory and the operating units, and the advisory group may act only upon instructions of the operating units.

Even if the operating units arrange their own hedging upon guidance or instruction by the advisory group, the parent company could still interfere in the day-to-day operating decisions of its subsidiaries. Furthermore, the local tax authorities of the operating units could take the view that losses, which the operating units incur while carrying out such hedging instructions, cannot be tax deductible.

If a centralized management approach is chosen, exposure must also be centralized. The remainder of this section will concentrate on currency exposure centralization techniques.

Centralization of currency exposure

The centralization of currency exposure as such does not ensure superior hedging results. It must go hand-in-hand with adequate management policies and procedures, and an experienced staff which can handle the task.

The task

The individual exposure centralization techniques at a U.S. corporation which has two manufacturing and three marketing subsidiaries overseas illustrate the point. In this simple example, the U.S. company supplies raw materials to the overseas manufacturing units, and the manufacturing units provide finished products to the overseas marketing subsidiaries. The marketing subsidiaries sell these products to independent distributors in their markets and bill them in their local currencies.

The merchandise flow and the billing arrangements are summarized below. The flow of funds shows the same pattern as the flow of the merchandise, except that the direction of the flows is reversed.

Such a structure is typical for many small and medium-sized multinational corporations, in that the currency exposure is concentrated at the overseas marketing subsidiary level which may be — and usually is — least equipped to handle such exposure in a professional way. The U.S. company, the manufacturing subsidiaries and the independent distributors are not

238

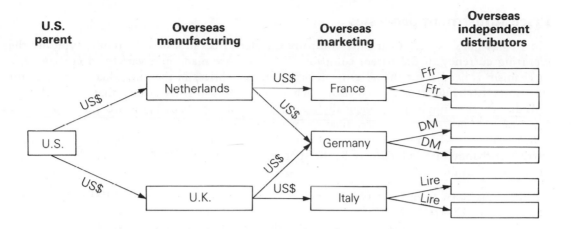

involved in currency conversions in our example. The lack of conversions, however, must not lead to the conclusion that they have no currency exposure. They are exposed to price fluctuations due to exchange rate movements. Traditional hedging techniques cannot protect against such exposures. In many cases, medium- to long-term contracts for the supply and sale of their products at fixed prices may be the only solution. However, such commitments often are not possible or desirable for other reasons. Price exposures, therefore, are the most serious unhedged currency exposures for many companies.

It is important to differentiate between inter-company exposures and exposures due to dealings with third parties. In our example, the only dealings of the company with third parties are the sales to the independent distributors. Though the currency exposure becomes visible in the transactions and cash flows between the overseas manufacturing and marketing subsidiaries, it is the sales of the manufacturing and marketing subsidiaries to the independent distributors which create the exposure for the company. If these sales could be billed in U.S. dollars, the cash flow imbalance would disappear. This, however, may not be possible for other reasons.

Before we can look at possible solutions, let us introduce one further dimension to our example. It cannot be realistic to assume that all disbursements of the manufacturing subsidiaries are made in U.S. dollars. Since they operate from an overseas location, they will incur a major share of their costs in overseas currencies. In many cases, these will be the currencies in which the marketing subsidiaries bill the independent distributors. Such a structure is undesirable: the marketing subsidiaries convert their local currencies into U.S. dollars to settle their liabilities to the manufacturing subsidiaries at the same time as the manufacturing subsidiaries are forced to buy those local currencies to cover their disbursements. There is no reason to believe that this selling and buying of the same currencies at different levels within the same company will have a positive impact on worldwide earnings.

Multicurrency billing systems

As a first step in the right direction, we could transfer the currency conversion exposure from the marketing to the manufacturing subsidiary level via a change of the inter-company billing arrangements. This can be accomplished by a replacement of the U.S. dollar as the billing currency with the currencies in which the individual marketing subsidiaries bill their customers — usually the local currencies of the marketing subsidiaries. Such a step has two immediate consequences: the marketing subsidiaries are no longer involved in currency conversions, and the manufacturing units now have a positive cash flow in a multitude of currencies.

This also brings most of the advantages of centralized currency exposure management described earlier. However, that multicurrency billing schemes accomplish full centralization of currency exposure only if all marketing subsidiaries are supplied from the same source. If there is more than one supply point, and all manufacturing subsidiaries bill under the described multicurrency billing system, the marketing subsidiaries are protected against the need for conversions. This gives only a certain degree of exposure centralization.

Price adjustment processes

Most companies express their inter-company transfer prices in a base currency, typically the reporting currency of the parent company. If billings are made in a variety of currencies, a mechanism is needed for the adjustment of the transfer prices in the individual currencies for significant exchange rate movements. Such periodic adjustments ensure that all marketing subsidiaries are supplied at essentially identical transfer prices. They are the appropriate response to concerns about discrimination or tax issues.

In most cases, the transfer prices in the individual currencies are arrived at by applying a current exchange rate (which may be the spot or a forward rate) to the base currency transfer price. For example:

Base transfer price	US$100
Current DM/US$ rate	2·40
Transfer price for shipments to the German subsidiary	DM 240

Some companies adjust the transfer prices in the individual currencies monthly, some quarterly, and others follow the short- to medium-term planning cycles. Because of the workload involved in any such adjustment, it is always advisable to test the exchange rate movements since the last adjustment.

Some companies have tried to move away from base transfer prices which are expressed in a single currency. In periods of sharp exchange rate fluctuations, such a system can cause substantial and unintended margin shifts between the manufacturing and the marketing subsidiaries. Such margin shifts can develop because a major share of the product cost of the manufacturing subsidiaries is not incurred in the currency in which the base transfer prices are expressed.

Frequent changes of the base transfer prices are one possible solution. However, some form of indexation may make more sense. In a simple example: the company involved expresses its base transfer prices in U.S. dollars; the average product cost structure of the overseas manufacturing subsidiaries by currency content is:

US dollars	60%
Dutch guilders	20%
Pound sterling	20%

Let us assume that the Dutch guilder has depreciated by 20% against the U.S. dollar, and sterling by 10%, since the date at which the current base transfer prices were established. The position of the index is calculated as follows:

Currency	Share	Relative currency value, expressed in U.S. dollars	(A) × (B)
U.S. dollar	60	1.0	60
Dutch guilder	20	0.8	16
Pound sterling	20	0.9	18
	100		94

The index position of 94 implies that the average product cost of the manufacturing subsidiaries in U.S. dollar terms has declined by 6% due to exchange rate movements, compared to the assumptions on which the established transfer prices were based. This reduced cost level means increased margins for the manufacturing subsidiaries. At the same time, however, the product cost in local currency to the three marketing subsidiaries (France, Germany and Italy) whose local currencies have depreciated with the Dutch guilder versus the U.S. dollar, has increased and their margins have fallen.

Some companies take the view that overseas manufacturing subsidiaries, since they are primarily involved in inter-company transactions and have only limited control over many of their activities, must be protected against adverse effects of currency movements. They also argue that the real impact of exchange rate fluctuation must be absorbed at the marketing subsidiary level. The other side of this argument is that the manufacturing subsidiaries cannot be entitled to any extra margins due to favourable exchange rate movements, and that such extra margins should be passed on in reduced transfer prices to the marketing subsidiaries.

The use of the index may be the most convenient solution for this problem:

$$\text{Basic Transfer Price} \times \text{Index} = \text{Adjusted Transfer Price}$$

Example:

$$\$100 \times \cdot 94 = \$94$$

We can apply the index also within the multicurrency billing system:

$$\text{Base transfer price} \times \text{index} \times \text{billing rate} = \text{Foreign currency adjusted transfer price}$$

Example for a transfer price in Deutschemarks:

$$\$100 \times \cdot 94 \times 2 \cdot 40 = \text{DM}225 \cdot 60$$

This system for transfer price adjustments is relatively new, and we know little about the reaction of the authorities in the individual countries. We can assume, however, that their attitude will be positive since this system is highly mechanical, it responds to developments which are outside the control of the company, the impact of arbitrary judgement is minimal, and the adjustment mechanism tries to maintain a useful margin balance between the subsidiaries with different functions in the individual countries.

Inter-company factoring

In our example of a U.S. company with two overseas manufacturing and three marketing subsidiaries: the company has decided that it wants to concentrate its currency exposure at the manufacturing subsidiary level, and it has accomplished this by billing out of the manufacturing subsidiaries in the currencies of the supplied marketing subsidiaries (multicurrency billing). At this stage, the currency exposure is concentrated at two points — the two manufacturing subsidiaries. Our objective is to transfer these exposures to a single point at which the combined worldwide exposure will be managed. This central point could be the parent company, one of the manufacturing companies, or any other subsidiary.

Of the many techniques for this purpose, two are particularly relevant: factoring and reinvoicing. Of these, factoring is the easiest and most economic solution in many cases, but few companies have made use of it.

Let us look again at our basic invoicing structure.

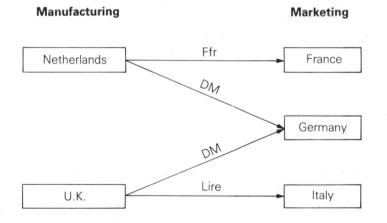

The company has decided that it wishes to centralize its worldwide currency conversion exposure at the Dutch manufacturing subsidiary. Under inter-company factoring, the U.K. manufacturing subsidiary sells its export receivables, which were generated under the multi-currency billing system, at their discounted value to the Dutch manufacturing subsidiary. Such inter-company trading of receivables is usually done once a month. The Dutch manufacturing company then holds all outstanding inter-company receivables from marketing subsidiaries.

The valuation of the receivables in this trading must reflect two factors: current exchange rate levels, and the cost of funding the receivables until their agreed due dates. Since the factoring of the receivables is a cross-border transaction, that discounting can only be done at arm's length conditions.

The interest charge, which covers the period from the date of factoring until the due dates of the inter-company receivables, is made at the inter-bank Euro-interest rate level of the currency involved, plus a surcharge for the discounting subsidiary. This surcharge, typically in the $\frac{1}{8}$–$\frac{3}{8}$% per annum range, covers handling costs and provides a small margin for the factoring unit. In the majority of cases, the collection risk stays with the subsidiary which issued the invoices initially. However, this will not create any problems in most cases, since all discounted receivables are receivables from affiliates.

The discounting is done for immediate settlement or for a deferred value date, depending on the funding needs of the two subsidiaries involved in the transaction. Settlements are usually made in a multitude of currencies, as required by the subsidiaries which sell their receivables. This avoids renewed conversions by those subsidiaries to cover their own disbursement obligations.

The most striking effects of inter-company factoring are the centralization of currency conversion exposure, and the fact that marketing subsidiaries, which are supplied by several manufacturing units, can now make their payments to a single address. These involve less work than most reinvoicing arrangements, but also miss some of the advantages of reinvoicing. Our example has dealt only with inter-company receivables, though this is not a restriction of the system itself. After some adjustments, it can also handle the factoring of receivables of affiliates from third parties.

Most authorities, such as central banks and tax authorities, have no objections to inter-company factoring systems. However, a few central banks continue to have reservations about payments to addresses which have not issued the initial invoices. And certain central banks require that the participation in such a scheme must not lead to an advanced or delayed inflow or outflow of funds into or out of their countries.

Reinvoicing

Reinvoicing is the best known and most widely used technique for the centralization of currency exposures. Under reinvoicing, the manufacturing subsidiaries ship directly to the marketing subsidiaries, but they bill a separate entity — a reinvoicing company — in the currencies in which they require funds. The reinvoicing company, in turn, bills the marketing subsidiaries in the currencies in which they generate funds. The currency conversion exposure is now concentrated in the reinvoicing company. In most cases, the reinvoicing company is a separate legal entity which usually operates from a low tax-rate location. The function of the reinvoicing company, however, can also be performed by any of the operating subsidiaries, and sometimes even by the parent company.

Since the reinvoicing company provides protection for the operating units against the impact of currency fluctuation, the prices at which the reinvoicing company bills the marketing subsidiaries are fixed for certain periods, usually for the duration of a planning cycle. Since the reinvoicing company must be in a position to dispose of its future exposures without a loss at

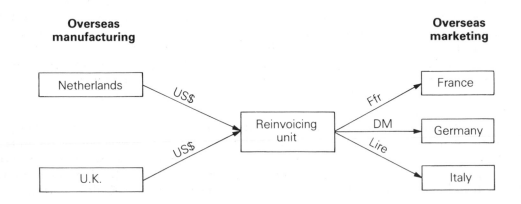

242

the time at which the transfer prices in the individual currencies are established, such transfer prices are set on the basis of the forward rates for the average protection period versus the currency in which the reinvoicing company is charged by the manufacturing subsidiaries.

The main disadvantage of reinvoicing, compared with factoring, lies in the workload involved. Two legal entities must issue invoices, instead of one, and the same applies to accounting. In some cases, the manufacturing subsidiaries also produce the second invoices, but this only marginally eases the administrative burdens. On the other hand, reinvoicing offers two advantages which we do not have in the case of factoring.

1. Some companies have used reinvoicing to reallocate margins. If the manufacturing as well as the marketing subsidiaries operate in high tax-rate countries, whereas the reinvoicing unit has a low tax-rate, a major margin for the reinvoicing unit in the reinvoicing process can reduce worldwide tax expenses. The room for such margin reallocations is limited for most companies.
2. Reinvoicing can transfer excess liquidity from the operating subsidiaries to the reinvoicing unit. Let us assume regular payment terms of two months between the manufacturing and the marketing subsidiaries. If the terms between the manufacturing subsidiaries and the reinvoicing unit are increased to three months, and the terms between the reinvoicing unit and the market subsidiaries are reduced to one month, we have transferred cash in the amount of a flow of two months to the reinvoicing unit. This may be beneficial not only because of a potentially lower tax rate on interest income but also because we may have more room for active cash and currency management in the reinvoicing unit than in the operating units.

Adjustments in payment terms within the reinvoicing process can also be used to move excess liquidity to locations within the worldwide organization which are in constant need of cash. If a company does not wish to use any of these options, factoring may be a better choice than reinvoicing.

Protection

The purpose of most hedging schemes is to protect the operating units against adverse impacts of future currency movements on cash flow or earnings. If the prices at which the manufacturing subsidiaries bill the reinvoicing unit, and the prices at which the marketing subsidiaries are billed by the reinvoicing unit are fixed for extended periods, both the manufacturing and the marketing subsidiaries are protected during these periods, and all currency exposure is absorbed by the reinvoicing unit.

The situation is different in the case of inter-company factoring. Depending on the adjustment system for inter-company transfer prices, the manufacturing or the marketing subsidiaries or both are exposed up to the date of billing. From that date up to the date at which the receivable is passed on to the factoring unit, the manufacturing unit is exposed, and the factoring unit carries the exposure during the remainder of the cycle. In most cases, factoring provides less protection against currency exposure to the operating units than reinvoicing. If a company is not concerned about the protection of individual operating units, but about its overall exposure, neither reinvoicing nor factoring may be necessary.

Some companies use a central unit, which could be the parent company or one of its subsidiaries, for two functions: for the management of the currency exposure of the group, and as a settlement facility for the individual operating units. Whenever a subsidiary has to settle a liability in a foreign currency or wants to convert cash in a foreign currency into its local currency, such transactions can be executed as inter-company transactions with the central unit. In the two examples, the central unit settles the liability and charges the subsidiary at the market rate in its local currency, and it buys the cash in the foreign currency and reimburses the subsidiary in its local currency.

The advantages are obvious: the currency exposure remains decentralized, but the management of the worldwide exposure is centralized. All currency conversions with third parties (banks) are executed by the central unit, and additional administrative work is kept at a minimum. Such a system can work only in an environment of liberal banking rules. Subsidiaries subject to strict exchange rules will not be able to participate in most cases.

Its main disadvantage lies in the fact that it protects the total company through the currency management activities of the central unit, but it does not provide any hedging protection for the individual operating units.

Organization

The central currency management function can be performed at various levels of the worldwide company: it can be organized at the parent company level, or it can be the responsibility of one of the operating subsidiaries or a separate subsidiary whose only function is the management of the currency exposure of the company.

While no one structure can serve as an ideal solution for every company there are some ground rules.

1. For tax reasons, it is generally not advisable to centralize the currency exposure of subsidiaries at the level of the parent company.

2. Companies which wish to keep their currency management operations at a low key will centralize the currency exposure at one of their major operating subsidies. This implies the acceptance of exchange control status of a resident of the country in which the subsidiary is located, and that the income due to the currency management activities is taxed at the statutory tax rate of that location. Such an exchange control and tax status are not necessarily bad: the resident status may provide access to a specific financial market, which a non-resident cannot use, and it may not seriously limit the access to other markets.

   Although hedging is expected to make positive contributions to earnings, sizeable losses during certain periods cannot be ruled out, and offsets by tax benefits may be welcome.

   There are other advantages: major operating subsidiaries tend to have more leverage in their dealings with authorities, such as central banks, than pure financial subsidiaries. Central banks may be prepared to grant a licence for certain export-related hedging activities which they would not consider in other cases. In extreme situations, central banks may even be prepared to apply certain non-resident rules to important resident companies.

   Since operating subsidiaries generally have a bigger equity base, relative to pure finance subsidiaries, it is possible to absorb major hedging losses without a capitalization adjustment. Furthermore, if currency exposure centralization and management are handled in an existing operating subsidiary, the legal, accounting and other headaches of a separate subsidiary are avoided.

3. Exposure centralization and management in a separate subsidiary which has no other functions is the most sophisticated structure. Most such solutions involve an offshore location (with no, or insignificant, exchange restrictions, and low income taxes or none at all). In some cases, the currency management function has been assigned to existing holding companies. Such structures were usually developed in response to tax considerations. Since many central currency management operations are involved in significant interest flows, the minimization of tax expenses on such flows is an important consideration, and explains the concentration of such operations in a few countries.

   As a compromise between the use of an existing operating subsidiary and the formation of a separate finance subsidiary, a branch of an operating subsidiary in another country with offshore characteristics may give the benefits, and avoid the disadvantages, of both solutions. The centralization and management of currency exposures in a separate finance subsidiary has not always produced better results than other structures. Most companies, or at least those with only a small to medium-size exposure in foreign currencies, may be well advised to integrate central currency management functions into major operating units.

5. Using computers in treasury management

Richard J. Hudson

External information suppliers

The institutional providers of computerized information supply services which fall into three categories. First, there is the currently traded or offered rates in a wide variety of instruments, exchanges or commodities. These may be collected both by the provider or by his agents close to the marketplaces of the world. The second service is the collection, editing and display of news both of general and specific nature. The third and more recent facility is in the making of a marketplace. For those areas where an open market does not exist, the computer can act as the marketplace and can readily supplement or run in parallel to existing facilities.

The treasurer and his corporation may have both the requirement and the capability to deal in multiple centres, and the desire to "follow the clock" in these times of currency volatility. In many organizations the central treasury, for organizational reasons, may not be the exclusive hedger, particularly for associated companies and far flung global outposts. A suitable information system can still enable him to monitor activity on a realtime basis around the world at minimum effort to himself.

Bank or service bureaux facilities

The next area are the services which may be offered to the treasurer by those with whom he does business, or by service bureaux. The major service bureaux, as the information providers, have large worldwide networks which, on their own or in association with others, provide global services to a degree and reliability that the treasurer needs.

Cash management facilities, perhaps bred out of the distinctiveness of the American banking system, and giving the ability to monitor balances and to effect payments, are now expanding. For dollar accounts they are available with global time-sharing or other interface. As more banking systems become realtime their introduction in other major currency centres must occur and must be allowed for in any five-year plans now being made. These systems will in their turn mean that a treasurer can have the information available to effect more accurately and speedily his overseas banking. It is not only the forces of competition that will encourage these systems but also the unabated decline in relative computer hardware and data communication costs.

Several bureaux are able to offer standard or personalized packages of interest and use to the treasurer in his dealing function — be it foreign exchange or loans and deposits. These systems may be a cost effective introduction to realtime processing, and supply an entry method which large, albeit sophisticated batch systems for general accounting or manufacturing processing, cannot readily encompass. Other bureaux may be specialists in other directions — such as the supply of computer readable databases on rates upon which independent forecasts and models may be based without the need for data capture by the treasurer himself, a task which he can well do without even if he had the resources.

In a more specialist field, banks, brokers and advisers have a variety of tools and models which are available or, in certain cases, can be tailored to or written especially for, corporate clients. For example, in addition to the services on information processing, there exist hedging calculation tools, contract monitoring, global asset management with the inclusion of tax constraints and assistance in the timing of currency dealing or the future consolidation of balance sheets — a battery of facilities to make the treasurer's actions more effective and more logically justifiable and leaving him and his staff more time to make the decisions where judgement and experience are of significant relevance.

Microcomputers

Finally, microcomputer technology now makes it possible to have a ready means to interrogate or capture a previously unavailable corporate database, or to maintain sophisticated calculating tools which far exceed those which previously might come from the more advanced hand calculators, i.e. discount yields and futures calculations. Languages such as APL can be used to devise complex "what if" type calculations.

An in-house computer system

An in-house computer facility can give the opportunity to harness together in a more coherent manner the various strands of information. What data does such a system require and what types of sub-system can be integral to it; what use can be made of the data in forecasting and variance analysis as well as for current and historical monitoring and optimization that can become available to the treasurer?

The data required

Such a system cannot operate in isolation from the operations management of the company. It is very much an integration of the operations as well as the accounting data that can make such a system both possible and viable in terms of cost and administration.

The chief constituent driving the action is the projected cash flow of the corporation and its subsidiaries. These may be both revenue or capital by nature. I shall assume them to be transactions for financial or commercial reasons as opposed to balance sheet translation where money transfers do not take place.

Monthly cash flows with computerized quarterly accumulation, may be input by various means. At its simplest the corporate treasurer's department may receive and input them. The department itself may make reasonable estimates from historical and other data. Present-day communications techniques make available a variety of other and more localized input methods which include direct dial-up as used in timesharing, packet switching (a means of moving data through communal networks such as offered by British Telecom), a tied line between the out-station and the central computer where data volume or importance is justified, or finally making use of an international bureau or network provider. Telex input will be introduced shortly in at least one treasury. Once on the computer, cash flows need to be updated on a regular basis and such updates carefully monitored — an excellent task for the system itself. It is a crucial decision whether the flows should be based on forecast sales, orders received or goods invoiced. However, there is nothing to inhibit the use of each at appropriate points in the future cash flow periods.

At the more immediate end of the flows, a cash book combining trading and monetary movements and hence equally an accounting and auditing tool or, alternatively, simple bank position inputs are required.

There is now in place sufficient data to handle any variation of multicurrency netting that may be required, and with suitable computer understandable knowledge national deviations from open market dealing can be allowed for. In designing an in-house system, sufficient care must be made to allow, as far as is possible, for a changing corporate management and organizational structure, by taking an intelligent view of the next five or more years.

Variety of inputs

First, there are spot, forward and future foreign exchange deals and loans and deposits with current and forward value dates. Exchange deals may involve one or more arbitrage deals between currencies.

In skeletal form the computer input of all the above, be it cash flow or more complex in nature, is fully identified for the database management given a relatively small number of attributes, i.e. company, currency, amount, value dates and rate. This minimal data input system will necessarily be able to assimilate any types of transactions or new instruments that futures markets or the like can introduce, albeit SDRs or ECUs might cause a temporary hickup.

Exhibit 5.5.1: Receipts and payments budget

						Period number						
	1	2	3	4	5	6	7	8	9	10	11	12
Property				1,000				1,000				1,000
Contract services		500		500		500		500		500		500
Sundry sales	2,000		9,000		15,000	600	21,000		4,000	17,000	8,000	10,000
Equipment on lease				400				400				400
Total	2,000	500	9,000	1,900	15,000	1,100	21,000	1,900	4,000	17,500	8,000	11,900
Hardware	4,000				5,500				18,000			
Royalty	400				500				1,900			
Commission	100				100				400			
Spares			700			900		400		700	600	400
Advertising					1,000							
Premises				400				400				
Personnel				5,000				5,000				5,000
Total	4,500		700	5,400	7,100	900		5,800	20,300	700	600	5,400

Net receipts periods 5–8 are 25,200

247

For the larger or more sophisticated treasury a "plug-in" type of approach may be useful. While a skeletal system can provide much of the raw data, it need not have sophisticated on-line systems for cash flow budgeting, exchange or instrument dealing. It need not have currency loans and deposits with real time printing of associated documents such as contract notes or deposit receipts, etc. These systems can be added at leisure to feed the skeletal system. Indeed, should these systems already exist, simple electronic transfer of the salient needs can be readily made. Neither user nor computer department relishes the prospect of an all-or-nothing new system; the time and effort in acceptance testing and parallel running are major efforts for a department such as a treasury that may not have a large office complement or may not be able to call upon adequate temporary resource allocation.

Forecasting and variance

The computer system will allow definitions of companies' currencies and types of cash flow. With these in place any company can input cash receipts for any currency or cash flow according to the periods in which they are expected to occur. In Exhibit 5.5.1, in which the company/currency is ignored for simplicity, there is a representation of 12 periods cash flows against four and seven types of flow for receipts and payments respectively. As indicated earlier, it may be that the most adjacent periods are driven by items invoiced, the middle periods by orders received and those further away by forecasts.

The cash flows needs to be separated between internal and external so that appropriate and relevant hedging operations can be implemented. From the total summary of periods five to eight inclusive there is a net surplus of 25,200.

The treasurer's or operating company's experience will allow varying degrees of reliability to be placed on the budgeted figures. Exhibit 5.5.2 demonstrates one method in which the differences from budget may be quantified. Thus, for property income we are not expecting the amount to vary but there is a possibility of it not being earlier and up to four weeks later. Sundry sales might be 20% greater or 20% less and may be received four weeks earlier or later.

Exhibit 5.5.2: Variance levels

| | Percent | | Weeks | |
	Better	Worse	Earlier	Later
Property	0	0	0	4
Contract services	0	0	4	4
Sundry sales	20	20	4	4
Equipment on lease	0	0	4	4
Hardware	20	20	4	4
Royalty	20	20	4	4
Commission	20	20	4	4
Spares	0	0	0	4
Advertising	0	0	0	4
Premises	0	0	0	4
Personnel	0	0	0	0

These potential variances could be entered for each company, for each currency, for each cash flow. It is not unreasonable to consider that the expected variances might increase as the periods extend into the future and this situation might be dealt with in two or more ways. First, there could be multiple sets of variances by future period or, secondly, some form of computing extrapolation technique might be used.

Exhibit 5.5.3 shows the results of calling for the maximum best results for the company. In this case all receipts are expected at their maximum and as early as possible, all disbursements are at their minimum and as late as possible. The net surplus for the same periods is now 39,500.

In Exhibit 5.5.4 the opposite possibility is assumed: all receipts less and delayed, all payments more and earlier. The net deficit is 20,860.

The figures show that it does not need much to blow the net surplus or deficit off course. It is on this estimated difference that the treasurer must make his decisions on both present and

Exhibit 5.5.3: Maximum best

	Periods				
	5	6	7	8	Total
Property				1,000	
Contract services		500		500	
Sundry sales	4,800	20,400	9,600	12,000	
Equipment on lease				400	
	4,800	20,900	9,600	13,900	49,200
Hardware	3,200				
Royalty	320				
Commission	80				
Spares			700		
Advertising					
Premises				400	
Personnel				5,000	
	3,600		700	5,400	9,700
Net surplus					39,500

Exhibit 5.5.4: Maximum worst

	Periods				
	5	6	7	8	Total
Property				1,000	
Contract services		500		500	
Sundry sales	1,600		7,200		
Equipment sales				400	
	1,600	500	7,200	1,900	11,200
Hardware	21,600				
Royalty	2,280				
Commission	480				
Spares		900		400	
Advertising	1,000				
Premises				400	
Personnel				5,000	
	25,360	900		5,800	32,060
Net deficit					20,860

future activity. It will be his judgement whether to more realistically expect a 40,000 surplus or a 20,000 deficit — it will help him to decide whether to hedge some, all or none of the budgeted 25,200.

If this exercise is compounded for many companies and currencies, with different variance possibilities in different marketplaces, together with varying degrees of optimism or pessimism, it is clear that only a computational solution is possible.

With a system such as this the treasurer need not be constrained in the assessments which he wishes to make, nor their frequency should operational or market forces dictate. He can decide on the grading of optimism or pessimism which might be applied and these could be influenced by either of these forces. He can also, perhaps with less embarassment and greater effectiveness, be in a position to monitor his entire department. The database can also provide in live mode or with suitable test data a means of management training and education.

The treasurer, as well as overseeing the day-to-day cash position, is likely to be heavily involved in the funding of local and overseas operations. For this purpose a specific capital investment tool would be most appropriate. A corporate asset and liability model may also be useful. It will be for the treasurer himself to assess whether or not the amount of time expended by his department on consolidations of actuals and budgets warrant this type of solution.

For international funding, the computer — from current borrowings and projected new alternatives — can arrive at hurdle rates for investment and view the corporate balance sheet effects. Given sufficient information, the computer can monitor longer-term asset and liability matching.

A by-product of the deposit and loan system or the foreign exchange system will be the ability to monitor with whom and in what quantity business is conducted. A treasurer may wish to keep open a variety of lines of credit, of channels of communication that can be opened should anything blow him off course. The computer would facilitate keeping a watch on individual activity levels.

Spot and forward exchange rates, futures and worldwide interest rates can be readily stored for periods of years. As previously indicated such data may be largely obtainable from a data bank. Given certain constraining parameters past periods can be interrogated to see how close the budgets have been, how well they have fallen within the variance patterns. From these the treasurer may extrapolate future variances. The data can be examined to see what better results might have been obtained with historical knowledge and whether there were any trends or factors that could be identified that could have steered his decisions to this optimization.

Conclusion

The first policy to be decided is the degree of integration of the treasury and the operation and accounting functions. The second is to decide on where the department wishes to be. The third objective will be to convince others that the treasurer's final proposals are viable and, if appropriate, cost effective.

But the most vital requirement of the system is that it can do enough clever things but at the same time not clutter up the decision makers with too much. It is for the treasurer to decide on the key pointers that effect his decision making — let the computer do the filing and the number crunching.

6. Control systems

R. Geoffrey Bardsley

Every few years, the financial press reports a new foreign exchange scandal, resulting in a multi-million dollar loss for some unfortunate bank. Brussels, Milan, New York, Lugano — the names are familiar to everyone in the world of foreign exchange. Occasionally the losses overwhelm the bank, which has to be closed or merged: Herstatt and Franklin National were the outstanding instances of the 1970s. Usually, however, the bank is big enough to survive the experience. The dishonest — or merely over-enthusiastic — trader is dismissed. A few top management heads may roll. There is a painful shareholders' meeting. And the episode is over — until the next time.

Dishonesty does not seem to be the chief cause of the catastrophies. Excessive zeal and greed for profits, followed by panic and attempted cover-up, are the more usual reasons.

Although all the cases that have so far made the headlines have involved banks, many corporate treasurers may shiver with apprehension when they read the stories. If they don't, they should. A corporation, active in the foreign exchange markets, operating with dozens of banks in two hemispheres, is exposed to very similar risks. Forward exchange limits for such companies at the banks are large — $100 million or more is not unusual — and the international banking system's combined limits for many a big multinational company undoubtedly exceed $1billion. An unskilled, unlucky or unscrupulous company trader can do a lot of damage within such broad limits.

Corporations really active in the foreign exchange markets, such as the huge oil companies and commodity firms, can be presumed to possess sophisticated internal controls which minimize their risk of loss. There are, however, many other companies which operate in the forward exchange markets but whose trading volume may not seem to justify the erection of a complex control structure. Although company management may consider exchange trading as a sideline activity, the company's outstanding forward exchange contracts may well total several hundred million dollars at times. Management may not have realized the extent of its exposure to loss from unauthorized trading.

People and rules

How can the corporation eliminate the risk of disastrous losses? The short answer is that it cannot, any more than the banks can. This is a telephone market in which contracts worth scores of millions of dollars are concluded within minutes. The written confirmation follows, but the contract is oral and it is binding. The risk of loss is always present. But it can be limited in a number of ways. These limitations can be grouped under two headings: people and procedures.

The most important decision facing the corporate treasurer is the choice of a trader. Not only must the trader understand the intricacies of the exchange markets and be a person of judgement, imagination and decisiveness. He or she must also possess maturity and integrity: maturity to resist the temptation of an apparent easy killing in the market, integrity to admit mistakes and acknowledge losses while they are still manageable.

But the trader cannot be expected to work in a vacuum. Clear rules must be established. They should state what exposures may be hedged by means of forward contracts. Most companies consider it appropriate to hedge transactional exposures resulting from known or expected future international remittances. Not all companies, however, hedge translation exposures arising from net assets or liabilities in foreign currencies, and the demise of FAS 8 has reduced even further the number of companies that hedge such exposures. But whatever the company's policy, the trader must know exactly what he is authorized to do, so that there can be no question of misunderstanding.

Two key recommendations are offered to the treasurer. First, to the greatest possible extent, centralize responsibility for foreign exchange trading in the office of the treasurer. Second, put all rules into written form.

Centralization has obvious advantages. The best available expertise is brought to bear on each purchase and sale of foreign currency. Small transactions referred to the centre by various operating units can be accumulated and traded as a single amount, usually resulting in a better rate. Purchase requests from one unit can be offset against sale orders from another unit. Most important, in the context of this chapter, the corporation retains control over its foreign exchange operations.

Written procedures

There are several areas in which written rules are advisable. These involve limitations on the amount, tenor and type of contracts that the trader may be authorized to execute. The trader himself may have no authority apart from what he receives each time he trades. The financial officers of the corporation are given written authorities by senior management, on the basis of which they in turn authorize the trader to operate in the market. These authorities typically increase in amount with the rank of the individual. If an operating unit informs the trader that it is embarking on a programme of purchases or sales of foreign currency, e.g. to cover a series of imports or exports, the trader may obtain a written authorization enabling him to accept instructions from the operating unit over an extended period of time. An upper limit on outstanding forward contracts will normally be included.

Having set up these internal rules, the treasurer should now consider whether he wishes to inform his bankers of any limitations placed on the exchange trader. Most treasurers are unlikely to do this as a routine matter, and it would be pointless in the case of really big companies, because it would be impossible in practice to notify every bank throughout the world with which the company might trade foreign exchange.

There is, however, one type of non-routine trading that the treasurer may wish to restrict. Banks themselves sometimes ask companies to provide them with special written authorization of trading outside normal business hours. Such trading occurs, for example, when a U.S.-based company wishes to trade in the European markets as soon as they open. This may entail phone calls from the U.S. trader's home at 4.00 am local time. When responding to a bank's request for written authorization of such trading, or when initiating the authorization himself, the treasurer may want to set limits on the amounts and tenors of contracts that the company's trader may write.

Contract confirmations received from banks should be checked to the trader's records by an independent internal auditor. If the bank asks for the return of a signed copy of the confirmation, the copy should be returned promptly and should be signed by someone other than the trader. Some companies send out their own contract confirmations as soon as a trade is made without waiting for the bank's confirmation to arrive. This is an excellent discipline which can also reveal mistakes before they become serious.

Most of the remaining internal disciplines should be automatic. Accounting entries will be made promptly, reports of outstanding contracts submitted regularly to the treasurer, and outstanding forward contracts revalued at current market prices at frequent intervals. This is all routine, or should be.

Reporting and communicating

One additional discipline is recommended. This is a regular foreign exchange meeting. It may be confined to treasury people, or it may include representatives of the controller's office and perhaps other areas such as purchasing. The important thing is that the meeting should take place at regular intervals, that it should never be omitted and rarely postponed, and that minutes of the meeting should be circulated promptly and become part of the permanent files of the treasurer's department.

The agenda will include a review of spot and forward rates of those currencies in which the company has exposures, with an analysis of recent rate movements. Next should come a review of expectations about exchange rate trends over the next few weeks. The exchange trader should then describe contracts into which the company has entered since the last meeting. A report should be presented of gains and losses on outstanding forward contracts, based on current spot and forward rates, and these gains or losses should be compared with the position at the time of the last report. A report should also be made of any uncovered exchange exposures and of the trader's intentions to hedge them or not. Each company will add items to the agenda according to its particular exposures and policies. The meeting serves as an excellent forum for the discussion of policy, and the minutes act as a vehicle for internal circulation of up-to-date information about the company's foreign currency exposures, its exchange gains and losses and its plans for the immediate future.

These meetings should be frequent, say once a week, and involve operating people and departmental management. A second, higher level meeting may be held at less frequent intervals, say once a month. This second meeting will be attended by the chief financial officer and possibly, depending on the corporation's size, by other members of senior management.

The purpose of the monthly meeting is to review exchange rate trends and market forecasts for the benefit of senior management. The most recent forecast of the company's future currency exposures will also be described, and the treasury representatives will recommend hedging actions. Once again, senior management decisions taken at this meeting will be recorded in writing and will act as the trader's authorization to execute contracts.

Conclusion

The risk of loss from unauthorized trading can never be eliminated. What can be eliminated, however, is the risk of loss due to uncertainty or misunderstanding. Furthermore, the chance of loss due to incompetent personnel can be reduced through the careful selection of the company's exchange trader. The establishment of the internal disciplines of regular reporting, prompt accounting entries and frequent, organized, open discussions will go a long way towards creating an atmosphere in which speculation is unlikely to flourish, and any unauthorized trading should come to light before serious damage has occurred.

7. Profitability analysis: currency variance

Gerald F. Lewis

One aspect of foreign exchange risk not easily understood is the impact of currency movements on the income statement, as presented by the parent company, especially where the parent company manages the currency risk. A way has to be found to isolate the effect of currency movements when explaining the results of operations to management at the end of a given period, be it a month, a quarter, or the full year. The method usually adopted is commonly referred to as variance analysis. It indicates the factors which have an impact on earnings, and how much each one contributes to the change in results when two periods are compared. For the purpose of this section, it is immaterial whether we compare one period against a like period in a previous year, whether we compare actual results with a budget or profit plan, or whether we are making projections for the future. The technique is the same and, if applied rigorously, it gives management confidence in the explanations offered.

Variance analysis concepts

Variance analysis can be made relatively simple, or can be extended to include detailed and sophisticated approaches, depending upon the requirements of management. For illustration purposes we assume a relatively simple approach, which is explained in detail, while the more sophisticated methods are only alluded to later in this section.

The two most common variances used by financial analysts are volume and price variances. We need these to analyse both revenues and costs, and the method is the same whether we deal with realizations or costs of sales. One way of arriving at a volume variance in revenues is to multiply the change in sales volume by the unit selling price of the base period. Similarly, when we wish to establish the volume variance arising out of costs, we multiply the change in cost volume by the base period's unit cost. The base period is the period against which we make our comparison, be it the prior year, the prior month, or perhaps the profit plan. To arrive at the revenue price variance, we take the change in selling price and multiply it by the current period's sales volume. The cost price variance is computed similarly: the change in unit cost is multiplied by the current period's volume. It is more descriptive to call the price variance relating to cost of sales a cost rate variance.

The foregoing variances give us the explanation as to what happened to the margin or gross profit realized in our business. In the simplest variance analysis one more aspect needs to be accounted for: expenses. The easiest method is to compare current period expenses with those of the past or comparison period, and call the result an expense variance.

This provides a very basic variance analysis only. More sophistication is frequently desirable and necessary. The price variance relating to revenues can easily be broken down into variances arising from price changes at the port of entry (assuming third party market prices are available) and the prices achieved at the final destination. Similarly, the volume variances can be divided between a true volume variance and the variance which arises from a change in the mix of products sold. A more elaborate variance analysis approach will include the change in volume-related expenses as part of the volume variance. The cost rate variance can be calculated in such a way that management can ascertain the effect of cost changes based on current or replacement costs, while the analyst segregates those changes which are due to the vagaries of the inventory valuation system. Finally, the expense variance can be made more useful by differentiating between fixed expenses, maintenance, gain or loss on exchange, gain or loss on the sale of assets, etc.

To simplify our illustration, we use only the four basic variances (volume, price, cost rate and expenses); any other approach would make the understanding of currency impacts more complicated. The formulas suggested above are those that have been found most useful by many businesses. Other formulas are possible and are recommended in various publications. No statement can be made as to the most correct calculation, as much depends upon the results that a given manager wishes to concentrate on or achieve.

254

Separation of conventional and currency factors

To arrive at an evaluation as to what the effects of currency are on income, it is necessary to go through the conventional variance analysis and then ascertain by difference how currency movements affected the stated results. We have again to establish a convention to determine the base on which we make our comparisons. Comparisons made against the currency translation in force during the base period are the most practical. Thus, for example, if the exchange rate in year 19X0 was LC 1 = PC 1, all local currency results of the current period are translated at that rate. In our example, we assume that the LC has depreciated by 10%, and the exchange rate in year 19X1 was LC 1 = PC 0·9.

Local variance analysis

First, it is necessary to establish the variance analysis as it would be done by the local subsidiary or affiliate. Exhibit 5.7.1 presents a simplified income statement of LC company for the first quarters ended 31/03/X0 and 31/03/X1. During the first quarter of year 19X0, the company sold 1,000 units at LC 1; its unit cost was LC 0·50; it had expenses, interest and depreciation of LC 200, LC 25 and LC 50, respectively. In the first quarter of year 19X1, the company's sales rose to 1,200 units at a selling price of LC 0·95 per unit, and its cost had dropped to LC 0·40 per unit. Expenses rose to LC 220 and interest charges to LC 30; depreciation was the same as in year 19X0.

Exhibit 5.7.1: LC company

| | 1st quarter ended | | | Variance analysis (LC) | | | |
	31/03/X0	31/03/X1	Total	Volume	Price	Cost rate	Expense
Revenues	1,000	1,140	140	200	(60)		
Beginning inventory	(500)	(380)	120				
Purchases	(500)	(600)	(100)				
	(1,000)	(980)	20				
Ending inventory	500	500	0				
Cost of sales	(500)	(480)	20	(100)		120	
Gross profit	500	660	160				
Expense	(200)	(220)	(20)				(20)
Interest	(25)	(30)	(5)				(5)
Depreciation	(50)	(50)	0				
	225	360	135	100	(60)	120	(25)

The first column of the variance analysis is a total column and shows the differences for each item in the income statement. The volume variance for revenues is computed by multiplying the change in sales volume, 200, by the base period selling price of LC 1, which results in a variance of LC 200. The related volume variance applying to cost of sales is ascertained by multiplying the change in volume, 200, by the base period unit cost LC 0·50. The result indicates that volumes added LC 100 to the company's costs. Therefore, our net volume variance is LC 100, relating to before-tax income. To identify the price variance, we take the current period's volume of 1,200, multiply it by the change in selling price, a negative LC 0·05, and obtain a negative price variance of LC 60. The cost rate variance is LC 120, which we obtain by multiplying the current period's volume of 1,200 with the positive change in cost of LC 0·10. Finally, the negative expense variances of LC 25 are shown in the last column.

The analysis of these results shows that the company improved its before-tax income by

LC 135, which is made up, as follows:

	LC
Higher volumes accounted for	100
Lower prices reduced earnings by	(60)
The cost rate was lower by	120
Expenses were higher by	(25)
	135

In many situations it is unnecessary, meaningless or very difficult to extend the variance analysis to include the tax line. In most business situations, management can affect transactions in terms of pre-tax realizations and outlays only. Prices to customers are always stated on a pre-tax basis, and merchandise is normally paid for on a pre-tax basis. Moreover, tax calculations are frequently complex: companies avail themselves of accelerated depreciation for tax purposes, but not always for book purposes. In the United States and some other countries, depletion allowances for tax have a different basis from that used for shareholder reporting purposes; various inventory systems, such as stock relief in the United Kingdom or LIFO (last-in, first-out) valuation in many other jurisdictions apply to tax calculations, but do not always find reflection in book income (to mention just a few of the literally dozens of book/tax adjustments that multinational companies face). Consequently, the variance analysis frequently stops on the before-tax income line, and we respect this convention in this section.

Parent company analysis

Exhibit 5.7.2 extends the example discussed above to the parent company. The illustration has been expanded to show how LC company's results would be reflected in the parent company's statements, if we assume an exchange rate of LC 1 = PC 1 in year 19X0 against a rate of LC 1 = PC 0·09 in year 19X1.

This illustration is based on the concepts included in FAS 8. It is equally valid for those situations under FAS 52 where the functional currency (see Chapter 1, section 5) is the currency of the parent company. For example, if PC company is located in the United States and LC company in Argentina, because of the extreme inflation in Argentina FAS 52 requires that the U.S. dollar be used as functional currency. The results of the Argentine subsidiary, under FAS 52, are shown in Exhibit 5.7.2.

The data in the PC column follow logically from the above exchange rate assumptions. Two lines need further explanations. The beginning inventory shown for the quarter ended 31/03/X1 has to be converted at the historical rate of exchange in compliance with FAS 8. For purposes of this illustration, we are assuming that inventories are valued on a FIFO (first-in, first-out) basis and that the historical rate is the same as that of the previous year, namely LC 1 = PC 1. The ending inventory has an average exchange rate of LC 1 = PC 0·09; the old inventories have been used up, and only the latest inventories are held in stock. The other line that shows an unusual exchange rate conversion is the one showing the depreciation expense; that item also follows the FAS 8 requirement of an historical conversion rate, which in our example is LC 1 = PC 1.

Before considering the variance analysis of the parent company, we restate our principle of using the base period exchange rate as that which underlies our comparison. It reinforces the highly desirable result that the basic variance analysis at the parent company office will look the same as that obtained by the local subsidiary or affiliate. Thus, if we look at the variance analysis columns of Exhibit 5.7.2, we see that the results of the analysis — the bottom line for volume, price, cost and expense — are exactly the same as those of Exhibit 5.7.1, except that all data are stated in PC. This is solely due to an assumption of a base period exchange rate of LC 1 = PC 1. In all real situations this is most unlikely, but proportionately the results will always have to be the same.

Continuing with our illustration: if we go through the analysis of our total revenue difference of PC 26, our volume and price variances of PC 200 and a negative PC 60, respectively, do not add up to the total of PC 26. As we have previously established that these identified variances are the appropriate ones calculated by the local company, the balance, a negative PC 114, must

Exhibit 5.7.2: LC company, a 100%-owned subsidiary of PC company—FAS 8

	1st quarter ended 31/3/X0			1st quarter ended 31/3/X1			Total	Variance analysis (PC)				
	LC	ER	PC	LC	ER	PC		Volume	Price	Cost rate	Expense	Currency
Revenues	1,000	1.0	1,000	1,140	0.9	1,026	26	200	(60)			(114)
Beginning inventory	(500)	1.0	(500)	(380)	1.0	(380)	120					
Purchases	(500)	1.0	(500)	(600)	0.9	(540)	(40)					
	(1,000)		(1,000)	(980)		(920)	80					
Ending inventory	500	1.0	500	500	0.9	450	(50)					
Cost of sales	(500)		(500)	(480)		(470)	30	(100)		120		10
Gross profit	500		500	660		556	56					
Expense	(200)	1.0	(200)	(220)	0.9	(198)	2				(20)	22
Interest	(25)	1.0	(25)	(30)	0.9	(27)	(2)				(5)	3
Depreciation	(50)	1.0	(50)	(50)	1.0	(50)	0					
Before-tax income	225		225	360		281	56	100	(60)	120	(25)	(79)

257

be due to currency. (This amount can be calculated: the exchange rate changed by 1/9th, or 11·11%; 11·11% of PC 1,026 equals PC 114.) In other words, the weakening of the local currency versus the parent company currency has resulted in a translation into fewer parent company currency units. Exactly the opposite is the case for cost of sales and expenses.

Our final conclusion is that, from a parent company's point of view, the total variance of PC 56 shows the same factors as the ones noted in Exhibit 5.7.1, only this time expressed in parent company currency, and that currency itself has caused the overall results to be lower by PC 79. This indicates that when a local currency depreciates in relation to the parent company currency, and where margins are positive, the translation process will result in lower earnings as shown in this illustration. By the same token, the opposite would happen if the local currency appreciated.

The summary presentation of the variance factors is:

	PC
Higher volumes accounted for	100
Lower prices reduced earnings by	(60)
The cost rate was lower by	120
The gross profit (margin) improved by	160
Expenses were higher by	(25)
Local factors accounted for an earnings improvement of	135
A weakened LC caused currency losses of	(79)
Before-tax income improved by	56

Each one of these factors may be analysed further. It is, for example, possible to segregate the currency effect between ordinary, or pure translation, and dual currency accounting. Dual currency accounting is practised for such factors as inventories and fixed assets where books are kept in both LC and PC.

In this example, the dual currency accounting effect would be PC 43, which is arrived at as follows: the opening inventory in year 19X0 was converted at a rate of LC 1 = PC 1; whereas in year 19X1 the current exchange rate was LC 1 = PC 0·9, with an effect of reducing costs by PC 38. Similarly, depreciation was held constant, while a translation at the current rate would have reduced the charge by PC 5. Altogether, as our overall currency variance is a negative PC 79, and dual currency accounting explains PC 43 of the variance, the pure translation effect between the two quarters is a negative PC 36.

While the foregoing example converted the LC results into PC, using the principles of FAS 8 or of FAS 52 when the functional currency is PC, Exhibit 5.7.3 uses the same LC data, but converts them into PC results, using the conversion principles of FAS 52. Under FAS 52, LC is designated as functional currency, and all elements are converted at the average exchange rate, LC 1 = PC 1 in 19X0 and LC 1 = PC 0·9 in 19X1. It should be noted that only two elements change (when compared with FAS 8), inventory and depreciation.

The analytical procedures are exactly the same as those illustrated above, and the volume, price, cost rate and expense variances continue to reflect the same relationships after translation into PC as they did in the original LC example. There is, however, a change in the currency variance between Exhibit 5.7.2 and Exhibit 5.7.3.

Under FAS 8, the currency variance is a negative PC 79; under FAS 52, the currency variance is a negative PC 36. The difference of PC 43 is, of course, the currency effect of using historical currency rates (dual currency accounting) for purposes of FAS 8 — a situation which no longer applies under FAS 52. (The negative currency variance of PC 36 can be arrived at independently by multiplying the pre-tax income of PC 324 with the 11·11% change in currency values.) It is evident that FAS 52 permits an improved analysis of results as the currency variance represents a true measure of the effect of the changed currency values without being encumbered with accounting conventions which have little meaning in the eyes of management.

258

Exhibit 5.7.3: LC company, a 100%-owned subsidiary of PC company—FAS 52

	1st quarter ended 31/3/X0			1st quarter ended 31/3/X1			Total	Variance analysis (PC)				
	LC	ER	PC	LC	ER	PC		Volume	Price	Cost rate	Expense	Currency
Revenues	1,000	1.0	1,000	1,140	0.9	1,026	26	200	(60)			(114)
Beginning inventory	(500)	1.0	(500)	(380)	0.9	(342)	158					
Purchases	(500)	1.0	(500)	(600)	0.9	(540)	(40)					
	(1,000)		(1,000)	(980)		(882)	118					
Ending inventory	500	1.0	500	500	0.9	450	(50)					
Cost of sales	(500)		(500)	(480)		(432)	68	(100)		120		48
Gross profit	500		500	660		594	94					
Expense	(200)	1.0	(200)	(220)	0.9	(198)	2				(20)	22
Interest	(25)	1.0	(25)	(30)	0.9	(27)	(2)				(5)	3
Depreciation	(50)	1.0	(50)	(50)	0.9	(45)	5					
Before-tax income	225		225	360		324	99	100	(60)	120	(25)	(36)

Conclusions

Variance analysis is a methodology which explains what has happened, or what is likely to happen, in the comparison of income statements for two different periods. As such, it reports on currency effects, but cannot guide as to future behaviour. By critically examining variance factors, especially the currency factor, an insight is gained into some operational matters which could have results with regards to exposure management.

The recommended basic methodology is not affected by any revisions of the techniques for translating local currency statements. The examples show that the basic operational variances are the same, regardless of whether FAS 8 or FAS 52 applies; only the variance attributable to changes in currency relationships differs in line with the translation technique employed. The portion of the analysis which deals with the events that occurred in the country in which LC Company was located will not be affected if the recommended method is used.

Author's biographies

Michael Adler is Professor of Finance at Columbia University Graduate School of Business. His teaching and research interests are corporate finance for the international firm, international finance, forward exchange and futures markets. He has been a Visiting Professor at Wharton School of Business and Finance, Stanford University, Hebrew University, European Institute for Advanced Studies in Management (Brussels), and London Graduate School of Business Studies. He has consulted for the U.S. Treasury, U.S. State Department, Board of Governors of the Federal Reserve System, and IBM. He obtained an MS at Carnegie-Mellon University and a DBA at Harvard University.

Robert K. Ankrom is Group Treasurer, Peugeot SA. Before joining Peugeot he worked for Chrysler Corporation, and for Chrysler International as European Treasurer from 1974–80. He attended Massachusetts Institute of Technology and Harvard Business School.

Boris Antl is a Vice-President in the Reserve Asset Management Program at J. Henry Schroder Bank & Trust Co., New York. He is presently on secondment in London with J. Henry Schroder Wagg & Co. Limited. While in New York he was responsible for the management of a number of multicurrency and all-dollar investment portfolios and also advised companies on international investment, borrowing and exposure management strategies. In London he is in charge of specialized financial transactions and also advises a number of central banks on the management of their international reserves. Previously, he worked with Chemical Bank's Foreign Exchange Advisory Service. He received his MBA in Finance and International Business from Columbia Business School.

R. Geoffrey Bardsley is Assistant Treasurer of Xerox Corporation, where his responsibilities cover both domestic and international treasury operations of Xerox and its worldwide affiliates, including financing, investment and foreign exchange. Before joining Xerox, he was Senior Vice-President and Manager of the International Division of the National Bank of North America, New York City, from 1967 to 1970.

Douglas E. Bender is a Partner in the firm of Price Waterhouse. He has extensive experience as an auditor of multinational corporations and works in the firm's national accounting services department. He is currently serving on the FASB's Statement 52 implementation group.

Brinsley Best is Director of Best & Associés S.A.R.L., Paris, which he founded in 1978 after eight years as Assistant Director of Economic Research for Eurofinance S.A., Paris, an economic and financial research company owned by Société Générale, Dresdner Bank, Crédit Suisse and others. Since the early 1970s, he has been active in the development of medium-term economic, financial and political scenarios and forecasts, and has specialized in the development of forecasting and of risk management methodology for exchange rates and interest rates.

John F. O. Bilson is an Associate Professor of International Economics at the University of Chicago's Graduate School of Business, and a Research Associate of the National Bureau of Economic Research. In 1980, he held the Robert Eckles Swain National Fellowship at the

Hoover Institution and was a visiting Associate Professor of International Economics at the Graduate School of Business, Stanford University. He was previously an economist in the Research Department of the International Monetary Fund, a consultant to the International Finance Division of the Board of Governors of the Federal Reserve System, and a member of the Economics Department of Northwestern University.

Joseph G. Blake is Treasurer, European Division, Diamond Shamrock Corporation. He joined their tax department in the United States in 1977, was promoted to Manager of European Finance in 1979, and moved to European headquarters in the U.K. Prior to this, he worked for Peat Marwick Mitchell and Co. as an auditor and tax specialist.

Victoria Blake is a Vice President in the Securities Origination and Currency Swap Department of Citicorp International Bank Limited in London. Before moving to London in January 1981 she worked in the Corporate Finance Department of the bank in New York for two years and the Treasury Division for six years prior to that. A graduate of Hollins College, she attended the Programme for Management Development at Harvard Business School in the autumn of 1981.

Mark Borsuk is Managing Consultant for Asia, Foreign Exchange Advisory Service, Chemical Bank. (FEAS advises central banks, trading companies and commercial banks in the region on international financial trends and treasury management techniques.) He is a specialist in the yen and Japanese financial markets. He previously held positions as a foreign exchange trader and institutional investment adviser.

Alan Clements is Finance Director, Chairman of the Paints Product Policy Group, Territorial Director for Sub-Saharan Africa, and a member of the Board of ICI.

He joined ICI in 1956 as a member of the Taxation and Rating Section of the Treasurer's Department at Head Office. In 1966 he became an ICI Assistant Treasurer, in 1971 the Deputy Treasurer, and in 1976 the Treasurer. He is a director of several ICI subsidiary and associated companies, including AECI Limited and ICI Americas Inc. He is Chairman of ICI Finance Limited, President of ICI International Finance Limited and Chairman of ICI North America Inc. He is also a director of Gillett Brothers Discount Company Limited, and of Trafalgar House Limited.

Graham Cocks is a Director of Syntec Economic Services Pty. Ltd., which he joined in January 1975. He has managed Syntec FX, Syntec's specialized foreign exchange consultancy service, since its inception six years ago. He also acts as a general economic consultant to two of Syntec's corporate clients and contributes to most of the Group's activities. In 1980, he co-directed and authored a study of Australia's exchange control system commissioned from Syntec by the Campbell Committee.

Jeffrey C. Donahue is Manager, Foreign Currency Operations, at Union Carbide Corporation. His responsibilities encompass all pertinent areas of foreign exchange exposure management, and his principal function is currency risk management strategy and market tactics. He was formerly with Chemical Bank and Commercial Credit Company in exposure management and international economics functions.

J. A. Donaldson is Deputy Treasurer, ICI, responsible *inter alia* for short-term cash and currency management. He qualified as a chartered accountant in Glasgow. Thereafter he joined ICI where he has worked in accountancy, distribution, data processing and finance. For a number of years he had specific responsibility for ICI's finances in Western Europe.

Gunter Dufey is Professor of International Business and Finance at the Graduate School of Business, University of Michigan. His research interests focus on financial management in multinational corporations and international financial markets. He also serves as a consultant for industry, financial institutions and government agencies.

Bernard Dumas is Professor of Finance at CESA, France. He has also been a Visiting Associate Professor at Wharton School, University of Pennsylvania, and Associate Professor at Columbia University.

Malcolm J. Finney is an International Tax Consultant with Thornton Baker, member firm of

Grant Thornton International. His previous work experience has included working as an international tax consultant with the City firm of international tax and finance consultants J. F. Chown & Co. Ltd.; as a corporate executive in the corporate finance department of merchant bankers J. Henry Schroder Wagg & Co. Ltd.; and with the London firm of consulting actuaries, Duncan C. Fraser & Co.

Ian Giddy is an Associate Professor at Columbia University Graduate School of Business. He has also been an Assistant Professor at the University of Michigan, a Visiting Assistant Professor at the University of Chicago, and a Professorial Lecturer at Georgetown University. He has served in the U.S. government as Financial Economist at the Comptroller of the Currency and as Senior Financial Analyst at the Board of Governors of the Federal Reserve System. During 1980–81 he was on leave as an economist at the International Monetary Fund. He is co-author of *The International Money Market* (Prentice-Hall, 1978) and co-editor of the forthcoming *International Finance Handbook* (Wiley, 1982), and is currently writing a book on international banking regulation.

Stephen Goodman is Senior Director, Business Investments, Singer Company, Stamford, Connecticut. Since joining Singer in 1977, his responsibilities have included the management of the company's worldwide currency exposure, including its hedging programme, and supervising the management of the company's pension fund. Prior to joining Singer, he was Vice-President, Policy Analysis, the Export-Import Bank, and spent six years as Director of International Trade and Monetary Research at the Office of Economic Research, CIA. He is a graduate in Economics of Cornell and Yale Universities.

Björn Holm has established his own company, Nova Regis AB, consulting primarily in the areas of business development and finance. Prior to this, he was Controller for Scandinavia for Corn Products Co., Copenhagen, and an internal consultant with the Kockum Group of Companies, Malmo, assisting in the restructuring of their industrial division. In 1972 he joined the Höganäs Group of Companies, Sweden, where he served as Deputy Financial Director, and in 1977 he joined Bohlin & Strömberg AB, Management Consultants in Stockholm.

Richard J. Hudson is Financial Products Manager, Geac Computers Ltd., concerned with corporate loan systems, insurance, retail banking and treasury management. Prior to joining Geac, he was City Manager, Business Computers Ltd., concerned with financial product software, and Assistant Manager, ICFC, Management Services Department.

Richard G. Hunt is Senior Treasury Associate, Foreign Exchange, Occidental Financial Services, responsible for the determination of worldwide corporate foreign exchange exposure and the subsequent role of foreign exchange and interest rate forecasting. He has been involved in corporate treasury management since 1966, when he joined Gulf Oil Company in London, after a spell with the merchant bank, Samuel Montagu. He joined Occidental Petroleum Corporation in 1974.

David Kern is Manager, Economic Analysis, Statistics and International Sections, National Westminster Bank Limited, London. He is responsible for preparing the economic and financial forecasts used in his bank's planning machinery and for co-ordinating the work on country risk assessment.

Richard M. Levich is Associate Professor of Finance and International Business at New York University Graduate School of Business Administration. He is also a Research Associate with the National Bureau of Economic Research in Cambridge, Massachusetts. He has been a visiting faculty member at the University of Chicago and at Yale University, and Visiting Scholar at the Board of Governors of the Federal Reserve System. He received his PhD from the University of Chicago in 1977, and is the author of *The International Money Market: An Assessment of Alternative Forecasting Techniques and Market Efficiency* (JAI Press, 1979), and the co-editor of *Exchange Risk and Exposure: Current Developments in International Financial Management* (Lexington Books, 1980).

Gerald F. Lewis is Deputy Controller of Mobil Corporation and Mobil Oil Corporation in New York City. He was employed as an accountant and auditor in London and New York from 1941 to 1953, when he became Controller of the Inter-American Grain Corporation in

New York. He joined Mobil in 1956 holding various controllership positions in U.S. and international operations. He has an MBA from New York University.

Gail F. Lieberman was staff Vice-President, Financial and Capital Planning for RCA Corporation. Previously she was Director, International Finance for Standard Brands, Inc., and an independent consultant. Since July 1982, she has been Senior Vice-President and Chief Financial Officer, Scali McCabe Sloves Inc., in New York.

Richard Mathews is Vice-President and Manager of the International Treasury Management Group of Marine Midland Bank NA., New York. He has been with the bank since 1977. Prior to joining Marine Midland, he worked for three years for Merrill Lynch Holdings in the U.K.

Nigel Meade has been a Lecturer in the Department of Management Science at Imperial College, London University, for nine years. A statistician by training, he specializes in forecasting and statistical model building for mainly financial application. He has acted as a consultant in this area to a wide range of companies.

Friedrich W. Meierjohann is Director of Cash and Currency Management, Polaroid (Europa) BV, Amsterdam, The Netherlands. He is responsible for the management of the currency exposure of the Polaroid group and the funding of the 25 overseas subsidiaries of Polaroid Corporation in 21 countries throughout the world.

Rolf Mirus teaches International Finance and Business Economics at the Faculty of Business Administration and Commerce, University of Alberta, in Edmonton, Alberta, Canada. He received his PhD in Monetary Economics from the University of Minnesota.

Jeffrey Mizrahi is Vice-President and Director of Investment Research, International Investment Management Service, Bank of America NT & SA. Prior to joining the bank, he worked for the Economist Intelligence Unit, Charter Consolidated and James Capel. He joined Bank of America in 1978, to head their international investment research effort.

David Morrison is Senior Economics Consultant at Simon & Coates, a leading London stockbrokers, where he is in charge of the firm's Currency Advisory Service. Between 1974 and 1978 he was an international economic adviser at the Bank of England, specializing in the U.S. economy and analyses of world trade flows. In 1978 he entered stockbroking and in 1980 was ranked top currency and international economist in the Continental Illinois survey of investment managers.

Bluford H. Putnam ia a Vice-President of Chase Manhattan Bank, heading the Financial Risk Management Division of the Economics Group. His responsibilities include planning strategies for managing interest rate risk, co-ordinating research studies into financial futures and options markets, and providing specialized consulting to both the Chase Manhattan Bank and its customers. His prior experiences include covering Eurocurrency market developments, actively participating in the forecasting process for foreign as well as U.S. interest rates for Chase, and sharing responsibilities for the Chase Economics Group's foreign report. He also served as an economist in the International Research Department of the Federal Reserve Bank of New York.

Michael R. Rosenberg is Director of International Fixed Income Research at Prudential Insurance Company of America. Prior to joining Prudential, he spent four and a half years as a senior foreign exchange market analyst for Citibank and a year and a half as an international economist for Chase Manhattan Bank. He has a PhD in Economics from Penn State University.

Adam Ruck was, until May 1981, a journalist on the *Euromoney* staff and an editor of the *Euromoney Currency Report*. He has degrees from the universities of London and Oxford and, before joining *Euromoney*, worked in the Investment Division of N. M. Rothschild and Sons Ltd. He is currently researching a study of France.

Gary Schlossberg is Vice-President and Senior Economist, Economics Department, Wells Fargo Bank NA, San Francisco, responsible for the U.S. and international function. He is responsible for the international function in the bank's Economics Department. Previously he was Assistant Vice-President, Planning Division, International Banking. Prior to joining Wells Fargo, he worked for the Federal Reserve Board in Washington, and the U.S. Treasury Department.

David K. Slifer is a Vice-President Team Leader with Bank of America's Forest Products Section. As Global Account Officer for the major companies in this industry, he has marketed international concepts such as parallel loans, foreign currency financing techniques and foreign exchange. Prior to joining the section, he was Manager, Global Treasury Management Services for North America. His four-year assignment in London allowed him to develop Bank of America's first fee-consulting services in international treasury management for corporate clients. He is a graduate of Wharton School of Business and Finance.

Claude Tygier is a Senior Vice-President and Head of Foreign Exchange Trading for J. Henry Schroder Bank and Trust Company. He gained his trading experience with the United California Bank, International, New York, from 1967–74. Thereafter, he became the Head of the Foreign Exchange Department at the Union Bank of Switzerland, New York branch.

Stanley C. Waldner is a principal of Waldner & Co., a Chicago-based research firm dealing in foreign exchange and domestic interest rate exposure management. The company has essentially three functions: (1) basic research and model development, (2) exposure management services for multinational corporations, and (3) active trading of both company and venture capital. He was formerly a partner with a New York Stock Exchange member firm, and subsequently an independent currency trader on the floor of the International Monetary Market of the Chicago Mercantile Exchange.

David Wyss is Vice-President and Chief European Economist for DRI Europe. Previously, he was Senior Staff Economist at the Council of Economic Advisers and Senior Economist at the Federal Reserve Board.

David Zenoff is a specialist in the management of international business. Since 1972 he has been President of his consulting firm, David B. Zenoff & Associates, Inc., which provides consultation on a variety of management challenges associated with international business expansion and operations. He is a part-time Lecturer in International Business at Stanford University Graduate School of Business. From 1966–72 he was a Professor of International Business at Columbia University Graduate School of Business. He received his MBA and PhD from Harvard Business School.